AMERICAN ENTERPRISE AND

SCANDINAVIAN ANTITRUST LAW

E. ERNEST GOLDSTEIN:

AMERICAN ENTERPRISE and
Scandinavian Antitrust Law

UNIVERSITY OF TEXAS PRESS, AUSTIN

Library of Congress Catalog Card No. 63–16059
Copyright © 1963 by E. Ernest Goldstein
All Rights Reserved

*Manufactured in the United States of America
by the Printing Division of the University of Texas*

I gladly dedicate this volume
to American enterprise in Europe.

INTRODUCTION

As more and more American enterprises consider entrance into the European Economic Community and expansion in other Western European countries, American executives and their American lawyers need to know something of the European antitrust laws. While this is being written, the first regulations interpreting Articles 85 and 86 of the Rome Treaty, which gave birth to the E.E.C., are being issued in Brussels, and one can only speculate as to what effect the developments will have on American business.

The legal systems examined here are those of Denmark, Norway, and Sweden. The variety of legislative devices employed in the three Scandinavian countries, the general willingness of all three governments to inform the public of their respective efforts to control restraints of competition, and the contrasting methods of approach to antitrust problems by equally able administrators—all provide ideal conditions for a comparative study.

Owing to restrictions, secrecy, or the lack of legislation in each of the six E.E.C. countries, a study of their legal systems could not be thorough and, consequently, would be relatively uninformative.

The laws, or lack thereof, of Belgium, Italy, and Luxembourg can provide us with absolutely no information or material in our search for a basis on which to evaluate antitrust developments under European legal systems. The Netherlands have a law of some vintage, but the absolute secrecy concerning their cartel register and the minimal information furnished by the Dutch Cartel Decrees provide few guidelines on which to evaluate the operations of the administrator.

France operates without a cartel register, so this country offers no help in understanding this major feature in most European systems for control of restrictive business practices. The growing French jurisprudence dealing with refusal to sell stands alone as the only instructive feature of French law. Current material concerning the French treatment of cartels and ententes generally is unavailable because the Commission Technique des Ententes has not published a report concerning its activities since 1957.

Germany does maintain a cartel register, but the Cartel Authority in Berlin is snowed under an avalanche of papers and subjected to various political and intergovernmental pressures. The indeterminacy of practice under the law is shown by the fact that from 1958 to 1961 the Federal Cartel Office in Berlin received 189 requests for cartel approval. Of these, 2 requests were refused, 83 were approved, and the rest are pending.

Since England and Eire share our common-law heritage and language, the reports of the British Restrictive Trade Practices Court and of the Irish Fair Trade Commission, which are easily accessible, are also easily understandable. However, the other countries of Western Europe present a language barrier. In addition their legal processes which provide control of restraints of competition or restrictive trade practices are administrative and thereby provide little if any of the case law which most American lawyers seek. This analysis attempts to provide a basis for an evaluation and understanding of the administrative process and of the European administrator.

This book is a break with scholarly tradition in that footnotes are, refreshingly I hope, absent. It is assumed that most American lawyers will normally be able to obtain the information they need by making use of the internal references which have been, for the most part, confined to the more easily obtained public documents.

The Appendices contain the text of statutes obtained from the excellent and indispensable *Guide to Legislation on Restrictive Business Practices*, published by the European Productivity Agency of the Organization for European Cooperation and Development in Paris. Unless indicated to the contrary, the cut-off date for the materials is 1 January 1961.

Traditionally books of this sort have been compilations of papers by learned experts who are native to the country on whose law they comment. A disadvantage of this mode of preparation is that the most learned foreign expert is not always able to present the facts and issues that most concern an American lawyer. Although my study may not be a wholly successful attempt to provide all the answers to all questions, it is hoped that it will enable other American-trained lawyers to venture into foreign fields with confidence.

This work literally could not have been written without the many hours freely given by managers and executives of American enterprises abroad, who talked freely and gave information generously. To honor their confidence, even where the disguise may wear thin, I have used no names of firms except where requested to do so. So that the reader may make comparisons, a consistent numbering system has been used to identify each firm.

This book and its research are the result of the generosity of the Ford Foundation in granting the author an International Legal Studies Fellowship for a year of research in Europe, 1959–1960. My work was further assisted by Dean Page Keeton of the University of Texas School of Law, who has provided financial and other assistance, and to whom I gratefully acknowledge my debt.

Many people who were helpful and generous with their time and their information are to be held blameless for any errors which appear in this work. Those who hold official position gave of their time and counsel as private individuals. I am happy to acknowledge the invaluable help and assistance of Messrs. A. Mikkelsen and P. Luchow of Copenhagen, A. Frihagen of Oslo, and B.-H. Kockum of Stockholm, who were more than generous with their great knowledge and time. The courtesies and kindnesses of other friends are acknowledged with many pleasant memories: Messrs. E. Klaebel, S. Gammelgaard, F. Nielsen, and W. Boserup of Copenhagen; the Hon. F. Öhman and Messrs. A. Skiöld and T. Odhe of Stockholm; and the Hon. W. Thagaard and Mrs. E. Bøe of Oslo.

E.E.G.

Horseshoe Bend
Austin, Texas

CONTENTS

TABLES

MAP

PART ONE:
DENMARK

CONTENTS

PRELIMINARY OBSERVATIONS

THE HISTORY OF Danish legislative control of restraints on competition, in a practical sense, began with the enactment of the Price Agreements Act of 1937. The Price Control Board (P.C.B.), the administrator of this Act, operated under transitional legislation from 1940 to 1955 or from World War II through the postwar era; it had authority not only to control restrictive agreements, but also to intervene, if necessary, in order to control prices and margins where no restrictions were involved.

Transitional and provisional legislation was enacted in step with the revival of the Danish economy. In 1949 legislation created the Trustkommission, composed of experts from academic life and the civil service, as distinguished from representatives of special-interest groups. This agency was given the task of surveying and reporting the extent and effects of restrictive practices in various industries.

At the specific request of the Parliament and the government, the Trustkommission surveyed the entire economy and the problems of controlling restrictive practices, and the results of this survey were published in its 1953 Report (No. 3). The bill based on this report was initially submitted to the Parliament on 11 December 1953 and, subsequently, became Law No. 102 of 31 March 1955, the Monopolies and Restrictive Practices Control Act. Under the 1955 legislation the Monopoly Control Authority (Monopoltilsynet, M.C.A.), with offices at Norregade 49 in Copenhagen, inherited some of the duties of the Trustkommission, which terminated in 1959.

The second chapter of the Trustkommission's 1953 Report deals with the government's policy of controlling restrictive practices and expresses three primary objectives which such a policy should seek to attain:

1. The abolition of unreasonable profit margins,
2. The maintenance of free entry into trade and industry, and
3. The termination of certain practices which impede efficiency in production and distribution.

The Trustkommission Report emphasized that the attainment of all three objectives in an always mutually compatible fashion was not likely. It was the view of the Trustkommission that the third objective, the promotion of efficiency, was most likely to receive general acceptance.

When the government first presented the bill to Parliament, each of the objectives received equal weight. In the final text, however, promoting efficiency as an overall objective is not mentioned. The debates do make it clear, nevertheless, that the Parliament intended that the Monopoly Control Authority consider this objective in reaching its decisions; the evidence shows that the M.C.A. has heeded this parliamentary admonition.

Section 1 of the 1955 Act states that its purpose is "to prevent unreasonable prices and business conditions and to secure the best possible conditions for the freedom of trade" by means of "public control of monopolies and of restrictive business practices." The issue of efficiency is assumed to be within the concept of "unreasonable prices," which means not only unreasonable margins, but also prices inflated through unnecessarily large costs. Inordinate advertising could be such an inefficient added cost factor.

Generally the Act embraces all forms of restrictive business practices which exert an effective influence in local or wider markets. The criterion for any M.C.A. negotiation, intervention, or injunction is the unreasonableness of the practice in question. The Act provides that the unreasonableness of prices is to be measured in terms of comparable enterprises operating with comparable commercial and technical efficiency. Since unreasonableness was also the criterion of the Price Control Board, the M.C.A. has an accumulated backlog of interpretation from which to obtain guidance.

As was true with the 1937 legislation, the 1955 Act is bottomed on the principles that restrictive practices are to be controlled rather than prohibited, and that the decision to control is to be based on the actual or probable effects of the practice in a specific case. The essential features of the control system are (1) the all-embracing duty of enterprises to notify the M.C.A. of restrictive practices and (2) the authority of the M.C.A. to demand a notification when it finds that an enterprise dominates its industry or trade through an essential restrictive practice, monopoly, or price leadership. It should be emphasized, however, that the registration that follows notification never connotes approval of the registered practice and the M.C.A. always has the power to evaluate this activity.

Accompanying the M.C.A.'s authority to demand notification and registration is its power to control prices set by those enterprises officially entered in the Register. The Act provides that such registered firms must obtain M.C.A. approval before they raise prices. A 1960 amendment, however, allows the M.C.A. to grant exemptions from this provision in special cases.

The Act applies also to restrictive practices of professional groups, such as price fixing by medical doctors, but it does not affect wages and labor conditions. Public utilities and other activities controlled by appropriate authorities in matters of price policy are also exempt.

One exception to the principle that restrictive practices be controlled rather than prohibited is the ban on the enforcement of minimum, vertical resale prices without the prior approval of the M.C.A. The prohibition, as recommended in the Trustkommission Report, is based upon the finding that resale-price maintenance normally results in unreasonable prices and may impede progress in the development of efficient distribution. This finding was made at a time when Danish distribution was undergoing a minor revolution: development of voluntary chains of wholesale distributors and a great increase in retail self-service establishments, all of which fostered desirable price competition along with cost savings in doing business.

Relatively few resale-price–maintenance agreements have been approved, and it is unlikely that the M.C.A. intends to expand its range of approval.

Maximum prices may be fixed vertically and reasonable horizontal price agreements are not prohibited.

In 1953 the Trustkommission also recommended that exclusive-dealing contracts be generally prohibited in the same fashion as re-sale-price–maintenance agreements. This proposal did not carry the Parliament, but, as was the case under the 1937 Act, few exclusive-dealing arrangements survive the test of the 1955 legislation.

Outside the field of monopoly and restrictive practices the M.C.A. is empowered, after consulting consumer and trade organizations, to order price marking or price posting for important consumer goods in trades where such marking or posting is not practiced to a reasonable extent. Under these powers the M.C.A. administers rules for the marking of canned foods and the posting of meat, chicken, vegetable, and fish prices.

If the M.C.A.'s investigation discloses that a restrictive business practice may result in unreasonable prices or business conditions, unreasonable restriction on freedom of trade, or unreasonable discrimination in trading conditions, it has the duty to intervene.

The intervention in the first instance is an attempt to modify or terminate the undesirable practices through negotiation. If negotiation fails, the M.C.A. is authorized to enjoin the practices or business conditions or to prescribe modifications of prices or business conditions. Such modifications may include the fixing of maximum prices or margins as well as ordering that prices, weights, measures, or composition of a product be indicated by clear marking or posting. Moreover, if negotiations have failed, the M.C.A. may exert what seems to be its strongest authority: to order one enterprise to supply specified buyers on terms comparable to those usually provided by the supplier.

If a party is dissatisfied with an M.C.A. injunction or order, he may appeal to the Appeal Tribunal, created by Section 18 of the 1955 Act. Subsequently, if he so desires, he may appeal to the regular courts. As a practical matter, only a few cases have reached the courts.

In connection with registration the second pillar of the Danish system is publicity. Over the years publicity and the resultant education of the Danish consuming public concerning restrictive practices have made it unnecessary for the M.C.A. to devote much of its energies to determining either the existence of unregistered arrangements, which are subject to notification, or violations of its decisions which require termination or modification of a practice. Because it is almost impossible to keep a restrictive arrangement secret in such a small country with a population sensitive to its rights as consumers, tradesmen, and producers, it would be safe to guess that more than 90 per cent obedience of the notification law is observed. Only in those cases where notification is dependent on demand from the M.C.A. may a marked number of notifications be missing, and this failure is in large part due to policy decisions rather than to weakness of the system.

The M.C.A.'s negotiation in attempting to modify unreasonable practices is conducted without public scrutiny, and, if it results in a conclusion satisfactory to the parties, the public is advised by the publication of the result in Meddelelser fra Monopoltilsynet (Communication from the M.C.A.), a monthly bulletin, and often by a full discussion in an annual report. Thus, beginning with either the announcement of a negotiated modification or an order, all, including the reasoning of the M.C.A., is public. At present only the actual votes of the M.C.A. members are withheld, but the question of also publishing this personal information is now under consideration. Of course the full publicity given to registrations often triggers a complaint leading to an investigation.

As earlier noted, matters notified and registered are open to the public, with the exception of the few secret registrations, and the education through publicity is believed to be an essential element of the Danish control system. Of course, as Section 9 of the Act makes clear, registration and publication do not mean that a practice is approved, and the M.C.A. has at any time the power to investigate a restrictive practice to determine if it is lawful, under Section 11.

The investigatory power of the M.C.A. is not, however, limited solely to those matters which have been notified and registered. The jurisdiction of the M.C.A. extends to any practice or condition encompassed within Section 2 of the Act. Acting under this power the M.C.A. undertook to investigate the trade in watches and the sale of radio receivers for home use. Upon the completion of these investigations in 1956 and in 1957, the M.C.A. published a brief summary of the results in the regular issues of Meddelelser, the M.C.A. bulletin.

Before the complete text of the investigation was distributed, the National Organization of Craftsmen asked the Appeal Tribunal to stay the publication of the full text of the investigations.

The ground for the request was the alleged absence of specific authority under the Act enabling the M.C.A. to publish the results of its investigations as the Trustkommission had done in a series of published studies of breweries, cement, flat glass, coal, brick and tile, and lime, whiting, and mortar. By the end of 1958 the matter had not been resolved as the complainant, through his attorney, delayed oral argument before the Tribunal.

It was not until May 1960 that the complainant withdrew his pleadings, at which time the Tribunal decided that it was legal to publish findings dealing with the optical trade.

The M.C.A. has now published a variety of reports in addition to those involving watchmakers and opticians. They include trade in radio receivers, the book trade, electrical engineering, and the observance of suggested retail prices in the grocery trade. Investigations likely to result in further published reports deal with the oil trade and trade in agricultural machinery.

The M.C.A. has also made use of the power granted by Section 1 of the Price Supervision Act, No. 135, of 25 May 1956. Under this legislation it has published reports on the potato trade, oil burners, prices for pork and bacon, and fruit and vegetable prices.

Moreover, the M.C.A., operating under Section 2 of Act No. 135, has completed a number of confidential studies of comparative pricing of products subject to import control and restrictions. These reports have been a major factor in the liberalization of Denmark's trade policy. Often they have indicated the areas of needed changes. Indications are that the M.C.A. finds the publicity developed by its reports to be most valuable. Thus, one can expect further judicious use of the power to publish the results of investigations.

> Sources: Meddelelser 1956 (No. 9, pp. 119–120), 1957 (No. 2, pp. 17–22; No. 3, pp. 25 ff.; No. 8, pp. 123–124), 1958 (No. 6, pp. 81–85, 86–88), 1960 (No. 2, pp. 19–29; No. 3, all; No. 6, pp. 81–98; No. 10, all); Monopoltilsynets Aarsberetning 1956 (pp. 46–47), 1958 (p. 103), 1959 (pp. 95–96), referred to hereafter as Aarsberetning.

The M.C.A., representative of a wide variety of interests and skills, consists of fourteen members and a chairman. In 1959 a law professor served as chairman and the members included lawyers and economists, civil servants, representatives of consumer, labor, trade, cooperative, employer, and similar groups. Three members were women, one of whom was a lawyer and a member of Parliament; another, the head of the National Board of Housekeeping; and, the third, the head of the Danish Women's Consumer Council. The M.C.A. members meet at least once each two weeks, and they are paid for their services.

The M.C.A. supervises the activity of the Directorate, made up of almost seventy-five staff members, whose top officers are trained in law and economics and are acquainted with a wide range of industrial problems. The Directorate maintains the Register, publishes the registrations, and conducts the preliminary investigations and staff work necessary for M.C.A. action and decision. The M.C.A. and its Directorate approach and resolve problems with a high degree of sophistication and practicality. Their work is carried on with but a very few regulations, of which the most important are the Ministry of Commerce Notice No. 193 of 18 June 1955, concerning notification and registration under the 1955 Act, and the instruction sheet accompanying the *Skema* (notification forms).

The succeeding sections deal extensively with the actual administrative practice involved in notification and registration.

I. REGISTRATION OF RESTRICTIVE BUSINESS PRACTICES

THE REGISTRATION of restrictive business practices has been a feature of Danish economic life since 1937, and under the present Act registration serves not only to inform the M.C.A., but also to provide such information for the public.

A. The obligation to register agreements and decisions

Sections 6 through 9 of the Act set forth the standards for notification and registration, and the key phrase is "effective influence" as used in Section 6, which in part reads: "agreements and decisions [which] exert . . . an effective influence on price, production, distribution, or transport conditions throughout the country" shall be notified to the Monopolies Control Authority. Just how broad is the meaning of these words will be seen through the decisions of the M.C.A.

The word "agreement," as it is usually defined by the M.C.A., means any arrangement, formal or informal, binding or advisory, which has been entered into between enterprises in order to restrict competition or which has the effect of restricting competition. The word "decision" refers to horizontal arrangements of a restrictive nature, binding or advisory, made between members of a trade group or organization or entered into by the participants in a financial combination. A reference to the words "restrictive practices of enterprises and associations," technically means vertical restrictions on competition between subsequent sellers.

1. GENERAL TYPES OF REGISTERED RESTRICTIONS

Some restrictions are almost per se subject to notification and registration, and they include price fixing, market sharing, and exclusive dealing. For other types of restrictive arrangements the criteria include both the content of the agreement and the economic power of the participants. If the restrictive agreement is binding, with provisions for enforcement, the presumption is that the participants wield sufficient economic power to render the agreement subject to notification.

Where the arrangement involves a suggested course of conduct, rather than a binding one, the factors determining registration include the proportion of trade controlled by the parties to the arrangement, the relative position and size of those not in the arrangement to those participating, the nature of the goods involved, and the pattern and potential of competition in that particular line of trade.

The statute establishes a duty to notify the M.C.A. whenever two or more enterprises enter into any arrangement which might restrict competition vertically or horizontally in any appreciable degree. For example, arrangements among hairdressers in a very small town have represented a degree of restriction that required notification.

The scope of the notification and registration procedure may be seen through an examination of the various types of practices registered. They include production quotas, exclusive dealing, aggregated rebates, boycotts, price fixing at other than the retail level, discriminatory rebates, joint sales agencies, product-specialization agreements, division of markets, customer allocation, profit pooling, limitations on free entry into trade or industry, service-price schedules, suggested price schedules, and agreements for collaboration on bids for construction contracts.

2. SPECIAL TYPES OF AGREEMENTS

a. Export cartel arrangements

At the present time export cartel arrangements are not required to be registered although no specific statutory exemption actually exists. The M.C.A. has chosen not to consider such arrangements within the scope of the notification provisions, but it does have the power to require registration of export cartels under Section 6. The reason for not requiring registration of export cartels involving manufactured goods is that the domestic controls are deemed so thorough that an export cartel would be unable to enter into domestic restrictive arrangements or to cause unreasonably high domestic prices without falling under the jurisdiction of the M.C.A. A few agricultural-product export arrangements may be registered, but they are limited exceptions.

An example of the way in which the M.C.A. deals with export cartels is found in its recent order to an unregistered export association controlling exports of Danish blue cheese. A Danish exporter who was denied a supply of cheese for export was upheld in his demand by the M.C.A., and the export association, faced with the possibility of being required to register, did not appeal the order to supply. The export association, now that it has complied, will not be required to register in all likelihood, since it no longer directly affects the domestic market.

Import cartels and some international cartels are registered.

The registration of dominant enterprises depends on a request from the M.C.A. that the enterprise submit a notification. This subject will be dealt with in II below.

b. Sole-agency agreements

A single exclusive-dealing agreement may not be of sufficient importance to require registration, but a series of agreements may have a total impact which makes them subject to registration. Thus, a series of sole-agency agreements in various market areas would be registrable because the total system in itself increases the probability of the dealers' compliance with the suggestions and stipulations of the manufacturer or distributor. The M.C.A. interprets the Act to give substance, rather than form, primary consideration.

c. Arrangements of trade associations and financial combinations

Trade associations which, by their membership, composition, and size, are able to exert an effective influence on competition must register as such. They must also register any decisions or restrictive practices which they employ.

Combinations between firms based on financial interdependence must also notify the M.C.A. of the restrictive practices and decisions they use.

With the enactment of Law No. 102 on 7 April 1936 Danish trade associations were given the right to obtain standardization or collective marks. An association and its members could use the mark for the purpose of distinguishing their commodities from others or of denoting their control over the quality of the goods.

To the M.C.A. the standardization marks presented a potential problem in that, once a mark was registered, the M.C.A. would have no way to supervise or to control unreasonable conditions or detrimental effects which might obtain from its use. Neither the 1936 col-

lective and standardization mark law nor the 1955 Monopolies and
Restrictive Practices Control Act contained a provision allowing
cancellation of the mark when used in a restrictive fashion. A group
of powerful retailers could build up the acceptance of a collective
mark, which they controlled, so as to monopolize the market in a
particular line of goods. Since the exclusive arrangement or monopoly
power would in this instance be legally based on the 1936 enactment,
the M.C.A. would be powerless to intervene.

In 1957 the M.C.A. examined three trades in which standardization
and collective marks were used, both to indicate quality-control
standards and to denote a common line of commodities. In the watchmakers', watch dealers', and the goldsmiths' trades the use of such
marks was found to be similar to a legitimate exclusive-dealing arrangement without unreasonable restrictions on trade. However, in
a third trade the M.C.A. found exactly those evil effects that it had
feared: a tendency to monopolization of some commodities by certain members of the trade.

The M.C.A. reported the results of this investigation to the Ministry of Commerce and suggested that the 1936 legislation, which had
authorized standardization marks, be amended. The proposed amendment provided the Ministry with authority to cancel a standardization or collective mark upon recommendation from the M.C.A. when
it was found that the use of such marks created or had a tendency to
create unreasonable conditions and detrimental effects proscribed
by Section 11 of the 1955 Act, and when these effects could not be
terminated by ordinary operation of the Act.

A strong protest against the proposed amendment arose from the
very moment it was announced. During 1958 the matter was the subject of many discussions involving the Ministry of Commerce, the
Directorate for Patents and Trademarks, and the M.C.A. As a result
of these conferences the amendment took a new form. The final proposal was a bill providing for the cancellation of a mark or an injunction against the use of a mark through a decision of the regular courts.
The standard to be applied by the courts was to be: the mark is
forfeit if its use involves restrictive business practices in restraint
of trade.

The final enactment, Law No. 212, 11 June 1959, represents a further change designed to meet Denmark's obligations under the rules
of the Paris Convention of 20 March 1883, concerning industrial property. Law No. 212 provides for the cancellation of a mark or the

enjoining of the use of a mark by the courts if its use is found to be "adverse to the public interest." It is generally agreed that this broad language includes, among other things, the harmful effects under Section 11 of the Monopolies and Restrictive Practices Control Act.

Sources: Aarsberetning 1957 (pp. 31–32), 1958 (pp. 12–13).

B. Registration formalities

According to the Ministry of Commerce Notice No. 193 of 18 June 1955, the duty to notify devolves upon the Board of Directors or managers of limited-liability entities; the responsible partner or partners of partnerships of various types; the operator-owner in one-man businesses; the Board, business manager, or individual members of combinations or associations; and the person in charge or representative of foreign enterprises or combinations doing business in Denmark.

1. NOTIFICATION FORMS

Notice No. 193 sets up provisions for the transmittal to the M.C.A. of copies of all agreements and decisions and for the completion of special questionnaire forms or schedules. These forms, five in number, are designated as *Skema*. All of the *Skema* call for routine name, address, and membership information. However, each has a separate function and in each instance calls for especially relevant information.

a. Agreements form

Skema I is used to register agreements or arrangements of ordinary enterprises, as distinguished from those of trade associations, dominant enterprises, or financial combinations. Information must be provided as to the conditions under which new participants may be admitted to the agreement, the rules which govern the withdrawal of participants from the agreement, the degree to which the agreement may be binding or merely advisory, the relationship of the agreement to other existing arrangements or understandings, and the proportion of the number of enterprises participating in the agreement to the total number of enterprises in the given trade or commerce.

b. Trade association form

Skema II is used to register trade associations or organizations. The required information includes the details of the internal structure of the association and the full membership list, including addresses. If the association reports that it has established arrangements involving restrictive practices, then questions such as those in Skema I must also be answered on Skema II. Additional questions, which establish the full scope of the practices, may be whether time limits are applicable to the arrangement and whether any rules for the settlement of disputes involve restrictive arrangements.

c. Dominant enterprise form

An enterprise which has been asked by the M.C.A. to declare itself as a dominant enterprise uses Skema III. This form calls for a detailed exposition of the enterprise's sales policy, with particular emphasis on the variety of prices and rebates available to various categories of customers. Specific information as to preferential treatment that may be given to special groups of customers is to be supplied. The enterprise is also required to report whether it is a party to any agreements which in themselves would be or are already subject to notification. If the enterprise maintains any sort of vertical control from production to ultimate consumption, the controls and the method for ensuring the observance of such controls must be reported.

d. Financial combinations and mergers form

Skema IV applies to mergers and financially interdependent combinations. Here the questions are designed to expose the structure of the combination and the full extent of the joint activities in question.

e. Amendments form

Skema V is used for amendments to registrations made on the other four forms. The rules require that all alterations in registered matters be reported to the M.C.A. Information reflecting changes in prices, margins, and ownership are to be made by ordinary letter. All other changes are made on Skema V, including notification of the discontinuance of a registered restrictive practice, detailed information as to the nature of the alteration, and the effective date.

A notification received by the M.C.A. is officially stamped to indicate the date of receipt and promptly examined to see whether it is procedurally correct as regards signature by qualified persons, completion of the appropriate *Skema,* and attachment of necessary related documents. Any errors noted at this point are rectified before further processing begins.

2. THE EXTRACT

Once a notification is found to be complete, an extract is entered into the Register. All extracts, after registration numbers have been assigned, are published in both the Danish Official Gazette and in the Registration Journal (Registreringer i Henhold Til Monopolloven), formerly a monthly but now published twice a year by the Ministry of Commerce. This extract contains the main features of the notification, using the original language as much as possible. Minimal information which must appear in every extract includes:

1. The names of the enterprises or associations participating in the notified restrictive practices, decisions, or arrangements,
2. The date of the commencement of the restrictive activity,
3. The goods, services, and trades involved in the restrictive arrangement,
4. The geographic area encompassed by the restriction and its contemplated duration,
5. The rules governing admission to the arrangement or decision and withdrawal from it,
6. The existence or nonexistence of a joint executive authority administering the restriction,
7. The regulations on fixing of prices, profits, rebates, quotas, and similar restrictions, and
8. The rules for the settlement of disputes and the measures designed to enforce and to prevent violations of the arrangement or decision.

Although the extract gives the general nature of the notified matters, normally any specific information as to the level of prices and the size of profits and rebates is omitted. The size of fixed quotas is usually given except in those lines of commerce where it is apparent that quotas will be frequently altered. Of course, all of the notified information not in the extract—such as level of prices, size of profits and rebates—is available in the public file, excepting the few cases where secrecy has been permitted.

The M.C.A. has adopted the practice of submitting a draft of the extract to the notifier, along with an invitation to comment, before publication. The few comments received have pertained to minor changes in language, and they have usually been accepted prior to publication.

3. TIME REQUIREMENTS

Sections 7 and 8 of the Act, which govern the time requirements involved in notification, state that agreements and decisions are not enforceable in the law courts if notification has not taken place within eight days of the making of the agreement or decision. This policy has proved to be an effective means of ensuring notification. If an agreement is found to be invalid by reason of a failure to notify on time, actual invalidation, as a practical matter, can be avoided by reconfirming the agreement; the time of notification can then be computed in relation to the time of reconfirmation.

When a notification discloses on its face that it was not made in due time, the extract reflects this failure with a note to that effect. An appended statement, referring to the operation of Section 8 of the Act, states the parties' inability to claim the protection of the courts for the agreement or decision.

Whenever the notifier knows that he cannot make a full and punctual notification, the M.C.A. practice is to accept a preliminary notification and to grant a postponement for a specific period of time which seems proper under the circumstances. The preliminary notification must be sufficiently specific to give the essential elements of the agreement, decision, or amendment of a registration. Then, if final notification is received within the prescribed period, the notification is treated as being fully valid.

4. FILING SYSTEM

Under M.C.A. procedure, registration takes place when the notification extracts are numbered in succession and placed in the loose-leaf ledgers and files maintained for such purposes. When the notifications are numbered, a copy of the notification is endorsed to show that registration has taken place and then marked with its number and the date. A copy of the extract is placed with the endorsed copy of the notification, and a list of the accompanying documents which are in the public file is added. Also placed with the file is a statement to the effect that registration does not imply approval of the notified material. Amendments or alterations of matters already notified and registered are likewise registered under the serial number of the original registration and so entered into the Register.

Information notified to the M.C.A. on forms other than the *Skema,* such as changes in prices or rebates, is placed in the registration file along with the notification and its related documents.

5. SECRET REGISTRATIONS

In the rare case of a secret registration, a regular number in sequence is assigned, and both the Gazette and the Registration Journal publish a notice to this effect. If a registration is secret only in part, the Gazette, Registration Journal, and the public files so disclose. Actually less than a dozen secret registrations in active status have been on the Register, which, at the end of 1960, involved some 2,300 registration numbers, including terminated and obsolete registrations.

6. ALTERATION OR TERMINATION OF A REGISTRATION

When the M.C.A., acting under the power granted to it by Part V of the Act, alters or terminates a registered restrictive practice, a copy of the letter from the M.C.A. or, in some cases, a summary is placed in the public file under the registration number. The intervention itself is also made public through the various government publications and sometimes in the public press.

When the M.C.A. is notified that a registered agreement or decision has been terminated or when reasons for continuing a registration no longer exist, the registration is so endorsed, and the ledger pages are moved to a special ledger. This information is also published.

7. APPROVAL OF PRICE INCREASES

Under the provisions of Section 24 of the Act, as amended in 1960, the M.C.A. must be notified, unless an exemption has been granted, of any price increase contemplated by any entity which is on the Register, and M.C.A. approval must be given before the price increase is valid. Such price-increase notifications are placed in the Register and the public file, and they are published in Meddelelser fra Monopoltilsynet, a monthly bulletin which also contains digests of all M.C.A. decisions, Appeal Tribunal decisions, and other matters relevant to control of restrictive business practices and monopolies.

II. REGISTRATION AND CONTROL OF MARKET-DOMINATING ENTERPRISES

FROM THE BEGINNING of Danish control of restraints on competition in 1937 the expressed legislative policy has been to make no distinction between obstructions to trade by collective action and obstructions to trade by the individual action of a powerful enterprise.

According to the Trustkommission's 1953 Report (No. 3, p. 92) the policy of requiring dominant firms to register under the amended 1937 Act was grounded on the need to exert control over those firms which fixed the trade procedures of their customers. With such binding arrangements the degree of market control was considered irrelevant, and became an issue only where the actions of the producer or seller or importer were in the form of recommendations. Where firms made no effort to dictate the actions of their customers, the main issue was the actual market control, but other factors were considered, such as the number of competing firms, price leadership, and personal or financial links between theoretical competitors. On this basis a major American shoe-machinery manufacturer, Firm *801*, doing business in Denmark was not required to register. In Denmark this firm has three competitors, two of whom are closely interrelated, thus giving the American firm less than dominant power by M.C.A. standards.

A. Registration of market-dominating enterprises

The Trustkommission's final report (No. 8, 1960, p. 15) observes that the present Register is far from complete in regard to dominant firms and their decisions. One might well expect to see during the next several years an increased number of requested notifications from dominant firms under the provisions of Section 6 (2) of the Act. The government's action is motivated by its desire to keep prices down by operation of Section 24. Naturally firms that have been requested to register under Section 6 will fight the registration, if at all feasible, so as not to be limited in their freedom to price. On the other hand, liberalized trade policies may increase competition to the point where dominant firms are fewer.

If the M.C.A. does become increasingly interested in requiring notification of dominant enterprises, further restrictions, beyond those inherent in the publicity and the limitation on the freedom to price which come with registration, do not automatically follow. The Trustkommission's 1953 Report (No. 3, p. 33), in a section dealing with effective competition, monopoly and public control, makes the point that, in the Danish view, monopolies may benefit the economy through efficiency and cost savings. Thus, in the Trustkommission's view the most efficient production and distribution of goods may be realized in a market where effective competition prevails or in a market where efficient, benevolent monopolies operate. It is on the strength of this outlook that the Danes do not totally prohibit market-dominating enterprises, mergers, and cartels. In the Danish view the economy will work best if such forces are brought under uniform lines of public control in order to prevent abuses.

1. GENERAL REGISTRATION PROCEDURE

The general means employed for the control of dominant enterprises are, in the first instance, notification with a view to inclusion in the public Register, and, secondarily, intervention in the economic activities of dominant enterprises and of cartels as well, when their practices involve unreasonable prices, unreasonable business terms, unreasonable restrictions on the freedom of trade, or unreasonable discrimination in trading conditions.

Under the provision of Subsection 2 of Section 6 of the Act, individual enterprises and financial combinations or mergers which exert or may exert an effective influence on prices, production, and distribution or transport conditions must, only on request of the M.C.A., make notification, so as to supply the M.C.A. and the public with information about the prices and terms of their businesses.

As is the case with registration of restrictive arrangements, registration does not imply approval. In simplest terms the effect of registration is to demonstrate that the registered matters come under the provisions of the Act, thus empowering the M.C.A. to take action if it so decides.

If an examination of the registration discloses actual or potential detrimental effects flowing from certain policies of the dominant enterprise, the M.C.A., proceeding under Section 11, attempts in private to negotiate the elimination or modification of these policies. Orders to terminate the practices are issued under Section 12 only if negotiation fails. Resale-price maintenance by a single dominant enterprise is barred equally with collective resale-price–maintenance schemes, thus leaving suggested prices as the only vertical price guidance device legally sanctioned.

2. POLICIES OR STATUS REQUIRING NOTIFICATION

No regulations or orders have been promulgated amplifying or interpreting the effective influence standards set forth in Subsection 2 of Section 6 of the Act. Thus, we must look to actual administrative practice and the views of former and present officers of the M.C.A. Directorate, as expressed in papers and a variety of publications—all of which are synthesized below.

Other than the size of market share and the pricing policies, which are the two primary considerations, special factors are given attention and analyzed as a whole in classifying an enterprise as dominant: the degree of concentration in the industry as shown through the number of enterprises involved, the relative distribution of the total volume of trade among these enterprises as well as the total sales of the enterprise in question, the quantity of imports, the trading conditions governing imports in the industry, or the importance of the industry to the economy as a whole.

a. Size of market share

The initial factor given consideration is the proportion of trade controlled by the enterprise in question to the total trade of the industry. In some instances the proportion may be so high—70 per cent, for example—as to render unimportant a variety of other factors. Commonly, however, an overall investigation of the industry is necessary because few enterprises enjoy such a high percentage.

In contrast to the Norwegian policy of not requiring registration by those with less than 25 per cent of the market, such a degree of control in the Danish market or even less, when considered in light of other factors, may influence a decision that a firm must register as dominant. For example, as a result of the M.C.A.'s policy of considering several factors, it has required registration by firms with as low as 10 per cent of the volume of trade, when such firms distribute goods through exclusive arrangements or other restrictive modes of distribution.

As discussed in the 1959 Annual Report (p. 30) a wholesale-watch company was found to be not dominant. The firm's total share of the imports of pocket and wrist watches was no more than 15 per cent. In addition, if the market computation were made in terms of the proportion of the total market in name-brand watches, the firm's percentage dropped to about 6 per cent. Being concerned about the possible dominance of the firm, the M.C.A. investigated, but it could not prove the existence of an alleged system of compelling observance of suggested resale prices. It is conceivable that, if such a system had been proved, the firm would have been classified as dominant, and notification would have been ordered with but 6 per cent of the market involved.

b. Growing industry, freedom of entry, downward price trend

In the Danish system a 25 per cent share has not been enough by itself to require the firm to notify as dominant. Size is less a factor when the industry in question is a growing one and when a record of freedom of entry for new firms is proved. If, in addition, signs of a downward price trend are discovered, particularly when the enterprise in question assists the trend, there is good reason to expect that notification will not be required.

c. Availability of product

Another factor of weight along with any or all of the considerations already noted is the availability of substitute products to the consumer. The greater the availability, the greater is the chance that the M.C.A. will not treat a firm as dominant.

d. Business policies

Policies in doing business may also be a factor in classifying enterprises as dominant. For example, exclusive sales agencies, important factors in ordinary registration, are here of great importance, for they exist to ensure compliance with the suggestions and conditions laid down by the producing enterprise. The existence of such a mode of distribution is a factor in determining whether notification is necessary.

e. Declining industry

In the 1958 Annual Report of the M.C.A. (p. 27) the Appeal Tribunal found that a firm in a declining industry, a manufacturer of dynamo-power bicycle lamps, was not required to register as dominant. The Tribunal considered pertinent factors, such as the relatively small annual sales by the firm and its proportional share—about 20 per cent of the total sales of dynamo lamps—against the background of the sales of many other kinds of bicycle lamps. In consideration of all these factors along with the decline of the bicycle-lamp industry, the Tribunal decided not to require registration.

f. Trademarked products

In the cases involving trademarked items the M.C.A. initially studies the degree of independence in pricing policy available to the particular firm. Thus, an enterprise which holds a small share of the market but which produces a price-leading trademarked item may be treated as dominant. On the other hand, an enterprise which holds the same small market share and which produces a trademarked item that is not a price leader normally will not be treated as dominant and, therefore, will not have to notify. An exception would be where the public acceptance of the trademark has become so great as to give the product the status of a special article for which there is no ready substitute.

g. Price leadership

Another consideration which has led the M.C.A. to treat firms with as much as 17 per cent of the market as not dominant is the extent of the enterprise's freedom to make its own prices. Thus, if the industry has a clear price leader, other than the enterprise in question, or, if factors beyond the enterprise's control determine its prices, the M.C.A. is not likely to find that a mere high percentage of market control constitutes effective influence.

h. Uniformity of industry practices

The Appeal Tribunal, created by Section 18 of the Act, has upheld the registration of an American importer, Firm 34, with only 14 per cent of the market in petroleum products. In this case, which will be discussed in the section dealing with case studies of the petroleum industry, the Tribunal's decision was based upon a finding of rigidity in this import market in that all importers fixed suggested resale prices, and in that the small number of importers facilitated the potential joint planning of sales.

Similarly, an exclusive importer of certain brands of agricultural machinery was required to register, even though other competing machines were available in Denmark.

B. Control of market-dominating enterprises

Because any sizeable American firm doing business in Denmark is likely, on the basis of present trends, to end up on the Register because of dominance, aside from the issue of participation in restrictive agreements, American executives should understand the criteria for control over dominant firms and the procedures in exercising it.

The M.C.A.'s main concerns in controlling dominant enterprises are refusal-to-deal problems and discriminatory practices. The M.C.A. can attempt to modify these restrictive practices through negotiations and persuasion, or it can interest itself in such problems with an eye toward possible future action through an order to deal.

Whatever the legal posture of the possible course of action by the M.C.A. the same considerations would apply when the M.C.A. evaluates the merits of the complaint and of the defense.

1. M.C.A. ORDERS TO DEAL

In Denmark many of the refusal-to-sell problems arise out of overall sales policies of dominant firms. The M.C.A. seeks to resolve this type of problem by modification of the offending trading terms and sales policies. Since refusal to sell can also arise in other contexts, the M.C.A. is empowered to order an enterprise to sell to specified buyers at terms applicable to similar sales.

The legislative history of this portion of the Act indicates that the Parliament was aware that the right to refuse to sell, if unchecked, could negate any legislative or administrative measures that might be taken against boycotts, exclusive agreements, and resale-price maintenance. The power to order an enterprise to sell was considered particularly important as a means of preventing dominant firms from dictating the modes or practices of the distribution of their products.

The power of the M.C.A. under Section 12, Subsection 3, to order a firm to deal is limited, by operation of Section 11 and Section 2, Subsection 1, to jurisdiction over dominant firms. Thus, a refusal to deal by a nondominant firm is subject only to the persuasive powers of the M.C.A. The result of this limitation on the power of the M.C.A. is to weaken the effectiveness of the prohibition of vertical price fixing under Section 10 in those situations where the supplier does not qualify as a dominant firm. The only situation in which the M.C.A.

could act against a refusal by a single nondominant firm would be under Section 10 when the refusal could not be justified on any other conceivable grounds except as a means of enforcing price. This situation is, of course, not likely to occur, and a variety of plausible reasons for a refusal to deal with a price cutter can normally be advanced so as to free the nondominant supplier from the operation of the law.

Of course an agreement among nondominant suppliers would provide the M.C.A. with jurisdiction that is absent when a single nondominant supplier refuses to deal.

2. MAIN CLASSES OF CONDUCT DEMANDING INTERVENTION

The principal classes of business conduct by dominant firms which have most commonly caused M.C.A. intervention are refusal to deal, discrimination in terms of delivery, discrimination in prices, and exclusive-dealing contracts—all four of which frequently lead to an order to deal.

a. Refusal to deal

The administrative practice of the M.C.A. has been to investigate and to intervene in refusal-to-deal practices of a dominant firm only when other enterprises have complained that they have been hampered by the firm's practices or power.

1. THE COMPLAINT. In its consideration of cases of discontinuance of supplies or refusal to deal, the M.C.A. is guided by a variety of private and public economic principles. As a prerequisite to M.C.A. intervention the complaining, potential buyer must be able to establish that he has a legitimate interest in carrying the goods in question. This is not to suggest that lines of trade or classes of dealers must be rigid, but a grocer who seeks to carry only one brand of television receiver, and who is refused, is unlikely to receive a sympathetic ear at the M.C.A. If, however, the same grocer has acquired additional premises and has shown a bona fide attempt to enter the electric-appliance field, his case receives consideration.

In the ordinary case the primary considerations in the M.C.A.'s evaluation of the complainant's point of view are the importance of the article to the consumer, the relevance of the article to the buyer's field of trade, and the availability of substitutes if the article is trade-marked. If a buyer can obtain delivery of goods similar to those in dispute and carry on his trade with the substitutes, the complaint has generally been rejected. The question of substitutes is handled on a factual, rather than theoretical, basis, and the actual ability to obtain substitutes and the actual degree of equivalence of the substitute are thoroughly explored.

2. ACCEPTABLE DEFENSES. The M.C.A. treats as possible acceptable defenses those reasons for refusing to deal which are objective and factually based. If it can be established that a refusal to deal is, in fact, based upon proven considerations of efficiency and rationalization in production and distribution, the refusal to deal will not be challenged by the M.C.A. Other acceptable reasons for refusing to deal may arise from the operation of a reasonable and uniformly applied policy, such as one establishing a minimum size of purchase orders. Similarly acceptable would be a refusal based on reasonable standards establishing minimum business or professional training for dealers. Such defenses are, in the opinion of the M.C.A., susceptible to objective proof, as are other defenses based upon poor financial or credit status of the dealer or upon the dealer's use of unfair methods of competition.

3. UNACCEPTABLE DEFENSES. The M.C.A. does not accept as a valid or objective reason for a dealer's refusing to sell the fact that his potential buyer may resell the goods at prices below suggested ones or below those prices at which others sell the same product. Loss-leader selling might be accepted as an objective excuse, but such a case must really be proved. The M.C.A. has not yet found a case in which the sale has been below cost, even when the cost concept includes a proper allowance for business expenditures.

The M.C.A. has not accepted a variety of other defenses raised in refusal-to-sell situations. For example, a refusal tied to a program of limiting output and supply will not be treated as valid. The same result would obtain if the refusal were either in consideration of the wishes of older, established customers or in response to pressure from the competitors of the would-be buyers.

One unacceptable defense is illustrated by a case in which manufacturers discontinued supplies to a chain in the radio and television retail trade in Denmark. The trade operates with relatively high suggested resale prices which permit confidential price reductions to individual customers. The manufacturers have generally not interfered with this method of retailing. In fact, it would appear that they prefer to maintain this system of trading, which, in effect makes competition between dealers less severe and less obvious. This lack of competition between retailers, in turn, relieves the suppliers of any pressures for lower prices that might come with more active price competition at the retail level.

One retail chain in the radio and television trade, however, drastically reduced its prices for all makes of television sets. The chain undertook this reduction in the first instance to reduce its inventory of slow-moving merchandise. Secondarily, the chain wanted to establish firm, competitive prices for television sets as a means of terminating the general trade practice of giving concealed rebates to customers astute enough to haggle over prices. As a consequence of the chain store's price reductions, five of the six suppliers of television sets discontinued dealing with the chain. At the same time the chain was expelled from the retailers' trade association.

The M.C.A. found that the discontinuance of supplies by the manufacturers was in large part motivated by a desire to oblige competitors of the chain rather than by a desire to maintain resale prices. It further found that the discontinuance of supplies had the same effect as a refusal by a dominant firm or by a group acting under a specific agreement. Negotiations with the manfacturers having failed, the M.C.A. ordered resumption of deliveries to the chain. This order was upheld on appeal (Meddelelser 1961, No. 3, p. 67).

The M.C.A. will not accept subterfuges designed to restrain competition as defenses in refusal-to-deal cases. Typical is the case of a dominant manufacturer of yarn who stopped supplying a retailer, making it clear that resumption of deliveries was contingent upon the retailer's willingness not to undersell the suggested resale prices. Simultaneously the manufacturer instructed his other dealers that they were not to give any rebates or reductions on the suggested resale prices that he had established. The M.C.A. ordered that this form of resale-price maintenance be terminated and that the dominant firm resume supplying the price-cutting retailer. The M.C.A. was upheld on appeal (Meddelelser 1961, No. 5, p. 105).

b. Discrimination in terms of delivery

A typical case of justified discrimination in trading terms is reported in the M.C.A.'s Annual Report for 1957 (p. 72). A producer of luxury porcelains, which might also be classed as art objects, had trading terms which, by favoring the specialty dealers in luxury goods, discriminated against the general dealers in household china, porcelain, and glassware. The Appeal Tribunal, in overruling the M.C.A., upheld the right of the manufacturer to discriminate as a means of promoting sales of a luxury item in luxury shops, which account for the largest amount of such trade. The Tribunal found the discrimination to be lawful because the luxury articles were not necessities and thereby determined that the general dealer in housewares could easily satisfy the greatest part of his customers' demands without stocking such items.

On the other hand, the M.C.A. will not accept as valid reasons advanced to justify the existence of discriminatory business terms and prices, which may be equated to refusals to deal and which have the effect of discouraging new and inexpensive modes of distribution. Thus, terms discriminating against supermarkets, discount houses, and voluntary chains are forbidden in the absence of some objective defense.

One of the postwar developments in the Danish distribution system has been the voluntary chain in which independent retailers or wholesalers band together to pool their resources and effect savings which are passed on to the consumer. Some dominant firms have refused to supply such chains on the theory that to do so would make it impossible for ordinary wholesalers to sell their goods on their usual terms. The M.C.A. has not found this view to be justifiable and has successfully negotiated the equal treatment of voluntary chains.

c. Exclusive dealing

Frequently the M.C.A. finds exclusive-dealing arrangements to be unjustified and orders the company to deal or orders that the company's contracts be revised.

The 1959 Annual Report (p. 65) reports a case involving a well-known vacuum cleaner manufactured in Denmark. Traditionally such machines were normally sold only by individual salesmen going to the customer. However, the factory in question, the leader in its field, had a system of distribution employing both direct salesmen and ordinary appliance retailers and it sold only to retailers willing to accept an exclusive contract. The M.C.A. found that the exclusive agreements precluded the dominant firm's competitors from placing their wares in appliance stores unless the retailer was willing to give up the best-known brand in the field. The M.C.A. decided that a retailer should be able to present to a customer all of the brands generally available, so that the customer could make his purchase on the basis of a sound comparison of all competing brands.

While the case was on appeal to the Tribunal the dominant firm resumed negotiations with the M.C.A. and revised its dealers' contracts to meet the views of the M.C.A.

The M.C.A. will not accept refusals based on maintaining traditional distributor-dealer relationships, as is shown in the radiator case. The largest of the five Danish manufacturers of heating radiators is registered as a dominant enterprise, Registration No. 2127. At one time the five manufacturers had entered into an agreement giving a wholesalers' trade organization exclusive wholesale rights to their radiators. This agreement had been terminated by an order from the M.C.A. Subsequently a wholesaler, who was not a member of the organization, was refused delivery on the ground that his relationship to a housing cooperative disqualified him as a wholesaler. The M.C.A. was unable to find a reasonable basis for the trading policies justifying the refusal to deal, and, therefore, ordered the five suppliers to deal with the complainant on the same terms as apply to other wholesalers. The Appeal Tribunal upheld this order (Meddelelser 1957, No. 4, p. 45).

The Parliament, anticipating a large number of refusal-to-deal cases, cautioned the M.C.A. to use sparingly its power to order sales and the M.C.A. has heeded this admonition. Despite a sizeable number of refusal-to-deal complaints, the power to order sales has been used in only three cases over a six-year period. Other situations involving refusals to deal or discriminatory practices have, as already described, been handled by a negotiated modification of trading terms.

d. Discrimination in prices

Price discrimination in Denmark has taken a variety of forms including aggregated rebate systems, quantity-discount arrangements, and rebates based on dealer classification. As developed in the American case studies in III below, the M.C.A. considers that it has control over most forms of unreasonable inequality and has intervened where there is evidence that the discrimination is in fact unreasonable.

If a firm were to reduce its prices drastically in a market area which, at that time, was a most important one for a competitor, the M.C.A. would examine such price discrimination to determine whether it was reasonable and the degree to which it may have overstepped the legitimate bounds of competition. A similar approach would be taken during a price war in which markedly low prices were set for an entire line throughout the country. So far such cases are only theoretical, for market conditions in the expanding Danish economy have provided no opportunities for them to arise. If they were to develop, the M.C.A. in its search for objective data would look to related price levels and trends. Thus, unreasonably low prices are deemed to be within the jurisdiction of the M.C.A.

e. Unreasonable prices

In the course of the parliamentary debate preceding the enactment of the Monopolies and Restrictive Practices Control Act of 1955, it was suggested that the M.C.A.'s power to intervene might well be used to provide a more permanent and continuing control over dominant enterprises. In this context it was suggested that price regulation applicable to dominant enterprises should be carefully undertaken so as to encourage rationalization. The M.C.A. was asked also to administer its price-regulation power in such a way as not to hamper the initiative and enterprise of the dominant firm. Obviously Parliament issued a large order, difficult to apply. It is equally difficult to judge the degree to which the M.C.A. has actually succeeded in meeting the broad objectives established by the Parliament.

Subsection 2 of Section 11 of the Act requires that the M.C.A., in judging the reasonableness of a firm's prices, take into account the conditions in other enterprises operated with comparable technical and commercial efficiency. As a consequence of this yardstick, in practice the general level of efficiency becomes the norm, and the more efficient firms are entitled to higher profits resulting from their excess of efficiency. This section has been administered by the M.C.A. so that prices or margins are not fixed at a level lower than that required to cover necessary operating costs, including depreciation and what is denominated as a "reasonable net profit" in Subsection 4 of Section 12 of the Act. The M.C.A., as Subsection 4 suggests, does consider the reasonableness of the profit in light of the financial risks involved in the trade or industry.

One of the more objective elements common to most price-regulation cases as well as to those involving margins and discounts, is the ratio of net profit to invested capital. The net profit with which the M.C.A. must deal is the "reasonable" one denominated in Section 12 of a statute devoid of any definition of "reasonable net profit." The M.C.A. practice, which has usually gone unchallenged, is to treat as net profit that which remains of the gross profit after deducting all costs of doing business, including depreciation and payment to the entrepreneur for his administration and enterprise. Income taxes and interest on loans are not deducted from gross profit under this formula. The scope of deductible costs is relative to the risk factors involved and to traditions or patterns of treating costs peculiar to a given trade or industry and thereby will vary from case to case.

While comparisons may be useful when considering prices or profits in a multienterprise industry governed by a restrictive agreement, the validity or possibility of comparison diminishes when dealing with a dominant enterprise that may in fact be a monopoly. In such a case a special standard of costs must be developed on the basis of a study of the dominant enterprise itself in light of generally accepted principles of good business practice.

As a means of encouraging dominant enterprises in their efforts to develop more economical and efficient means of doing business, the M.C.A. attempts to work out with them individual long-range schemes for price regulation. Prices based on standard calculations are allowed to vary in accordance with general trends in wage rates and costs of raw materials. Through the stability and certainty that a dominant enterprise gains from such a plan, the M.C.A. believes the enterprise will be encouraged to devote its energies to promoting efficiency, which will in turn be rewarded by higher and retainable profits.

3. REGISTRATION OF NET PRICES

The extent of M.C.A. authority over the price policies of dominant enterprises has recently been tested in connection with an M.C.A. request to a dominant enterprise in the glass industry to notify and be registered under the provisions of Subsection 2 of Section 6 of the Act. The dominant enterprise conceded that it must register, but it resisted the M.C.A. demand that it include the net prices charged for the goods it manufactured and sold. The enterprise further asserted that such net prices, not being subject to registration, were therefore not subject to the provisions of Section 24 concerning prior approval of price rises.

The Appeal Tribunal upheld the M.C.A.'s authority to require the registration of such net prices even if the language of the 1955 Act was not specific as to this point. The Appeal Tribunal grounded its finding on a reading of the present Act and the earlier 1937 legislation. The 1937 legislation had been interpreted, without challenge, as requiring the registration of net prices. The Tribunal noted that the parliamentary comments on the enactment of Section 6 of the 1955 Act demonstrated that the provisions were intended to be applied in the same way as were those of the previous legislation. Thus, it decided that the present Act gave the M.C.A. the right, within certain broad limits, under which it could determine the precise character of the registration. The Tribunal further found that the 1955 changes in the registration provisions, first enacted in 1937, were not made for the purpose of limiting the duty to register (Meddelelser 1961, No. 2, p. 43).

An appeal in a similar net-price–registration controversy was withdrawn as soon as the result in the glass-industry case was known. The industry involved in the second appeal was the production of meal, and official notice of the withdrawal of the appeal appears in Meddelelser 1961 (No. 2, p. 51).

4. AMENDMENT OF SECTION 24 TO ALLOW EXEMPTIONS

The key to price regulation of dominant enterprises lies in Section 24, which provides that increases in prices, margins, and discounts in regard to goods and services, covered by agreements or supplied by dominant enterprises, cannot be carried into effect without prior approval from the M.C.A. The section thus covers everything that is registered. Consequently, this limitation on the freedom to determine prices has been considered irksome.

Not until the summer of 1960, when Denmark entered the European Free Trade Association (E.F.T.A.), was the Act amended to allow certain exemptions under Section 24. Law No. 231, of 10 June 1960, added a third subsection to Section 24 empowering the M.C.A. to grant exemptions when warranted by market conditions, the nature of the commodity, or its relative importance to the total volume of trade. The amendment also allows an exemption to be granted on the basis of rationalization agreements which are deemed to be of material importance in furthering efficiency. The amendment, though primarily designed to provide Danish trade and industry with a greater degree of flexibility within the competitive framework of the E.F.T.A., has already been used to accomplish a variety of purposes.

If classified in terms of goods and services approximately twenty exemptions have been granted from the requirement that price raises by those on the Register must be approved in advance by the M.C.A. Involved in these exemptions are twenty-two dominant enterprises and six registered agreements.

The single Danish producer of fertilizer was granted an exemption for a mixed fertilizer consisting of potash and phosphate because each component part is itself already price-controlled, and each product is available separately for individual use (Meddelelser 1960, No. 9, pp. 135–137).

A manufacturer of horseshoes had his prices freed because reduced barriers to imports had created effective price competition at a time when the market for the product was beginning to dwindle (Meddelelser 1960, No. 9, pp. 145–146).

An agreement under which the prices of field and garden seeds were fixed by two cooperative societies was freed from M.C.A. control, because the M.C.A. found that the bargaining strength of the buyers and sellers was so nearly equal that no further government surveillance was needed (Meddelelser 1960, No. 11, pp. 190–191).

The M.C.A. exempted the lists of suggested prices for soling shoes that had been established by local societies of master shoemakers and footwear dealers. The increased availability of low-priced footwear so changed the competitive situation in the trade that profit possibilities markedly diminished for those depending on resoling for a livelihood (Meddelelser 1960, No. 11, p. 191).

The Association of Danish Clogmakers' was granted an exemption. Its price list suggesting the repair prices for the wooden-soled shoes was freed. In the view of the M.C.A. the relative unimportance of the products justified the move. Similar reasoning led to the freeing of oyster prices. The prices of crisp bread baked in Copenhagen were also freed because liberalized trade policies had opened the Danish market to highly competitive Norwegian and Swedish products (Meddelelser 1960, No. 11, pp. 192–193).

A society of carrot growers whose prepackaged trademarked carrots are important to the food trade in Copenhagen was given freedom to price. This exemption was granted, in the face of the registered agreements fixing prices and restricting the areas of carrot production, on the theory that the supply of carrots would be disorganized if price changes could not be made rapidly (Meddelelser 1961, No. 4, pp. 91–93).

Additional goods and services which have been granted exemptions include coke, herrings, sea freight rates, certain structural shapes of nonferrous metals, psychological services, coal, paper, tile products, regular gasoline, ball bearings, petroleum, and tobacco.

As can be seen from the nature of the exemptions, the amendment to Section 24 has provided the M.C.A. with flexibility enabling it to discontinue control where legally it has jurisdiction, but where it recognizes that it can accomplish little of significance. The cases also illustrate the trend toward eventual freedom from the operation of Section 24 for those portions of the economy that become subject to effective foreign-based competition through the operation of the E.F.T.A. or Denmark's possible entry into the European Economic Community.

C. Evaluation of the Danish attitude toward dominant firms

The Danes recognize that they have a limited market in which one or a few domestic enterprises will often be able to satisfy the nationwide demand. Thus, the outright prohibition of monopolies would be neither reasonable nor feasible. Only abuse of power, as distinguished from power itself, is the target of the Danish legislative and administrative system of control. The only type of power which is considered in itself an abuse is resale-price maintenance; for this reason it is prohibited and subject to the very few exceptions that the M.C.A. has allowed for heavily taxed or controlled goods.

Moreover, the M.C.A. recognizes that the very nature of a monopoly is to try to limit the market supply and to maintain the highest possible prices and profits. This is why the power to intervene against unreasonable prices has been given to the M.C.A. and has been exercised.

Mergers have not become troublesome in Denmark for a variety of reasons. Consolidations and combinations that have been made before 1955 are in most cases now subject to control as dominant enterprises. Some mergers may be discouraged by the possibility that the resulting firm will then qualify as a dominant enterprise. Whatever the reasons may be, the Act is interpreted as providing for control of mergers and financial combinations as much as it does for control of dominant firms.

Under the usual analysis of the difference between the American system of prohibition of certain activities and the European model, in which only abuse is penalized, one might assert that an enterprise in the United States has the burden of proving the reasonableness of its activities, while European administrators, such as the M.C.A., have the burden of proving that the enterprise has acted unreasonably. In actual Danish practice, this asserted difference in the burden of proof is hardly discernible.

Americans in Denmark, critical of the system, allege that in some instances an M.C.A. demand to a dominant enterprise to notify is related to M.C.A.'s wish to be able to control price rises of the enterprise through the operation of Section 24. Thus, some American firms not yet registered as dominant, but potentially subject to a demand to notify, indicate that they are, in some instances, inhibited in their pricing policies because of the potential of a demand to register.

The M.C.A. is very much aware of the criticisms, complexities, and difficulties that are the inevitable result of any attempt to find a rational solution to the problems created by dominant enterprises in an economy as small as that of Denmark. It is not at all unlikely that the otherwise normal business and trading terms when employed by a monopoly or dominant firm may exert an effective influence on the free play of competition by leading to discrimination and thus to the detriment of other enterprises. It is in such cases that the M.C.A. is called upon to weigh carefully and to balance delicately a large number of public and private considerations and interests. The M.C.A. would be the first to admit that in some such cases it has not always found the perfect solution. However, no one else has come up with a more acceptable substitute. When questionable features have been present in a case the M.C.A. has on occasion been overruled by the Appeal Tribunal. The M.C.A. fully understands that price questions demand the careful scrutiny of a large variety of accounting factors. Even though certain general indications concerning unreasonable prices have emerged from the experience under the 1937 and 1955 Acts, each concrete case requires the most painstaking inquiry.

The Danish policy and hope is to avoid having to take the final step to total price control in exercising control over dominant enterprises. It is this hope that justifies the expenditures of time and detail in administering the regulation of dominant enterprises.

III. CASE STUDIES OF AMERICAN FIRMS

A. Introduction

In 1959 and early 1960 I surveyed forty-five Danish enterprises in which there was a substantial, direct or indirect, American financial interest. Twenty-eight of these enterprises were registered, and at least one more seemed a likely candidate for registration in the near future. About half of the registrations were for dominant enterprises. In several instances firms that are considered among the giants of American industry did not appear on the Register because, in the context of the Danish competitive situation, they were something less than dominant.

Among the firms interviewed or queried through questionnaires, two firms producing and dealing in business machines, Firms 51 and 53, which were not on the Register, reported that there was too much competition in their industry. Among the registered firms a dominant manufacturer of toilet articles, Firm 23, indicated that in its trade the competition ran from "none" to "sufficient." A registered, dominant petroleum importer, Firm 33, indicated that competition was "sufficient." A registered importer of automobiles, Firm 101, found too much competition present, though the government effectively controlled all prices. An American tire manufacturer, Firm 92, whose trade terms are registered, also found too much competition.

The registered firms, which are required to ask for prior approval for price hikes under Section 24, indicated that their price rises had always been approved. This fact was explained by the managers of Firm 101, by the observation that it is usually apparent how much of a price increase the M.C.A. will approve in any given case. In every instance the conduct of the M.C.A. was sincerely respected, though most American firms found the Danish legislation even more restrictive than the American antitrust laws. In all interviews in Denmark the American laws seemed to emerge as the ideal form of legislation.

In describing the American experience in Denmark, the material will be organized on a trade basis, rather than a practice basis. In accordance with the promise made to those courteous enough to fill out questionnaires and to grant interviews, no direct identification of their firms will be made. Because nothing concrete will be gained by giving the names of those firms to which no promises were made, they also will be treated anonymously.

B. Perfume and toilet articles

Trade association—Collective resale-price maintenance—Permitted resale-price maintenance—Price list—Dominant registration—Agreement to boycott—Refusal to sell—Special market through name-brand dominance

An industry trade association, made up of some fifty manufacturers, importers, and wholesalers, is registered under No. 160. Until the enactment of Section 10, which prohibits resale-price maintenance, this association maintained a collective system of enforcing the resale price of its commodities, dating back to the 1920's.

A large number of the products which the association's members sell or produce are subject to special taxes and excise taxes, as well as a number of indirect taxes. Goods subject to this sort of taxation are normally granted an exemption from the ban on resale-price maintenance. Therefore each member of the association may set the resale prices for its goods which are subject to special taxation. The association publishes a price list showing these legally fixed prices for the leading brands of its members. The association itself is very careful not to participate in the pricing, and collective enforcement is totally terminated. Each member has the right to enforce his own prices, and collective or joint enforcement is cause for M.C.A. intervention.

Firm 21, a member of the association, imports, produces, and sells perfumes, cosmetics, and various beauty aids; it, along with the rest of the trade, does not fix the prices of products not subject to tax.

Firm 23, whose line includes soap and toothpaste as well as cosmetics, also has joined in Registration No. 160. Firm 23's legal resale-price–maintenance program for articles outside the scope of the perfume- and toilet-article trade association is Registration No. 509, a dominant-enterprise registration, covering taxed items on which it has the right to fix prices.

Firm 23 has adopted a policy of giving the same quantity discount prices, to wholesalers and retailers, when the latter are able to purchase in the same quantity and under the same payment terms as wholesalers. As a result a group of wholesalers located outside of Copenhagen have entered into an agreement not to stock Firm 23's products until the sales policy is terminated. This agreement to boycott Firm 23 is Registration No. 2104. As far as can be ascertained, the M.C.A. has not received a complaint from Firm 23 asking that it intervene against the boycott, which is apparently ineffective.

Distribution policies in the toiletries and cosmetics field seem to be undergoing a degree of change, as the above boycott and a further case involving an imported, American-made nail polish indicate. The Danish importer of an American nail polish maintains his own wholesale department. The importer, at one point, stopped supplying a variety of imported items, including the exclusively controlled American nail polish, to wholesalers outside of Copenhagen. This discontinuance resulted in a complaint by a wholesaler whose supply had been cut off. In responding to the complaint, the importer-wholesaler defended itself through its policy based on the fact that it had itself been cut off by other importers and producers, who had previously sold to its wholesale department and who now acted as wholesalers. While the matter was under discussion with the M.C.A., evidence was adduced that the American nail polish truly dominated the market to the extent that no substitute was available, as measured by public demand. Thereupon the importer-wholesaler agreed to resume sales to other wholesalers at the old terms. On this basis, and because of the reasonable nature of the importer's original motive for not supplying other wholesalers, the M.C.A. decided that governing the importer's future activities through intervention was not necessary.

Sources: Registration Nos. 160, 509, 2104; Aarsberetning 1956 (pp. 40–41), 1957 (p. 69); Meddelelser 1956 (No. 5, p. 55); Priskontrolraadets Beretning (1938–1943, pp. 37 ff.), referred to hereafter as Beretning; Trustkommissionens Betaenkninger (No. 8, 1960, pp. 221–223), referred to hereafter as Betaenkninger.

C. Motion pictures

Trade association—Licensors' uniform licensing terms—Licensees' uniform licensing terms—Boycott

Registration No. 2187 reports an agreement involving seven American producers and distributors of motion pictures, Firms 61, 62, 64, 66, 67, 68, and 69, and a trade association controlling American film exports, Firm 63. The agreement, which became effective in February 1957, provides a uniform system of licensing the exhibition of films owned by the American firms.

By this agreement motion picture theatres are classified into three categories, and minimum exhibition fees are established in most cases at 40, 36, and 30 per cent of gross box office receipts, after deduction of amusement taxes. The terms for first-run theatres, which initially pay at the rate of 40 per cent, include minimum playing-time requirements and a scale of reduced rentals to 36 and 35 per cent when films are held over for extended runs.

The rental terms upon which the Americans agreed initially were not fully acceptable to the associations of Danish theatre owners,

Danish film producers, and distributors of foreign films other than those produced in America. Currently the terms established by Registration No. 2187 prevail.

Registration No. 1869 for the film distributors' association originally included the American firms along with the other importers and distributors of foreign films. The Americans have withdrawn from this organization, and it is their new arrangement that is reflected in the later registration.

The Danish theatre owners in 1952 joined together in two agreements, Registration Nos. 1870 and 1871, relating to Copenhagen and provincial theatres. These agreements, which are generally still in operation, establish the relative maximum rentals that the members must pay for motion pictures. To ensure compliance with the maximum rental restrictions of the agreements and to prevent highly competitive bidding for pictures, the members undertake to maintain uniform ticket prices and not to raise prices for special films that might otherwise command premium ticket prices. The agreement does not mean that all members charge the same ticket prices. Ordinarily a member will not deviate from his own particular ticket-price policy for the purpose of obtaining potential added revenue which would enable him to make the high bid for an exceptionally desirable feature film. The exhibitors' trade organization, registered under the agreements, is empowered to grant exemptions from the uniform-pricing provisions.

The agreement registered as No. 1871 is also concerned in part with the competition between television and motion pictures. Certain provisions prohibit portions of films shown in theatres to be shown on television, and, reciprocally, they ban theatre exhibition of a film already shown on television. Exemptions from this prohibition may be granted in special circumstances by the governing board of the exhibitors' trade organization.

In the view of the Price Control Board the restraints on television were unreasonably restrictive. The matter was taken up with the government-owned television authority, which informed the P.C.B. that negotiations were already underway with the theatre owners. Through an informal understanding the Danish Television Authority broadcasts several films a week. However, the formal restrictions are still registered and still binding upon both the distributors and exhibitors of films.

Registration No. 1871, which primarily concerns the Copenhagen theatre owners, also contains provisions for a boycott of certain Copenhagen newspapers whose advertising rates were, in the view of the theatre owners, too high. The P.C.B. initiated inquiries and the parties soon came to terms, without any formal intervention. The theatres now place advertising in all papers on four days of each week, and on the remaining days the papers carry program information without charge to the exhibitors.

> Sources: Registration Nos. 1869, 1870, 1871, 2187; Beretning (1951–1952, pp. 35–36); Betaenkninger (No. 8, 1960, pp. 154–117).

D. Petroleum

Dominant registration—Small firm registered; large firm unregistered—Controlled prices—Formula pricing—Suggested maximum prices—Exclusive dealing—Appeal from order to register—Price leadership—Approved price raises—Request to be removed from register

Denmark has six major importers and refiners of petroleum products. Four of these are American firms, of which only two are presently on the Register as dominant. Two non-American firms are also registered as dominant, leaving two major American firms off the Register. According to figures published in 1954 American Firm 33, Registration No. 1466, controlled 36.4 per cent of the entire market in all petroleum products. American Firm 34, Registration No. 1685, had the lowest percentage of market control of the four registered firms with 14.1 per cent. At present it is estimated that American Firm 32, which has not been required to register, has a larger percentage of the market than registered Firm 34. It is expected that Firm 32 will be asked to register as dominant in the near future. The Trustkommission estimated that the four leading petroleum firms control 90 per cent of the market.

Until the end of 1960 the M.C.A. effectively controlled petroleum-product prices through a formula calculating wholesale prices on the basis of F.O.B. prices in export countries, freight rates, and approved, import profit margins. This method of price calculation establishes what is called the maximum price, which, until 1960, was in fact the minimum price, according to one of the American oil companies. It was the view of the same company that this form of control may well have kept prices abnormally high.

During 1959 and 1960 the registered petroleum refiners began to feel competition from lower-priced products originating in Germany and Italy. The increased competition, which became evident through the growth of new firms and the abundance of products available in Denmark, led to the granting of an exemption to the registered firms under the provisions of the 1960 amendment to Section 24. Thus, free pricing was instituted for most petroleum products. In 1959 the maximum price margins, as established for the oil firms, lost their meaning in light of a competitive situation which had brought to an end the operation of the synonymous maximum and minimum prices.

Much of the complicated petroleum-industry picture can be more readily understood by examining the history of how the M.C.A. and its predecessor, the P.C.B., handled petroleum problems.

In May 1950 the four presently registered oil companies, including Firms 33 and 34, were told by the P.C.B. that they were to register as dominant firms because of their controlling position in trading gasoline, kerosene, and fuel oil. In addition, the system of exclusive-dealing contracts with dealers, the then legal fixing of resale prices, as well as other restrictive trade terms, were considered by the P.C.B. as further justification of such registrations.

Firm 33 and the two non-American firms registered as the P.C.B. requested. Firm 34, however, raised a variety of objections that led to a series of negotiations which involved the Ministry of Commerce. Firm 34 claimed that it was unlike the others in that a certain amount of its trade was by sales to wholesalers, while the other petroleum firms, which had registered, sold directly to the retail dealers or industrial consumers. Firm 34 posed the question in terms of whether it must register in view of its contracts with wholesalers, and whether registration was to be limited solely to its business terms with retailers.

The Appeal Tribunal found that the wholesalers who bought from Firm 34 resold the products, usually gasoline and diesel fuel, under its trademark. Further, the wholesalers were subject to a contract with Firm 34 through which they undertook to protect its trademark and its right to this mark and to follow its established business policies. Firm 34 was therefore ordered to register in terms of all its trade. Since 1950 the importance of the firm's wholesale trade has greatly diminished, and it is no longer in itself legally significant.

In 1957 Firm 34 asked that it be dropped from the Register as a dominant firm. Without specifically mentioning Firm 32's increased market share, Firm 34 showed that its share of the gasoline market had dropped from about 13 to 10 per cent, its share of the kerosene market stood at 7 per cent, and its fuel-oil share dropped from 15 to 10 per cent. Nevertheless, the M.C.A. refused Firm 34's request. Among the reasons given by the M.C.A. was that the trader's ability to influence price and other conditions of doing business in the petroleum industry was not measurable solely in terms of the percentage of sales. The M.C.A. was of the opinion that the question must be viewed against the entire context of the trading and competitive conditions in the petroleum industry. Such important contextual considerations included, in the M.C.A. view, the very small number of importers, which could facilitate collusion if the industry decided to embark on such a course, and the universal practice of all importers of suggesting resale prices.

Firm 33 had a further registration in 1951, No. 1583, as a dominant firm in the refining and extraction of gasoline, benzine, and mineral spirits. This registration, apparently dormant, is not cross-indexed to Firm 33 in the 1958 Registreringer (Index to the Register).

In 1955 the M.C.A. reviewed the state of the petroleum industry. In its Annual Report it described the Danish demand for gasoline and mineral oils as being entirely supplied through imports, with Danish production being limited to such by-products as asphalt and gases. It also observed that large industrial users of fuel oil import directly for their own needs. Five nonregistered oil companies were listed as doing business in Denmark, including Firm 32.

Firm 33, which has the largest percentage of market control of each petroleum item, except heavy fuel oil, was treated by the M.C.A. as being the price leader in the sense that the conditions of trade established by this firm set the standards for the terms, prices, and margins which the M.C.A. approved until the end of 1960.

At the present time no horizontal price agreements or any other agreements between the oil companies exist, as far as the M.C.A. can ascertain, and this lack has fostered competition in ways other than by price. Competition in gasoline has expressed itself through the proliferation of service stations to the point, some said, of overcapacity. In fuel oils competition has been expressed through the granting of rebates from the officially quoted maximum prices. This device was chosen instead of lowering the official maximum price, so as to avoid the possible necessity of asking permission to raise the price at some future date. The granting of rebates continues in fuel oil despite the 1960 freeing of prices.

Except for the usual adjustments upward in price, the M.C.A. on the surface indicated little interest in the petroleum industry until the end of 1960. In 1957 the M.C.A. announced the initiation of an investigation of the petroleum industry for the purpose of determining whether the competition between firms has led to an excessively large number of service stations. In 1958 the M.C.A. stated that its investigation and report were not complete, and in 1959 it was silent on the matter.

The failure of the M.C.A. to issue a report on service stations may be attributed to a variety of factors. It is unlikely that a satisfactory measure of capacity or overcapacity could readily be devised. Even with such a yardstick, the issues became moot because of labor shortages and a variety of legal restrictions on the building of new service stations. This almost complete halt in the construction of new stations came at a time when Denmark began to experience an almost explosive growth of its motoring population. Thus, no further need for any investigation is apparent. A report may be published in the spring of 1962.

Sources: Registration Nos. 1466, 1583, 1685; Aarsberetning 1955 (July 1–December 31, pp. 76–80), 1957 (pp. 18–19, 76), 1958 (p. 84); Beretning (1949–1951, pp. 62–63); Betaenkninger (No. 8, 1960, pp. 88, 91–92, 232–234); Meddelelser 1956 (No. 5, p. 62), 1959 (No. 4, pp. 68–70), 1960 (No. 12, p. 214).

E. Farm machinery

Dominant registration—Suggested prices—Exclusive dealing—Horizontal and vertical trade association agreement—Resale-price maintenance with rebate—Discrimination against cooperatives—Modification of restrictive agreement—Freedom from prior approval for price rise—Variable rebate system—Freedom of entry—M.C.A. special procedures

Two American firms are registered as dominant in the trade in tractors and farm machinery. Automobile Firm *101* is registered under No. 719 because of its pre-eminence in the import of tractors. Registration No. 1470 is assigned to American Firm *201* for its control of the market in the importation of mowers and reaper-binders. As initially registered, both firms followed the then legal practice of fixing resale prices, and both began with highly restrictive exclusive-dealing arrangements. Registration No. 719 remains in force today because of its sole-agency, exclusive-dealing, and territorial-allocation provisions. As the chronology below discloses, not only has resale-price maintenance been prohibited by law, but also exclusive-dealing arrangements have been considerably modified on the basis of findings that such arrangements were in effect a form of price fixing. It should be kept in mind that Denmark is greatly dependent on its agriculture, and it is therefore quite sensitive to high prices for farm machinery.

Present arrangements in this industry have their roots in agreements dating back to late 1943. It was at that time that an agreement was concluded among the respective organizations representing producers and importers of farm machinery and dealers and master-smiths selling farm machinery. The agreement established a system of resale-price maintenance for both Danish and imported farm machinery, including tractors. Under this agreement, Registration No. 702, the individual producers and importers fixed the prices, as distinguished from a collective, horizontal price agreement. In order to maximize sales the agreement permitted the granting of a rebate of up to 10 per cent of the fixed price for cash sales.

A feature of the agreement was a provision forbidding sales to Dansk Landbrugs Andels-Maskinindkøb (D.L.A.M., Danish Farmers Cooperative Purchasing Association for Agricultural Implements) unless the cooperatives would agree to maintain the resale prices and to withhold directly the cash rebate, of up to 10 per cent, from its members. This provision meant, as a practical matter, that the farmers' buying cooperatives could not trade in farm machinery without changing their status, and that such cooperatives were effectively barred from the business of dealing in farm implements and machinery. In 1951 the Price Control Board decided that the agreement could not stand because of the provision barring cooperatives. The P.C.B determined that the parties to the agreement could give rebates even higher than 10 per cent to the cooperatives, and that the cooperatives were not barred from passing the rebates on to their members.

Under the then applicable legislation, the parties to the registered agreement were unable to increase their prices without the prior approval of the P.C.B. In 1952 the parties to the agreement, Registration No. 702, asked the P.C.B. for the right to raise prices without the prior approval of the P.C.B. The grounds for this request included the increased market supply of farm machinery and implements and the resultant heightened competition. As a bargaining point the parties offered to annul the part of the agreement binding dealers to obey the prices fixed by the producers and importers. Fixed prices would then be supplanted by recommended prices. The P.C.B. accepted these conditions and freed the industry at that time from the requirement of prior approval of price increases.

In a parallel development, an agreement was entered into in September 1951 among the members of the Danish Farm Machinery Manufacturers Association, Registration No. 1639, establishing a varying schedule of rebates for farm implements and machinery. The amount of rebate varied not only with the article in question, but also with the classification of the purchaser of the machinery.

The rebate schedule appeared to be unfavorable to the mastersmiths, and their organization complained of the discrimination. Acting on the request of the P.C.B., the manufacturers rewrote the various definitions establishing the status of buyers so as to make such definitions more objective and not purely discriminatory. The efforts led to further dissatisfaction on the part of other buyers' groups, so that the manufacturers dissolved the entire agreement in 1952.

The agreement, Registration No. 702, which had been modified for the benefit of the farmers' buying cooperatives, and then made to cover recommended prices, was abandoned in 1954. It was at that time replaced by a new agreement, Registration No. 2033. This new agreement was between the producers and the importers on the one hand, and the dealers and mastersmiths on the other. Its main effect was to limit producers, importers, and dealers solely to buying from and selling to:

1. Members of the organizations and firms taking part in the agreement, or
2. Firms that would undertake in writing to abide by the rules of the agreement, or
3. Dealers accredited by the three leading tractor producers and importers, including those accredited by American Firm *101*, a participant in the agreement.

The agreement further provided for the establishment of a special committee to screen those applying for the right to be buyers or sellers under Class 2 above.

When the farmers' cooperative-buying societies, D.L.A.M., asked to be classified as qualified sellers and buyers, the screening committee refused them on the ground that the special character of D.L.A.M. rendered it something other than an ordinary member of the trade.

By the time D.L.A.M. had exhausted its efforts to gain admission under the terms of the agreement, the new and current legislation on competition and monopolies came into effect under the administration of the M.C.A.. The D.L.A.M. then complained to the M.C.A., alleging that the effect of the agreement was to prevent the cooperatives from obtaining supplies from Danish manufacturers and importers, and also to foreclose the market for the implements and machinery which D.L.A.M. itself either produced or imported and formerly had sold to dealers and mastersmiths covered by Registration No. 2033.

The M.C.A., utilizing its powers under Section 11 of the Act, found that the rules established by the agreement were unreasonable restrictions on trade in that such rules unreasonably foreclosed the D.L.A.M. from an essential part of its trade.

In a somewhat unusual procedure, the M.C.A. did not follow its finding by an immediate intervention under the powers granted by Section 12 of the Act. For reasons about which we can only speculate, the M.C.A. decided to make a sweeping investigation of the general effects of the agreement on outsiders, such as D.L.A.M., and also on the participants themselves. It is a safe guess that the M.C.A. had reason to believe that some participants in the agreement had joined and accepted the rules only because they knew that they would otherwise be forced out of business.

As a result of the full investigation, the M.C.A. did intervene and ordered that all exclusive-dealing rules contained in the agreement be abolished, thus effectively terminating the industry's exclusive-dealing practices grounded on compulsory arrangements. Further, the M.C.A. nullified the provisions governing the right to be admitted to the agreement and barred the continuation of the screening committee. Thus, anyone ordinarily qualified as a seller or buyer, who wished to accept the remaining, viable portions of the agreement, could enter.

The participants thereupon filed an appeal, and the Appeal Tribunal ruled in 1958 that the M.C.A. decision in its entirety was valid.

In July 1959 Registration No. 2033 was amended by the registration of a new agreement, Registration No. 2294, replacing the one that the M.C.A. had ordered modified. This has in turn been replaced by Registration No. 2327 of January 1961. The new agreements are very general and even vague in nature. In part they set forth rather imprecise rules concerning dealer margins. Similarly, vague provisions are characterized as "promoting the common interests of the branch of trade including the maintenance of good practices in the branch of trade." Just what the agreements do mean will probably be seen only by measuring them against the actual practices in the trade. It would not be unlikely that in the future the M.C.A. might again investigate farm machinery. One has the impression that the M.C.A., as is the case with similar agencies in other countries, believes that certain industries or trades seem to be prone to following practices that might become restrictive.

Further insight into policy considerations which are important to the M.C.A. can be obtained by comparing the M.C.A. treatment of the arrangements in farm machinery to the matter related to automobiles as set forth in L in the Denmark case studies. The historical distribution pattern for farm machinery may be termed as collective discrimination or control except in the trade in imported tractors. All importers have attempted to follow the same forms of trade terms and conditions, and this attempt has been on an across-the-board basis of agreement at the various levels of the industry. In turn, each level of industry has been tied to the others. In the automotive and tractor field, the importers including firm *101* have, by and large, each developed exclusive-dealing and sales-districts arrangements that are quite similar, but there is no evidence of total collective action at the import level or at other levels. The closely knit connections between all levels of the farm-machinery industry make it difficult for a new firm to enter the trade. Such affiliations have frequently caused M.C.A. intervention. This is not the case with automobiles where new imports and changes in dealer franchises have caused turnover, and the M.C.A. has, therefore, not touched the automobile industry's exclusive-dealing and related arrangements.

Sources: Registration Nos. 702, 719, 1470, 1639, 2033, 2294, 2327; Aarsberetning 1957 (pp. 58–63), 1958 (pp. 23–27), 1960 (pp. 83–87); Beretning (1949–1951), pp. 83–84; 1951–1952, p. 31; 1952–1953, pp. 57–58); Betaenkninger (No. 8, 1960, pp. 88, 92, 93, 273–275); Meddelelser 1961 (No. 4, pp. 77–82).

F. Photographic articles

Dominant registration—Resale-price maintenance—Horizontal and vertical agreement—Collective rebate scheme—Approved purchasers—Freedom of entry—M.C.A. interim relief procedures

American Firm *401* was registered very early—in 1938—as a dominant firm, Registration No. 29, because it fixed the sales conditions of its customers as well as resale prices, which were legal then. Since 1938 this firm has been a party to a variety of other registered agreements.

Firm *401* participated in an agreement, Registration No. 1185, fixing the minimum prices for developing and printing of photographs. This agreement has been rendered unenforceable by Section 10 of the current Act which prohibits resale-price maintenance.

In an agreement registered in 1942, Registration No. 1178, Firm *401* also participated in a group comprising fourteen importers and one Danish manufacturer of photographic materials. The organization, which still exists, is known as "Fotim." As originally registered, the Fotim agreement stipulated detailed conditions governing both the wholesale and retail trade in photographic articles and a collectively organized and controlled system of rebates, which varied by article and by class of customer. With a few exceptions the agreement permitted members of Fotim to grant rebates on individually fixed resale prices only to those customers specifically recognized by Fotim. Moreover, such special customers were given the rebates subject to various conditions designed to ensure price maintenance of trademarked items. Much of this agreement was also rendered meaningless with the enactment of Section 10.

Fotim and its agreement, Registration No. 1178, continued to expand in the years after 1942 and entered into an implementing, supplementary agreement, Registration No. 1179 for the photo trade. By 1957 the membership of Fotim had grown to include twenty importers of photo articles, with the four leading firms controlling 66 per cent of the trade. Each importer handles his line or lines on an exclusive basis. In addition there is one Danish manufacturer of photographic paper and film.

By 1957 the Fotim collective rebate system had come to depend on the operation of the approved list of those eligible to enjoy the rebate system. A wholesaler, in order to qualify for a rebate, had to be a member of the Danish Photo Wholesalers Trade Association.

A retailer or professional photographer, in order to qualify for rebates, had to be a member of a trade or professional organization recognized by Fotim.

Because the exclusiveness of this system of rebates worked a sufficient hardship on outsiders who were wholesalers, retailers, and photographers, a considerable number of complaints reached the M.C.A. early in 1957.

The M.C.A.'s initial evaluation of the complaints and of the rebate system disclosed some features that were clearly in conflict with Section 11 of the Act. On the other hand, there was evidence that the agreement and the industry involved a number of complexities that warranted a full-scale investigation, which was bound to be time-consuming. The time factor appeared to be of great importance as the spring and tourist upsurge in photographic trade was only weeks away, and the M.C.A. wanted to give the quickest possible relief to the complainants.

Thereupon the M.C.A. negotiated with Fotim an agreement removing the restrictions on rebates that applied to films, papers, and chemicals consumed by the amateur picture-taker. This agreement gave immediate relief to the outsiders and gave the M.C.A. time to do a full investigation of the rebate system. The investigation, running through 1959, resulted in a series of further modifications which drastically reduced the number of rebate classifications and rendered them more functional. Also the character and quantity of business done by the purchasers seeking to qualify for rebates was more objectively determined. The key change was the termination of the practice of basing qualifications on membership or nonmembership in trade organizations.

> Sources: Registration Nos. 29, 1178, 1179, 1185; Aarsberetning 1957 (pp. 50–51), 1959 (pp. 59–61); Betaenkninger (No. 8, 1960, pp. 88, 92, 285–286).

G. Coal and coke

Foreign export cartel—Import cartel—Market sharing—Joint purchasing agency—Secret registration—Price control—Financial combination

American Firm *501* is one of seven firms in Denmark licensed or selected by Koksexport Norden (the German Coke Export Cartel) as exclusive buyers of coke. The German cartel in question is organized to control exclusively German coke exported to all of Scandinavia. The seven companies make their coke purchases from Germany in common and have agreed, Registration No. 2176, upon each firm's share of the market.

The M.C.A. has apparently shown no great interest in the restrictions created by the agreement, recognizing that the Danish importers have no real freedom of action in dealing with the German export cartel. Denmark's dependency on outside sources for fuel is a further complicating factor motivating the cautious approach.

Firm *501* is also a shareholder in a firm known as Polimport, which has six classes of shareholders comprising some thirty-one importers of fuel. Polimport controls the entire Danish importation of coal and coke from Poland. The market share of each importer is determined by his proportionate shareholding and class. No trade in Polimport shares may take place without the unanimous consent of the Polimport Board of Directors. The provisions concerning the conditions of import are among the few on the secret Register. The other portions appear under Registration No. 2239, which is an example of a registration by a financial combination.

The M.C.A. maintains control by supervising the price of coal and coke, which currently is under a Section 24 exemption because of fuel-oil competition. It is believed that by this device, the consuming public is given the greatest possible protection under the rather special circumstances.

> Sources: Registration Nos. 2176, 2239; Betaenkninger (No. 8, 1960, pp. 70, 71, 86, 92, 232, 234–235).

H. Oatmeal

Dominant registration—Market-sharing agreement—Price control

American Firm *83* is registered under No. 760 because it dominates the market for a basic Danish staple, oatmeal. Prices for this commodity are, by operation of Section 24, controlled by the M.C.A., as they were by the P.C.B. under special legislation.

Under Registration No. 1717, which was last amended early in 1960, Firm *83* controls 36.6 per cent of the oat market pursuant to an agreement which provides for market sharing of the production of bulk oatmeal. Sales above and below the established quotas are subject to regulation under the agreement. Rules provide for reimbursing producers who have sold less than their quota by those whose sales exceeded the quotas. This agreement, which itself does not fix prices, dates from 1952 and replaces an earlier agreement registered as No. 1491, which was both a market-sharing and a price-fixing agreement.

The present market share of Firm *83*, 36.6 per cent represents a drop in its proportionate strength. In 1952 three mills, of which Firm *83* was the largest, controlled the entire production of packed oatmeal in Denmark. The share of Firm *83* was at that time 53 per cent of the market, with a second firm accounting for 34 per cent and a third, for 13 per cent. The second largest firm presently has 20.7 per cent of the market assigned to it by agreement

> Sources: Registration Nos. 760, 1491, 1717; Beretning (1951–1952, pp. 25–26); Betaenkninger (No. 8, 1960, pp. 43, 57, 63, 181–182); Meddelelser 1956 (No. 5, p. 6); Registreringer (1960, No. 4, p. 21).

I. Household and industrial sewing machines

Dominant registration—Suggested prices—Prohibited repair of competing product—Trademarks—Rebates—Agency—Limits on registration—Limits on publicity—Resale-price maintenance and consignment sales—Request for removal from the Register—Special market through name-brand dominance

Since 1955 American Firm *601* has been registered because of market dominance under Registration No. 2084. The dominance covers the use of its sewing machines both for household and for craft and industrial purposes. Resale prices are suggested by the company. The registration discloses that distributors of the firm's products are obligated not to undertake the repair of machines manufactured in Japan. Competing machines are imported into Denmark from countries other than Japan, and the problems raised by machines produced in Eire by subsidiaries of Japanese firms seem not to have been contemplated.

The P.C.B. in its final report (1953–June 1955) reviewed the general market conditions for sewing machines. It found that, both for household and craft use, imports filled the Danish demand, and that machines which originated in those countries which were members of the Organization for European Economic Cooperation (O.E.E.C.)

were, commencing in 1952, imported into Denmark with no tariff restrictions.

The P.C.B.'s analysis by brand names of machines imported during 1953 and 1954 disclosed that more than 25 per cent of the imports bore Firm *601*'s trademark, and that the second largest imported brand represented close to 20 per cent of the imports. The study also showed that the two major importers were fixing binding resale prices, operating rebate schemes, and imposing strict agency conditions.

Then in 1955 the P.C.B. asked both firms to register under the provisions of Section 6 of the Act which was then in force. Firm *601*'s registration was among the last to take place before the current Monopoly Control Law became operative. The new Act, according to Firm *601* and the other major importer, raised some new questions as to the extent of the information that had to be registered, and the P.C.B. left these in abeyance until the M.C.A. took office. The sewing machine importers argued that the size of the rebates and the provisions governing agency contracts should not be made public. Both importers alleged that the public dissemination of such information would hurt them and their dealers in machines because competing suppliers, upon learning the trade terms of the two importers, might offer greater profit margins. In turn, customers, once they knew the size of the dealers' margins, might create pressure for lower prices.

As soon as the new Act came into effect, the two sewing machine importers further advised the M.C.A. of their opinion that Section 10 of the Act, banning resale-price maintenance, did not apply to their method of doing business and to their dealers. The importers alleged that their dealers were not truly dealers, but rather consignees with no property rights in the sewing machines. In addition, Firm *601* said that its dealers were really agents because all contracts were entered into in the name of the trademark owned by Firm *601*. Further, the other importer said it would be unfair if independent dealers who purchased machines for resale from it could sell at prices lower than those of the importer's own fully controlled affiliates, who appeared to the public as ordinary dealers. The M.C.A. found that none of the arguments justified the exemption of the firms from the provisions of Section 10. They were both ordered to end price fixing as of 1 July 1956.

In 1956 the question of what should be made public was also decided by the M.C.A. Its decision was that all margins, rebates, and provisions governing the importers' relationships with dealers and agents should be made public.

Subsequently Firm *601* and the other importer asked in October 1956 to be removed from the Register on the ground that each had lost a portion of the market, with Firm *601* averaging between 25 and 20 per cent for the period 1948–1955, and the second importer averaging less than 20 per cent. It was also argued that since resale prices were no longer binding the need for registration had disappeared.

The M.C.A. rejected this request. It took the position that percentage of the total market in sewing machines was no longer meaningful. The M.C.A. found that Firm *601* and the other importer had each so widely advertised and exploited their respective trademarks that their products could no longer be classed with sewing machines in general, but rather they must be treated as special machines, each in its own individual class.

In February of 1962 American Firm *601* won its battle and was removed from the Register as a dominant firm. The American firm had dropped to second place in the market, and its share of the market had diminished considerably. The non-American competitor that had been in second place now remains on the Register as the only dominant firm in the industry.

> Sources: Registration No. 2084; Aarsberetning 1956 (pp. 24–25), 1957 (pp. 19–20); Beretning (1953–1955, pp. 37–41); Betaenkninger (No. 8, 1960, pp. 79, 81, 88, 275–276).

J. Automobile tires and tubes

Horizontal and vertical agreement—Approved dealers—Fixed prices—Freedom of entry—Collective resale-price maintenance—Control of gross profit margins—Discrimination in export prices—Aggregated rebates with fixed prices—Rebates unsupported by purchases—Recommended rebates—Aggregated rebates and suggested prices—Refusal to deal—Purchaser's qualifications—Loss leader—Horizontal agreement to observe suggested prices

Denmark does not produce automobile tires, though it does produce bicycle tires. Practically all brands of American tires have their import representatives in Denmark, and one large American producer maintains his own import organization, Firm 92. As of 1952 about one-third of the entire tire market was controlled by this American firm, by a British firm, with which Firm 92 has working arrangements in other countries, and by an Italian firm through a Swiss holding company. In 1952 the top four importers controlled 54 per cent of the market and the top nine, 76 per cent.

The currently rather complex arrangements in the Danish tire industry have their roots in the pre-World War II practices of the importers. For our purposes, however, they begin in October 1950 when Firm 92 and some other importers entered into an agreement with the Tire Dealers Association, Registration No. 1387. The importers agreed to sell only to those dealers who signed a declaration binding themselves to 1) observe the retail prices established by each importer, 2) abide by the special conditions and terms of sale fixed by a commission of importers, 3) deal only in those brands imported by importers participating in the agreement, and 4) pay a fee to the Association of .5 per cent of the value of the combined purchases from the importers taking part in the agreement, with a maximum not to exceed five hundred kroner. This last provision was designed to finance the collective enforcement activities under the agreement.

In many respects this agreement closely followed the agreement which governed the trade before the last war. Shortly after Registration No. 1387 came into force, the P.C.B. received complaints both from the importers outside the agreement and from dealers. As a result of its investigation, the P.C.B. ordered that Provision 3, listed above, be deleted from the agreement. Because of this order from the P.C.B., the parties cancelled the entire agreement.

Then in November 1951 the importers who were parties to the terminated agreement, including Firm 92, concluded a new agreement establishing rules for a scheme of collectively enforced resale prices, Registration No. 1686. To supplement and implement Registration No. 1686, the parties entered into an agreement registered as No. 1687, which provided for the creation of a committee of importers and dealers to police the enforcement of the collective resale-price–maintenance scheme. Up to this time American Firm 91 also was a participant in the agreements; at present, however, it is not directly active in Denmark.

During the post-World War II period, the P.C.B. controlled and regulated the profit margins of tire importers and dealers. Some of the P.C.B. decisions were appealed and the Tribunal generally found that the parties were entitled to a higher rate of earnings. The entire matter of tire prices was complicated by the fact that in the period 1948–1952, when Denmark suffered a severe dollar shortage, the export prices of American tires to Denmark were from 5 to 10 per cent higher than the export prices applicable to other countries with less of a dollar problem. This particular peculiarity did not endear the American tire industry to the P.C.B., for Denmark depended to a great extent on American tires.

By the end of 1952, through a series of decisions by the P.C.B. and appeals by the tire industry, some of which failed and some of which succeeded, the total profit margin for dealers and importers inched up to 35 per cent of the importers' delivered-in-Denmark cost price. This method of computing profit margins may have encouraged the abnormally high American export prices at a time when the P.C.B. made efforts to keep profit margins down. Prices for American tires exported to Denmark fell into line when the 35 per cent margin was allowed.

Once the 35 per cent margin was established, the importers involved in agreement Registration No. 1686 advised the P.C.B. that a further agreement, which was never approved, had been entered into with the Tire Dealers Association. The dealers were to receive an average profit of 13.9 per cent of the retail price and a portion of this profit was to be derived from a rebate of 10 per cent on each purchase. This rebate was, in part, to take the form of an aggregated rebate, based on the dealer's annual purchase from importers taking part in the agreement.

TIRE DEALERS REBATE SCHEDULE

Total Kroner Value of Annual Purchases		Rebate
Up to	2,500	3.0%
2,500	10,000	3.9%
10,000	50,000	4.4%
50,000	100,000	5.0%
100,000	350,000	5.5%
350,000 and above		6.5%

The arrangement would have permitted all importers to join if they wished, so long as they agreed to fix and enforce retail prices for tires and tubes—an arrangement closely approximating the prewar trading conditions. The P.C.B. examined the arrangement and found it contrary to the legislation governing restrictive practices. The P.C.B. was particularly critical of the aggregated rebate feature and enumerated a variety of reasons for finding this unreasonably restrictive. After indicating that the aggregated rebates did not reflect real economies in production and distribution, the P.C.B. found that the real vice lay in the way the aggregated rebate system impeded competition of those importers who were unable or unwilling to join the scheme because of the resale-price–maintenance restriction. According to the P.C.B. the aggregated rebate system worked against such independents, by providing buyers a strong economic incentive to confine their purchases to members of the group giving the aggregated rebates. Even lower prices offered by independent sellers would not alone help them compete against such a system, for the pricing would have to depend on the amount of rebate a buyer could be expected to earn if he did not buy from the independent. This reasoning was later considered by the British Monopolies and Restrictive Practices Commission in its 1955 report Collective Discrimination.

Both the importers and the Tire Dealers Association appealed the decision of the P.C.B. During the hearing clear evidence was adduced that the importers outside the agreement found the arrangement very harmful. Thereupon the Tribunal affirmed the P.C.B.'s decision, and the projected agreement with its aggregated rebate arrangement never came into being.

In January 1955 the importers who participated in the attempt to set up an aggregated rebate scheme advised the P.C.B. that they wished to make revisions in a 1949 agreement, Registration No. 1063, which in 1953 was modified and registered as Registration No. 1982. This agreement, in which Firms 91 and 92 both participated, established the maximum amount of rebates that the importers could give to dealers in auto, truck, and tractor tires. They now wished to revise the agreement so as to give to those dealers, who purchased not less than 25,000 kroner yearly from any one of the importers, extra rebates varying between 2 and 5 per cent. The scheme further provided that once a dealer qualified for the extra rebate, solely on the strength of his purchases from one importer, all of the importers would be entitled to give an extra rebate to the dealer, without reference to the actual size of their sales to him. This variation on the classic aggregated rebate system encouraged purchase from a limited group.

The P.C.B. and the importers negotiated over this scheme to the point where the importers gave up the arrangement. Instead they amended Registration No. 1982, so that the size of a dealer's rebate was only recommended or suggested, but at the same time the retail prices charged by the dealers were fixed by the importers. A further provision was that if an importer wished to grant a larger rebate than the recommended one, he had to notify the Tire Importers Association, and the reasons for such a grant had to be stated. This amendment was not opposed by the P.C.B.

The importers also agreed that membership in Registration No. 1982, as it was now amended, was to be limited to the parties to the agreement, Registration No. 1686, which established the scheme of collective enforcement of resale prices. Membership in a 1950 agreement, Registration No. 1483, was also required for importers. This agreement, which counted Firms 91 and 92 among its participants, spelled out the way in which guarantees were to be honored and the uniform manner of treating complaints from dealers and consumers concerning the wear and defects of tires and tubes. Thus, an entire complex of agreements, Registration Nos. 1483, 1686, 1687, and 1982, served to govern practically every facet of the tire industry and trade and to provide the maximum possible uniformity in the relationships between importers, between importers and dealers, and between dealers.

As the various agreements were taking form, the profit margins on tires fluctuated and reached a high of 38 per cent in the spring of 1955, before dropping to the current 36 per cent.

As soon as the present Monopolies and Restrictive Practices Control Act came into effect, banning resale-price maintenance as of 1 July 1956, the system of collective resale-price maintenance was no longer enforceable. Thus, agreements under Registration Nos. 1483, 1686, 1687, and 1982 were cancelled. Also about this time Firm 91 ceased to participate directly in import matters, and its line was turned over to a Danish firm.

Earlier in 1956, and prior to the termination of the four agreements, the importers sought the approval of the M.C.A. for a new aggregated rebate scheme on the theory that the ban on resale-price maintenance would change the restrictive nature of the scheme. The M.C.A. found the new scheme unacceptable, and it was dropped. At about the same time the M.C.A. received a complaint from a hardware dealer, who dealt in tires and tubes for carriages and wheelbarrows, alleging that the importers would not supply him with automobile tires at the regular terms for ordinary dealers in automobile tires. The M.C.A. found no cause to intervene in the matter because there was no basis for treating the hardwareman with his minute demand for tires as if he were a regular dealer in automotive tires.

In 1956 after terminating all prior agreements, some twenty importers of tires and tubes, representing what is today about 70 per cent of the import market, formed a new agreement, Registration No. 2194, in which Firm 92, still the leader of the industry, participates. The participants are obligated to deal only with authorized dealers. Each importer sets his own suggested resale prices. Maximum rebate limits are established for each class of buyers. For delivery to the Danish Army, a system of net prices without rebates is established, and each party to the agreement participates in a pool, taking an equal share of the sales to the Army.

A companion agreement to Registration No. 2194, is Registration No. 2195, which was concluded by the Tire Dealers Association. This group of dealers, which the importers in Registration No. 2194 recognize, agreed not to sell tires at prices below those suggested or recommended by the importers. Since horizontal price fixing is not prohibited, the agreement was legal unless it had unreasonable effects. The agreement, Registration No. 2195, was abandoned by the parties in June 1959.

A pair of agreements such as Nos. 2194 and 2195, in a practical sense, avoids the prohibition on resale-price maintenance. Until now the M.C.A. has not followed the Norwegian example of obtaining a ban on horizontal price fixing. Thus, Section 10 of the Act is limited to a ban on vertical fixing of minimum prices and can be circumvented in part by dual or even triple horizontal agreements.

In 1957, while No. 2195 was in effect, the M.C.A. acted on a complaint from an authorized dealer who had cut prices of tires to the point that some were alleged to be loss leaders, though the existence of an actual loss leader has never been established in Denmark. The dealer complained that as a result of his price cutting, a group of importers had collectively stopped delivery of tires. As a result of negotiations with the M.C.A., the importers agreed not to stop deliveries again without prior approval of the M.C.A.

Horizontal combinations to fix prices are not, however, totally immune. The M.C.A. has intervened in price-fixing situations not within the purview of Section 10. Thus, an agreement among the members of the Danish Goldsmiths Guild, retail jewelers, to abide by the suggested prices of a manufacturer of plated silverware was ordered cancelled. Underlying the agreement to fix prices was another agreement giving the members of the Guild the exclusive right to sell the plated silverware. Thus, a cut price meant loss of membership in the Guild and automatically loss of the right to sell the silverplate. The M.C.A. determination that the agreements constituted an unreasonable restraint on trade was made in July 1956. This order was confirmed on appeal and the Guild withdrew a subsequent appeal to the High Court in 1957.

The intervention of the M.C.A. seems to have been clearly predicated on the effect of the two interrelated agreements, which was to cut off a source of supply from price cutters. However, since the tire agreement and the automobile arrangements in Registration No. 2195, discussed in Section L of the Denmark case studies, do not encompass the entire trade, these agreements are set apart from that of the Guild.

The enforcement of Section 10 is probably the most difficult problem faced by the M.C.A.

Any evaluation of the treatment accorded tire importers by the Danish authorities must be made with the realization that for a long time the Danish trade has been subject to the restrictive arrangements emanating in Britain from the Tyre Manufacturers Conference, Ltd., and from the Webb-Pomerene Rubber Export Association of America. The price leadership and control effected through these arrangements have long been factors requiring consideration by the Danish government.

Sources: Registration Nos. 1063, 1387, 1483, 1686, 1687, 1982, 2194, 2195; Aarsberetning 1955 (July 1–December 31, pp. 83–84), 1956 (pp. 19, 33–34, 37–38), 1957 (p. 41); Beretning (1949–1951, p. 79; 1951–1952, pp. 135–136; 1952–1953, pp. 58–59, 79–80; 1953–1955, pp. 97–98); Betaenkninger (No. 8, 1960, pp. 68, 69, 70, 88, 92, 225–226); Collective Discrimination (The Monopolies and Restrictive Practices Commission, London, July 1955, pp. 72–76); Report on the Supply and Export of Pneumatic Tyres (The Monopolies and Restrictive Practices Commission, London, December 1955).

K. Telephone and telegraph equipment, cables, and electronics

No registration—International cartel—Agreement to allocate markets

The telegraph system of Denmark is state-controlled, and the telephone system is operated by three concessionary companies. Thus, the government has an element of control over cables and telephone equipment.

A subsidiary of American Firm *301* is not registered because the M.C.A. believes that a power balance exists in the industry. The M.C.A. and the Trustkommission have, however, from time to time investigated the operations of Firm *301* through its Danish subsidiary in which it holds 70 per cent of the stock. This subsidiary is one of the four firms supplying telephone equipment, which together control 88 per cent of that market.

Firm *301* is not represented in Denmark in its traditional role of cable maker, particularly telephone cables, because of an agreement between Firm *301* and a major Danish firm with a monopoly in such cables. By means of this agreement, in which there are reciprocal promises as to exclusive markets, Firm *301* has agreed not to compete in Denmark in the production of cables. This agreement is not registered, but it is known to the Danish authorities.

The patent licensee of American Firm *301* is the Danish participant in an international cartel agreement known as the Lausanne Agreement. This international agreement has Danish Registration No. 1624 and is also registered in Norway and Sweden. A description of the Lausanne Agreement appears in Norwegian Case Study F, *infra.*

The published reports concerning Firm *301* and its subsidiary demonstrate that even without registration, the Danish agencies concerned with restrictive practices make an effort to investigate all areas which might potentially raise questions of control. It is for this reason that the status of Firm *301* was discussed in the final report of the Trustkommission. Inasmuch as the M.C.A. now has the general investigatory function of the Trustkommission, and since the M.C.A. Directorate personnel in large part staffed the Trustkommission, there is every reason to expect that the M.C.A. will continue surveillance of this industry.

Sources: Registration No. 1624; Betaenkninger (No. 8, 1960, pp. 266–268).

L. Automobiles and parts

Dominant registrations—Allocation and protection of dealer territories—Exclusive dealing—Comprehensive trading conditions— Price control—Agreement to observe suggested prices—Gross profit margins—Authority of the M.C.A. under Section 23—Removal from the Register in whole and in part—Request for special legislation— Termination of sole-agency agreements

The two largest American producers of automobiles, Firms *101* and *102*, are dominant in the Danish market of automobiles and parts. Registration No. 719 has been assigned to Firm *101* and Registration No. 720 to Firm *102*. Both registrations concern not only automobiles, but also spare parts. In the case of Firm *101*, as previously noted in Section E of the Denmark case studies, Registration No. 719 also includes dominance in tractors.

Both firms import both American-made and European-made automobiles and parts from plants which they control. Other American cars are imported into Denmark by apparently Danish-owned import houses. The Danish importer of the products of the third largest American automobile producer, Firm *103*, is covered by Registration No. 1390. One of the smallest American producers, Firm *104*, has its products imported under Registration No. 1524. These registrations are given as they stood in January of 1954, prior to the major changes in the dominant registrations in the automobile industry.

The registrations for Firms *101* and *102* were initially required in 1944, not only by reason of the share of the market involved, but also because of the various trading rules that each had established. These rules included the allocation of districts to dealers, so that if a dealer sold to someone resident outside his assigned territory, the dealer in whose territory the purchaser's residence was located would be compensated. In a large city such as Copenhagen the region might be divided into several parts, with compensation for sales determined by the home address of the purchaser. This territorial-compensation device was designed to discourage price competition and customer shopping within a brand of car. The registrations also typically reflected the dealer's agreement not to sell competing cars or parts.

Registration No. 720 is illustrative and typical of the degree of control initially maintained by the importers over their dealers.

Maximum resale prices were fixed. The manner in which show-rooms were to be arranged and maintained was stipulated, and the nature of the service available to customers was prescribed. Certain dealer obligations were to be measured in terms proportionate to their volume of business. Among such obligations were the duty to advertise and the requirements concerning the maintenance of a stock of parts. In addition, the importer reserved the right to sell directly to certain public institutions.

All of these provisions of Registration No. 720 except those fixing price are still in effect along with a system of territorial allocation, sole-agency restrictions, and a variety of exclusive-dealing arrangements.

In 1952 the Price Control Board reported that through the registrations and the concomitant control over price raises, similar to the present provisions of Section 24, the prices of about 90 per cent of the new cars imported into Denmark were under control.

About this time the availability of cars in Denmark began to reach a point approaching a balance between supply and demand. In order to prevent supply from running away with demand, 443 of about 600 authorized automobile dealers entered into an agreement, Registration No. 2003, binding themselves not to accept used cars as part payment for new cars. By 1955 the participants in the agreement dropped to 204, and then, pursuant to the terms of the agreement, it was no longer binding on those who remained as participants. The agreement officially terminated in 1957.

In 1953 the effort to stabilize automobile prices was increased. To implement the prohibition against used cars as trade-ins, the dealers handling the most popular imported German automobile in the Lolland-Faster area of southern Denmark agreed, Registration No. 1971, to maintain the recommended resale prices established by the importer. In Copenhagen the dealers handling Firm *101*'s cars entered into a similar agreement, Registration No. 2103, as did the dealers of Firm *102*, Registration No. 2038.

In its first six months of operation, in 1955, the M.C.A. surveyed the automobile import industry and noted that up to January of 1954, nine importers controlled 80–90 per cent of the total market. Those nine importers were all registered because of dominance and because of the trade terms by which they controlled their dealers. Until January 1954 all registered importers fixed minimum resale prices. Subsequently minimum resale prices were abandoned, with two exceptions, and recommended retail prices in the form of recommended maximum prices were substituted. The two exceptions involved the importer of cars produced by American Firm *104*, Registration No. 1524, and the importer of a French line, Registration No. 1636.

After its survey the M.C.A. reported that, as a consequence of the law requiring approval of price raises—a system which is still applicable—the gross profit margins were figured for automobile importers at 12–13 per cent of the cost of the car delivered to the Danish warehouse. Dealers' profit margins were computed at 16–17 per cent of their cost.

The M.C.A. investigation of the trade disclosed that spare parts are imported by the importers of the vehicles, and that the prices are controlled and calculated in the same way as those for the automobiles. Thus, the importers set recommended retail prices. The margins are, however, considerably different. As reported in 1955 the total margin of profit above the landed price of a spare part—a profit shared by importer, dealer, and mechanic—varies between 90 and 130 per cent. This fact is pointed to as an improvement over the prewar margin of 200 per cent or more.

Beginning in 1946 the P.C.B. had required car repair shops to specify in writing the parts used and the prices of such parts on all repair bills of ten kroner or more, and the M.C.A. continued this administrative rule when it took office. The car dealers' trade association appealed to the Appeal Tribunal on the ground that the M.C.A. lacked authority to make such a ruling. The Tribunal, upholding the M.C.A., ruled that the M.C.A. derived competence in this matter by operation of Section 23 of the Act which provided for the transfer of authority from the P.C.B. to the M.C.A. This power terminated by the summer of 1961, and Section 13, under which the M.C.A. has authority to order price posting, is insufficient to sustain the repair-bill ruling.

In 1956 a series of price changes took place in the automobile import trade. Firm *101* advised the M.C.A. that it proposed to lower the recommended retail prices on a popular line which it produced in the United Kingdom and imported into Denmark. These reductions included a 22 per cent reduction on a sedan model and convertible. Import prices, importer's margins, and dealer's margins were all reduced proportionately.

At the same time Firm *102* asked for and obtained approval of higher prices on automobiles and trucks on the strength of higher import prices. Four other importers reported a variety of price changes at the same time.

In December of 1956 the importer of a line of British and German cars, of a British tractor line, and of the cars of American Firm 103 asked that it be removed from the Register where it held No. 1390 as a dominant firm. The argument on behalf of the importer was that his imports amounted to less than 5 per cent of the market, that his prices were only recommended, and that he had no control over dealers. In support of his position, the importer cited the 1952 decision of the P.C.B. which cancelled a French import firm from the Register. The M.C.A. agreed to cancel the registration.

Other small importers who gave a degree of liberty to their dealers also were permitted to leave the Register. Four firms then remained on the Register in 1957, of which Registration Nos. 719 and 720 represented Firms 101 and 102 respectively. The other two dominant registrations represented the largest-selling German car, Registration No. 1645 and Registration No. 1524, which relates now solely to its dominance in the tractor market.

In April 1957 the terms of Registration No. 1645 were also reduced by deleting the provisions concerned with large motor trucks. This change in registration was prompted by the fact that the German's share of the large truck business was now less than 3 per cent, but the dominant registration for automobiles, small panel trucks, and spare parts still continued. With this change, only the three largest importers of automobiles remained on the Register because of market dominance.

In August 1958 the trade association for the wholesale vehicle dealers in the Provinces asked the Ministry of Commerce whether it would consider proposing legislation governing the sole-agency and exclusive-dealing contracts of the automobile dealers. The association acted as a representative for the automobile dealers' trade groups and for an association of retailers of tractors, whose problems were similar to those of the auto dealers. It was pointed out that the United States had recently enacted special legislation concerning automobile dealers, Auto Dealers Franchise Act of 1956 (15 U.S.C.A. 1221 et seq.), and that France had revised some rules as well. The association asserted that it was motivated by an interest in seeing that sufficient legal protection was given to the dealers through a standard contract with the importers.

The questions were then referred to the M.C.A. for its opinion of the rather complex dealer contract, which, as we have seen from the description of Registration Nos. 719 and 720, includes territorial allocations, showroom conditions, and parts-stockage requirements. The specific question put to the M.C.A. was the degree to which the M.C.A. could control such contracts under the provisions of Sections 11 and 12 of the Act, which empower the M.C.A. to control unreasonable conditions of doing business.

One defect in the contractual arrangements, from the dealers' viewpoint, was the absence of any fixed time limit to the agency, so that as a practical matter the importer could cancel the agency with or without extremely short notice.

The M.C.A. took the view that, for the most part, the general rules for interpretation of bilateral contracts were applicable to these contracts. Only where provisions affected others could the M.C.A. intervene. Thus, one would be free to bargain away his own rights if he saw fit, but if the same bargain meant higher prices or reduced competition, then the M.C.A. could intervene. The M.C.A's essential position was that it would not bar a particular contract provision without showing that the effect was unreasonable under the meaning of that term in Section 11 and in Section 12. Therefore, before the M.C.A. could act it must be able to find, for example, that the importer's almost absolute right to cancel an agency encouraged dealers to maintain higher prices and to reduce competition more than would otherwise be the case. Such a finding would then mean negotiation and intervention by the M.C.A. under Section 11.

The M.C.A. further advised the Ministry that it had exercised its power under Section 11 and had, in several limited cases, modified the rules limiting a dealer's territory and providing compensation for violating another dealer's trade area.

The M.C.A. concluded its report to the Ministry by stating that it intended to make an investigation into the present content and effect of the contracts between dealers and importers. The M.C.A. further found that no special legislation was necessary. This view was adopted by the Ministry, and, as of January 1962, no special M.C.A. report has been published. The sole-agency contracts remain in force, presently unchallenged.

The automobile-industry trading terms have evolved rapidly in Denmark after having followed a traditional European pattern of price fixing and territorial allocations. Denmark has attempted to ensure some competition and price freedom in an industry which depends entirely on imports. It has recognized that only a few major firms now dominate the world market, and for that reason close supervision is maintained over the three major firms. It is assumed that the general freedom granted to the smaller firms will impel them to compete actively against the three larger ones.

Certainly an element of handicap comes with registration. American Firm *101* has stated that it would be happier if it were no longer on the Register. It argues that it has no monopoly in automobiles and spare parts, and that prices are only recommended maximums. Under those circumstances it would like to be free to make its arrangements and prices as it pleases.

> Sources: Registration Nos. 719, 720, 1390, 1524, 1636, 1645, 1971, 2003, 2038, 2103; Aarsberetning 1955 (July 1–December 31, pp. 80–83), 1956 (p. 21), 1957 (p. 20), 1958 (pp. 58–59); Beretning (1952–1953, p. 58; 1953–1955, pp. 109–110); Betaenkninger (No. 8, 1960, pp. 42, 47, 81, 86, 88, 92, 279–281); Meddelelser 1956 (No. 5, p. 63).

M. Tobacco

Dominant registration—Exemption from resale-price–maintenance prohibition—Exemption from prior approval of price raising

American Firm *11* along with its nearest Danish competitor controls 90 per cent of the Danish cigarette market. This among other factors has led to the 1954 registration, Registration No. 2074, of the American manufacturer as a dominant firm. The Danish competitor is also registered as a dominant firm, Registration No. 2075.

Cigarettes in Denmark are subject to a very high ad valorem tax. In keeping with the general rules for granting exemptions to the prohibition of resale-price maintenance under Section 10, the two major cigarette producers have been allowed to fix resale prices because of their tax burden, providing a second reason for requiring registration.

The M.C.A., in its analysis of the Danish cigarette trade, has seen a continued shift in consumer preference back and forth between the two major competitors, which are of about equal size and strength. Although recognizing the danger that collusion between the two is a possibility, the M.C.A. has deemed this to be unlikely. Moreover, since the cigarette manufacturers have been permitted to fix resale prices, changes in prices to the ultimate consumer are subject to M.C.A. approval. Therefore, when the 1960 amendment to Section 24 was enacted, the M.C.A. gave the two cigarette companies the right to raise their own, immediate sales prices without prior approval. The Danes, in terms of kroner value, consume almost as much tobacco in the form of cigarillos and cigars as they do in the form of cigarettes. The cigar and cigarillo trade is slightly more competitive than the cigarette trade. So for the time being the M.C.A. considers its control sufficient.

Sources: Registration Nos. 2075, 2074; Betaenkninger (No. 8, 1960, pp. 188–189); Meddelelser 1960 (No. 7/8, pp. 101–102).

N. Titanium oxide

International market agreement—Prohibition of exports

Since 1921 American Firm 701, its Norwegian subsidiary, and a Danish importer of titanium oxides and whites have been registered through an agreement, Registration No. 1092, restraining the right of the Danish party to export the products which are the subject of the agreement.

In 1916 Firm 701 created a Norwegian subsidiary which is registered in Norway under Registration No. 3.27 as a market-dominating firm. This subsidiary in turn entered, on behalf of itself and its American parent, into an agreement governing the sales of products to Denmark. The essential feature of the registered agreement is the condition that the Danish party will not re-export its imports from the United States or Norway. This obligation is undertaken by the Danish party in return for the supplier's giving the Danish party an exclusive right to deal in his products. Such an agreement, barring other circumstances, is legal in Denmark, and the only requirement is that it be registered and that price raises be approved before becoming effective. Other trade terms of the agreement were modified in 1946, 1949, and 1957.

Sources: Registration No. 1092; Norwegian Registration No. 3.27; Betaenkninger (No. 8, 1960, pp. 226–227).

PART TWO:
NORWAY

CONTENTS

PRELIMINARY OBSERVATIONS

NORWAY CAN BOAST the longest history of continuous legislation controlling restrictive business practices in Europe. Beginning with emergency legislation in 1920, or the 1926 Trust Law—depending on which group of scholars one favors—Norway's control system evolved through a variety of legislative and administrative forms to its major enactment of 26 June 1953. The Act on Control of Prices, Dividends, and Restrictive Business Arrangements (the Price Act) has been amended and implemented by a series of orders of the King in Council (Cabinet). The order of the King in Council of 18 October 1957 prohibited the vertical fixing of minimum prices, and the order of the King in Council of 1 July 1960 banned horizontal price-fixing agreements. Both prohibitions are, however, subject to some exemptions.

The Norwegian policy permits restrictive practices, except for price fixing, if they can be justified and if they are not unreasonable or against the public interest. All restrictive arrangements, formal and informal, must be registered as well as dominant firms, which fill a major part of the Register.

The Price Act is designed to apply to all kinds of business activities, including even those business activities operated by national or local government authorities. Its purposes, according to Section 1, are to achieve full employment, effective utilization of productive capacity, and equitable distribution of national income and to avoid economic crises. One means of accomplishing these objectives is to safeguard "against improper marketing or competitive conditions, and against restrictive business arrangements which are unreasonable or detrimental to the public interest."

The legislation operates primarily through two main agencies, the Price Council and the Price Directorate, which have separate areas of jurisdiction as well as an overlap of interest. In addition, the legislation provides for an annual parliamentary participation in establishing policy lines, thus subjecting the operation of the Act to a variety of influences.

Much of the power to establish regulations and rules, as denominated by the Price Act, lies with the King. Section 3 states that "the King shall lay down the general instructions governing control and regulations," and Section 24 enumerates his specific powers of regulation. The word "King," not to be taken in a literal sense, refers to the Norwegian Council of State.

This body, which is made up of the entire government (similar to our Cabinet, but unlike the smaller British Privy Council committees), issues orders in council which are denominated as orders or decrees of the King. Henceforth the phrase "King in Council" will be used in connection with decrees or orders which are issued pursuant to the delegation of authority to the King as provided in the Price Act.

The rather complex and comprehensive Price Act has been reduced in part, as of 1 July 1960, by the termination of the provisions relating to control of dividends, but price control, even in the absence of restrictive practices, is a power still available to be exercised under the Act.

The Norwegian Register, maintained by the Price Directorate at its offices at H. Heyerdahls Gt. 1, Oslo, is open to the public. Publicity does play a role in the Norwegian enforcement scheme, though not to the full extent that one finds in either Denmark or Sweden.

The basis for decisions not to require registration are not made public in Norway. In fact, most such decisions by the Price Directorate concerning inaction are kept confidential. The extent of this preference for secrecy will be demonstrated in the case history of shoe machinery.

The public receives news of the administration of the Price Act from a variety of publications including Pristidende (the Price News), a periodical report on registrations, important decisions, regulations, and matters germane to the administration of the Act. The public may keep informed also by means of occasional press releases, Rundskriv, with summaries of important decisions, as well as by means of cumulative summaries of all of the registrations in the form of special supplements to Pristidende, denominated as Oversikt or surveys of the Register.

I. REGISTRATION OF RESTRICTIVE BUSINESS PRACTICES

SINCE THE ENACTMENT of the 1920 legislation Norway has had a system of registering restrictive practices and dominant enterprises, which after forty years of experience, seems to be fully accepted and is subject to very few unresolved problems.

A. The obligation to register agreements and arrangements

Section 33 establishes the obligation to report to the Price Directorate, under regulations to be issued by the King in Council. Subsection 1 enumerates certain specific practices which are to be reported. Subsection 2 makes it clear that the effect of the restriction and not the form determines what is to be registered.

1. RESTRICTIVE ARRANGEMENTS

On 19 March 1954, as reported in Pristidende 1954 (No. 6), two sets of regulations or decrees were issued governing registration. The first set forth the conditions under which the duty to register obtained, as set forth immediately below, and the second prescribed the actual registration procedures.

The obligation to report exists in the following cases: 1) Where the arrangement or agreement concerns regulation of prices, rates of profit, rebates, bonuses, discounts, terms of delivery and payment for goods, and other conditions governing trade and commerce applicable to members of an association or group or applicable to non-members, 2) If an arrangement gives the members of the association either exclusive or preferential-dealing arrangements with another group or with a single enterprise, 3) If an arrangement involves any limitation on freedom of entry into a trade or industry or involves any form of allocation of production or quotas for the partition of sales, or 4) If a refusal to deal or any form of punitive or coercive measure is part of a restrictive arrangement and is used as the means of enforcing the restriction or punishing a violation of the arrangement.

The form and practice of a restrictive arrangement are not controlling factors in determining the obligation to notify. Thus, the obligation is not diminished if the arrangement is merely oral or if it is couched in terms of suggestion or recommendation, as distinguished from a contractual undertaking.

The duty to notify carries with it the duty to advise the Price Directorate of all changes, including additional restrictions.

Any association or enterprise is, pursuant to Section 33 of the Price Act, obligated to report on its own initiative to the Price Directorate if it establishes or intends to set up a scheme or arrangement of restrictive business practices. This term, as used in Norway, connotes both vertical and horizontal arrangements or agreements. The obligation exists both for formal associations or organizations and for informal groups, whatever their form, as long as restrictive practices are involved.

2. DOMINANT AND FOREIGN-CONTROLLED ENTERPRISES

Section 34 of the Price Act places the duty on enterprises to register as dominant if they control one-fourth or more of the production or distribution of a commodity or of a service. In computing the extent of control over the trade, the fact that an enterprise may operate through various subsidiaries is disregarded. Generally the obligation to register is determined without reference to legal fictions.

Thus far the Norwegians have not considered it important to apply any special tests in determining the precise size or limits of the market in which dominance is to be measured. Thus, private motor vehicles, trucks, and motor scooters would be treated as three separate markets. However, further refinement, such as the Danish treatment of a highly advertised sewing machine as a commodity in and of itself, is not presently considered by the Price Directorate or Norwegian legal scholars.

The Price Directorate does have the power to require registration of firms not engaged in restrictive practices or which control less than one-quarter of the market if the enterprise's trade is important to the Norwegian economy.

As a result of the secrecy attached to Price Directorate decisions concerning registration, and in the absence of any appeals from orders to register issued under these Price Directorate powers, there is no way to be certain whether this power has ever been used.

A second category of enterprises required to report by Section 34 encompasses subsidiaries of foreign firms and organizations under the influence of foreign firms which may be assumed to have an influence on the prices of commodities or services in one or more countries. The obligation also applies when a Norwegian firm is associated with foreign firms or cartels, and when such an association may be assumed to have an influence on prices.

Section 34 does not indicate what percentage of the market controlled by a foreign-owned firm or affiliate makes registration mandatory. Although no regulations or rulings have been issued, apparently the practice of the Price Directorate is to treat foreign-controlled firms as it does the purely domestic firms—under the 25 per cent rule, applied by statute. This policy is best demonstrated by the American-owned petroleum Firm 32 which controls just under 25 per cent of the trade in petroleum products, but which has not been required to register as dominant.

The Price Directorate maintains a watch over the economy to determine whether there are unregistered restrictive arrangements or unreported dominant firms. Its decision not to require a report is usually not made public, but its demands for registration are often publicized through appeals from its decisions. These appeals to the Price Council, as provided by Sections 33 and 34, have thus far been fruitless, for in no case has the Price Directorate been overruled.

3. EXEMPTIONS FROM THE OBLIGATION TO REPORT

Where an enterprise's business activities are of so little significance to the economy that supervision is not needed, the Price Directorate may grant an exemption from the duty to report. No public record of such an exemption exists however.

Section 33 also provides that regulations may be issued to exempt certain minor restrictive practices from the obligation to report, but no such regulations have been promulgated.

a. International trade agreements

Exemptions from the obligation to report are given by Section 43 to associations or to agreements of a restrictive nature in export or international trade, not affecting the Norwegian domestic economy. The Directorate may terminate the exemption in the event that it is contrary to an international undertaking. Norway, it might be noted, has long been interested in the development of an international system for control of restrictive practices.

Another major exception of primary interest in the international field, though not necessarily limited to it, involves restrictions ancillary to trademark and patent rights. The Price Directorate practice, which has no statutory basis, is to exempt from registration highly restrictive agreements known to be in restraint of trade when it can be shown that the restriction is connected to a transfer of patent or trademark rights. This policy has exempted from registration a large number of agreements which have been put on the Register in other countries. As far as can be ascertained, the bulk of the agreements that are exempted in Norway are classified as licenses.

b. Agreements concerning wages and other conditions of work

Employers' and employees' associations or groups which concern themselves only with wages and other conditions of employment are exempt by operation of Section 2. If, however, these associations or groups should enter an agreement which discriminated against a price-cutting employer, such an agreement would not be exempt from the operation of the Price Act, for it would be competition regulating. Fees for professional services are not exempt.

4. FAILURE TO REGISTER

Failure to report under the obligations imposed by Sections 33 and 34 is punishable in the case of an individual by fines or imprisonment under Section 52—the applicable penalty depending on the intent of the accused. Legal entities may be fined or deprived of the right to do business by operation of Section 53 of the Act. In theory Sections 52 and 53 would also permit punishment for initiating a restrictive practice before reporting it.

The Oslo book-printer case illustrates one of the few occasions when Section 33 was invoked. The Ministry of Wages and Prices charged that the printers failed to register a restraint of trade and, further, that a restrictive agreement was put into force before registration, contrary to the provisions of Section 36. The Oslo District Court on 15 December 1960 sustained these charges and fined three of the officers 3,000 kroner.

Upon appeal the Court of Appeals of Eidsivating acquitted the officers on 19 June 1961. The Court held that the unregistered restrictions were an informal variation of the firm's registered practices and not sufficiently different as to constitute a violation. Furthermore, the Court's view was that the overall registration by the trade included the Oslo association. The basis for the acquittal was the finding that the defendants had not intended to violate the law.

B. Registration formalities

The Price Act precisely places the burden of reporting restraints on competition to the Price Directorate in relation to the nature of the restraint reported. Accordingly in the case of an association or cartel organized to regulate competition the obligation to report lies with the managing board of the association and not on the individual enterprises which participate in the cartel. If the association which must report is an international cartel with headquarters outside Norway, the obligation rests on the association's Norwegian representative and on the Norwegian member enterprises. Where an arrangement regulating competition operates without an association or central organization, the duty to report is incumbent upon all of the enterprises which participate, including foreign participants who must report through their Norwegian representatives. When a dominant Norwegian enterprise is asked to report to the Price Directorate, the burden lies with the enterprise itself, and the rule is similarly applicable in the event the report is to be made by the Norwegian subsidiary of a foreign enterprise. When the obligation is upon an enterprise to report, it is generally understood that the duty lies specifically with the managers and officers whose status is cognizable as such under the applicable commercial law.

1. REPORT FORMS

Three separate report forms, *Skjema*, are available and each is to be filled out in triplicate. Skjema A is to be used by a competition-regulating association, Skjema B is for a report by a competition-regulating group of enterprises without a separate Board of Directors or without managers, and Skjema C is to be used by a dominant enterprise.

a. Association form

Skjema A, for the ordinary organization or association regulating competition, calls for the submission of the following data:

1) The name and address of the association, of the chairman of its managing or governing board, and of the chairmen of any committees or agencies established for the purpose of executing restrictive business practices,
2) The names and addresses of members, if fewer than fifty,
3) If more than fifty members, the number of members,
4) If the organization is a foreign cartel, the names and addresses of domestic members and cartel representative,
5) The date of the founding of the association,
6) The subdivisions of the association and lists of its participations in other associations,
7) The geographic district encompassed by the association and the proportionate extent of the association's membership in the area,

8) The membership qualifications, responsibilities and rights of members, terms for the settlement of disputes, and the penalties that the association may impose, and

9) The aims and operating policy of the association.

Copies of the articles of association and the text of all provisions concerning restrictive business practices which have been established must be submitted with the *Skjema*. If the restrictive arrangement was not originally reduced to writing, the registration must be accompanied by a complete, written description of the arrangement. The Norwegian concept of restrictive business practices includes suggested or recommended actions as well as those that might be contractually binding.

The duty to report includes the duty to complete the appropriate *Skjema* form, to provide supplementary reports reflecting changes and alterations in any aspect of the association's activities or purposes, and to notify the Directorate of any new restrictive arrangements.

Under the regulations of the King issued on 19 March 1954, pursuant to the initial sentence of Section 33, the association has the duty to report to the Price Directorate for purposes of registration within fourteen days before the arrangement or restrictive practice or association takes effect. Registrations antedating the Price Act are by Section 35 incorporated in the Register if they continue to qualify for registration.

Under the 1954 regulations, which are the subject of supplementary reports, new price schedules, changes in rebates, and new terms of business must be notified to the Price Directorate on the day when such alterations or new terms are adopted.

b. Arrangement form

Skjema B, for groups which lack the formal organization or governing board necessary for a Skjema A registration, calls for the same information as is required in Skjema A. A further requirement is to name an officer who is empowered to represent the group before the Price Directorate in all matters under its jurisdiction.

c. Dominant enterprise form

Skjema C, the form for dominant enterprises, calls for the following information.

1) The name and address of the firm and names and addresses of shareholders, owners, and board members,
2) The legal form of the entity and when it was formed,
3) A full description of any changes that may have taken place in the form or structure of the enterprise from the date of its inception,
4) An outline of the major activities and business policies of the firm and a list of its major products,
5) A statement concerning any restrictive practice arrangements, foreign or domestic, which the enterprise may have a duty to report, and
6) Full information concerning all entities, foreign or domestic, which may have an influence, interest, or control in the reporting enterprise, and full information concerning all entities, foreign or domestic, over which the reporting enterprise may exercise influence or control.

Upon their receipt at the Price Directorate, the *Skjema* are carefully examined to determine whether the answers are complete. In some instances the Price Directorate will ask for clarification or expansion of information.

2. DIVIDED REGISTER

When the Price Directorate is satisfied with the amount and quality of information supplied to it, the *Skjema* and its enclosures are entered into the Register, which is divided into two parts—one for the public and one with which the Directorate works.

Both the public and working Registers contain the original *Skjema,* the enclosures, and supplementary reports. The public Register may also contain Price Directorate reports and decisions affecting the registrant. The Price Directorate will, upon a showing of good cause, withhold from the public Register certain trade secrets.

The working Register contains all of the materials available in the other one plus information which is not open to the public—such as copies of correspondence with the registrant, internal office memoranda, and confidential reports.

3. FILING SYSTEM

Numbers are assigned to the registration under a system which identifies the nature of the registration by the first digit. A registration beginning in "1" is for associations, "2" is for groups, and "3" is for dominant enterprises. The remaining numerals denote the consecutive number assigned within the given category. Thus, Registration No. 2.144 refers to the 144th registered group. A registration number is permanently assigned to the particular association, group, or dominant enterprise, even though the Register may disclose that the obligation to report has been terminated.

The actual filing system for both registers involves the creation of separate files in alphabetical order within each of the three classes of registrations. The registration numbers are entered into two indexes. The first index is alphabetical by name of the association, group, or enterprise and is subdivided by the three major classifications. The second index is arranged in terms of the commodities or services that are the subject of the restrictions.

Each registration is coded, and information of major importance is placed upon punch cards, which are used for surveys of practices or preparation of other indexes.

Documents reflecting abolished or supplanted restrictive practices are placed in special files which are maintained separately from the main registers. The public has full access to the public Register, and copies or photostats of the contents may be obtained for a fee.

C. Registration statistics

Special supplements to Pristidende, Oversikt, contain a cumulative survey of each active registration as of the end of 1959. They disclose the number of registered associations, groups, and enterprises within particular trades or commodity groups. This data is prepared in separate tables for nationwide and local arrangements. Twenty-eight categories of trades and services are listed, making for rather broad groupings, such as "XIV. Automobiles, tires, and repair shops."

Typical and informative tables, containing data as of 1 October 1958, appeared in the supplement to Pristidende 1959 (No. 3). The excerpts from these tables, as set forth below, give only the totals of agreements or arrangements, each of which may encompass several varieties of restrictions.

As of 1 October 1958, 240 agreements or arrangements were registered because they contained one or more restrictions on prices and conditions of delivery. Of the 53 governing prices to consumers, 32 were binding and 21 were recommended. The binding prices were exemptions from the prohibition on resale-price maintenance primarily in the fields of health and veterinary services, banks and insurance rates, and transport. Another 147 restrictive clauses dealt with manufacturers' or wholesalers' prices of which 120 were binding and 27 were advisory. The largest number of binding agreements were in forest products, fish and sea food, transport, and banks and insurance. Next in frequency were 84 price-differential restrictions and 11 undertakings for price equalization. The major industries utilizing price-differential agreements were ferrous and nonferrous metal products, forest products, and building materials. Almost half of the 11 price-equalization schemes involved fish and sea food.

As of 1 October 1958, 170 nationwide agreements and arrangements affected production and sales through seven major categories of restrictions other than those involving price. The 24 territorial-allocation agreements were for the most part in processed food products, agricultural products, and chemicals. The majority of the 31 production-quota schemes were in chemical products, metallic ores, and agricultural products. The trades represented by the 4 specialization agreements were processed foods, metal products, chemicals, and building materials. Forest products, ferrous and nonferrous metal products, and building materials were the major subjects of the 55 exclusive-dealing arrangements. Of the 13 restrictions-on-entry agreements, publishing and machine and mechanical trades had a greater than average number. In the 6 registered restrictions involving tenders and bids, the building and installation trades led the list. Finally, agricultural products, fish and sea food, and processed foods represented the major commodities involved in the 37 joint-sales or purchasing-agency agreements.

In the period from 1 January 1954 through 1 October 1959, 239 registrations terminated by reason of the end of the obligation to report or by reason of a dominant firm ceasing to do business. Of the total terminated registrations 135 involved associations, 101 involved groups or arrangements, and 3 concerned dominant enterprises.

In making any appraisal of total registration figures, attention should be given to the Price Directorate's practice of registering local associations, which report an affiliation with a nationwide association, as part of the nationwide registration. Thus, the actual number of associations involved in restrictive practices is much higher than the registration figures indicate.

ACTIVE REGISTRATIONS

	1 Jan. 1955	1 July 1957	1 Oct. 1958	1 Oct. 1959
Associations	411	502	529	555
Groups	117	202	191	212
Dominant	43	78	79	79
	571	782	799	846

The increase in the number of active registrations is not evidence of inability to curtail retraints of competition on the part of the Price Directorate or the Price Council. If anything, the indications are of greater activity by the Price Directorate in ensuring compliance with the registration requirements. The larger number of registrations also reflects the increased Norwegian commercial activity and stabilization of the economy, which has made the control over dividends no longer a necessary feature of the general control over economic activity. It would seem that these figures serve best as an indicator of economic growth as well as of the extent to which restrictive practices are a feature of Norwegian economic life, for we must bear in mind that few practices are illegal per se in Norway.

II. LEGISLATIVE FRAMEWORK FOR CONTROLLING RESTRICTIVE BUSINESS PRACTICES

A. Introduction

The present system of controlling restrictive business practices is a rather complex compromise between two views, and it is in part based on the experience under the Trust Act of 1926.

The Trust Act of 1926 created a Trust Control Council (Trustkontrollraadet) with the power to make rules and to decide individual cases. The Council had broad power to decide when general regulations were necessary, the principles on which a regulation would be based, and the actual contents of such regulations. The Council had no power to declare that a person or association had violated the law. It was only effective *in futuro* by deciding that the continuation of a practice would be illegal. The powers of the Council were not subject to an appeal to the appropriate ministry, though general principles of judicial review of administrative acts applied.

The second agency created by the Trust Act was the Trust Control Bureau (Trustkontrollkontoret). The Bureau, headed by Mr. Wilhelm Thagaard, had the duty of making the necessary investigations and preparations in presenting cases for decision to the Council. The Bureau was in reality a strong and independent agency, not subject to the control of either the Council or of regular agencies of government. In practice it made policy while exercising its investigative powers. Indeed, the Bureau displayed such energy and drive in the accomplishment of its tasks that many considered it to be the preeminent Norwegian agency controlling restrictive business practices.

The dual-agency system, represented by the Council and the Bureau under the 1926 Act and extant under the 1953 Act, is not unique, for the United States also has a duality and Sweden utilizes several agencies. The existence of two Norwegian agencies with direct responsibilities in the control of restrictive business practices is probably a result of a long-standing political dispute over whether the power to lay down general rules and regulations and the power to decide individual cases should be vested in the ordinary agencies of government, or whether these powers should be confided to an independent quasi-judicial body.

In the Norwegian view this dispute is relevant not only to the procedural nature of enforcement, but also to the fundamental philosophical approach in controlling restrictive business practices. It is argued that the very complex nature of restrictive-business-practices problems requires the legislative body to give wide authority to an administrative agency to make rules and regulations and to establish norms. An independent body would be expected to have a more direct or parochial interest in its task than would a division of an already established governmental agency, subservient to a ministry.

This conflict was resurrected during the consideration of the proposals for the current legislation. The committee proposing the legislation which is now the Price Act recommended that the power to lay down general rules and the power to decide specific cases should be given to the government generally and should be administered through existing regular agencies, such as those in the Ministry of Finance. The proposal for a Price Council envisaged a wholly consultative body with no more than advisory powers. The Price Directorate would thus be established as an ordinary agency of government, and its head would be, under the proposed legislation, also the chairman of the Council. The committee's minority was of the view that the chairman of the Council should be a judge and that the Council should be independent of the government in general.

B. The Price Act of 1953

The Price Act of 1953, retaining the dual system, is a compromise between the two views. The power to lay down general rules was given to the King in Council—the entire Cabinet of the government. The power to decide individual cases was granted to the Price Council, which serves also in an advisory capacity. The Price Directorate received the broad power of investigating the economy and of supervising subordinate agencies.

1. REGULATORY POWER, DIRECT AND DELEGATED

The King in Council, having the power to issue general rules, may delegate this authority to the ministry and to the Price Directorate under the provisions of Section 9.

Delegations that have been made pursuant to Section 9 include giving to the ministry the power to set up committees to assist in control of restrictive practices under Section 8, Paragraph 2, and the implementation of this authority through the grant of power to committees to demand information under Section 15, Paragraph 3.

The Act does not designate the ministry which is empowered to take action. The ambiguity has a purpose since the determination of jurisdiction rests with the King in Council. Until the Royal Decree of 29 July 1955 the ministry involved in trade regulation was the Ministry of Finance. After the Decree the authority was given to the recently created Ministry of Wages and Prices and still remains with it.

The ministry is empowered to redelegate such powers as it may have to the Price Directorate. By the Royal Decrees of 18 December 1953 and 29 July 1955, and through a Ministry of Finance Resolution of 24 December 1953, the Price Directorate has received the sweeping powers derived from Section 24, general powers of regulation, and Section 42, which concerns prohibition and abolition of restrictive business arrangements.

The King's authority to be consulted on decisions involving general principles has been delegated to inferior bodies and to the ministry, with no remaining need to consult the King in Council. The King in Council has delegated the right to levy assessments under Section 25, Paragraph 3, Sentence 1, to support the regulation of prices and costs not enumerated in the statute, and the right to assess interest in the case of such levies. Further, the King has delegated the authority under Section 26, Paragraph 1, to issue regulations governing the keeping of accounts as part of the system of regulation of prices and profits.

In all instances the delegating authority has residual power. The resolutions effectuating the delegations are the Royal Resolution of 18 December 1953 (Pristidende 1954, p. 3), the Finance Ministry Resolution of 24 December 1953 (Pristidende 1954, p. 6), and the Royal Resolution of 29 July 1955 (Pristidende 1955, p. 382).

2. SCOPE OF THE ACT

Only a limited number of defined restrictions on competition are directly made the subject of administrative action under the Act. Unreasonable prices and conditions of business contrary to the public interest are generally forbidden by Section 18, and middlemen activities that cause unnecessary price raises are prohibited by Section 21.

The right to refuse to deal is circumscribed by operation of Section 23.

Long-term restrictive arrangements are subject to control under Section 37.

When restrictive arrangements are made by those submitting bids or tenders to those offering contracts on a bid basis, the bidders are required by Section 39 to advise the purchaser of the implications of the regulation or control exercised by the arrangement. Now under the provisions of Section 2 of the Royal Decree of 1 July 1960, banning horizontal price fixing, tender cartels are prohibited. No exemptions to the prohibition have been granted.

Section 40 gives the Price Council specific control over fines, penalties, and other measures imposed by associations or groups to ensure compliance by members with the restrictive arrangements of the association or group.

The last of the specifically controlled practices is covered by Section 41, which allows the Price Council to intervene in cases where a restrictive association has excluded or refused to admit an enterprise.

All of the remaining activities that could be classified as controls over restrictive business practices are governed by Sections 24 and 42 of the Price Act.

C. The Price Directorate

The Price Directorate, staffed by lawyers, economists, and civil servants and headed by the vigorous Mr. Thagaard until 1 January 1961, was granted very broad powers under the Price Act, enabling it to take an active part in every conceivable aspect of the control of restrictive business practices.

The statutory authority of the Price Directorate, provided by Section 5, includes supervision and regulation of a variety of subordinate bodies—such as the County Price Committees, controlling restrictive practices at the local level, and the Price Inspectorate, the local investigatory and enforcement agency. The Price Directorate's more important powers are generally stated as being to:

a) Assist in the preparation and implementation of matters decided by the Storting (the Parliament), the King in Council, or the Ministry concerned;

b) Prepare cases for decision by the Price Council and carry out its decisions;

c) Prepare and implement measures of control and regulation within the jurisdiction of the Directorate;

d) .   .   .   .

e) Assist in other ways in implementing the Act.

1. POWERS OF SUPERVISION AND REGULATION

Under Section 33 the Price Directorate has direct responsibility for supervising the reporting and registration of restrictive agreements, groups, and dominant enterprises, subject to an appeal to the Price Council.

Section 24, authorizing some two dozen types of regulations, ranging from business terms to packaging, grants all of this authority to the Price Directorate. Only the power to regulate and set minimum prices and the power to rationalize production are withheld from it. Otherwise the Directorate can regulate such controversial areas as unnecessary middleman activities, quality control, and the weights and measures to be used in standard packages.

The authority delegated to the Price Directorate includes all encompassed by Paragraphs 1, 3, and 4 of Section 42. Thus, the Price Directorate may prohibit or amend a provision made by a restrictive association where it may be contrary to the public interest or harmful to the economy. Furthermore, this power applies equally to provisions of arrangements that are not cartels.

Dominant firms—those firms producing or distributing 25 per cent or more of the total production or distribution—are required to register under Section 34; registration as a dominant firm under this section makes the enterprise's terms of business with its suppliers, competitors, and customers subject to the Price Directorate's power to prohibit or amend. The power to prohibit not only includes the power to prohibit restrictions in being, but also reaches restrictions not yet in effect.

Delegation has been made under Section 9, Paragraph 6, so that the Price Directorate need not consult the ministry in making decisions.

The authority of the King in Council under the Price Act includes the issuance of regulations concerning the organization and functions of the Price Directorate. The clear implication is that these functions may be extended to include those functions not specifically given to any other agency under the Act.

2. INVESTIGATORY AUTHORITY

The general supervisory power granted to the Price Directorate under Section 32 enables the Directorate to undertake, if it wishes, rather sweeping investigations into any aspect of economic life bearing on competitive conditions or on the effects of restrictive business practices. Investigations into the activities of dominant enterprises are also authorized. Moreover, the Price Directorate has very broad authority to implement or propose any public measures of regulation and control authorized by the Price Act for the public good and to give all assistance permissible under the Price Act to those enterprises found to be endeavoring to implement arrangements for the public good.

3. INFORMAL PROCEDURES

The Directorate's activity in controlling restrictive business practices often takes the form of informal negotiations with the parties engaging in restrictive arrangements. For the most part the Price Directorate operates on the basis of complaints from those aggrieved by a practice or arrangement, though this is not necessarily its sole basis. Because of the weighty persuasive powers of the Price Directorate, a large number of controversies never reach the point of formal proceedings before the Price Council, or never require orders from the King in Council.

4. RELATION TO THE PRICE COUNCIL

Decisions of the Price Directorate requiring registration, under Sections 33 and 34, may be appealed to the Price Council, but otherwise the Directorate is not subordinate to the Council. The Council may neither issue orders to the Price Directorate nor specify the nature of the investigation to be made, even when the Directorate is preparing cases to be decided by the Council.

A close reading of the Price Act, particularly of the very general terms of Section 5, would seem to indicate an overlap in authority between the two bodies. In practice this is not the case. For example, the Council, taking the position that sales price levels are within the sole jurisdiction of the Directorate, will refuse to consider the economic and competitive effects of an actual level of sales prices even as part of a refusal-to-deal case. Similarly, as a matter of official practice, the Directorate leaves all refusal-to-deal problems to the Council, but there is reason to believe that the Directorate may be involved informally in such problems, although no documentation to this effect has been made public.

Unlike the Price Council, the Price Directorate works in an aura of secrecy which may be contrasted to the widely documented activities of the Danish M.C.A. The Price Directorate policy is in part a reflection of general Norwegian administrative practice. However, this practice has certainly been modified in relation to the work of the Price Council, whose decisions, along with extensive abstracts from the arguments of the parties and related materials, are published in Pristidende.

D. The Price Council

The Price Council consists of five members appointed by the King in Council pursuant to Section 4 of the Price Act.

Though the specific proposal that a judge head the Council was omitted from the Price Act, the practice has been to use a Supreme Court justice as chairman. Until 1 January 1962 the other members were a professor of economics at the University of Oslo, the director of Norway's largest chocolate manufacturer, the chief of a district agricultural bureau, and a member of a municipal administration. A professional expert, a representative of the Price Directorate, attends the meetings as a nonvoting participant in the Council and prepares cases for it. No doubt he is highly influential in the deliberations of the Council, whose members have other duties to perform. Having such an expert assist in the formation of Council policy is another example of the very broad practical power of the Price Directorate. Since 1 January 1961 the chief of the Price Directorate has appeared in person before the Price Council in major cases.

1. AUTHORITY

The Price Council, having a dual function, serves in an advisory and consultative capacity, and, as a quasi-judicial body, it is responsible for decision-making. The four classes of cases in which the Council is empowered to exercise authority under the 1953 Act are advisory opinions under the provisions of Sections 4 and 42; appeals under Sections 33 and 34; exemption requests under Section 37; and disputes under Sections 23, 40, and 41.

a. Advisory opinions

The general provisions of Section 4 enable the Price Council to serve as an advisor to the government in all areas of policy development relating to control of restrictive business practices and price regulation. Section 42, reiterating this advisory role of the Price Council, bespeaks its authority to advise the King in Council, and the general language of Section 16 is read by some Norwegian authorities as requiring such cooperation from the Price Council.

In the Ministry of Finance's proposals for legislation, which were a basis for the Price Act, great emphasis was laid on the advisory function of the Price Council as a desirable legislative feature.

Many legal scholars, however, have criticized this role. They argue that the function of the Price Council as an independent, quasi-judicial body is damaged if it also maintains an intimate relationship with the government, albeit only as an advisor in formulating policy.

Apparently the validity of this criticism has been recognized, for the Price Council has not been asked to function as an advisor, and it has never on its own initiative exercised its prerogative and offered advice.

b. Appeals from decisions of the Price Directorate

The cases before the Price Directorate concerning the obligation to register, either for concerted activities under Section 33 or as a dominant enterprise under Section 34, are basically problems of statutory interpretation of the type normally encountered in the courts.

Issues raised on appeal concern the extent of the powers of the

Price Directorate. There is no issue of either the reasonableness of a certain practice or the extent to which the practice leads to a public detriment. Such issues on appeal may arise from special orders by the Price Directorate calling for the filing of unusual quantities of information, not normally called for in most registrations. In all of these appeals the Price Council acts more as a judicial body than as an administrator.

As of 1 January 1958, after almost four years of experience under the Price Act, the Council had received only five appeals under Section 33, and each had been sustained. As of the same date the Council had received no appeals under Section 34.

The Price Directorate's practice of not disclosing either its decision not to require registration or the reasons underlying the decision places a lawyer at a disadvantage in counseling a client. Only those registrations which are demanded and thereafter appealed to the Price Council enter the public record. Obviously, if the Price Directorate decides not to require registration after negotiation with the parties, the case will not be appealed, and therefore will never serve to guide others to whom a request for registration might be made. Thus, the operation of Section 34(3) cannot be evaluated unless and until a Price Directorate decision is appealed. Until that time, one cannot know how the legislation has been interpreted.

c. Exemptions: long-term arrangements

Long-term restrictive arrangements, as distinguished from single transactions, are subjected to control by Section 37. The maximum duration of a restrictive arrangement is fixed at one year unless the arrangement includes a provision allowing cancellation by up to three month's notice. The absence of such limitations renders an arrangement unenforceable, and only the Price Council may grant an exemption from the time prerequisites. Arrangements of one year's duration may, of course, be renewed and remain enforceable.

Section 37 of the Price Act is identical to Section 16 of the old Trust Act. The practice of the Trust Control Council under that Act was to grant exemptions freely, on the ground that long-term agreements were not inherently dangerous.

The Price Council, acting under the Price Act, has taken the position that exemptions to Section 37 are to be granted only in very special circumstances. Because there must be a showing of some technical necessity for the agreements to be binding longer than a year, the majority of approximately twenty exemptions have been granted to agreements dealing with agricultural and forest products. The seasonal markets involved and the special problems of agriculture are found to call for long-range agreements. It is argued that any effective action under the agreements would be forestalled if arrangements could be terminated after just one season.

Direct or indirect horizontal price fixing is the key feature of most of the long-term agreements. Therefore, the value of Section 37 as a means of controlling restrictive practices has diminished considerably since the 1960 Order of the King in Council, banning horizontal price-fixing agreements

d. Powers of intervention

Under operation of Section 23 the Price Council may intervene when a refusal to deal is detrimental to the public interest or when it has an unreasonable effect on the refused party. The concept of refusal-to-deal or refusal-to-have-business-connections includes an apparent willingness to deal coupled with unreasonable terms. The Price Council has the authority to enjoin such unreasonable and detrimental refusals to deal and to require commerce between the parties.

Section 40 gives the Price Council specific control over fines, penalties, and other measures imposed by associations or groups to ensure compliance by members with the restrictive arrangements of the association or group. Again the standard to be applied is the public detriment or the unreasonable effect on the party concerned. The Price Council's authority to cancel, reduce, or modify the penalty extends to those coercive measures undertaken by dominant enterprises as well as to those employed by groups and associations.

Section 41 allows the Price Council to intervene in cases where a restrictive association has excluded or refused to admit an enterprise. The standard to be applied is the unfairness to the one excluded or the extent to which the exclusion is contrary to the public interest.

2. JURISDICTION

The powers of the Price Council and of the Price Directorate are as limited as those of their predecessors under the Trust Act, in that they lack authority to find that there has been a punishable violation of the law. This power still remains in the regular courts, where private parties or the state may proceed on the basis of either general criminal or tort law against those employing restrictive business practices.

The two bodies may prohibit only certain future actions. If these prohibitions are violated, then a further basis for criminal or private action in the courts is established. Only one criminal case has been instituted since the adoption of the 1953 Act, the book-printer case.

All decisions under the Price Act are appealable to the courts, though not all decisions of the Price Council are appealable to the appropriate ministry or the King in Council.

The general bases for judicial overruling of the administrative decisions include a finding that procedural rules have been violated, that a decision is not based on true facts, that a decision is based on a misuse or abuse of power, or that the decision does not accord with the general principles of law and equity.

Under Section 4 the Council is empowered to make decisions in those cases involving Sections 23 (refusal to deal), 33 (registration of restrictive agreement), 34 (registration of dominant enterprises), 40 (imposed penalties), and 41 (exclusion of organization). In conjunction with this delegated authority, Section 50 states that the decisions of the Council taken under Sections 23, 33, 34, 37, 40, and 41 may not be appealed to the appropriate ministry or to the King in Council, unless the King has issued regulations to this effect.

a. Judicial review

The Price Act carefully leaves to the Price Council and to the Price Directorate broad powers to determine or define what is unreasonable or likely to cause detriment to the public. The effect of this broad power is to limit radically the opportunity to perfect an appeal to the courts. Section 23 allows the Price Council to determine when a refusal to sell is unreasonable. The power to establish the standard of reasonability has meant that only one Section 23 case has gone on appeal to the courts since the enactment of the Price Act.

The Court of Appeals of Eidsivating has made it clear in the Section 23 case that it does have complete authority over the Council under the Price Act. This appealed case involved a central distributor of newspapers and periodicals who was ordered to sell to a dealer. The Court of Appeals in its decision of 4 April 1961 upheld a lower-court determination that the Council was in error.

The Appeal Court first ruled that the central distribution agency was not a restrictive association within the meaning of Section 41, and not an organization regulating competition. Secondly, the Court indicated that it was not satisfied that the Council decision was sufficiently clear as to the ownership of the complainant. Finally, the Court found that the Council order granting the complainant an interest in the central agency was unconstitutional because the Price Council had not been given authority to grant an ownership interest.

b. Administrative review

Decisions of the Price Council, except those under Sections 33 and 34, may be overruled by the appropriate ministry. A decision of the Price Directorate to require registration is appealable to the Price Council. According to Section 50 the Council decision is final to the extent that the decision could not be appealed to the Ministry of Wages and Prices, but an appeal could be made to the courts on the grounds applicable to judicial review of administrative decision.

One aspect of the Council's power that has not as yet been clarified is the extent to which it can be instructed in its handling of cases. Certainly the Ministry may set forth procedures to be followed by the Council. It is assumed by some scholars that the Ministry of Wages and Prices may also in the abstract set down general rules interpreting the Price Act, similar to the French Circulaires. However, most scholars assume, and the practice so far bears them out, that no ministry has the power either to order the Council to follow certain principles or to take a specific stand in a given case.

In one case a Price Council decision under Section 23 was appealed to the courts and was thereupon suspended by a ministerial order. This order was issued after a recommendation from the Council, which found that it did not have the authority, *sui generis*, to place its own decision in abeyance.

In all other cases related to Section 23, the Ministry has until now taken the stand that it cannot and will not evaluate or review the decisions of the Council. This attitude, however, does not apply to Section 37 cases, exemptions from limitations on long-range restrictive agreements; the Ministry has overruled a Section 37 decision by the Council.

No cases concerning Section 40 have appeared before the Council and, as a result, the Ministry has not had occasion to be involved. Only three cases concerning Section 41 have been before the Council and these decisions were not appealed.

3. DECISIONS ON REFUSALS TO DEAL

The Price Act provides uniform procedures to be applied by the Price Council in disputes under Sections 23, 40, and 41.

In contrast to the numerous refusal-to-deal cases which the Council has had to consider, the disputes under Sections 40 and 41 have been almost negligible. Until now the Price Council has had no case involving penalties imposed by trade organizations under Section 40, and only three cases under Section 41, concerned with exclusion from membership in a trade group. Musical goods, electrical appliances, and newspapers and periodicals were the trade groups involved.

The cases of refusals to deal, penalties imposed by trade groups, or refusals to admit to membership in a trade group—including those which never reach the Price Council—normally are in the form of disputes between private parties. However, the dispute may also take the form of a controversy between a private enterprise and a government enterprise. It is also possible that a dispute may arise from a matter presented on the initiative of the Price Council or the Price Directorate, so that the dispute would number the Price Directorate as one of the parties. This situation has in fact happened once in 1959: the Price Directorate considered a case on its own initiative when a dealer was effectively excluded from participation in the Electrical Dealers Trade Association. Thus far the Price Council has not taken up a matter on its own initiative.

a. Procedure

In its handling of cases the Council conducts a hearing that is neither wholly administrative nor wholly judicial. The extensive use of briefs and submissions through documentary evidence are more the hallmarks of an administrative tribunal than of a trial court. Having a Supreme Court justice sit as chairman has had its influence.

The Price Directorate, which participates in the internal deliberations of the Council, examines and evaluates the facts of the case in advance of the Price Council hearing. This evaluation results in a trial memorandum to the Council which is not shown to the parties prior to the Price Council's decision.

The features of the procedure that smack more of the trial court include each party's access to all statements and arguments of the other party and each party's opportunity to rebut its adversary's arguments. Facts are found through the adversary process. This procedure ensures speedy justice at a minimum cost to the parties.

Through the participation of the Price Directorate and through something akin to our judicial-notice concept, the procedure also provides for consideration of consumer interests.

The role of the Price Directorate in the operations of the Price Council greatly enhances the Price Directorate's power to negotiate informally for the modification or termination of a restrictive practice. Parties often decide that little is to be gained in going before the Price Council on an appeal, or even in an original case, when it is clear that the Price Directorate will take an adamant position.

b. Cases

The bulk of the Council's work arises from Section 23, refusal-to-deal cases. About twenty such cases a year, dealing with everything from advertising to woodenware, are the standard work load.

The 1926 Trust Act provision that refusals to deal were illegal if they were unfair had the effect of enabling the courts to hold a given refusal unlawful and even criminal. The Trust Control Council could decide that a given refusal would violate the Act if continued in the future.

The Price Act of 1953 authorizes the Price Council to prohibit refusals when such refusals are detrimental to the public interest, or when they have an unreasonable effect on the party refused. A refusal under the Price Act does not become unlawful unless it is continued after being prohibited by the Council, or is initiated after the Council has given an advance opinion that a specific refusal would be prohibited.

The Council has power to give an advance ruling, if requested by a party intending either to refuse to deal or to urge others to refuse to deal. Absent such a request, the Council is without power to act unless a refusal, a threat of refusal, or an incitement to refusal has occurred. A private party may seek in the courts compensation for injury arising from a refusal, unless the refusal has been specifically approved. Compensation may be had even if the Council has neither approved nor prohibited the refusal.

The limitation on the Council restricting its power to deciding what refusals will be illegal in the future is duplicated under Sections 40 and 41. The Council cannot rule a past activity unlawful.

The courts in giving compensation for damages arising from a refusal to deal are guided by the usual standards of detriment to the public interest or unreasonable effect on the party refused. Thus far the courts have not awarded damages in any case. The Price Council has heard no refusal-to-deal case involving dominant American enterprises. Trade groups involved in refusals to deal hardly ever include American participants.

The use of government power to force enterprises to deal with other enterprises is an increasingly important feature of many European systems of controlling restrictive practices. The Norwegian methods are among the most illuminating and their procedures are among the best documented, for the problem has had legal significance since the enactment of the 1926 Trust Act.

Although not bound by our doctrine of *stare decisis*, the Price Council seems to maintain a continuity and a consistency in its own decisions. It also takes cognizance of decisions made under the 1926 Trust Act, which made refusals illegal if unfair.

The present statutory standards are rather general—"detrimental to the public interest" and "unreasonable effect on the other party." The Price Council has read these standards so as to include refusals to deal conditioned upon compliance with unreasonable conditions. The Price Council may prohibit refusals but, unlike its predecessor, it may not make them unlawful.

Thus, the Price Council has applied its powers under Section 23 in some twenty cases a year to prohibit, as refusals to deal in various guises, price discrimination, restrictions on the development of new forms of distribution, exclusive-dealing agreements, restrictions on freedom of entry into a trade, and misuses of monopoly power.

From such cases one can discern certain consistent Price Council principles.

Very few defenses are available if the Council establishes that the purpose of a refusal to deal is to force participation in a restrictive association or group, or is to ensure that prices, markups, or terms of business fixed by an association or group are followed. Arbitrary refusals are also without defenses.

On the other hand, a refusal to deal as a means of implementing a scheme to limit the number of retailers of a particular trade in a locality has been permitted when a reasonable case for such a limitation could be established. The mere subjective view that a trade is crowded is no justification. A refusal to deal with anyone except a person having specific technical training may also be justified if some objective and clear-cut need for the training can be established.

A refusal to deal may also be a legitimate and justified defense mechanism against a cartel or a dominant enterprise, if the refusal can be shown to be promoting competition or to be defending against unfair competition.

Price cutting by a retailer is not now an acceptable reason for refusing to deal. Prior to 1940, if a retailer treated a product as a loss leader for a long period of time, thereby causing other retailers to drop the product, then a refusal to deal was considered justified. This result is not likely to obtain under the 1953 Act.

Discrimination in discount terms has been treated as a refusal-to-deal device. Discrimination, in order to be legitimate, must be based on a provable fact such as actual cost savings. The Price Council is unmoved by discounts related to mere word descriptions of the status of the purchaser as wholesaler or jobber or by considerations related to a history of previous dealings between the favored purchasers and the suppliers.

1. MILK CASES. Over the years the Price Council has been presented with two sizeable groups of refusal-to-deal cases, those involving sales of milk to food stores for resale, and those concerning the efforts of power plants to limit the electrical installation trade. These cases have been thoroughly analyzed by Arvid Frihagen in his book, *Fra Prisraadets Praksis*, published in Oslo in 1960.

Norwegian milk producers are closely knit together through a series of marketing agreements and organizational rules that create exclusive-supply areas for each dairy. As a result each dairy is prohibited from selling in another dairy's geographic territory. Thus, if an ordinary food store is refused supply by a dairy, it has no alternative source of milk. The classic conflict is between the efforts of dairies to limit their sales to specialty shops handling only dairy products, and the efforts of general food stores to obtain a source of milk for resale purposes.

The argument of the general food store is that to exclude the food store from the chain of distribution is unfair to consumers. It is also argued that the exclusion maintains an inefficient system of distribution by artificially subsidizing the dairy specialist, an obsolete type of retail distributor.

The evidence is clear that, while the general food store makes little direct profit in selling milk, the availability of milk is a major factor in inducing customers to enter a general food store. In the few cases where one or two general food stores in a locality have been allowed to sell milk, the rest being excluded, the argument is advanced that an unfair handicap has been placed on those refused milk.

As a result of these and similar arguments, the Price Council has with but a few minor exceptions consistently ruled that such refusals are unjustified and therefore prohibited. Its decisions are usually based on arguments grounded on consumer interest and on convenience in being able to buy milk where a wide variety of other food articles is available also. The unfair-handicap argument has also been accepted by the Council in relevant cases.

From 1926 to January 1960, fifty-three milk refusal-to-deal cases were decided, nineteen of which have been under the 1953 Act.

Swedish investigations of a similar problem have brought forth, subject to the differences in Swedish legislation, the same result as in Norway. Lacking the ability to prohibit the refusal, the Swedish government enforces its view by conditioning its subsidies in the dairy industry on delivery to all general food stores desiring service.

In Denmark, whose Milk Act limits the sale of milk to special milk stores in the urban areas, the M.C.A. has no jurisdiction except in those cases arising in rural areas beyond the reach of the Milk Act. The few Danish cases involving refusal to deal have all resulted in orders to deal as long as standards of hygiene are met.

The Price Council seems to have little difficulty with the milk cases, though one member has dissented in almost every decision prohibiting a refusal to deal. Generally there is no great area of disagreement among the Price Council members in disposing of such cases.

2. ELECTRICAL CASES. Norwegian district power plants have refused to deliver power to a consumer who has had his installation work done by an electrician who was not authorized by the power plant. Most Norwegian power plants are owned and run by a municipality. Their rules, often the result of action by the municipality itself, are established against a background of rules, regulations, and standards which the central government has promulgated. It is only the municipal rules which are sought to be enforced by threats of refusal to deliver power to customers. These threats have the effect of limiting the number of electricians for any given district or may even limit access to the trade to the employees of the power plant, to the point that private individuals are excluded. Altogether some thirty-nine

cases have been brought since 1926, of which twenty have been decided between the adoption of the 1953 Act and 1 January 1960.

Although the refusals are directed against the power consumer, the Price Council has treated electricians as the proper parties in interest.

The Price Council has from time to time indicated that it doubts that the municipal electric works can make such rules and regulations. However, the specific decision as to whether such rules are *ultra vires* has been avoided, and it is the general Price Council view that this issue is primarily a problem for the legislature.

Price Council prohibitions of refusals to deal are therefore bottomed on considerations of public interest and of fair treatment of electricians, rather than on the issue of the right to make rules.

Refusals in cases where the power plants acted to ensure that all installation work was to be done by the plant itself have been prohibited in all but two cases. Both cases involved thinly populated districts lacking good communications. The basis for the Price Council's allowing refusals in such cases was the practical one—that such districts were unlikely to foster any real competition. Any electrician would in every sense of the word have a monopoly in such a district. However, if a thinly populated district with poor communications does in fact have conditions which foster practical competition, then a refusal will be prohibited.

A further reflection of the Price Council's wary treatment of the power to regulate is found in those cases where the refusal centers on the establishment of standards of skill and experience considerably beyond those generally established throughout Norway by law. Generally the Price Council does not touch this type of regulation, seemingly not wishing to substitute its judgment in a technical matter. However, where a power-plant rule or regulation has required that an electrician have an office in the locality where the work is done, the Price Council has not hesitated to treat such a rule as unreasonable. Throughout the electrician cases, one notes that the Price Council is usually willing to accept rules and regulations based on general objective standards, which can be reasonably applied in advance to all applicants on a nondiscriminatory basis.

In all the electrical cases the evidence shows that the primary consideration in Price Council policy is to ensure actual competition in the electrical installation trade. Consumer interests, as in the milk cases, is also stressed in the electrical cases, despite the fact that consumers are not complainants. Over the years the members of the Price Council have become more and more unanimous in their decisions in electrical cases. Initially, a considerable number dissented.

The Price Council is by no means deterred in arriving at a decision prohibiting a refusal because it will thereby change a traditional way of doing business. Norway, as did many other European countries, began with the system whereby the power plant was the sole source of electrical installation. This situation has radically changed, for which the Price Council has been in part responsible.

The Norwegian system is in contrast to the practice in Denmark and Sweden, where general statutes require authorization from the power plant for installation work. However, authorization cannot be withheld from an electrician who has fulfilled the general, professional requirements established by the laws of the central government.

3. NONMONOPOLY SUPPLIER CASE. It is generally accepted that a supplier who has a monopolistic or possibly a dominant role in an industry is less likely to be permitted to refuse to sell than a producer in a more competitive trade or industry. Yet the fact that one is in a competitive trade is no guarantee of freedom to choose customers.

A case reported in Pristidende 1960 (p. 159) demonstrates how far the Price Council may go in prohibiting a refusal to sell. A men's clothing store in Stavanger, a city of 50,000 inhabitants, complained to the Price Council that a manufacturer refused to supply a costly brand of hats.

Hat sales represent only a very small part of the complainant's sales, and the high-priced items represent a tiny part of the total value of hat sales. The trade pattern is generally the same throughout Norway. Imported hats, competitive in price and of equal quality to the line refused to the complainant, were available to him. Norway's other major hat manufacturer also had available a line competitive to that refused to the complainant.

In the proceedings before the Price Council, the Price Directorate in its memorandum took the position that the refusal was unreasonable and should be prohibited. In this the Price Council concurred unanimously.

In the argument presented by the Price Directorate, it was asserted that in principle a producer or wholesaler should be generally free to select his customers when his products are in active competition with similar products. The distinction between the general principle and the case at bar was that the supplier had no systematic scheme for selecting his customers on an impartial basis. Thus, on the basis of the facts no objective justification could be found for the decision to cut off the complainant who had sold the high-priced line for some two years previously. In Stavanger some eight other stores, three of which were on the same street with the complainant's shop, sold the same brand of hat. The value of sales by the complainant was not noticeably different from that in other shops (Pristidende 1958, p. 62).

Thus, when one who is not in a monopoly position arbitrarily refuses to sell, a risk is involved that the refusal will be prohibited. If, however, the selection process is objective, openly announced, and applied, then a refusal is likely to be upheld. It may well be that behind the Price Council's unwillingness to sanction an apparently arbitrary or whimsical refusal is its fear that such a refusal may be used as a device for circumventing the prohibition against horizontal and vertical price fixing.

4. PRIVATE ENFORCEMENT. Although no criminal cases have been brought by private parties to the courts under the Price Act, several private cases seeking damages for refusal to sell have developed. Two such cases, arising in district courts, were decided by the Court of Appeals of Eidsivating in October 1960. In both cases the Court of Appeals upheld the lower courts' refusal to grant damages. One ruling has not been further appealed to the Norwegian Supreme Court. The second case may be appealed. The Court of Appeals' ruling was based on the insufficiency of evidence of monetary loss to sustain a claim for damages, arising from a refusal to deal in the electrical installation trade.

E. Prohibition of price fixing

The original Price Act does not contain any general provisions banning either vertical or horizontal price fixing. However, the legislation does empower the King in Council, either directly or by delegated authority under Sections 24 and 42, to take action against price fixing in general or in particular instances. This general power has been utilized almost exclusively in cases of horizontal price fixing.

Thus, the Price Directorate on 7 January 1956, utilized authority delegated to it under Section 42 to prohibit price fixing in bidding on government contracts for potatoes (Pristidende 1956, p. 54). On

4 November 1957 this same authority was used against price agreements on the saturated fats used in margarine production (Pristidende 1957, p. 585). More recently Sections 24 and 42 were invoked by the Ministry of Wages and Prices in an action taken on 28 May 1959, prohibiting all restrictive agreements of any significance in the book-printing trade (Pristidende 1959, p. 40). Agreements in this trade were the subject of a special report to the Storting (Storting Melding 1959–1960, No. 65).

1. PROHIBITION OF VERTICAL PRICE FIXING

Norway has always been preoccupied with the problem of price fixing. Being largely dependent on imports, Norway has from time to time felt imposed upon by artificially maintained prices. Such a condition led to the short-lived Decree of 25 September 1925, which banned fixing of minimum prices and related restrictive practices, such as refusal to sell, likely to foster price fixing. With that exception Norway lacked until 1957 an overall ban on price fixing, although various legislative acts provided the power to attack specific pricing practices.

Shortly after the enactment of the Price Act, the Ministry of Finance, using its powers derived from Sections 15 and 24, decreed on 22 June 1955 that all suggested resale prices, recommended or binding, were to be reported. This action was actually a major element in the investigations by the Ministry and the Price Directorate which finally led to the ban on resale-price maintenance (Pristidende 1955, p. 263).

One may surmise that in 1955, or even earlier, the Price Directorate under its general powers set out to investigate whether a ban on vertical price fixing was needed. Technically, not until 11 January 1957 did the Ministry of Wages and Prices order the Price Directorate to determine whether any general restrictive practices should be prohibited. On 14 January 1957 the Price Directorate filed a broad and comprehensive report with a full analysis of the Norwegian economy. This report, suggesting a ban on vertical price fixing and the power to grant exemptions, went to the Ministry, then to the King in Council. The King in Council submitted the report and recommendations to the Storting under the provisions of Sections 3 and 14 of the Price Act. The Storting unanimously approved the report and recommendations. The Decree of 18 October 1957 was promulgated under the authority of Section 24, and thus the ban on resale-price maintenance came into being, effective as of 1 May 1958.

a. Price Directorate Report of 14 January 1957

Because the Price Directorate's chief, Mr. Thagaard, has for many years been among the leading spokesmen for the European view that some restrictive practices may be valuable and therefore no restrictive practice should generally be banned, the Price Directorate's analysis of the effect of price fixing on the economy is significant. The analysis by the Price Directorate is also valuable for the insight it gives into the policy considerations that hold pre-eminence in Price Directorate thinking.

1. VARIATIONS IN DISTRIBUTION COSTS. The Price Directorate reported that it had found considerable variations in the costs of distribution between different types of stores and between various localities. Thus, Oslo and other major cities generally have higher overhead and higher distribution costs than smaller towns and rural districts. Specialty shops and luxury stores with extensive stocks and first-class premises have higher distribution costs than simpler establishments with rapid turnover items. Further variations in distribution costs were found to arise from differences in management techniques and operational methods.

Against this background of wide variations in distribution costs, the Price Directorate found that the supplier would fix the profit margins of all retailers at one and the same level, and the margin for all wholesalers similarly. Differences in distribution costs never entered into the calculations in the fixing of prices by suppliers for their resellers.

2. PROTECTION OF HIGH-COST DISTRIBUTORS. The Price Directorate found that most suppliers calculated resale prices so as to provide a good profit for dealers with the highest operating costs. Such high margins ensured the good will of high-cost dealers. Thus, self-service and lower-overhead establishments reaped higher profit margins than they needed, while at the same time being unable to attract customers with cheaper prices.

The suppliers argued to the Price Directorate that the normal consumer price was not inflated by establishing high profit margins. They reasoned that such margins were an incentive to the dealer to sell more high profit goods. The resultant increased volume, they argued, would lower the supplier's base price, so the consumer's ultimate price would not really be out of line, even with a high profit margin to the retailer.

The Price Directorate found that in actual practice this argument was unrealistic. It disregarded the fact that competitors of the high-margin supplier also want preferential treatment, so in the absence of a supplier's monopoly all suppliers normally offer equally high terms, and no one supplier is sufficiently benefited in volume as to be able to reduce his base price. Experience is clear that a general increase in dealer's profit margins inevitably means higher consumer prices.

The Price Directorate found that when competition reached a saturation point, the suppliers, in trying to provide high profit margins through high, fixed retail prices, introduced rebate schemes. All of the evidence seemed to indicate that such rebate schemes were usually undesirable and likely to be used in a manner that might be characterized as unfair competition.

3. COLLECTIVE RESALE-PRICE MAINTENANCE. The evil of rebates, born of the rivalry for high profit margins, is likely to spawn another type of restriction, collective resale-price maintenance. This device appears when the suppliers' costs of competing with rebates and high profit margins keyed to fixed prices gets out of hand. The Price Directorate found that collective price-maintenance schemes were an even greater restraint on competition than the evils they sought to supersede. Such schemes not only continue the exclusion of price competition among dealers, but also terminate the existence of price competition among suppliers. The conclusion of the Price Directorate was that collective resale-price maintenance meant higher prices at the suppliers' level.

4. SUBSTITUTES FOR PRICE COMPETITION. Whether prices are maintained by individual or collective action, the Price Directorate found that the result is that a dealer is not permitted to engage in price competition if he should so desire.

Proponents of price fixing advanced the view that in place of price competition came service competition. Absence of price rivalry, it was argued, gave an opportunity to provide the public with better stores, better equipment, better inventories, and better service.

The Price Directorate did not find, however, that such service competition was an inevitable or even a likely result of the absence of price competition. It considered the fact that a store selling a price-fixed commodity obtained the same price regardless of its service. The system of delivering on a nationwide basis prepackaged trademarked items with no variation in quality or price between dealers is a deterrent to the offering of additional services for which no additional return can be obtained. It was the Price Directorate's conclusion that true service competition inevitably meant higher costs. Higher costs mean pressure on the supplier to raise the profit margin, and this in turn means a new, fixed higher price to the consumer.

The Price Directorate found that some consumers will always prefer to shop in well-equipped stores, even if it means higher prices. This consumer habit did not seem a sufficient reason to prevent the rest, the great majority of consumers, from buying commodities more cheaply in stores able to sell at lower prices.

5. MAINTENANCE OF LOW PRICES. Certain suppliers told the Price Directorate that they used price maintenance as a device to hold dealers' profits down. In fact, the Price Directorate found that if competition among suppliers of a commodity is effective it will be difficult for a supplier to offer to a dealer a margin of profit that is lower than that offered by a competitor without incurring a reduction in sales to that dealer. Moreover, the Price Directorate noted that if a particular supplier's product was in demand because of its quality or low price, setting a minimum retail price would not be the best method of ensuring a low profit margin. The most effective device would be the use of a maximum-price limitation, thus allowing the dealer to reduce price if he wished. At the time of the investigation such limitations were nonexistent, though legal.

6. LOSS LEADERS. The Price Directorate examined the validity of using resale-price maintenance to stop loss leaders.

Having defined a "loss leader" as a specific article sold at less than cost price, or at less than cost plus a minimum profit as a means of attracting customers, the Price Directorate admitted that upon analysis of actual situations, it is difficult to specify what in fact constitutes loss-leader selling. The Directorate indicated that where price competition is effective the sale of a commodity may be made at a loss without in fact being a loss-leader sale. Certainly sales at less than the price fixed by a supplier are not automatically loss-leader sales. If the objective is to prevent them a refusal to sell to a dealer making loss-leader sales could be justified under operation of Section 23.

Over the years the Price Directorate, as was the case with the Canadian Combines Commission, has not been able to assess practices submitted to it and its predecessors as loss-leader sales.

7. EXCESSIVE NUMBER OF RETAIL ESTABLISHMENTS. The Price Directorate found that a long-run effect of resale-price maintenance was the establishment of superfluous new outlets. Experience has shown that the absence of price competition brings high profits which attract newcomers into the commercial field. The creation of new establishments marketing in areas of relatively inelastic demand means that sales per store will generally decline, and costs will go relatively higher. The result is finally a pressure for new and higher profit margins. When the pressure is satisfied, new enterprises are again attracted and the cycle continues at increased cost to the consumer.

8. SUGGESTED OR ADVISORY PRICES. The Price Directorate examined the likely results of allowing advisory or suggested prices if fixed prices were to be banned. It pointed out that experience has shown that most price fixing is based upon a scheme of collective enforcement that obviates competition among suppliers. The power of the collective action of suppliers, even if involving advisory rather than binding prices, is so great that the Price Directorate recommended that, in any scheme permitting suggested prices, the suggestions should be on an individual basis and not the result of collective action among suppliers.

9. PRICE DIRECTORATE CONCLUSIONS. The Price Directorate closed its Report saying:

the Price Directorate has concluded that binding resale price regulations must, in general, be regarded as counteracting a rational organization of distribution consistent with the public interest and moreover as entailing higher prices to the consumers. The Directorate is therefore of the opinion that there is justification for laying down a general prohibition of such regulations. On the other hand, the Directorate is aware that cases can occur where binding resale price regulations can be justified. The possibility of granting exemptions to this prohibition should therefore be left open, in cases where special considerations are present.

b. Report of the Ministry of Wages and Prices

On 18 January 1957 the Ministry of Wages and Prices sent its Report on resale-price maintenance to the Storting. The Ministry accepted the findings and conclusions of the Price Directorate and added some new arguments and new emphasis to the evaluation of the problem. The Ministry expressed concern over the fact that price fixing was widespread and covered a large part of the most important everyday consumer goods. It agreed with the Price Directorate's view that a superfluity of establishments was encouraged by the price-maintenance schemes and then pointed to the adverse effect on a rational organization of commodity distribution. This effect was found to be inconsistent with the public interest in that it meant unnecessarily high prices to consumers.

The Ministry found that collective price regulation was undesirable, and it opposed collective suggested prices. Because of its fear of collective action at the supplier level, it suggested that all collective arrangements in a trade or industry should be considered in passing on any individual request for exemption from the prohibition on vertical price fixing. Further consideration should be given, according to the Ministry, to the nature of the restrictions in force among the suppliers, the type and significance of the commodity, and the potential advantages and disadvantages flowing from an exemption.

c. Report of the Storting Finance and Tariff Committee

The Committee recommended the prohibition of binding vertical resale prices and other features of the Decree of 18 October 1957, which is set forth in the Appendix. The Committee noted also that horizontal price fixing at the producer, wholesaler, and retailer levels remained untouched and that such horizontal arrangements had a marked, adverse impact on competitive conditions. It further expressed the fear that the prohibition on vertical price fixing would encourage more restrictions through use of the horizontal agreements. Therefore, it recommended that horizontal price fixing should be placed under control. The Committee expressed satisfaction with the news that the Ministry shared its concern and that the Price Directorate had already initiated a study of horizontal price fixing.

The ban on horizontal price fixing was decreed in 1960, and it will be discussed in the succeeding section.

The Committee in its discussion of the proposed control of vertical price fixing stated that the work of the agencies regulating and limiting restraints on trade "seemed to show little results." At that time the Price Directorate was operating under a heavy burden of price-control activities, which had the effect of preventing restrictive agreements from pushing prices too high. At the same time the Price Council was operating under a full load of refusal-to-deal cases and handling some twenty applications for long-term arrangements under Section 37.

It is my view that the somewhat reduced price-control load of the Price Directorate has enabled it to operate more effectively than was possible in 1957.

d. The Royal Decree of 18 October 1957

This comprehensive Decree, prohibiting resale-price maintenance, is designed to cover all forms of price regulation by suppliers including suggested prices. Indirect or devious means of attempting to fix prices vertically are all apparently anticipated and controlled.

Suggested or advisory prices are permitted as long as the supplier makes it clear in writing to dealers that they are free to price as they please. The reason for this allowance was the general feeling that in some instances an individual supplier could effectively give constructive guidance to a retailer.

However, the right to give advice is not unlimited. The Price Directorate may, under the authority of Section 2 of the Decree, prohibit advisory activities if a supplier does not make it clear that a retailer may set his own price, or if a supplier engages in activities, as delineated in Sections 5 and 6 of the Decree, which are designed to induce or coerce a dealer to follow the suggested prices. Moreover, if the Price Directorate finds that advisory or suggested prices result in too high prices or profits or counteract effective price competition, it may prohibit them. To date, no such prohibition has been issued.

Foreign suppliers are subject to the ban on resale-price maintenance and to the limitations on suggested prices if they sell their goods in Norway either through their own subsidiaries or through representatives.

1. EXCEPTIONS TO THE PROHIBITION. Section 9 of the Decree gives the Price Directorate authority to grant exceptions under special circumstances consistent with the public interest and also to rescind them. The exceptions granted to date under the Decree are few in number. For a short period of time, the right to set prices of radio and television sets was granted, but it has since been rescinded.

The book trade, as is the case in Denmark, Sweden, and in other countries, has also received an exemption. The general theory favoring price fixing of books is that the trade is enabled to provide a wide variety of books that help the public. The best sellers, in effect, are considered as subsidizing good but less popular books. Price competition in best sellers, it is felt, would so reduce profits that it would not be possible to print and stock educational and other necessary works at reasonable prices. The exemption includes newspapers, magazines, and other periodicals sold in bookstores.

The exemption given to the scrap-iron trade represents what might be called a defensive use of the exemption power. Scrap iron is the subject of a major international cartel, and for self-protection the trade has been deemed worthy of special treatment.

A quasi-governmental enterprise, the monopoly handling alcoholic beverages, has been given the right to set prices for certain classes of industrial alcohol. This exemption, probably a recognition of the monopoly status of the supplier, also serves some regulatory purposes.

No time limit is placed on exemptions and they are subject to review at all times if an abuse is indicated or if the exemption is no longer needed. Furthermore, exemptions may be granted either to one trader with a trademarked product or to all or some of those in a particular trade for one or more of the commodities common to the trade.

2. EFFECT ON AGGREGATED REBATE SYSTEMS. In general aggregated rebate systems became less prevalent in Norway after 1 May 1958, when the Royal Decree of 18 October 1957 became operative. The effect of the Decree was to outlaw any collective system of price fixing or price recommendation on which a rebate system is normally based.

Aggregated rebate systems which are based on different retail prices recommended by an individual supplier are, however, still legal. The extent to which such systems restrict competition in Norway is far from clear. Only when the results of an expected Price Directorate study are made public will any authoritative information be available.

3. ENFORCEMENT OF THE PRICE-FIXING PROHIBITION DECREES. Under general principles of Norwegian law, violators of either the Royal Decree forbidding vertical price fixing or its counterpart involving horizontal price fixing are subject to criminal process in the courts.

No cases have yet been reported. The Price Directorate would normally function as the agency responsible for detection of violators and informal policing of the rules. A breach would be reported by

the Price Directorate, through appropriate channels, to the prosecut-
ing attorney and to the police of the jurisdiction in which the defendant is to be found. The case would then go to courts in the
normal fashion.

2. PROHIBITION OF HORIZONTAL PRICE FIXING

Section 32 of the Price Act gives the Price Directorate the power to
conduct investigations into all aspects of restrictive business practices. One of the few published reports made under this statutory authority led to the Royal Decree of 1 July 1960, prohibiting horizontal
regulation of prices, profits, and restrictions on bids.

One portion of the report dealt with a survey of the effect of the
1957 Decree banning vertical price fixing. The Price Directorate
found that in only 8.8 per cent of the cases were retailers using prices
different from those suggested by the supplier. The main reason
for the discrepancy, as shown in 3.3 per cent of the instances, was the
retailer's failure to keep up to date with price changes. Another major
reason for variance was the retailer's wish to use a price that was
easier to handle in an arithmetical way, such as rounding off to the
nearest multiple of 10 (Pristidende 1959, p. 469).

Considering that Norway has a population of about three and a
half million spread rather widely, even this tiny variation in price is
significant. Price cutting as we know it in the United States has not
yet appeared in Norway, though Oslo does have some electrical appliance stores selling at cut rates.

Although inertia and small markets and the like explain some of
the rigidity in following suggested prices, there was also clear evidence that the uniformity at the retail level reflected legal, horizontal price agreements at the production, wholesale, and retail levels.
It was clear to the Price Directorate that any effective system of freeing prices vertically called for a similar freedom horizontally.

Agreements regulating price play a major part in the Norwegian
economy, as is demonstrated by the fact that of the over seven hundred registered agreements in force in 1958, approximately 75 per
cent contained some form of price agreement. This widespread private regulation of price was found to have a greatly restrictive effect
on the economy. In the past the Price Act through its variety of controls, such as those over profits and dividends, has served to lessen
the impact of the private price-fixing arrangements. However, since
efforts were underway to end such governmental controls, the

importance of these arrangements loomed large. Dividend controls ended on 30 June 1960 and many other governmental controls over prices and profits are in the process of being terminated.

The Price Directorate often consults with major representative groups in the course of its investigations that may lead to new regulations. Very often drafts reflecting various approaches to a problem are prepared in advance to serve as a point of reference and to bring the various views into focus.

Alternative proposals for controlling horizontal price-fixing arrangements were prepared in 1958. One prohibited the implementation of horizontal arrangements regarding prices and profits without Price Directorate approval. The other proposal prohibited all binding horizontal restrictions on prices and profits and permitted advisory activity without prior approval, subject to the limitation in the Royal Decree of 18 October 1957.

During the summer of 1958 the Price Directorate consulted with leading representatives of industrial, commercial, and labor organizations as well as with the Council of Consumers. Except for the labor and consumer organizations the representatives strongly opposed any form or degree of prohibition of horizontal price agreements.

a. The Royal Decree of 1 July 1960

About a year later the Price Directorate's draft legislation was ready for submission to the Ministry of Wages and Prices. The report, submitted to the Ministry in August of 1959, stressed the detrimental effects to the economy stemming particularly from those horizontal price arrangements affecting consumer goods. However, in accordance with policies of control and subsidy in certain sectors of the economy, specific exemptions were provided for agriculture, forestry, and fishery activities as well as banking and insurance. It was also recommended that export activities be exempt. The class entitled to exemption was expanded in the final proposal to include joint sales agencies.

The Price Directorate drew heavily on the German Act against Restraints on Competition as a model. Previously the government had had the burden of proving harmful effects of price-fixing agreements in individual cases, whereas under the new Decree the involved parties would have the burden of demonstrating the benefits of the agreement to the public and the economy.

The Ministry of Wages and Prices, following the procedure described in the discussion of the Royal Decree of 18 October 1957, sent to the King in Council and through the King in Council to the Storting a message explaining the proposed Decree. This procedure was taken under the provisions of Section 3 and 14 of the Price Act. The Storting indicated its approval of the proposed Decree, and the King in Council issued it on 1 July 1960.

Discussion in the Storting would seem to indicate that the members expect a large number of exemptions in addition to those specifically provided in the Decree.

The Decree, unlike the earlier one banning resale-price maintenance, placed initial responsibility with the Ministry rather than the Price Directorate. The apparent reason for giving primary authority to the Ministry was the Ministry's desire to be able to lay down the basic principles of administration. As of 1 February 1961 the Ministry delegated its power to the Price Directorate, under operation of Section 9 of the Decree.

b. Analysis of problems arising from the Decree

The 1960 Royal Decree is, from some points of view, less clear than the earlier Decree concerned with vertical price fixing. Indeed the Decree seems to raise a number of questions for which no apparent answers are present.

Section 1 is the key provision. All forms of agreements or arrangements—binding or advisory, dealing with prices, profits, methods of calculating prices and profits, rebates, and the like—are prohibited. Section 2 prohibits all conceivable agreements restraining competition in tendering bids for goods or services. Section 2 prohibits agreements concerning conditions to be used, agreements to divide sales territories, and agreements as to production quotas, and thereby its impact seems far greater than that of Section 1. The true scope of Section 2 is unclear and warrants further clarifying regulations or decrees.

Section 3 is aimed at forestalling any forms of pressure that might be used to force higher prices. The provisions are applicable not only to trade groups, but also to members and individuals in the group who might try to influence someone to charge higher prices. As noted in the discussion of enforcement of the Royal Decree of 18 October 1957, individuals can be prosecuted in the courts for breach of this section.

Foreign-based cartels and associations are dealt with in Section 4. The foreign locus of the association or arrangement is no insulation against the operation of the Decree.

Section 5 sets up the exemptions for fisheries, agriculture, and forestry. It is understood that the exemption goes only to the primary level of production. Thus farmers, fishermen, and lumbermen may set the price horizontally for the initial sale of their produce. However, once the fish are sold to a cannery the exemption is ended. No horizontal price fixing of a can of herring is permitted at the retail level or at the wholesale level, and no horizontal price agreement among canneries is tolerated.

Section 5 contains an exemption for joint sales agencies. It is not yet clear just how comprehensive this exemption is nor to what extent it creates a loophole in Section 1.

Section 6 will make or break the Decree, for here is the authority, now delegated to the Price Directorate, to grant exemptions. This section gives very general criteria for granting exemptions, which are to be given "only for a limited period of time." The criteria include (1) necessary technical and commercial cooperation leading to public benefit in terms of better products or lower prices, (2) defense against unfair methods of competition, foreign or domestic, and (3) general public interest.

As already noted, the Storting voted its approval assuming that the exemptions would be easily obtained. The basis for the Storting's attitude is the belief that such exemptions are necessary if Norway is to take her place effectively in the European Free Trade Association, and if Norwegian business is to be able to compete with foreign firms in Norway.

The indications are that the generous policy toward exemptions is not intended to apply to tenders under Section 2 of the Decree. In 1958 twenty-one tender agreements were registered, and so far none has been granted an exemption.

c. Termination of price-fixing agreements

On 5 September 1960 the Ministry of Wages and Prices issued an order concerning the procedure for terminating price agreements by the time the Decree became effective, 1 January 1961. The ministerial order required all associations having proscribed restrictions to take formal steps to abolish them. All members were to get specific notice of the changes made. The formal changes in rules and a copy of the notice to members was to be filed with the Price Directorate. The Ministry also warned that organizations and their employees must not take any steps to induce members or others to charge high or higher prices or otherwise obstruct the full abolition of the restrictive agreements.

As this analysis is being written early in 1961, no regulations or guidelines have been issued which would indicate how the provisions allowing exemptions are to be administered.

III. CASE STUDIES OF AMERICAN FIRMS

A. Introduction

In 1959 and 1960 I surveyed, initially by questionnaire, twenty-two Norwegian enterprises known to have a significant number of shares under direct or indirect American control. Seventeen of the twenty-two firms are registered on the Norwegian cartel Register.

Representatives of American Firm 32, upon receiving the questionaire, discussed it with members of the staff of the American Embassy in Oslo to ascertain whether anything official was involved. It might be noted that the letter accompanying the questionnaire made it clear that my survey was wholly unofficial. Somehow the result of this conference between representatives of petroleum Firm 32, which is not yet registered as dominant, and the Embassy staff was a general understanding by members of the American business community in Norway that they should not reply. As a result only six of the Norwegian questionnaires evoked a reply, four of which were refusals to provide information in any form.

The two full replies were from subsidiaries of very large American enterprises. The Norwegian subsidiary of Firm 52, dealing in business and office machines, while erroneously denying registration, gave an otherwise full response, despite the fact that its Danish sister firm had refused to answer. The smelter subsidiary of American Firm 702 erroneously reported that it was registered as a dominant firm. Its reply stated a desire for a uniform, international, antitrust standard based on the American legislation.

The poor response to questionnaires in Norway may be contrasted with the thirty-three replies received in response to forty-five questionnaires sent to Denmark, and to Sweden's reply ratio of forty out of sixty-five.

Because of the unsatisfactory response from American firms in Norway, it has been necessary to rely on government and secondary sources in building the case histories. If the case histories do not adequately reflect the viewpoints of the American enterprises, the reason is apparent.

In this connection, it is interesting to note that there seems to be no consistent policy governing the decisions of American subsidiaries to reply or not to reply. The Danish subsidiaries of petroleum Firm 33 and electronics and cable Firm *301* were most cooperative, but their Norwegian counterparts refused any information. The same pattern of inconsistency was revealed in the treatment of other questionnaires, not dealt with in this book, which went to France, Germany, Eire, Austria, the Netherlands, and the United Kingdom. With the exception of petroleum Firm *32* American parent organizations have no consistent policy concerning the extent to which subsidiaries are free to give information.

B. Toilet articles

Dominant firm—Price lists—Suggested prices

In 1938 American Firm *24* organized a Norwegian corporation with two hundred shares valued at 1,000 kroner each, holding, then and to the present, all but two of these shares. The remainder are held by two who are referred to on the cartel Register as "Bostoners." The subsidiary was created to import and sell in Norway safety razors, razor blades, related shaving articles, cosmetics, and surgical knives on behalf of the American parent.

Because of the more than 25 per cent control that this import sales agency has over the Norwegian market, the enterprise has had to register as dominant, Registration No. 3.68. As early as 1956 the registration stated, "There is no agreement on regulation or control of competition." The registration was accompanied by a price list and a further statement: "Our retailers have assumed no obligation nor are they bound to maintain our stated prices." In subsequent years revised price lists, subject to the previously stated conditions have been filed.

With the promulgation of the Royal Decree of 18 October 1957, which forbade vertical price fixing, the dominant firm filed a statement with the Price Directorate reporting that, in accordance with the Decree, it had specifically advised its customers that they were not required to follow the prices calculated by it.

Although not called for by statute, the pricing practices of dominant firms are registered on the theory that the very dominance of the firms exerts an influence on prices in a direct sense.

In this instance, if any suggested prices are cut, the reduction is so infinitely small as to be insignificant. The factors in the observance of price are the relatively low profit margin in the suggested prices, the great public demand, and the relatively low prices of the items making up an individual sale, such as a package of razor blades.

There is no evidence that being forced to register as a dominant firm has harmed this American-owned enterprise.

C. Motion pictures

Refusal to deal—Patents—Uniform licensing agreements—Automatic renewal—Territorial restrictions

Three major American motion-picture producers, Firms 62, 64, and 65, maintain distribution facilities in Norway. These firms are not individually registered, nor is their export association, Firm 63. However, all of these entities are participants in two major agreements registered as Nos. 2.187 and 2.188.

Norwegian control authorities first concerned themselves with motion picture imports in 1938. An importer of films which were produced according to a patented method sought royalties of approximately 25 cents per yard of film. The Control Council, operating under the then applicable Trust Act, reduced the royalty to about 7.5 mills per yard. This reduced rate led to a refusal to deal, which the Control Council found was also unlawful.

Today in Norway a significant number of theatres are operated and controlled by municipalities or other administrative district agencies. As disclosed in Registration No. 1.571, a formal association or cartel registration for the National Association of Municipal Theatres, 131 communities have municipally operated theatres. Membership in the association is open to all of them, and 126 have joined. These members in turn control 188 of the approximately 600 motion picture theatres in Norway. However, the 188, being the major theatres, represent about 85 per cent of the total income from motion picture exhibitions. Thus, distributors of films are without any real bargaining power as long as there is no effective competition among exhibitors.

The agreement registered as No. 2.187 is for one year's duration, with a provision calling for automatic renewal as long as no participant in the agreement has withdrawn. On the distribution side all of the American firms making up the association, Firm 63, participate, as do distributors of films imported from the rest of the world. The exhibitors represented in this agreement are the members of the National Association of Municipal Motion Picture Theatres.

The agreement, dating from 1954, includes among its parties the Norwegian Film Bureau Federation and the Free Norwegian Film Distributors Association. The agreement specifies that it is open to all distributors of films.

The limits of film rental fees are established by the agreement, so that ordinary films are rented at 40 per cent of the gross receipts less taxes. Provision is made for different fees for special films. The agreement also regulates charges for advertising posters and other publicity materials, transport of film, and the like.

Specifically exempted from the agreement and subject to separate terms are films produced in Norway.

The distributors agree that they will lend or rent films only to those theatres that have been authorized pursuant to applicable law to give public performances. Further, they accept the provisions of the agreement as binding in all of their dealings with all motion picture theatres in Norway. On the other hand, the members of the National Association of Municipal Motion Picture Theatres agree not to rent films under terms other than those established by the agreement.

The agreement registered as No. 2.188 involves most of the motion picture theatres not controlled by the National Association of Municipal Theatres. Being a companion to No. 2.187, it includes all of the parties in No. 2.187. No. 2.188 governs rental terms—on the average fixed at five hundred kroner a month—for the Norwegian District Theatres Corporation, and establishes terms for all other charges.

Since many of the small Norwegian communities lack permanent motion picture operations, they depend on mobile exhibition units. The agreement governs the activities of such units by requiring that permission be obtained if an exhibition is to take place within fifteen kilometers (about nine miles) of a permanent theatre.

The Royal Decree of 18 October 1957 and the Decree of 1 July

1960 have had no effect on these agreements. Cartel Registration No. 1.571 is unchanged and agreements No. 2.187 and No. 2.188 have been exempted from the provisions of the Decree of 1 July 1960, banning horizontal price fixing. The balance of power between exhibitors and distributors seems to call for the exemption.

D. Petroleum

Dominant firm—Registered restrictive contracts—Government subsidy—Maximum prices—Base price—Contract restrictions —Dealers Association—Price lists

At least five major petroleum refiners and importers are active in the Norwegian market. Three are registered as dominant—American Firm 33 under cartel Register No. 3.5, a British-controlled firm under No. 3.15, and a Dutch-controlled enterprise under No. 3.6. Each of the dominant refiners is further registered by reason of restrictive contracts involving the trade in petroleum products. Firm 33's registration for such agreements is No. 2.144. American Firm 35 is registered solely because of its agreements under No. 2.190. American Firm 32, which has long sought to avoid registration in Denmark, remained unregistered in Norway until 1961, as to both its dominance and its contracts. Firm 32 has registered, but no registration numbers have so far been assigned.

Maximum prices and government controls have been the hallmark of petroleum marketing in Norway for a long time. At present government-established maximum prices remain as the last vestige of a rather broad control system, which also encompassed general profit and dividend controls. Maximum prices are set by the Price Directorate pursuant to its authority under Section 24 of the Act. For example, the Price Directorate's Announcement No. 34 of 7 September 1959 sets forth maximum prices at tank wagons, to consumers, at depots, and at airfields—for all types and grades of petroleum products. Oslo serves as the base in all price calculations (Pristidende 1959, No. 14, pp. 432–438).

Until 20 December 1957 petroleum suppliers had to contribute to a special government fund designed to assist in the maintenance of stable prices (Pristidende 1958, No. 1, p. 2). Now abolished are the systems of delivered prices under which the cost of transport to out-of-the-way distributors was absorbed by the refiners (Pristidende

1957, No. 7, p. 181). Another earlier form of control over petroleum-product sales was a government-subsidy arrangement designed to assist certain classes of consumers, such as the operators of small fishing vessels (Pristidende 1958, No. 1, p. 8).

All similar funds are now obsolete and the only remaining restrictions, aside from the general controls over profits, are those arising from the maximum-price dictates of the Price Directorate and from the agreements entered into between the refiners and their customers.

The petroleum trade has been notably free of involvement in restrictive practices cases. Only one case involving a refusal to deal under earlier legislation has been found. A distributor of petroleum products complained in 1950 that his Dutch-controlled supplier refused to give him products at jobber's prices. The two American firms on the Register, through affiliates, also refused to supply at the requested terms when the complainant, seeking an alternative source of supply, approached them (*Prisdirektoratets Avgjørelser i Boikotts-aker 1946–1953*, Oslo, 1958, pp. 273–277).

By a decision on 11 April 1950 the Price Directorate ruled that there was no collective refusal to deal because the complainant had not established a right to jobber prices.

Dominant Registration No. 3.5 for American Firm 33 shows that its Norwegian subsidiary was founded in 1893, with 36,615 shares of stock—20,397 are held by the parent corporation, 561 shares are held by other Americans, and the remainder are in Norwegian hands. Since the refinery is separately incorporated, Firm 33 has two Norwegian subsidiaries.

The agreements which are registered under No. 2.144 consist of a variety of standard contracts, all of which contain provisions declaring that the retailers or distributors of the products will not buy petroleum products from any other refiner or importer. Another provision binds the distributor or retailer not to transfer any property to any competitor of Firm 33. This is a general provision which seems somewhat ambiguous, though it is thought that "property" is meant to be limited to the location where the products are dispensed, in the sense of real property.

One of the contracts registered under No. 2.144, General Contracts of Sale, covers the trade in mineral oils and all classes of mineral-oil products. Normally it is used for service stations. Firm 33 has reported approximately 2,800 of these contracts to the Price Directorate in this registration. The British dominant firm reports 1,300 such contracts, and the Dutch-controlled firm 1,000.

Heating Oil Contracts, which number about 3,000, are usually concluded with the ultimate consumers.

Coastal Station Contracts are for the general sale of mineral oil and for all mineral-oil products to vessels. The 220 contracts of this class contain special conditions in connection with the tanks, pumps, and equipment which the refiner places on the dealer's property. If the dealer in any way violates his contract, the supplier, on a declaration that the contract is terminated, has the option of either removing the tanks and equipment, or of continuing the enterprise of selling and distributing on the dealer's premises.

The Agency Contracts, of which there are 55, and the 1,200 retailer Contracts Concerning Pumps and Equipment also contain provisions giving the refiner the option of removing his equipment or taking over the sales if the retailer or agent violates his agreement.

Prior to the promulgation of the Royal Decree of 18 October 1957 the General Contracts of Sale, Coastal Station Contracts, and the Agency Contracts all contained a provision by which the dealer would undertake to follow retail prices established by the refiner. Of course, the maximum-price provisions, which are obeyed as if they were for minimum prices, had long rendered these clauses meaningless. It might be noted that not every request for a price increase by the refiners has met with government approval.

The contracts registered under No. 2.190 merely reflect the fact that the Norwegian subsidiary is an agent for its American parent, Firm 35. Unlike a dominant registration, no information is given as to the history or control of the Norwegian entity.

These contracts generally provide that the dealers are not bound to follow the prices or profit margins suggested by the refiner. In this regard the Register contains some ambiguous correspondence concerning the possibility that prices might actually have been stipulated by the supplier. The control through maximum prices and the ban on resale-price maintenance make this question moot.

The reported contracts under No. 2.190 are simpler and fewer than those under No. 2.144. Under the 175 Gasoline Station Contracts the refiner either lends or rents equipment to the dealer. The Subtank Contracts, which number approximately 65, are concluded with those who either borrow or rent tanks—normally with large-scale consumers of petroleum products. Also included in No. 2.190 are 15 Heating-Oil Retailer Contracts.

The contracts for gasoline stations and subtanks contain clauses binding the dealers to give first preference to the refiner in mineral-oil products. The retailer is further obligated to carry only the refiner's products in his retail establishment. The heating-oil dealer is more specifically bound not to engage in any business in which, either directly or indirectly, he deals in a competitor's products. Violation of the agreements by either party may entail abrogation of the contract.

The contracts that are registered for the other two dominant firms, the British-controlled enterprise and the Dutch-controlled firm, are basically similar to those already discussed. These contracts are varied to include Peddler Contracts, Tractor-Fuel Contracts, and Technical-Chemical Contracts. The dominant registration of the Dutch refiner lists the corporations which it influences or controls.

Approximately 5,000 service-station contracts for gasoline are disclosed by all of the registrations. Many of these are in reality contracts for one or two pumps located at small country stores. Some 1,500 of the service-station and garage-gasoline dealers have joined the Gasoline Dealers Association, Oslo, which has cartel Registration No. 1.186. The Association was founded in 1932 and is subdivided into forty-nine district associations, which have locally applicable rules and regulations. A common form of association-policed restriction concerns the hours during which the service stations operate. The rules fix the premium price that is to be paid by the consumer when sales are made after closing hours, and the closing hours themselves are carefully regulated.

Prior to the prohibition on price fixing, many of the district associations had registered suggested, collectively enforced price lists for various forms of service on automobiles. Such price lists were most common in the major urban areas. Many of these price agreements were abandoned in 1958.

The Association, which includes among its members many of the major dealers, also was itself a participant in the pre-ban agreements concerning automobile tires, Registration No. 2.54, and automobile accessories, Registration No. 2.66. Because the Royal Decree of 18 October 1957 forbade horizontal or collective suggested resale prices, the automobile tire agreement, which will be discussed in a subsequent section, was changed to a series of agreements with the individual members of the Gasoline Dealers Association. However, it still appears that the Association is a party to the agreement on rebates concerning auto accessories, Registration No. 2.272.

The high degree of government control over the petroleum industry—which has included price—and the general profit and dividend control, has left the industry in a fairly static state. The market shares of the larger firms have not altered appreciably over the years, and the general pattern of trade terms has become somewhat rigid. The organized power of the major service stations has also served to maintain a balance in the trade.

E. Soft drinks

License—Sales territory—Exclusive dealing—Coca-Cola and other cola beverages—Uniform pricing—Exception to price-fixing ban

The registration concerned with bottled soft drinks, cartel Registration No. 1.345, does not directly involve any American firm. American Firm *84*, Coca-Cola, which will be discussed at length in the Swedish materials, is not here involved. Rather American Firm *85* is involved in this agreement through a license agreement relating to the supply of syrup and coloring for a beverage sold under a Norwegian trademark. It is because of the increased use of licenses that this case study is included.

The Norwegian-registered enterprise has a Norwegian name and trademark. The cartel is in the form of a corporation, founded in 1949 and reorganized in 1957 when several of the original stockholders withdrew. The present nineteen stockholders include major mineral-water producers and well-known breweries. Shares of the corporation are issued with a restriction requiring shares to be offered to other shareholders before sale to outsiders. The registration makes it clear that all shares are held in Norway, thus no foreign ownership interest is involved.

The pattern of operation of the corporation follows in the tradition of the highly cartelized Norwegian breweries. Indeed, the restrictive practices of the breweries are of such classic proportions that the Report of the Ministry of Finance to the Storting in 1952, in behalf of the legislation that became the Price Act, singles out the brewers' agreements as prime examples of private anticompetitive restrictions in Norway and quotes from them at length.

New bottlers may be admitted to the cartel arrangement upon a vote of the majority of the stockholders at a regular general meeting. Prior to admission, however, the new bottler's sales district must be determined. If an agreement between the newcomer and the corporation is not possible, then the matter will be brought before the general meeting of the shareholders. In accordance with a policy calling for equitable spreading of the new burden among the existing shareholders, their final resolution makes the loss of any one shareholder's sales district negligible.

The corporation has entered into an agreement with bottlers-shareholders, which permits the bottlers to process and distribute a cola drink of a quality and composition specified by the corporate management. The bottlers may not produce any other cola beverage or distribute a competing cola beverage. The sales district is normally limited to the bottler's mineral-water sales district. All bottlers are required to sell the cola drink in a uniform bottle, at uniform rates, and under uniform sales conditions. The syrup must be purchased from the corporation and must be supplied to all bottlers at the same price. All requirements for ingredients such as coloring and syrup will be taken care of exclusively by the corporation either through importation or its own production under license.

Failure by a bottler to observe the regulations established by the corporation may mean fines of up to one hundred kroner per day ($14). Violation of the agreement may mean immediate cancellation of business relations. Any disputes under the agreement are to be resolved by an arbitral tribunal.

Some evidence supports the proposition that some of the restrictions in the agreements between the corporation and bottler are inspired by the initial license agreement under which syrup is supplied to the corporation. Since this license agreement is not registered, it is not possible to specify which restrictions have been imposed by the foreign syrup supplier.

The agreement between the corporation and its bottlers requiring uniform pricing and uniform business terms seems to have been left undisturbed by the ban on price fixing. There is no record of an amendment to the original cartel registration after the Decree of 18 October 1957. This would indicate that restrictions ancillary to the licensing of a trademarked product and of a process, even if not patented, may be treated by the Price Directorate as exempt through operation of law.

American Firm *84*, Coca-Cola, has faced in Norway the question of whether its Bottlers Agreements are subject to cartel registration. These agreements embody the franchise under which the Coca-Cola Export Corporation supplies concentrate to those who prepare and bottle the beverage. The features of the agreements that concern the Norwegian authorities are the provisions giving a bottler territorial exclusivity and the provisions designed to maintain what the American firm considers the integrity of its trademark.

Coca-Cola Export and the foreign bottlers have entered into a series of vertical agreements under which the bottlers agree to develop the trade in the drink and satisfy the demand in their territory. In operation the agreements generally tend to keep prices at a minimum in order to encourage volume sales of concentrate, which is to the advantage of the American firm.

However, the general position of the Price Directorate, in seeking to order registration of the Bottlers Agreements, is that the effect of the vertical agreements is the same as that of a horizontal agreement dividing territory, and that, further, the territorial limitations on any bottler may be an unreasonable restriction on his freedom.

The issue to be resolved in Norway is not whether Coca-Cola Export must register as a dominant firm, but whether the agreements with its bottlers must be registered under Class 2 of the cartel Register. The Norwegian position is questioned because of the general administrative exemption normally granted to restraints ancillary to trademark licenses.

By the end of 1961 there was apparently no final decision as to whether registration would be required. The appeal was then pending, but informed opinion is that ultimately registration will be ordered.

It should be noted that the Coca-Cola Export Corporation has specifically requested that it be identified. A further and more detailed discussion of the problems of Coca-Cola appears in the Swedish case studies.

F. Telephone and telegraph equipment, cables, and electronics

Dominant registration—International cartel—Domestic agreement with foreign participants—Producer-wholesaler agreement—Customer classification—Price fixing—Requirements contracts—Rebates—Delivery terms—Agreement abolished—Adminis-

tration of agreements by committees—Penalties—Domestic cartel—
Exemption from price-fixing ban—Freedom of entry—Interlocking
agreements

This industry illustrates an interlocking network of restrictive
agreements and a variety of changes wrought by the Royal Decree of
18 October 1957, banning vertical price fixing and collective horizontal activities designed to maintain vertical prices.

American Firm *301* operates in Norway through two subsidiaries.
The first subsidiary is registered as a dominant firm under No. 3.22
and controls the second, which is registered as dominant firm No.
3.29. The entity registered as No. 3.22 will be referred to as "Electric,"
and No. 3.29 as "Fabrikk."

Electric was established in 1920 with a share capital of 200,000
kroner, with 1,000 shares issued. Except for 25 shares, the entire issue
is owned by the American Firm *301*. Electric serves Firm *301* by
registering and licensing patents on its behalf. Through a control of
the majority of Fabrikk's stock, Electric directs the affairs of that
company in accordance with Firm *301*'s policies.

Fabrikk, founded in 1915, today has issued 5,000 shares of preferred stock and 15,000 shares of common stock, all with a par value
of 1,000 kroner each. Electric owns 75 per cent of each class of shares.
Fabrikk is the operating entity and manufactures and trades in a variety of cables, conductors, and electronic parts. Further, it is the
subsidiary which participates in all of the agreements with which
we are concerned. Of all of the firms manufacturing similar products
in Norway, only Fabrikk and Electric are registered as dominant.
Fabrikk is also registered as a participant in a variety of agreements,
both international and domestic, some of which have recently been
abolished or amended.

1. THE INTERNATIONAL AGREEMENT REGULATING COMPETI-
TION IN HIGH VOLTAGE CABLES

In 1950 Fabrikk joined the 1947 Lausanne Agreement. This is a sales
agreement involving cable makers in Sweden, Denmark, Holland,
Belgium, the United Kingdom, France, Spain, Italy, Austria, Switzerland, and Finland. The affiliate of American Firm *301* in Denmark
and its subsidiary in England are also members. Later adherents to
the agreement include the makers from the West German Republic.
The agreement requires its participants to consider domestic market

prices of other participating countries when negotiating export orders to them and to consult representatives of the cable industry in these countries before deciding on prices. Further, the participants must, by means of this agreement, report to members from whose country requests are received for bids on cables of seventy kilovolts, or of greater capacity. Price lists for sales in nonmember countries are also made effective.

It is estimated that about 70 per cent of the high-voltage cable trade in Norway passes through the hands of participants in the Lausanne Agreement.

The Lausanne Agreement, unlike its predecessors of the pre-World War II period, contains no provisions calling for penalties in the event of violations. It only establishes a standard by asking that members abstain from substantially undercutting local prices. In general there is no evidence that members do undercut or that an enforcement scheme needs to be established. This agreement has not been affected by the ban on price fixing.

2. AGREEMENT ON INSULATED LEAD CABLES

This agreement, Registration No. 2.27, came into effect in 1934 and survived until the Royal Decree of 18 October 1957 became operative.

In order to qualify for membership in the agreement, a Norwegian or foreign factory had to have its products approved by the Norwegian Electrical Material Control. In July of 1957 the membership was composed of the sole Norwegian producer, Fabrikk, who was deemed to dominate the market, sixteen foreign cable manufacturers, and forty-four Norwegian wholesalers. The agreement established a Lead Cable Committee whose major function was to fix wholesale prices, to issue a price list, and to classify customers.

To qualify as a wholesaler, a firm had to have the reputation of a leader in the electrical trade and annual total purchases of at least 75,000 kroner ($10,500) from member producers. Wholesalers agreed to keep the prices fixed by the Committee and to abide by all regulations established by the agreement or under it. They further bound themselves to purchase all their needs solely from other participants in the agreement. The producers, in turn, agreed to sell only to the wholesalers, with the exception of direct sales to the Norwegian State Railways and the Norwegian State Telegraph Works.

Goods were supplied to wholesalers with a rebate of 24 per cent given on the list price. Additional rebates to wholesalers were provided on the basis of the total annual purchases from participants in the agreement.

WHOLESALE REBATE SCHEDULE

Total Kroner Value of Annual Purchases	*Rebate*
75,000–150,000	4.25%
Over 150,000:	
On the first 150,000	5.50%
On the next 150,000	6.00%
On anything more	6.25%

The association had a list of preferred customers, which was normally called the "special list." Persons on this list and other groups were also entitled to rebates.

PREFERRED CUSTOMER REBATE SCHEDULE

Class of Buyers	*Rebates*
Important buyers on the special list	. 7.5–15.0%
Power plants and authorized installers	15.0%
Larger firms with established electrical needs from the special list	15.0%
Other firms with established electrical needs, ship radio installers	7.5%
Norwegian State Railways and Telegraph Works . . .	24.0%

Agreement No. 2.27 forbade the giving of further rebates, such as those for cash payment. Delivery of goods from manufacturers to wholesalers was solely on the basis of freight paid to Oslo. The wholesaler was required to pay the additional freight charges on sales delivered to other localities. Similarly wholesalers made their deliveries F.O.B. Oslo. Additional charges on deliveries to other localities were calculated according to the terms specified in the agreement.

When the Royal Decree of 18 October 1957 became operative, an announcement was sent as shown by the cartel Register, to all of the participants in the agreement, advising them that they were free to calculate prices and profits as they pleased. This is not to say, however, that any noticeable changes in the pattern of business have since taken place.

3. THE INSULATED CONDUCTORS AGREEMENT

The Insulated Conductors Agreement, No. 2.16, is now abolished. It was between Norwegian cable makers and foreign cable makers with

Norwegian sales agencies on the one hand, and wholesalers in electrical goods on the other hand. Coming into force in 1930, the agreement was open to all manufacturers whose products were approved by the Norwegian Electrical Materiel Control. Members included Fabrikk, three smaller Norwegian manufacturers, fourteen foreign manufacturers, and fifty-nine wholesalers.

It is estimated that the Norwegian manufacturers produced the major portion of the goods traded under the agreement, and that all of the participants controlled between 75 and 80 per cent of the nationwide trade in insulated conductors.

The administration of the agreement was provided through the creation of the Conductors Committee, whose duty was to fix the prices for the goods covered by the agreement and to establish the gross prices to be paid by installers and electric works.

The agreement had a rather complex customer-classification system coupled with a product-classification system.

Group A consisted of wholesalers who principally served as suppliers to installers and electric works. A requirement for its membership was a minimum, annual individual volume of trade no less than .5 per cent of the total Group A trade.

Group AR consisted of wholesalers selling primarily to the radio and television industry. To qualify for this Group, one had to be affiliated with a participating Norwegian manufacturer and listed as such.

Membership in both groups was limited to those firms trading principally as a wholesaler and maintaining a staff of salesmen. Of course, one had also to agree to all of the terms of the agreement.

All wholesalers participating in the agreement agreed to purchase all of their requirements solely from foreign or domestic member manufacturers. In return the manufacturers agreed to make all of their sales through participating wholesalers, except for sales to other manufacturers, and except for sales to the Norwegian State Railways and the Norwegian State Telegraph Works.

Group AR wholesalers received a 20 per cent rebate based on the gross price of fixed or movable plastic insulated conductors of various dimensions. This rebate was also given to Group A on the same conductors and other goods classified as Ia. Goods classified as Ib, such as plastic-guarded, corrosion-proof conduits, were sold on the basis of a 24 per cent rebate.

The scheme for giving rebates on annual purchases of goods was developed along somewhat complex lines because most qualified wholesalers did most of their business in goods that were not the subject of this agreement. Rebates for the individual wholesaler were computed according to his percentage of the total volume of wholesale trade in the articles covered by the agreement. If a wholesaler did less than 1 per cent of the total trade, his rebate bonus was at the rate of 1.6 per cent.

WHOLESALE REBATE SCHEDULE

Percentage of the Total Sales	*Rebate*
Up to 2.5%	4.3%
For the next ½%	5.8%
For the next ½%	6.3%
For the next ½%	6.8%
For anything more	7.3%

PREFERRED CUSTOMER REBATE SCHEDULE

	Rebates According to Product Classification	
Class of Buyers	*Ia*	*Ib*
Registered large buyers	16.0%	20.0%
Electric works and authorized installers	12.5%	15.0%
Firms with established electrical needs from a special list	12.5%	15.0%
Other firms with established electrical needs	5.0%	7.5%
Radio industry (only for fixed or immovable, plastic insulated conductors)	12.5%	
Telephone companies, special firms, electronics dealers, electric-motor dealers	12.5%	15.0%
Registered equipment makers	12.5%	20.0%
Norwegian State Railways and Telegraph Works	20.0%	24.0%

The rebates, applied according to the accompanying rebate schedule, were to be given only on sales involving goods which the purchasers would directly consume and not resell. No extra rebates, including those for cash sales, were permitted.

The agreement also established freight-prepaid terms of delivery to wholesalers in Oslo and Drammen (Norway's fifth largest city, a manufacturing center). Deliveries elsewhere called for payment of freight charges by the wholesaler. A similar scheme applied to the delivery of goods by wholesalers.

Finally, the parties bound themselves to follow all price lists and other fixed terms of trading without preference to any customer. Violation by a dealer could mean lowering of his price classification. Disputes were to be settled by the Committee.

With the promulgation of the Royal Decree of 18 October 1957 the agreement was abolished and announcements were sent to all participants informing them that they were free to deliver and price as they saw fit.

Again it may be observed that the almost thirty years of enforced dealing according to fixed patterns has shown no appreciable change, and none is immediately foreseeable, absent some major economic dislocation.

4. THE RADIO FURNISHERS NATIONAL ASSOCIATION

This Association, with headquarters in Oslo, is sufficiently close-knit as to require a Class 1 cartel Registration as No. 1.239. The Association was not abolished by the Royal Decree of 18 October 1957, but it was required to modify some of its terms while, at the same time, enjoying a special exemption from the operation of the Decree. Eventually it was terminated by operation of the Royal Decree of 1 July 1960.

The Association was founded in 1938 and reorganized in the summer of 1955. At that time it subdivided into four groups, and a member could belong to more than one. Three of these groups were active until the end of the agreement—Radio and Television Receivers Group, Marine Electronics Group, and the Radio Parts Group.

The Radio and Television Receivers Group was made up of radio and television set manufacturers, importers representing foreign manufacturers of radio and television receivers, and authorized Norwegian wholesalers. An authorized wholesaler was one who did at least 80 per cent of his business in the Group's products, amounting initially to a minimum of 100,000 kroner ($14,000) per annum. In 1959 the sum became 250,000 kroner and the percentage requirement was dropped. The entire Group comprised thirty members.

The Marine Electronics Group with eight members was made up of makers and importers of apparatus.

The Radio Parts Group was made up of firms dealing mainly in radio and electronic parts, which maintained country-wide regional divisions, which carried a full assortment of goods, and which maintained a country-wide sales organization. Excluded from membership were those firms that either maintained retail sales departments or imported and sold goods on an agency basis. The Group had twelve members.

Each Group acknowledged in the cartel registration statement that it had substantial control over its respective market.

The Radio and Television Group agreed to deliver sets only to wholesalers who are members of the Association and to serve only those retailers who are authorized in the radio trade. They further agreed to allow sales of radio sets for permanent mounting in automobiles to those automobile dealers who were also authorized as radio dealers and who maintained a permanent staff of auto-electric specialists.

The Association was authorized to deprive any wholesaler member or any authorized radio or television dealer of his normally applicable rebate in the event that he was found purchasing from a non-member, unauthorized supplier at terms more favorable than those operable within the Association.

Approved or authorized members of the radio trade, as the term was used by the Association, included those whose business was solely in radio and television receivers, those dealing in electrical appliances or musical goods, and those in other types of retail establishments with separate departments for the retail sale of radio and television sets. It was further required that such departments be run by at least one qualified full-time employee with knowledge and training appropriate to the business. Requirements were established as to the amount of equipment that must be maintained, the location of the establishment, and minimum capital. Thus, the Association was able to control effectively new entry into the retail trade in radio and television receivers.

All the members agreed to abide by the retail prices fixed for radio and television sets. These prices included two types of taxes. One was a turnover or transaction tax, which was accumulated in the process of manufacturing the receiver, and the other was a stamp or excise tax, which was also levied. These taxes are an important consideration, as is the case under the Danish law, in administering exemptions to the prohibition on vertical price fixing.

The rebates which the members enjoyed on the fixed retail prices —their profits—were calculated after deducting the turnover and stamp taxes from the retail price. Retailers purchased sets at the retail price, without taxes, less 22 per cent. The wholesaler's profit margin varied with the value of the individual transaction. Thus, if a wholesaler's purchase was valued at between 100,000 and 250,000 kroner, he was entitled to a rebate calculated at 27.5 per cent. This rebate could climb to 30 per cent on purchases of a million kroner or more.

The Association also agreed to deliver to dealers on a freight-free basis to the dealer's nearest railroad station or ship landing. A variety of other regulations controlled terms of payment, advertising allowances, guarantees, and closing-out sales. The authorized dealers all agreed to abide by these terms. In the event of a violation by a dealer, his suppliers were accorded the right to refuse to deal with him.

Members of the Radio and Television Group agreed that they would maintain only one agency in each of the sales districts into which the country is divided. However, where a member already had more than one representative in a district, other members had the right to establish an equivalent number of agencies if they wished.

The Radio and Television Group, acting for its Association, entered into a formal agreement with the Norwegian Radio Dealers National Association, which itself had cartel Registration No. 1.255. This agreement terminated with the effective date of the Royal Decree of 1 July 1960. The Radio Dealers National Association was made up of 27 local associations with 541 members plus 171 unaffiliated members, who together controlled about 90 per cent of the nationwide trade.

The agreement between the two Associations provided that each would assist the other in enforcing the terms of trade under which they both operated. These terms further included provisions for controlling service and guarantees on the receivers. The Dealers Association agreed to seek to favor and encourage its membership to purchase only from members of the Radio and Television Group. In turn the Radio and Television Group agreed to deliver receivers only to those who were members of the Dealers Association. The Group also agreed that it would not give rebates to a dealer who engaged in unfair competitive tactics, such as price cutting, when the Dealers Association so requested.

The Marine Electronics Group agreed in No. 1.239 to sell only to registered dealers. To qualify as a registered dealer, a firm must have in its employ a professionally qualified, licensed, marine electronics technician. This requirement was absolute. Additional requirements called for a minimum inventory, for selection of products, and for a permit allowing the making of tax-exempt sales.

The Marine Electronics Group developed and applied its own rebate schedule to transactions with a single supplier.

MARINE REBATE SCHEDULE

For radio transmitters, radio receivers, and direction finders:

Annual Purchase in Kroner Value	Rebate
Up to 25,000	18%
25,000 to 50,000	20%
50,000 or more	22%

For sounding equipment:

Annual Purchase	Rebate
Up to 4 sounders	12.0%
5 to 9 sounders	13.0%
10 or more sounders	14.5%

The rebates were computed on the consumer prices set by the suppliers. The dealers had to obey the consumer prices, but they had the right to give to their customers up to 20 per cent of the rebate which they received when they made sales to ship yards, boat builders, and the like. Additional regulations concerned price calculations for installation in construction, bidding for such work, and guarantees. A major violation of the regulations by a dealer entitled a supplier to refuse to sell, either wholly or partially.

The Radio Parts Group agreed that prices were to be fixed through a net-price list. All suppliers agreed that they would not offer products on a clearance-sale basis without giving other suppliers a month's notice and that the products would be offered in advance to other suppliers at the projected clearance price. In all matters the members agreed to attempt to calculate prices on the identical basis or formula.

In the case of a parts shipment valued at less than 1,000 kroner ($140.00), all prices were F.O.B. the supplier, but on larger orders shipments were freight-free to the purchaser's nearest railway station or steamship landing. Guarantees and terms of payment were also subjects of regulations.

Certain of the Association's terms of agreement were denominated as laws, and violations of them meant exclusion from membership. On the other hand, less drastic penalties were invoked in the case of violations of the common terms covering transactions. In the Radio and Television Group and in the Marine Electronics Group, fines of up to 25,000 kroner and 50,000 kroner, respectively, could be assessed. The Radio and Television Group established a separate committee to assess penalties, while in the other two groups a membership meeting assessed the penalty. Any penalty decision was appealable to the Complaint Bureau of Commerce and Industry.

With the coming-into-effect of the Royal Decree of 18 October 1957, which outlawed vertical price fixing and the establishment of collective terms of doing business, the rebate scheme of the Radio and Television Group was granted an exemption. The exception was based upon the special circumstances that obtain in the industry because of the collection of taxes by the supplier on the component parts. Thus, the suppliers were allowed to adopt a general price level and, through a rebate schedule, to fix their prices to retailers. However, as a condition of this exception, all regulation of retailers' prices, either by suppliers or other retailers, was prohibited.

This granted exemption is not unlike the Danish exemption permitting the price fixing of cigarettes, cosmetics, and other high tax items. It also resembles the general Norwegian exemption given to setting of agricultural prices at the primary level.

The agreement between the Association and the Norwegian Radio Dealers National Association was amended so as to terminate the provisions that indirectly controlled retail prices. The Radio Dealers amended their internal regulations accordingly.

The Marine Electronics Group was also initially given an exemption from the prohibition on collective trade terms, which has since been revoked.

Many of the regulations as to rebates and the like continued in the three Groups without change.

As noted earlier, the Royal Decree of 1 July 1960 terminated the part of No. 1.239 that still remained after the granting of the conditional exemption from the provisions of the Royal Decree of 18 October 1957. Dealers in Oslo are cutting some prices for radio and television receivers, but no clear indication of major changes in distribution has appeared since the termination of the agreements.

5. THE NATIONAL ASSOCIATION OF ELECTRICAL WHOLE-
   SALERS AND AGENTS

This venerable Association was founded in 1918 and continues its Class 1 cartel Registration No. 1.323, unchanged by the Royal Decree of 18 October 1957. The Association draws its membership from firms that have as their principal activity the sales of electrical machines, electrical apparatus, electrical materiel, and lighting fixtures.

To qualify, one must maintain a warehouse capable of ordinarily supplying the needs of the trade, and one must have a sales force adequate to call upon the principal dealers in the larger districts of the country. No firm is accepted for membership that has a total annual income of less than 500,000 kroner ($70,000). At least 80 per cent of this annual income must be derived from wholesaling goods which are subject to the agreement. The firm's manager must have a minimum of three years of experience in the wholesaling of such products. Others eligible as members include those firms that serve as the direct agents or distributors of manufacturers. Any firm that does business as an installer or that maintains a retail establishment is ineligible for membership.

The Association's ninety-one members represent between 80 and 95 per cent of Norway's total electrical trade. Fabrikk, on its own, as an agent for its American grandparent Firm *301*, and as an agent for some of its European cousins, is a leading participant in the Association.

The Association has established common delivery terms for the wholesaling of installation materials and various electrical goods that are not the subject of such special agreements, as those already examined in the prior portions of this case study. The goods encompassed by this agreement must all be delivered F.O.B. The Association regulates also the payment of packing costs and the terms of payment for goods. Delivery of goods on commission or consignment is forbidden.

Certain patterns of Association regulation emerge from its various circulars and bulletins. Thus, it would appear that firms outside the electrical trade, such as hardware stores, are not permitted to obtain full wholesale terms. On the other hand, the firms doing installation work are forbidden to purchase from manufacturers and may purchase only from wholesalers; the wholesalers, in turn, may deliver only from their warehouses and are forbidden to order direct delivery from a manufacturer to the installer.

As discussed in an earlier section concerning refusal to deal, in many cases authorization to install electrical equipment or lines may depend on the local electric works. The Association, recognizing the existence of these problems, has given wholesalers two choices of delivery to follow when a professionally qualified installer who lacks the electric works' authorization has placed an order for installation materials. The wholesaler in such cases may effectuate delivery through an authorized installer and then allow the two installers to agree on the terms under which the authorized installer is to be compensated for his assistance. The other alternative allows wholesalers to deliver to the unauthorized installer, while providing reasonable compensation to the authorized installer concerned.

The installation service, of great economic significance by itself, has a special agreement, cartel Registration No. 2.235, concerning the accreditation of wholesalers of installation materials. The National Association of Electrical Wholesalers and Agents is a party to this accreditation agreement, and thereby Fabrikk and other Association members are directly involved.

Neither the regulations of the National Association of Electrical Wholesalers and Agents nor the Installation Accrediting Agreement has been amended or changed by the Royal Decree of 18 October 1957. The Association and its agreement, No. 1.323, are typical examples of the high degree of organization that exists in every aspect of the electrical trade. There are, moreover, in the electrical trade additional associations and agreements in which Fabrikk does not participate, such as those dealing with flexible and inflexible tubes, light bulbs, and automobile lights. Most of these arrangements are over twenty years old, and some are more than forty years old. All of them represent a formalizing of business relationships and a division of functions which are likely to continue even if the legal agreements are abolished. Change, even where it may be desirable, will be slow in coming. Any impact of the abolition of agreements that is likely to be felt at an early date will probably be in the area of freedom of entry.

In those industries and trades which do not have agreements such as the Lausanne Agreement there is a possibility that as tariff barriers diminish, new import sources will appear for Norwegian traders. These new sources may very likely provide an opportunity for breaking down the barriers to freedom of entry which the present close-knit suppliers have been able to maintain at both wholesale and retail levels.

G. Automobile tires and tubes

Importers' cartel—Vertical agreement—Rebates—Regulated terms—Bonus—Trade-in—Substitute agreements—Multiple trade association control—Vertical control through interlocking horizontal agreements

Norway, unlike Denmark which does not produce automobile tires, has at least one tire manufacturer, cartel Registration No. 3.30. Nevertheless, a major portion of the tire and tube trade for automobiles, cycles, and tractors, is carried on through sales of imported tires. American participation in the trade is quite noticeable in that all major and many minor American brands, including the house brand owned by American petroleum Firm 33 are present. The agreements controlling the trade have had to be revised by reason of the Royal Decree of 18 October 1957, banning vertical price fixing and collective enforcement of trade terms. It is in the substitute agreements that we find some new departures in agreements regulating restrictive practices.

1. THE AUTOMOBILE TIRE IMPORTERS UNION

The Union, which has cartel Registration No. 1.113, was founded in 1935 and reorganized in 1950. Its members included the importers of practically every major brand of American tires. The brands not represented in this agreement are the private one of the American petroleum Firm 33 and a minor brand, which in the United States is in part owned by a major mail-order and retailing organization. Moreover, it would appear that American Firm 91 has an interest in one of the seventeen member import houses.

Although the Union itself is abolished, its complex membership requirements are still of interest because its members participate in current agreements. The membership was generally limited to those who imported tires on a nationwide scale and who were affiliated on an established basis with a foreign tire manufacturer. At least 90 per cent of the business of these importers was at the wholesale level. Old established firms needed only to certify that their wholesale turnover approximately met this requirement. Newcomers into the trade had to have at least 50,000 kroner ($7,000) of their own capital to qualify for membership. All members had to employ at least one traveling salesman who was on the road at least two hundred days a year. Each member had a manager as well. Members were required to maintain good-sized, well assorted inventories. The Union set up standards which must be met by each member-firm's owner or executive manager. If the owner or manager was not already well known as a leader of the trade, he had to be able to prove by affidavit that he had had at least five years of theoretical and practical business and field training.

Membership was not static, and it recently went from fifteen to seventeen. Together the importers represented about 40 per cent of the trade in automobile tires, with the balance held by a Norwegian producer and nonmember importers, including the representatives of major Austrian and Swedish brands.

Members were permitted to help each other by furnishing tires to fill an order, but they were limited in dealings outside the Union. They could sell automobile and motorcycle tires only to those who acted solely as retailers and who bought all of their requirements from the participants in the Automobile Tire Agreement, cartel Registration No. 2.54, which has also been replaced since the Royal Decree of 18 October 1957.

A Union member was allowed to sell directly to consumers only with the express authorization of the Automobile Tire Committee, which was established by the Tire Agreement, No. 2.54. Any business dealings with nonmember wholesalers, retail-importers, or producers were forbidden, including those with their subsidiaries. However, in four instances exceptions from this prohibition were granted.

The Union had over the years adopted a variety of regulations limiting advertising and public-relations activities by its members. For example, one regulation, adopted in 1950, permitted a member to mention a retailer's name in his advertising if the retailer paid at least 50 per cent of the cost of the advertisement.

Another example of regulation and mutual agreement came with the agreement to raise all tire prices on 15 October 1955. The members of the Union agreed to raise the prices for all of their products at the same time, making the hike simultaneously and universally effective.

Union members were not allowed to be members in name only of associations, groups, and like organizations sponsored by their customers. The Union deemed this passive membership to be a form of indirect financial assistance to the customers and, therefore, forbade its members to provide such aid.

The Union was entitled to fine its members for violations of the rules and regulations by fines of up to 2,000 kroner ($280) for a first offense, and up to 5,000 kroner ($700) for additional offenses. Exclusion from membership was another possible sanction.

2. THE AUTOMOBILE TIRE AGREEMENT

The Automobile Tire Agreement, No. 2.54, being a companion agreement to No. 1.113 had the Union as one of its members. It was an effective device for controlling the Norwegian trade in tires from the time it came into force in 1938 until it was superseded in 1958, as a result of the Royal Decree of 18 October 1957. The single Norwegian tire manufacturer and twenty-nine importers of tires participated in the Tire Agreement. These participants are referred to as the suppliers, and the dealers, whom they supply, are known as the Automobile Tire Committee.

The Automobile Tire Committee consists of the Automobile Dealers National Association, Registration No. 1.271, the National Union of Automobile Wholesalers, Registration No. 1.92, the National Association of Auto Repair Shops, Registration No. 1.229, the Service Stations Association, Registration No. 1.186, and the National Association of Tire Repairers, Registration No. 1.518.

The agreement encompassed about 95 per cent of the suppliers of tires and almost all of the retail outlets for tires, thus controlling about 90 per cent of the total, nationwide trade in automobile tires.

A supplier who accepted the agreement could do business only by selling to retail establishments which were parties to the agreement through their associations and unions. The dealers could not sell tires obtained from suppliers outside the agreement. American Firm 33 was listed as one of the twenty-nine supplier-importers, and it was thus able to sell its brand of tires through the Service Station Association members who market its petroleum products.

Membership in the agreement was open to any supplier willing to abide by its terms. Service stations, dealers in automobiles and accessories, tire repairers, and vulcanizers were all entitled to join as dealer-members, even if they were not members of one of the associations making up the Automobile Tire Committee.

The Tire Agreement prohibited direct or indirect sales by suppliers to consumers, unless special approval had been given by the Automobile Tire Committee.

Suppliers were required to set their prices through printed price lists. Dealers received a 12.5 per cent rebate on the list price plus an annual bonus computed on the basis of the dealer's total, annual tire sales of all brands included in the agreement.

Total Sales Kroner	Dealer's Bonus
2,500	2%
5,000	3%
15,000	4%
30,000	5%
50,000	6%
80,000	7%
120,000	8%
170,000	9%

Dealers were permitted to give a 4 per cent consumer rebate on sales to state and municipal agencies and to those with licensed transport or conveyance concessions.

Large-scale consumers who could show purchases of new tires of over 15,000 kroner ($2,100) yearly could be given rebates of up to 7 per cent. Those consumers with even greater annual purchases of new tires were given additional bonuses that ranged from 2 per cent on 20,000 kroner to 9 per cent on 170,000 kroner.

The dealer's bonus at the end of the year was calculated on the basis of his total sales to consumers of those brands covered by the agreement. That portion of his sales which was derived from purchases made by large consumers, entitled to extra rebates, was treated separately to allow for the rebates and bonuses given to the special customers.

The Tire Agreement stipulated the conditions of payment that dealers had to meet, and it set up special terms to cover the sales of tires for mounting on new cars. Dealers taking a tire in trade were forbidden to give more than could be realized on the sale of the used tire, and suppliers were forbidden to accept used tires in trade or payment. Prices lower than those fixed under the agreement and dealing at terms more favorable to the dealer or consumer than those established by the agreement were forbidden.

Dealers who violated the agreement could be punished by loss of their rebates, which meant that their tire sales would be without any profit. The duration of such a penalty could be determined by the Committee and fines of up to three hundred kroner per violation could be levied.

Now this agreement is abolished and two new agreements have taken its place as well as that of the Importers Union.

3. AGREEMENT AMONG IMPORTERS AND THE MANUFAC-
TURER OF TIRES

This agreement was made in 1958 among twenty-seven suppliers of automobile, tractor, and cycle tires. The single Norwegian manufacturer, the major importers who made up the Union, plus other importers who formerly participated only in the now abolished Automobile Tire Agreement are the sole participants in this horizontal arrangement, cartel Registration No. 2.279. The same American firms participating in the prior agreements are also members of this one. The agreement controls about 90 per cent of the tires traded in Norway.

The suppliers agree that they will issue printed price lists governing their dealings with retailers. Dealers are to receive a year-end bonus computed on the basis of their total sales of tires bearing the trademarks of the participating suppliers.

The annual bonus to dealers was computed, until 1959, on exactly the same sales and percentage figures as set out in the previous agreement, No. 2.54. Under the new scale the bonuses begin with 2.5 per cent for sales of 2,000 kroner and rise to 11 per cent for sales of 140,000 kroner. The previous and similar bonus arrangement for motorcycle tires has been terminated and replaced by one which reduces wholesale prices by 7 per cent. The arrangement concerning the calculation of bonuses to dealers who sell to large-scale consumers continues. Also continued are the regulations on terms of payment as well as the prohibition against selling to dealers on terms more favorable than permitted in the regulations. One new feature of No. 2.279 is the allowance of clearance sales when permitted by the Automobile Tire Committee, whose existence was continued in Registration No. 2.280.

The suppliers have agreed not to sell to dealers unless they participate in the Agreement among Automobile Tire Retailers, Registration No. 2.280. A reciprocal provision concerning purchases in No. 2.280 makes the agreements operatively effective. The Automobile Tire Committee is empowered to determine when it might be proper for a supplier to sell directly to a consumer.

The suppliers' agreement, No. 2.279, is administered by a Committee. In the event that a complaint is filed with the Committee, alleging that a supplier has violated the agreement, the Committee may order inspectors to conduct an investigation. These inspectors are required to operate under professional secrecy. The agreement imposes on its members the duty to report violations to the Committee.

To ensure that suppliers will abide by the agreement, and thus in effect guaranteeing payment of a potential fine, each supplier is required to draw a trade acceptance in favor of the Committee in the amount of 5,000 kroner. The maximum penalty for a breach of the agreement is 5,000 kroner. An exemption from the provisions of the Royal Decree of 1 July 1960 has been given this agreement.

4. THE AGREEMENT AMONG AUTOMOBILE TIRE RETAILERS

This agreement, No. 2.280, was entered into simultaneously with the previous agreement, No. 2.279, so as to replace the abolished Automobile Tire Agreement, No. 2.54, and so as to render effective the Agreement among Importers and the Manufacturer of Tires, No. 2.279. No. 2.280, now superseded by No. 2.363, is important in arriving at an understanding of current practices.

The participants in this agreement included almost 1,200 retailers of tires—service stations, automobile dealers, repairers of automobiles and tires, and the like. Its membership, although noticeably less than the combined membership of the original Automobile Tire Committee in Registration No. 2.54, nevertheless represented about 85 per cent of the retail trade in tires.

The Automobile Tire Committee, continued after No. 2.54 was abolished, administered this agreement. It consisted of representatives from the same five trade associations that participated in the form of associations in the now defunct Registration No. 2.54.

The dealers were required to fix their retail prices, including the turnover tax, on the basis of the supplier's price list.

	Retailer's Margin	
Total Sales to:	Until 1959	After 1959
Regular consumers	27.0%	30.0%
The state or municipalities . . .	22.0%	24.5%
Large-scale consumers	18.0%	19.5%

Provision was also made for year-end bonuses to large consumers in addition to their benefiting from an initially lower price. The figures on which this bonus was calculated were, until 1959, identical with those that were provided in the now abolished Automobile

Tire Agreement, Registration No. 2.54. After 1959 the scale ranged from a bonus of 2.5 per cent on purchases of 17,000 kroner to 10.5 per cent on purchases of 140,000 kroner.

The agreement fixed terms of payment that were identical with those followed in the suppliers' agreement, Registration No. 2.279. Similarly No. 2.280 prohibited its dealers from giving consumers better terms than those permitted by the agreement. Clearance sales, also agreed upon by the suppliers, could take place only with the approval of the Automobile Tire Committee. The dealer was forbidden to pay more than the resale price of a used tire taken in trade. Also, the trade-in allowance on mounted equipment had to be at least 10 per cent of the sales price.

The Automobile Tire Committee received all complaints of violations by dealers, and it had the right to assign an inspector to investigate. The inspector was bound by terms of professional secrecy. Violations of this agreement were penalized by fines of up to three hundred kroner.

Of crucial importance in making both this agreement and the previous one effective was the provision requiring that participants purchase tires only from suppliers who participate in the suppliers' agreement, Registration No. 2.279. This stipulation completed the link between the two agreements. Together they recreated, until No. 2.280 was superseded, the situation the members had enjoyed under the abolished agreement, Registration No. 2.54—vertical control through horizontal agreements. It was as if the Royal Decree of 18 October 1957 had never been promulgated.

The tire trade in Norway had by means of two agreements accomplished what before was done by one agreement. The vertical agreements were absent, but the effect was obviously vertical as well as horizontal.

The only flexibility introduced through the new arrangements is derived from the reduced retailer membership. This reduction indicates that some potential of new competition may arise. On the other hand, the taxes involved in the sale of tires would seem to be an argument for governmental approval of continuing rigidity in the tire-price structure.

The agreement registered as No. 2.280 was a victim of the Royal Decree of 1 July 1960. It has been replaced by an agreement registered as No. 2.363 between the Norwegian manufacturer and the tire importers on the one hand and the automobile tire dealers association on the other. The main operative feature of the new agreement is an undertaking by the retailers to sell only tires supplied by parties to No. 2.279, the only agreement mentioned which was not abolished by the Decree. The vertical control element thus remains unchanged and will probably continue to be permitted as long as tires bear a heavy tax.

H. Malleable-tube cartel

British and French subsidiaries—International price list—Uniform international net prices—National groups—Registered dealers—Continuation of cartel after dissolution

Norwegian cartel Registration No. 1.368 is assigned to an international cartel in cast-iron tubes and fittings, such as sewer pipe. It is primarily concerned with the wholly Norwegian producing participant in the international agreement. If the Norwegian registration is read with No. 664 in the British Restrictive Trade Practices Register, the combined statements show that the British and French subsidiaries of American Firm 44 are among the leading participants in the cartel. They actively supply administrative leadership. The price lists of the American parent firm play a major role in setting prices. This interrelated registration on a country-to-country basis provides a means for cross-checking, which national cartel control authorities are now employing on an increased scale.

The International Malleable Tube Fittings Cartel, known as Imatufia, was organized in Switzerland in 1932 and 1933 and was thoroughly reorganized in 1947, after the close of World War II. The actual seat of the cartel is Schaffhausen, Switzerland.

Membership in Imatufia is open to any manufacturer of cast-iron-tube goods. The association usually regulates prices on the basis of a price list devised by American Firm 44. Other terms of payment, discounts, and delivery are fully regulated on all orders shipped by members to importers in other countries, and likewise on orders shipped to wholesalers within their own country.

To facilitate market sharing, a major feature of the agreement, the producing plants are organized into national groups or trade associations. Norway, with only one producer, has no need for a national association. The British Malleable Tube Fittings Association, registered under British No. 661, was presided over by the officers of the British subsidiary of Firm 44. In 1958 the Association reported that it had severed connections with Imatufia. This Association was dissolved in 31 October 1959, as a result of the British Restrictive Trading Practices Act.

Two or more national groups operate as the regional price-regulating organ. The single Norwegian producer constitutes the Norwegian national group, and he cooperates with the Swedish national group in setting prices and other terms for the region.

The Norwegian and Swedish groups set their regional prices in accordance with an international price list, based on American Firm 44's price list. This basic international price list is then converted, according to a predetermined scale, to fix the prices in each of the member countries. The conversion tables are calculated so that the net prices to importers or wholesale distributors are identical everywhere the agreement operates, regardless of the origin of a shipment or the currency in which prices are quoted. Obviously, this identity of prices renders the market-sharing agreement feasible.

A special registry of customers is maintained by the Imatufia secretariat, and customers coming under the agreement are given certain quantity discounts. The prices and discounts under the agreement are binding on the members. A member, prohibited from selling to an unregistered purchaser and from selling through exporters, must sell only to the importer or the domestic wholesaler. Norway has forty qualified wholesaler-importers. New firms can qualify for the registered list if, over two successive years, they have bought seven tons of malleable tubes and fittings from other registered dealers. If a registered firm fails to buy in this quantity, it is dropped from the list. Price maintenance by the customer seems to be an implicit membership qualification.

Any violation of the statutes of the cartel may entail fines to compensate the injured members, and each member has been required to post a security bond. Arbitration is agreed upon as the method of settling disputes.

Finally, one provision in the cartel statutes, which is seldom seen, concerns possible termination of the cartel; in effect, members are bound, if the cartel is terminated, to play the game as before. It may be assumed that this provision applies to the dissolution of national groups as well as to that of the entire cartel. Thus the actual status of the severed and dissolved British participants is far from clear.

Norwegian participation in Imatufia remains unchanged after the coming-into-effect of the Royal Decree of 18 October 1957.

I. Titanium oxide and paint

Dominant registration—Rebate scheme—Product classification—Freedom of entry—Interlocking agreements—Rebates based on packaging

American Firm *701* operates in Norway through a subsidiary which has dominant firm Registration No. 3.27. The Norwegian subsidiary in turn controls two daughter corporations. For sake of clarity we will refer to the direct subsidiary as "Oxide."

Oxide was established in 1916, with a seven million kroner share capital divided into 100-kroner shares. Common stock amounting to 35,000 shares was issued, and two series of preferred shares, A and B, were issued with 25,000 and 10,000 shares respectively. All of the preferred shares and 34,894 of the common shares are owned by American Firm *701*. The remaining common shares are in Norwegian hands.

Oxide has a daughter, "Mine," which it controls through ownership of all but 3 of the 3,000 issued common shares with a par value of 1,000 kroner each. Mine extracts and refines magnetite titanium ore using power from a wholly owned power plant. Oxide produces and sells titanium oxide, paints, varnishes, and pigments and also takes all of Mine's production.

Oxide stated in its original registration that it only advised its customers as to terms of business, rather than binding them to such terms. Prices, instructions for discounts, terms of delivery and payment, and other sales conditions were given only for the guidance of wholesalers and retailers. Now it has expressly advised its dealers of their freedom to set prices and to establish their own terms of delivery.

In January of 1954 Oxide wrote to the Price Directorate and stated that it did not participate in any arrangement which obligated it to regulate prices, distribution, or production. The letter noted that Oxide was a member of the Paint and Varnish Manufacturers Association, which will be described below. Oxide argued, however, that its participation, being limited to the paint and varnish part of its business, did not affect the production of titanium oxide, of which it was the sole producer. Further, Oxide argued that its participation should be of no significance in the matter of registration.

The Price Directorate has, however, required not only Oxide's dominant registration, but also has noted on the record its affiliation with the Paint and Varnish Manufacturers Association. The Association's interlocking arrangements with Oxide's customers and competitors is of greater significance than Oxide claimed in its letter to the Price Directorate.

The Paint and Varnish Manufacturers Association is registered as a cartel under Registration No. 1.133. It was founded in 1929 with membership drawn from manufacturers with a minimum capital of 100,000 kroner. Additionally, in order to qualify as a member, one must be engaged principally in the paint and varnish business, maintain a laboratory with a permanently employed chemical engineer, and maintain a staff of at least five regular employees whose exclusive occupation is the manufacture of paints. Further minimal requirements pertain to plant conditions and machinery. The Association has sixteen members.

A variety of regulations concerning the sale and distribution of products have been agreed upon by the members. These regulations cover paints, varnishes and lacquers (excluding those with a cellulose base), marine preservatives, oils, siccatives, primers, and finishes. Each member is to establish his own prices independently, file his price lists with the secretariat of the Association, and advise of all changes or amendments.

The members of the Association may set up agency stores only in those districts where retailers operate under the Agreement Controlling New Establishments in the Paint Trade, Registration No. 2.76. The new Establishments Agreement is between the Association, the Oil and Paint Dealers of Oslo, Registration No. 1.60, and other trade groups and paint producers. In general it lays down qualifications, such as minimum capital and limits of experience, which must be met before a new paint dealer will be permitted to operate. A board is created to oversee the agreement and administer it. The agreement covers the Oslo and Drammen Districts, and the political subdivisions of Vestfold, Östfold, and Telemark.

In those areas where the New Establishments Agreement is operative, the members of the Paint and Varnish Manufacturers Association have agreed to sell only to approved dealers.

Association members have also agreed not to give away their products or to make gifts to charitable organizations or charity bazaars unless the action is purely one of charity. If it is determined after investigation that a member has violated this provision, the matter will be brought to the attention of the other members. The implication seems to be that social pressures and similar sanctions will then serve to prevent future violations.

The classification of dealers as wholesalers and retailers is a function of the Association's Rebate Committee. The composition of the Committee, its procedures, and the principles it applies in classifying are all set forth in an agreement entered into in 1948. Parties to the agreement are the Association, Oxide in its individual capacity, two dominant producers of zinc oxide, and two dominant producers of oils used in paints. The Rebate Committee is composed of two representatives of the Association, two from the oil producers, two from the zinc-oxide producers, and one from Oxide. The Chairman of the Rebate Committee is always one of the two representatives from the Association.

The decisions of the Rebate Committee are binding on all participants, including individual members of the Association. Six paint manufacturers who remain outside the cartel are bound through an agreement with the Association to do business in a manner consistent with the bonus and discount systems operated by the Association under the decisions of the Rebate Committee.

As a result of this interlocking arrangement, between 90 and 95 per cent of all Norwegian paint and varnish is distributed in accordance with the decisions of the Rebate Committee.

Approved wholesalers of paint are denominated as B Customers, and approved retailers are denominated as C Customers. In the C category are both traditional retailers and stores that operate on mixed wholesale-retail lines, without being entitled to being recognized as B Customers. The Rebate Committee has laid down minimum capital requirements.

Location of Establishment	B Customers	C Customers
Oslo and Bergen	100,000 kr.	25,000 kr.
Rest of the country	70,000 kr.	25,000 kr.

These requirements for retailers are higher than those called for in the New Establishments Agreement.

Dealers are required to meet minimum standards of professional training and credit rating. To be classified as a B Customer, one must engage exclusively in the wholesale trade in paints and varnishes and similar coatings, and must employ one full-time traveling salesman in addition to the owner. Mixed operations, in which wholesale and retail sales are combined or in which the wholesaling of paints is combined with the wholesaling of other goods, are required to meet minimum annual turnover rates for linseed oil, zinc oxide, and other products in order to keep a B rating.

The original maximum rebate schedule for paints and varnishes was divided into two product classifications. Product Category A included varnishes, aluminum paints, metal coatings, shellacs, bronze tinctures, finishes, and floor paints. Product Category B included other paints, primers, and finishes. The original maximum rebate schedule was organized according to the accompanying table.

Customers							Rebate for Product A	Product B
B	.	.	.	.	.	.	31%	26%
C	.	.	.	.	.	.	27%	22%
Others	.	.	.	.	.		21%	18%

The rebates were applied to the individual price lists issued by each manufacturer. However, the rebate schedule did not apply to white oil paint and other exterior finishes, latex-based paints, and alkyd-resin finishes when delivered in ten-liter cans. In case of such deliveries, the individual manufacturer was free to determine the net prices to his customers. For customers such as contractors, industrial plants, and large consumers the net price was increased by the inclusion of special service items.

Until 1957 B and C Customers received an annual bonus calculated on the amount purchased from manufacturers participating in the Association.

AGGREGATED REBATE SCHEDULE

Total Kroner Value of Annual Purchase							*Bonus to B Customer*
At least 145,000	.	.	.	.	.	.	1%
At least 230,000	.	.	.	.	.	.	2%
At least 460,000 ($64,000)		.	.	.	.	.	3%

							Bonus to C Customer
At least 35,000	.	.	.	.	.	.	1%
At least 52,000	.	.	.	.	.	.	2%
At least 70,000	.	.	.	.	.	.	3%
At least 95,000	.	.	.	.	.	.	4%

When a manufacturer makes a shipment of twenty-four kilograms —the equivalent of twenty-four tins, each containing one liter—to a customer the shipment is on cost, insurance, and freight (c.i.f.) terms when forwarded to northern Norwegian destinations having regular steamship landings. Smaller quantities are delivered at F.O.B. prices.

The Association has also established uniform regulations governing terms of payment, return of merchandise, and advertising allowances.

A Marine Group, made up of ten members of the Association, has entered into a separate agreement concerning rust preventives, marine primers, marine paints, and special marine coatings. The agreement is designed to promote uniformity in marine sales in Norway, in deliveries to Norwegian-flag ships, and to ships sailing under foreign flags, but owned by Norwegian interests. It establishes rules for discounts and regulations governing conditions of payment and delivery from the factory. Only marine workshops and other members of the Association are given a special 5 per cent discount on copper primers and hull paints, the only discount given on these items. In contracts requiring a lump-sum bid, a special scale for calculations of total paint costs is used.

Participants in the Marine Agreement have obligated themselves not to have more than one sales agency in any one town and not to set up permanent inventories in any marine workshop.

In December 1957, prior to the 1 May 1958 effective date of the Royal Decree of 18 October 1957, the Paint and Varnish Manufacturers Association set up a new, simplified discount system. The new program did maintain the old customer classifications. The simplification came with the abolition of the product category distinctions between paints and varnishes and with the introduction of new distinctions in discounts to be based on the size of the container in which the product was sold.

Customers	Base Rebate for Packages of	
	1 liter or less	2.5 liters or more
B	31%	25%
C	27%	22%
Others	21%	18%

The price for paints delivered in cans larger than 2.5 liters was further reduced, whereas the consumer price of paints packaged in quantities under one liter was increased.

When the Royal Decree of 18 October 1957 became effective on 1 May 1958, the Association ended its practice of setting the discount terms of its members. Instead the manufacturers now set their own net prices for each group of customers, but they still agree not to charge different net prices to customers who fall within the same classification.

With the change in the law, it was expected that each manufacturer would set his suggested consumer prices on an independent basis. However, the members are obligated to compute their prices in such a way that the reseller, wholesaler or retailer as the case may be, will realize the same profit margin on similar goods of different producers. This computation will provide higher profit margins for goods packaged in one-liter cans than in larger ones. Thus, the December 1957 discount scheme is not really dead.

When the manufacturers make direct sales to consumers, they are obliged to observe maximum discounts on their own suggested retail prices, as shown in the accompanying table.

PREFERRED CUSTOMER DISCOUNT SCHEDULE

Purchaser	Maximum Discount from Retail Price
Registered	
State railways, Dept. of Defense	27% or 22%
Industrial plants	17%
Shipyards	3%
Public institutions	17%
Unregistered	
Industries, public institutions, individual contractors	
At least 150 liters/kilograms	12%
Less than 150 liters/kilograms	10%

Under the present state of the law, Association members have now freed themselves to price as they please in transactions involving special classes of paint sold to registered industrial shops and shipyards. Manufacturers are also free to price without reference to the scale of maximum discounts in the case of contracts for such public agencies as the State Railways, the Department of Defense, or the Post Office.

The penalty for violating the terms of the Association remains the same as ever, and members may be excluded in serious cases.

The Agreement Controlling New Establishments, Registration No. 2.76, unaffected by the Royal Decree of 1 July 1960, remains in force, and thus at least in the major trading areas of Norway, freedom of entry into the paint trade is effectively limited. Since this condition makes it relatively simple to maintain the systems controlling the trade, no appreciable changes are seen or foreseen.

By establishing a simplified discount system during the interim period between the promulgation of the Royal Decree of 18 October 1957 and its effective date on 1 May 1958, the Association was able to acclimate its dealers to a new and easily administered fashion of doing business after the Decree became effective.

J. Shoe machinery

Dominant registration—Order to register lease agreements —Order revoked

The Norwegian subsidiary of American Firm *801* is registered as a dominant firm in the shoe-machinery field, Registration No. 3.7. It was founded in 1910 with a capital of 700,000 kroner represented by 700 shares of common stock. All but 2 of the common shares are held by the American parent.

The Norwegian subsidiary dominates the field in selling and renting machinery for shoe production and in selling shoe-repair supplies and materials for the shoe industry. Another line of its business includes the furnishing of machinery and accessories for use in the radio, furniture, and construction industries. The machinery handled by the Norwegian subsidiary comes almost entirely from the American parent.

No competing firm is registered as dominant, and the registration indicates no participation in agreements or arrangements that are registrable.

One item in the files illustrates the method by which the Price Directorate operates. Shoe-machinery lease agreements between the subsidiary and a large number of Norwegian shoe manufacturers contain clauses which the Price Directorate in a memorandum described as "prohibiting the lessees to use machines from other companies when the lessor's machines can be used."

An analysis of these clauses caused the Price Directorate on 11 December 1954 to decide that such contracts and leases should be registered under the provisions of Section 33 of the Price Act.

The lessor asked the Price Directorate to reconsider on the grounds that the clauses in the leases had not been enforced for a great many years and further assured the Directorate that such clauses would not be enforced in the future.

The Price Directorate then agreed not to demand the registration of the lease agreements. However, the question remained of whether lessees of shoe machinery would know that they were free to use competitive machines. The files do not disclose either a requirement that the lessees be so advised or that an announcement was sent to them.

As far as can be ascertained, the lessees operate as if they were still bound by the clause. They are apparently ignorant of the fact that the clause is nonenforceable.

K. Office and business machines

Dominant registration—Cartel—Suggested prices—Uniform discounts—Uniform trade-in prices

Two major American producers of office and business machines are active in the Norwegian market through subsidiaries. American Firm 54's subsidiary is registered as a dominant firm, Registration No. 3.71, because of its sales of business machines and electric-shaving devices. American Firm 52's subsidiary is not registered as a dominant firm, but it is on the cartel Register, along with the dominant firm, as a participant in a restrictive association.

The dominant registration discloses the existence of a corporation formed in 1911, capitalized at 300,000 kroner, with 3,000 shares of common stock issued. Two shares are held by a Norwegian, 166 shares are owned by an American individual whose address is the same as that of the parent, and the balance of 2,832 shares are held by the American parent Firm 54. The Norwegian subsidiary is listed as producing and selling typewriters, calculators, bookkeeping machines, and electric razors. Prior to the ban on vertical price fixing, the firm fixed the retail prices of all of its products, but it now stipulates that all prices are advisory or suggested. The fixing of prices was accomplished by a detailed control over cash discounts and trade-in allowances on electric razors. The terms on business machines followed those established by the Association.

The National Association of Office Machine Agents is registered as Registration No. 1.131. The subsidiaries of both American firms are members of this organization, which was founded in 1927. In addition to its main office in Oslo, the Association has local offices in Bergen and Stavanger. It has fifty-four direct members and thirty-nine further members through the affiliation of the local organizations in Bergen and Stavanger.

Membership in the Association is open to all importers who are exclusive agents for lines of business machines, office machines, or filing systems, to retailers of such items, to retailers of office furniture, and to local trade associations of these retailers. The sale of office or business machines must constitute the major part of the dealer's business to qualify him for membership.

The Association controls almost all of the trade in office machines and involves all of the major brands.

The Association suggests a uniform system of computing trade-in allowances and resale prices of used machines, based on the serial number of a particular brand of machine. Clearance sales of all older models permit a dealer to sell below the usual suggested resale price of used machines. The sale must be bona fide and not a means for favoring an individual customer.

Since 1959, members have agreed that sales of demonstrators and superseded models may be made at lower than list price and, therefore, are free of the rebate provisions of the agreement.

Another area in which the Association guides its members relates to the discounts to be given to special classes of customers. Originally the only discount allowed was a 10 per cent discount to the Norwegian government and to the municipality of Oslo. This condition has been changed to treat municipalities as ordinary private customers who are not entitled to discounts. Sales of most machines to the Norwegian government are at a discount rate of only 5 per cent, but a 15 per cent discount is allowed to schools which will use the machines for instruction. Under no circumstances is anyone entitled to a discount on bookkeeping machines. The discount rules operate along with the individual importer's or producer's suggested retail price list. Obviously the rigid discount system has meaning only if one assumes that retailers follow the suggested retail prices religiously.

Dealer members of the Association have pledged not to seek franchises already enjoyed by a competitor who is also a member of the Association. However, if a franchise is offered without any initiative on the part of the offeree, then he is free to take it. Members pledge themselves also to good conduct in advertising so as not to refer in a derogatory manner to another member, his firm, or the machines he sells.

Any violation of the agreement can lead to a fine of from 100 to 5,000 kroner, or to exclusion from membership. Any disputes about the provisions of the Association's agreement are to be settled either by the Litigation Court of the Oslo Stock Exchange or by the fifty-member panel of the Oslo Trading Estates.

With each supplying member of the Association setting his own suggested prices, the uniform discount and trade-in system of the Association promotes the maintenance of such prices. Some suggested prices are likely to be identical, as are the profit margins, for reasons arising from the general nature of the competition in the trade.

L. Miscellaneous

Several minor registrations and a significant area of non-registration do not warrant an exhaustive treatment, but they are worthy of note in order to round out the Norwegian picture.

1. AUTOMOBILE IMPORTS

The Norwegian automobile import trade is governed by more than a dozen, highly involved agreements controlling the most minute of details. However, no importer of the leading American brands of automobiles, produced by American Firms *101* and *102*, participates, so the portion of the cartelized trade in new cars is only about 50 per cent of the total trade.

Some evidence suggests that the American manufacturers felt that they would be better served by following their own notions as to the type of control necessary to enhance the sales of their own products. Certainly the contracts entered into between the importers of such American automobiles and their dealers are not so restrictive as to require registration in and of themselves.

2. HEARING AID IMPORTERS ASSOCIATION

This Association, formed in 1949, is registered under No. 1.605. Of the eight members, at least two are recorded as having imported trademarked products from American manufacturers into Norway.

The Association agreement called for uniform fixed prices on batteries and for limitation of battery sales to registered distributors of hearing aids. Until 1958 the members fixed their retail prices for hearing aids and set the distributor's profit at 25 per cent of the retail price after deduction of taxes. They permitted a special class of dealers to receive an additional 10 per cent profit under terms to be established by the individual importers.

On 5 September 1958 the members agreed to terminate all cooperation in pricing, thus each importer now prices as he pleases. The indications are, that in lieu of issuing suggested retail prices, each importer sells to his dealer at a net price, and the dealer determines his own retail price and profit.

3. SEWING MACHINES

The Norwegian subsidiary of American Firm 601 is the only manufacturer of sewing machines registered as dominant, Registration No. 3.37. No practices in the trade in sewing machines are deemed so restrictive as to warrant registration.

The subsidiary is the successor to a Norwegian firm originally established in 1881. All but 2 of the 550 common shares representing a capital of 550,000 kroner are held by American Firm 601's holding company.

The Norwegian subsidiary operates primarily as importer and distributor of goods produced by the parent and maintains its own repair facility for repair and reconditioning of sewing machines.

The cartel Register specifically discloses that the subsidiary does not participate in any agreement designed to limit competition or prices. For a long time, dealers were free, as they are now, to price as they please, and the subsidiary has made its free-pricing policy applicable to machines and all accessories.

Some observers consider this form of bare dominant registration to be highly useful. It conclusively shows the public that a dominant firm is operating without restrictions on competition, and, in turn, serves to enhance goodwill and forestall any unfair criticism that might be engendered by the mere size of the enterprise.

4. BOTTLE CAPS AND CLOSURES

A Norwegian subsidiary of American Firm 901 participates in a classic market-sharing agreement, registered as No. 2.50. For sake of clarity, the subsidiary of the American firm will be called "Cork" and the other party to the agreement "Cap."

The agreement to share markets was first entered into in 1937. In its present form the agreement represents a revision made in 1942, while Norway was occupied.

Because of the provisions of Section 37 of the Price Act, limiting agreements to one year in length, or requiring provisions permitting cancellation on three months' notice, this agreement is subject to automatic renewal for one year. Provision is made for revision or adjustments to meet changes in economic conditions.

Cork and Cap, which produce 75 per cent of the Norwegian trade in bottle caps and closures, have agreed upon the quotas for sales to all members of the Norwegian Brewers Association, excluding sales to the three major Oslo breweries. On sales to the members of the Norwegian Brewers Association, the American Firm's subsidiary, Cork, is entitled to 298/450 of the sales and Cap 152/450. Cork and Cap are apparently free to compete for the favor of the three big breweries.

At the time the first agreement was entered into, in 1937, Cork had an agreement with a third firm which obligated that firm to discontinue its competitive production. Cork's agreement with the third party served as part of the consideration for its contract with Cap.

Twice a year Cork and Cap exchange reports concerning sales to those customers encompassed by the agreement. Compensation for deviations from quotas is then made.

Mediation is the means provided for settlement of disputes, and the agreement stipulates that Law for the Settlement of Litigation shall apply.

The agreement has not been affected by the Royal Decree of 18 October 1957. However, provisions concerning cooperation in price calculation were seemingly terminated under the Royal Decree of 1 July 1960. Yet, since the sales quotas can effectively continue only if prices are uniform, price leadership has probably been substituted for cooperative price calculations and the continuation of uniform pricing.

PART THREE:

SWEDEN

CONTENTS

PRELIMINARY OBSERVATIONS

PUBLICITY IS THE DOMINANT FEATURE of the Swedish system of controlling restrictive business practices. Other features, interdependent with publicity, are the Cartel Register, which dates back to 1946, the prohibition of resale-price maintenance and of cooperation in tendering of bids, enunciated by the 1953 legislation, and the termination of other restrictive practices through negotiation—all of which are themselves interdependent.

In Sweden publicity is almost a substitute for the administrative or judicial process which, in other countries, decides whether a restrictive practice is harmful and is to be terminated. Public opinion is the ultimate tribunal. Even some of the strongest partisans of the Swedish approach say that the system could work only in this country, implying that the Swedish public has cultivated a high degree of sophistication.

As restrictive business practices become more publicized in other Western European countries, an understanding of the unique Swedish policy may be particularly useful in evaluating the public attitudes that one may expect to develop. The new regulations of the European Economic Community with reference to restrictive practices will probably call for a relatively wide use of publicity. It is fair to assume that over a period of time, Common Market enforcement activities will reflect to a degree public attitudes toward restrictive practices. In part these attitudes may be anticipated by a careful scrutiny of the results obtained in Sweden.

Three agencies of the Swedish government participate in the control of restrictive business practices under two major statutes. Private agencies also are concerned with the decartelization of industry.

The State Price and Cartel Office (Statens Pris- och Kartellnämnd, S.P.K.) maintains the Cartel Register at its offices at Strindbergsgatan 36–40, Stockholm. Here are employed about one hundred investigators, clerks, and economists, who have additional duties of investigating and reporting on prices and on the degree of competition prevailing in various sectors of the economy. There are no enforcement powers in the S.P.K., which also maintains twenty-four district offices, each staffed by a manager and assistants. The reports of the S.P.K. and summaries of cartel registrations are published in Pris- och Kartellfrågor (Price and Cartel Questions, PKF). Appearing nine or ten times a year, PKF carries also the reports and summaries relating to the activities of the other two agencies.

The Freedom of Commerce Board (Näringsfrihetsrådet) serves as the administrative body which has the power to decide whether a restrictive practice is harmful. It cannot order the discontinuance of a restrictive practice, but it can negotiate for its termination. The nine-member Board has its offices at Stora Nygatan 2A, Stockholm.

The Commissioner for Freedom of Commerce (Ombudsmanna-ämbetet för Näringfrihetsfrågor) is the representative of the public in proceedings before the Board. In addition to making use of the investigative facilities of the Price and Cartel Office, the Commissioner maintains a staff of about ten, which serves as a secretariat and special investigating force. This office is at Storkyrkobrinken 7, Stockholm.

Both the Commissioner and the Board are creations of the Act To Counteract Restraint of Competition in Business in Certain Instances of 25 September 1953. This legislation, which has since been amended, is herein referred to as the "1953 Act."

The major industrial organizations and federations have created a committee of economic and business experts to work out methods for terminating restrictions in industry. The unofficial efforts of this group supplement the government's attempts to negotiate the end of certain restrictive practices.

In most general terms it can be said that the government depends on public reaction to publicized restrictive practices to force the practitioners to change their policies. This process calls for the publication of extensive reports concerning the practices of a particular sector of trade or industry or concerning an individual enterprise.

The impact of this form of reporting cannot be fully understood without actually seeing such a report. For this reason the case studies will be kept fairly short, and one particular case study dealing with the problems of American Firm 84, the Coca-Cola Export Corporation, will contain in extenso the complete text of the government's report on the Corporation's methods of doing business as well as related documentation. The report will not be edited to conceal the name of the American enterprise involved and its trademarks, pursuant to a direct request from Coca-Cola Export Corporation. The

Corporation's Western European area office was most cooperative in allowing free access to information.

I. REGISTRATION OF RESTRICTIVE BUSINESS PRACTICES

A. Historical development of the registration policy

Investigation has long been a major method of dealing with restrictive business practices in Sweden. The earliest attempt to handle problems of competition and monopolies was the formation of an investigating committee in 1911. A similar committee was appointed in 1920, and from its efforts came the Law of 1925, Providing for the Investigation of Monopolistic Enterprises and Amalgamations on a Regular Basis. The 1925 Act authorized the King in Council to order inquiries into the effects of monopolistic enterprises and organizations on price formation and competition. Little that was fruitful came of this legislative attempt.

In 1927 political groups and representatives of the cooperative movement initiated requests to the government to require the cartels to make their activities public. The rationale behind this request, which ultimately resulted in the Cartel Register of 1946, was that those competing with cartels would have less of a handicap if they knew just where and how the cartels existed and the scope of the agreements. It was also thought that consumers would react against the misuse of power by monopolies. The 1927 proposal was rebuffed by the government with the support of industry and trade groups.

The question of restrictions on competition came to the fore with the depression of the 1930's. In 1936 the "Expert Committee on Industry and Commerce" was appointed to investigate the existence of organized private monopolistic activities within industry and commerce and to propose methods for the elimination of anticompetitive activities. The Committee filed a full report on cartel organization and related restraints then prevalent, but World War II forestalled any possible action on the few conclusions that the Committee drew concerning measures that the government might take to counteract anticompetitive practices.

As World War II drew to a close in 1945 the Committee on Economic Postwar Planning proposed that restrictive business practices in commerce and industry be controlled. The main features of the proposal became the Act Concerning Supervision of the Restriction of Competition in Industrial Life, No. 448 of 29 June 1946.

The 1946 Act in Section 2 called for the reporting of "any cartel agreement or other similar agreement tending to restrict competition, . . . affecting prices, production, distribution or transport in the realm."

Such agreements, as is the case under the current legislation, were reportable only when the authorities so requested. The participants in a cartel had no obligation to report on their own initiative.

Section 1 indicates the purpose of the 1946 legislation:

With a view to preventing the detrimental effect of the restriction of competition in industrial life, supervision shall be exercised . . . by the registration of agreements tending to restrict competition and by means of special inquiries.

A Monopoly Investigation Bureau was created within the Board of Trade to maintain the Cartel Register and to perform the investigative activities called for under the 1946 Act.

The Committee on Economic Postwar Planning concluded that a cartel registration system would provide any eventual control body with the basic material necessary for surveying problems of competition. Publication of the contents of a Cartel Register, both in official publications and in the daily press, was considered a means of drawing public attention to cartels, so as to enable competitors of the cartel, if any, and the public to determine whether the cartels were abusing their freedom to operate.

The 1946 Act employed the specific term, "cartel agreement or other similar agreement," as a means of limiting the types of contracts to be registered. The purpose was to register only those agreements that actually restrained trade in the broad sense, rather than ordinary business contracts that set terms and conditions or literally restrained trade, but did not, for example, directly cause price fixing.

Once the authorities requested information concerning an agreement, the participants were under a strict obligation to supply full details of the agreement and other documentation. The argument for placing the burden on the government to request registration was that otherwise the Cartel Register would be swamped with thousands of irrelevant agreements. Also, it was argued that the system of request by government would allow a more methodical search for agreements that should be registered.

Under both the 1946 Act and its 1956 successor, the official view is that registration of agreements in itself is no indication that an agreement is harmful to the public interest. The public does not always share the neutrality of the government, and very often adverse public reaction appears when a cartel agreement is disclosed.

B. Agreements subject to registration

Under the Act Concerning the Obligation To Submit Information as to Conditions of Price and Competition, 1 June 1956 (the Registration Act), the current Cartel Register came into being as a successor to that created under the 1946 Act as well as a continuation of it. The 1956 Act vested the administration of the Register in the newly created State Price and Cartel Office, thereby changing the status and designation of the office maintaining it, and delegated, to the Office, the investigative authority in economic control.

Another important change, provided under the new Act, was a clarification in the definition of what had to be reported upon request. Now the Act does not contain the limiting term "cartel agreements." The information to be submitted, pursuant to Section 3, concerns "restraint of competition . . . and relates to the conditions of price, production, commerce or transport in Sweden."

The Board of Trade opposed the new text because it considered the language so broad as to call for the request of any contract between business men. However, the legislative history of the 1956 Act makes it clear that the intention is to follow the practices under the 1946 Act. The need for a change in language is based on the ambiguity flowing from the word "cartel," which might be read to mean that only horizontal agreements need be registered. The new language is designed to make it clear that vertical as well as horizontal restraints are encompassed.

A further clarification appears in Section 8, Paragraph 3, of the 1956 Act. Here it is stated that bylaws and restrictive regulations adopted by an association are comparable to agreements in restraint of trade and hence registrable. The 1946 legislation was not clear on this point though the practice was to require the registration of such restrictions.

The purpose of registration, as stated in Section 1, is "to promote the public knowledge of conditions of price and competition in the national economy."

The 1956 Registration Act places a duty on "entrepreneurs" to report and submit information upon the request of the authorities. The concept of entrepreneur as set out in Section 2 includes manufacturers, distributors, sellers, purveyors of services including insurance, and transferors and dealers in securities, licenses, and a variety of incorporeal rights. The definition also embraces those licensing the use of a commodity or utility and those licensed to operate hotels and rooming houses. Thus it may be said that Section 2 of the Act makes it applicable to all forms of agreements in trade, commerce, and industry with the exception of wage and condition-of-work agreements provided in Section 14.

Only agreements which affect the Swedish domestic market are the concern of the Cartel Register. Thus most export cartels, unless tied to the domestic market, are exempt from registration under a rigid interpretation of Section 3 of the Act.

Now it is generally understood as a matter of practice that agreements covering day-by-day business transactions and using customary trade terms, such as agreements to purchase, are deemed nonregistrable. An agreement must contain specific provisions designed to limit competition in price formation and freedom of entry and to restrain competition by division of territory in order to be registrable.

C. Registration formalities

The notice sent to the entrepreneur from the State Price and Cartel Office defines the information that must be submitted. Only trade secrets of a technical nature need not be disclosed, according to Section 4. Penalties for failure to provide information are provided through the operation of Sections 6, 10, and 13. Privacy and necessary protection against disclosure of technical information are provided through operation of Sections 9, 11, 12, and 13.

1. REGISTRATION FORMS

The usual practice of the State Price and Cartel Office is to send requests for information simultaneously to all engaged in a particular trade or line of commerce and to all related trade associations and groups. The formal letter which accompanies the registration form reads as follows:

In accordance with the law of 1 June 1956 concerning the obligation to submit information as to conditions of price and competition . . . the State Price and Cartel Office hereby requests that you return before . . .

[usually twenty-one days are given] the enclosed form advising us concerning restrictive agreements into which you have possibly entered (see further the enclosed form). If you have not entered into such an agreement, please furnish a declaration to this effect.

Associations must report agreements among their members, as for example agreements in the form of decisions made at a meeting, and also restrictive rules or other measures adopted by the association, as for example by a representative or committee on behalf of the association.

[At this point the form letter has a blank space in which the State Price and Cartel Office inserts special requests or questions.]

When reporting a restrictive agreement, the following ought to be noted:

1. Facts are to be given concerning every agreement still in force and concerning all agreements which were in force on 1 January 1957 or which have been entered into since then, even though the agreement has been subsequently abolished. The obligation to report includes both written and oral agreements. Also, occasional or local agreements, as for example price agreements within a certain village or community, must be reported.

2. The obligation to report is not dependent on whether the agreement has or has not harmful effects within the meaning of the cartel legislation.

3. An agreement which involves only the export market need not be reported. The obligation to report, however, does include agreements between Swedish and foreign entrepreneurs that affect the Swedish market.

4. The obligation to report also includes agreements on manufacturer's suggested prices, recommended prices, as well as uniform methods of calculation of prices and profits, understandings concerning the time to hold sales and advertising practices. The obligation also includes agreements on the norms or standards to be applied to pricing, calculations, quotas, market divisions, and the like.

5. The following kinds of documents must be submitted:

a) In the case of a written agreement a copy, and in the case of an oral agreement a detailed report of its contents.

b) Copies of other documents necessary to an understanding of the agreement, as for example price lists, rules governing rebates, or extracts from minutes; in the case where a report is made by an association a list of members and a copy of regulations and rules.

6. An entrepreneur who is a member of an association that has entered into a restrictive agreement may refer his report to that organization.

Stockholm the [date]
On behalf of the State Price and Cartel Office
[Signature]

Two copies of a report form are enclosed with the letter. One is to be sent to the Price and Cartel Office and the other is for the registrant's files. The form, a single sheet of paper, is divided into five columns whose headings are as follows:

1. When did you enter into the agreement and for what period is (was) it in force? Is the agreement written or oral?
2. Does the agreement replace any earlier, similar agreement?
3. What commodities or services are embraced by the agreement? If the agreement involves anything other than commodities or services (for example, the right to intangible property), please provide full information.
4. Please advise as to the general character of the agreement. Does it concern prices, quotas, division of territory, specialization, cooperation in selling or purchasing agencies, control over freedom of entry, cooperation in bidding, measures against outsiders or any other activity of a restrictive nature?
5. Please list the names of entrepreneurs or associations of entrepreneurs taking part in the agreement.

The report form allows also for a statement by the entrepreneur that he has never participated in registrable agreements or that he has not participated in registrable agreements after 31 December 1956. Just above the place for date, address, telephone number, and signature is a reminder of the penalties for providing incorrect or incomplete information as set forth in Section 10 of the Registration Act.

2. PROCESSING THE REGISTRATION

The State Price and Cartel Office prepares a summary of the material furnished in a registration statement and in related documents. The Office has discretion as to whether the summary shall be merely a general descriptive statement or a detailed précis. It is obvious that in exercising this discretion, the Office may influence public opinion by the nature of the publication. The summary will often contain, in addition to the data relating to restrictive conditions, other material which may illustrate and define the contents of the agreement and the economic effects of the restrictions. Here again, since the ultimate power rests with the public, the editorial policy is of great importance.

Those who are the subject of the summary are given a copy in advance for comment. If they are not satisfied with the summary, they may attempt to convince the State Price and Cartel Office that changes are necessary.

A number is assigned to the registration, the summary, and all related documents, including correspondence about the summary. All of these are entered into the public Register and the summary is published in Pris- och Kartellfrågor.

3. AMENDING THE REGISTRATION

Just as the registrant is not obliged to register without a request from the State Price and Cartel Office, he is similarly under no obligation to report changes in agreements. The State Price and Cartel Office periodically sends questionnaires to registrants designed to bring the Register up to date. The results obtained are then published in PKF.

In between the periodic checks, the Office notes in the Register any changes that a registrant may have voluntarily disclosed or any changes disclosed by its investigations.

In the case of a first registration the Price and Cartel Office automatically requests notification of all changes during the first two years after registration.

An agreement is deemed cancelled when formal notification to this effect has been made. The government, in evaluating the effectiveness of the publicity system, considers the totals of cancelled agreements to be of great significance, and, as we shall see in the statistical portion of this survey, the figures are subjected to a variety of analyses.

4. SECRET REGISTRATION

Secret registration, although permitted under the Act if it can be justified, has always been the exception in Sweden. The general view is that secrecy is justified only if it will prevent foreign interests from obtaining information that would harm the national interest of Sweden or would harm domestic business.

At present seventeen registrations are secret for a given period of time. One of the seventeen is secret *in toto* and the remainder are secret in part. Fifteen appeals to the King in Council for secrecy have been refused.

D. Appeals from an order to register

A registration does not indicate that a restriction is either good or bad. The issue on appeal from an order to register is not the effects of a restrictive practice. The issue is whether a "restraint on competition," as that term is used in the Registration Act, is involved.

The Act, however, contains no definition of "restraint on competition." The legislators believed that, because no practical definition could be devised, no purpose would be served by attempting one. The legislative history of the 1956 Act indicates that the objective is to register every restrictive practice—every practice which, as the subject of some form of agreement, implies or results in competition not being completely free.

The King in Council has received eighteen appeals from requests to register under the provisions of Section 13 of the Act. Seventeen of them were totally rejected, and in the eighteenth case, a change in the text of the summary was ordered. Thus, in no case has the request of the State Price and Cartel Office for a registration been overruled. Registration No. 1776, for Coca-Cola, was appealed and the registration summary, which is set forth in the case studies, was published pursuant to an Order of the King in Council of 25 September 1959. The original publication was predated to 30 September 1958, the date when the State Price and Cartel Office requested registration.

It is, however, uncertain whether the Swedish authorities have uniformly resolved the status of agreements ancillary to patent, trademark, and copyright assignments and licenses. Indeed the registration of agreements concerning the trademarks "Coca-Cola" and "Coke," Registration No. 1776, reflects this uncertainty. Although the Freedom of Commerce Board has found that territorial exclusivity ancillary to a trademark of a fruit drink is not a restraint with a harmful effect, the other control authorities seem to question such ancillary provisions and call for their registration.

E. Registration statistics

The arrangement and classes of information disclosed by the six statistical tables which follow reflect what the Swedish authorities consider significant and supply some facts upon which one can begin an evaluation of the effectiveness of a system that gives the public the job of passing judgment on restrictive practices.

All of the statistics presented in the tables are as of 1 November 1961 and appear in PKF 1961 (No. 10). Three totals are constantly used as points of reference in these official tables. The total of all agreements registered by 1 November 1961 was 1884; of this number, 940 are still operative and 944 are terminated. Each of the agreements registered normally embraces a variety of restraints, so the totals concerning types of restraints frequently exceed our three key totals wherever normally applicable. The same multiplicity affects the figures dealing with parties to agreements, for an agreement may involve several levels of distribution and more than one trade or industry.

Table 1 illustrates that most of the agreements registered immediately after the Cartel Register became operative have been terminated. However, some very ancient agreements, which are included in the registration totals for 1947 and 1950, are still in effect. The Foundry Convention (No. 62) was established in 1904, the Swedish Newsprint Union (No. 461) was formed in 1917, and the Radiator Convention (No. 12) in 1929. These three agreements, with some modifications, are operative today.

As an example of the way Table 1 is to be read, the first line discloses that 169 agreements were registered in 1947 and that 148 of them are now terminated, representing 87.6 per cent of all of the agreements entered into that year. Column 4 shows the total agreements terminated in a year.

TABLE 1: REGISTRATION STATISTICS

Yr.	Annual Regis.	Cumul. Annual Regis.	Agts. Term. Annually (re Col. 3)	Agts. Oper. at Yr. End (re Col. 3)		Agts. Terminated as of 1 Nov. 1961 (re Col. 2)	
1	2	3	4	5	6	7	8
				No.	%	No.	%
1947	169	169	17	152	90.0	148	87.6
1948	69	238	31	190	79.8	63	91.3
1949	103	341	44	249	73.0	82	79.6
1950	169	510	98	320	62.7	87	51.5
1951	111	621	66	365	58.8	92	82.9
1952	202	823	75	492	59.8	90	44.6
1953	309	1132	123	678	59.9	111	35.9
1954	115	1247	102	691	55.4	59	51.3
1955	370	1617	168	893	55.2	180	48.6
1956	78	1695	112	859	50.7	18	23.0
1957	31	1726	45	845	49.0	3	9.7
1958	28	1754	14	859	49.0	1	3.6
1959	35	1789	15	879	49.1	4	11.4
1960	42	1831	29	892	48.7	5	11.9
1961	53	1884	5	940	49.9	1	1.9

TABLE 2: TERMINATED AGREEMENTS

Registrations		Agreements Terminated			After Registration (re Col. 2)												
					Lapse of Years:												
Yr.	Annual	Prior to Reg.	As of 1 Nov. 1961	Same Yr. as Reg.	1	2	3	4	5	6	7	8	9	10	11	12	13
1	2	3	4	5													
1947	169	5	148	12	14	13	36	28	12	13	4	2	4	1	—	—	4
1948	69	9	63	8	7	16	3	3	7	3	1	—	2	—	1	1	2
1949	103	9	82	15	11	4	8	10	2	6	4	6	—	2	1	—	—
1950	169	26	87	9	4	22	6	6	3	5	2	3	—	1	5	—	—
1951	111	18	92	9	9	8	33	9	4	1	—	—	1	—	—	—	—
1952	202	18	90	3	19	17	6	3	19	2	2	3	—	—	—	—	—
1953	309	17	111	43	14	6	20	2	4	3	1	—	—	—	—	—	—
1954	115	11	59	12	11	11	6	3	4	—	—	—	—	—	—	—	—
1955	370	73	180	51	50	4	1	2	2	1	—	—	—	—	—	—	—
1956	78	10	18	1	2	3	—	—	1	—	—	—	—	—	—	—	—
1957	31	—	3	—	—	—	—	—	—	—	—	—	—	—	—	—	—
1958	28	1	1	—	—	—	—	—	—	—	—	—	—	—	—	—	—
1959	35	—	4	1	3	—	—	—	—	—	—	—	—	—	—	—	—
1960	42	2	5	3	—	—	—	—	—	—	—	—	—	—	—	—	—
1961	53	—	1	1	—	—	—	—	—	—	—	—	—	—	—	—	—
TOTALS	1884	199	944	168	144	105	119	66	58	33	14	14	7	4	6	1	6
Percent of the entire total of terminated agreements		21.1	100.0	17.8	15.3	11.1	12.6	7.0	6.1	3.5	1.5	1.5	0.7	0.4	0.6	0.1	0.6

Table 2 shows, as of 1 November 1961, the number of agreements terminated between the time of a request for registration and the date of actual registration, and subsequently.

TABLE 3: AGREEMENTS ACCORDING TO INDUSTRIAL OR SERVICE GROUPS

Industrial or Trade Groups	Operative Total	% (re 940)	Terminated Total	% (re 944)	Total Total	% (re 1884)	Percentage of Terminated Agreements (re Col. 1)
	1	2	3	4	5	6	7
Metal Industry	109	11.6	338	35.8	447	23.7	75.6
Earth and Minerals	53	5.7	90	9.5	143	7.6	62.9
Wood Products	69	7.3	28	3.0	97	5.1	28.9
Paper and Graphic Prods.	60	6.4	43	4.6	103	5.5	41.7
Food Products	374	39.8	234	24.8	608	32.3	38.5
Textiles and Clothing	85	9.0	31	3.3	116	6.2	26.7
Chemicals	59	6.3	59	6.2	118	6.3	50.0
Leather, Hair, and Rubber Prods.	10	1.1	38	4.0	48	2.5	79.2
Service Groups							
Handcraft	53	5.6	46	4.9	99	5.2	46.5
Transport	35	3.7	20	2.1	55	2.9	36.4
Entertainment	3	0.3	4	0.4	7	0.4	57.1
Miscellaneous	30	3.2	13	1.4	43	2.3	30.2
TOTALS	940	100.0	944	100.0	1884	100.0	50.1 Avg

The percentages shown in Columns 2, 4, and 6 of Table 3 are percentages of all agreements in the class considered in Columns 1, 3, and 5. Thus the 109 agreements in force in the metal industry are 11.6 per cent of all effective agreements, the 338 terminated agreements represent 35.8 per cent of all terminated agreements, and the 447 agreements, both effective and terminated, in the metal industry represent 23.7 per cent of all registered agreements.

TABLE 4: CLASSES OF AGREEMENTS

	1			2		
	Price Fixing Oper. Term. Tot.			Market Division Oper. Term. Tot.		
Industrial or Trade Groups						
Metal Industry	73	253	326	27	108	135
Earth and Minerals	40	70	110	16	25	41
Wood Products	53	21	74	3	3	6
Paper and Graphic Products	53	33	86	5	7	12
Food Products	148	78	226	29	85	114
Textiles and Clothing	22	10	32	1	3	4
Chemicals	19	40	59	10	16	26
Leather, Hair, and Rubber Products	4	6	10	2	----	2
Service Groups						
Handcraft	52	45	97	----	33	33
Transport	25	2	27	11	2	13
Entertainment	1	2	3	----	----	----
Miscellaneous	27	11	38	1	5	6
Total	517	571	1088	105	287	392
Percent of operative and terminated	47.5	52.5		26.8	73.2	
Percent of all registrations (1884)			57.7			20.8
Percent of all operatives (940) and all terminated (944)	55.0	60.5		11.1	30.4	

SIX CLASSES OF AGREEMENTS ARE CONSIDERED IN TABLE 4

1) *Price Fixing.* This term must be considered within the context of the ban on vertical resale-price maintenance and the continued legality of horizontal price-fixing agreements. Examples of the forms of limitation on competition that the term encompasses, as given by the State Price and Cartel Office, include agreements on fixed prices, minimum prices, or suggested prices. The concept also includes agreements on a common rebate system or on uniform accounting and price calculation principles.

2) *Market Division.* This term embraces agreements concerning production and sales quota allocations, territorial allocations, agreements limiting capacity or production, specialization or rationalization agreements, and agreements protecting the home market.

3) *Exclusive Dealing.* Generally the term applies to an undertaking by one party to buy certain goods only from the other party or to sell only to him. The concept also refers to mutual undertakings

	3			4			5			6	
	Exclusive Dealing			Joint Agencies			Freedom of Entry			Miscellaneous	
Oper.	Term.	Tot.	Oper.	Term.	Tot.	Oper.	Term.	Tot.	Oper.	Term.	Tot.
40	165	205	2	2	2	—	2	2	1	1	2
8	29	37	12	12	24	1	—	1	—	4	4
—	13	13	3	1	4	—	2	2	14	—	14
2	8	10	1	1	2	3	2	5	3	3	6
79	53	132	7	7	14	—	20	20	131	32	163
—	—	—	1	1	2	1	1	2	60	18	78
15	11	26	5	5	10	1	4	5	16	8	24
3	33	36	—	—	—	1	3	4	2	—	2
—	—	—	—	—	—	1	1	2	—	—	—
7	15	22	—	—	—	2	—	2	—	1	1
—	1	1	—	—	—	—	1	1	2	—	2
—	1	1	—	—	—	1	2	3	1	1	2
154	329	483	31	29	60	11	38	49	230	68	298
31.9	68.1		51.7	48.3		22.4	77.6		77.2	22.8	
		25.6			3.2			2.6			15.8
16.4	34.9		3.3	3.1		1.2	4.0		24.5	7.2	

of an exclusive nature as well as to provisions in an agreement conferring benefits in the form of special rebates and favoring a particular buyer or seller.

4) *Joint Sales or Purchase Agencies.* This term relates generally only to domestic agencies unless those concerned with international trade affect the domestic market.

5) *Freedom of Entry.* This term includes all agreements which are designed to exclude certain persons from entering a trade or industry whether or not the exclusion is grounded on sound technical reasons or an arbitrary intention to restrict competition.

6) *Miscellaneous.* This category includes limitations on competition through agreement. An example would be an agreement between an advertiser and an advertising medium not to carry news, publicity, or advertising about a competitor of the advertiser. Excluded would be a policy of refusing to deal arrived at unilaterally by a single entrepreneur.

Table 5 provides a tabulation of the registered agreements, distinguishing between horizontal, vertical, and multi-level agreements. The percentages in Column 2 are based on the total number of registrations, 1884. Column 4 reflects the percentage of the terminated agreements based on the total number of agreements in Column 1 on the same line. Finally, Column 6 represents the percentage of all agreements presently in force, 940.

TABLE 5: MULTI-LEVEL AGREEMENTS

Participants belong to one category of trade, industry, or commerce	Registered 1 No.	2 % (re 1884)	Terminated 3 No.	4 % (re Col.1)	Operative 5 No.	6 % (re 940)
Industry	613	32.5	389	63.5	224	23.8
Handcraft	126	6.7	49	38.9	77	8.2
Wholesale	83	4.4	41	49.4	42	4.5
Retail	304	16.1	69	22.7	235	25.0
Producers Cooperatives	75	4.0	9	12.0	66	7.0
Consumers Cooperatives	----	----	----	----	----	----
State and Commune	1	----	----	----	1	0.1
Miscellaneous	79	4.2	15	19.0	64	6.8
Totals	1281	68.0	572	44.7	709	75.4

Participants belong to two different categories	Registered 1 No.	2 % (re 1884)	Terminated 3 No.	4 % (re Col.1)	Operative 5 No.	6 % (re 940)
Industry—Handcraft	7	0.4	7	100.0	----	----
—Wholesale	121	6.4	88	72.7	33	3.5
—Retail	70	3.7	52	74.3	18	1.9
—Producers Coops	101	5.3	14	13.9	87	9.3
—Consumers Coops	5	0.3	4	80.0	1	0.1
—State & Commune	2	0.1	2	100.0	----	----
—Miscellaneous	6	0.3	6	100.0	----	----
Handcraft—Wholesale	5	0.3	4	80.0	1	0.1
—Retail	4	0.2	4	100.0	----	----
—Miscellaneous	2	0.1	1	50.0	1	0.1
Wholesale—Retail	73	3.9	63	86.3	10	1.1
—Producers Coops	40	2.1	30	75.0	10	1.1
—State & Commune	1	----	1	100.0	----	----
—Miscellaneous	2	0.1	1	50.0	1	0.1
Retail—Producers Coops	69	3.7	37	53.6	32	3.4
—Consumers Coops	1	----	1	100.0	----	----
—Miscellaneous	6	0.3	4	66.7	2	0.2
Producers Coop—Consumers Coop	19	1.0	8	42.1	11	1.2
—State & Commune	1	----	----	----	1	0.1
—Miscellaneous	29	1.5	13	44.8	16	1.7
State and Commune—Misc.	9	0.5	4	44.4	5	0.5
Totals	573	30.4	344	60.0	229	24.4

	Registered		Terminated		Operative	
	1	2	3	4	5	6
Participants belong to three different categories	No.	% *(re 1884)*	No.	% *(re Col.1)*	No.	% *(re 940)*
Industry—Handcraft—Wholesale	1	----	1	100.0	----	----
" —Retail	3	0.2	3	100.0	----	----
—Wholesale—Retail	18	1.0	18	100.0	----	----
" —State & Commune	1	----	1	100.0	----	----
Handcraft—Wholesale—Retail	1	----	1	100.0	----	----
" —Miscell.	1	----	----	----	1	0.1
Retail—Producers Coop— Consumers Coop	2	0.1	1	50.0	1	0.1
Totals	27	1.4	25	92.6	2	0.2
Participants belong to four different categories						
Industry—Handcraft—Wholesale— Retail	2	1.0	2	100.0	----	----
Participants belong to five different categories						
Industry—Handcraft—Wholesale— Retail—Producers Coop	1	----	1	100.0	----	----

Table 6 makes use of the same categories employed in the Table 5 analysis, but it deals in total numbers on category participation. As is apparent from Table 5 some agreements are tabulated more than once. Nevertheless, the percentage figures in Column 2 of Table 6 are based on the total registration of 1884 agreements, though the figures of Column 1 total more than 1884. The percentages in Column 4 are computed on the basis of the total of agreements appearing in Column 1 on the same line, so that Column 4 shows the percentage of terminated agreements in each category. Column 6 reflects the percentage of operative agreements based on the operative total of 940.

TABLE 6: MULTI-LEVEL AGREEMENT TOTALS

Category	Registered		Terminated		Operative	
	No.	% *(re 1884)*	No.	% *(re. Col. 1)*	No.	% *(re 940)*
Industry	951	50.5	588	61.8	363	38.6
Handcraft	153	8.1	73	47.7	80	8.5
Wholesale	352	18.7	252	71.5	100	10.6
Retail	553	29.4	256	46.3	287	31.6

(Continued on following page)

Producers Coops	337	17.9	113	33.5	224	23.8
Consumers Coops	27	1.4	14	51.9	13	1.4
State & Commune	15	0.8	8	53.3	7	0.7
Miscellaneous	134	7.1	43	32.1	91	9.7

In any appraisal of the Swedish economy, of the prevalence, and of the nature of restrictive trade practices in Sweden based on Tables 1–6, a *caveat* should be noted. The Swedish registration of cartels depends on the request of the S.P.K. This being the case, one cannot be certain that the Register accurately reflects the actual restrictive trade practices in force. In this sense the Swedish Register is to be contrasted with the Danish and Norwegian, both of which are allegedly almost universal in scope. Nevertheless, some Swedish authorities believe that their Register is accurate because they catch those who through misunderstanding fail to register under the compulsory systems.

II. ORGANIZATIONAL FRAMEWORK FOR CONTROLLING RESTRICTIVE BUSINESS PRACTICES

THE SWEDISH SYSTEM for controlling restrictive business practices utilizes three agencies in addition to some private organizations.

The State Price and Cartel Office (S.P.K.), established under the 1956 Act, has varied duties consisting primarily of maintaining the Cartel Register, and publishing Pris- och Kartellfrågor (PKF). Furthermore, it maintains an investigative branch which studies prices and works closely with the Commissioner for Freedom of Commerce.

The Commissioner for Freedom of Commerce is the key agency under the 1953 Act. He initiates investigations, receives complaints from the public, and acts as the representative of public interest in proceedings before the Freedom of Commerce Board.

The Board, also created under the 1953 Act, is the negotiating body and the agency empowered to grant exemptions from certain prohibitions embodied in the 1953 Act.

A. The State Price and Cartel Office

The State Price and Cartel Office has a wide ranging role in the Swedish scheme of control of restrictive practices. In addition to keeping the Cartel Register, it publishes Pris- och Kartellfrågor, usually ten times a year, in which the Cartel Register summaries appear along with various reports and price indexes, domestic and international, for raw material, wholesale, and consumer prices.

The price indexes reflect only a part of the price-watching mission of the S.P.K., which, since 1960, has accelerated its study of price trends as a result of the enactment of a retail purchase tax.

1. ORGANIZATION

The S.P.K. has four bureaus, each with special duties. The First Investigating Bureau carries out the investigations of restrictive practices when the Commissioner for Freedom of Commerce so requests. During 1960 and 1961, the S.P.K. published in PKF reports dealing with restrictive practices in the distribution or production of motor scooters, optical goods, cemented-carbide tools, plastics, cola beverages, trade association circulars, and furniture. Conversely, the S.P.K. annually refers more than a dozen matters, usually relating to prices, to the Commissioner for Freedom of Commerce.

The Second Bureau is concerned with trends of prices and production, current price supervision in various commodity fields, and price studies in specific branches of trade. At the end of this chapter are some excerpts of the reports published by this Bureau in 1960 and 1961.

The Third Bureau is itself subdivided into three sections. The Administrative Section, concerned primarily with internal matters, handles staff and organizational problems. The Investigation Section is concerned primarily with profit and cost structures of industry and among its recent reports is a major study of the profits in the automobile industry. The Cartel Register is also within its jurisdiction.

The Publications Section publishes not only PKF, but also the press releases which furnish the basis for national newspaper coverage of restrictive practices problems. In a normal year about forty press releases dealing with cartel registrations and reports will be sent to 180 daily newspapers and almost 100 weekly and technical journals.

In 1960 approximately thirty of the forty press releases led to one or more published stories, many in leading papers of nationwide circulation, concerning restrictive practices or prices. Ten newspaper stories were based on the State Price and Cartel Office's report on recommended prices and a like number reflected the findings from the investigation of advertising and prices for both fresh and cured meats. Reports on the cemented carbide cartel and on recommended prices for motor-scooter parts each led to nine newspaper articles. The results of the investigations of hearing aids, table potatoes, and fresh and cured meats each garnered eight news stories. The total number of published stories based on the 1960 reports of the State Price and Cartel Office totalled 132.

Finally the Statistical Bureau maintains the statistical data derived from the retail trade surveys and various investigations. The Bureau keeps a register of 85,000 retail establishments. From this register it selects the shops to be used in the various retail price surveys. The surveying techniques are established and supervised by the Statistical Bureau.

2. REPORTS

Both the published reports of the S.P.K. and the publication of Cartel Register summaries are major factors in shaping Swedish attitudes toward current restrictive trade practices and the Swedish opinion of specific industries, trades, or services.

When a report is made on a particular trade or industry, the usual practice is to make it available to the parties concerned before publication in PKF. Thus, the parties have an opportunity to change their practices prior to publication. Not infrequently, notices in PKF advise the changes resulting from an investigation and report.

In addition to its reports on restrictive practices the S.P.K. issues a great number of reports which are primarily concerned with consumer goods.

In 1960 and in 1961 five reports were published on prices and trade practices in meat, both fresh and cured. Four reports dealt with bread and other baked goods, and one discussed potatoes for table use.

A general price study of food was made as part of the research into the effect of the new, retail purchase tax of 4.2 per cent. The S.P.K. investigated and reported food prices in specific localities as well as the extent to which recommended prices are followed in the food trade and the nature of food profit margins.

During 1960 and 1961 the S.P.K. published eight reports dealing with textiles, ready-made clothing, knitted wear, and hosiery. Prices and price trends, recommended prices, and industry structure, along with quality factors were all fully discussed and examined. Footwear merited two reports during the same period.

Additional subjects for study in 1960 and 1961 were housewares, hearing aids, motor-scooter spare parts, radio, and television sets, heating oil, and building materials.

Reports were also issued concerning services such as stevedoring in Göteborg, retail purchasing groups, the weekly press, barbering and hairdressing, and driving schools.

Miscellaneous reports evaluated studies by a government committee dealing with price trends and with problems of how to have a more effective watch over prices.

The complete text of the report by the S.P.K. on Coca-Cola, in the Swedish case studies, provides a clear view of the extent to which the editorial views of the S.P.K. are discernible in its reports.

S.P.K. publishes, in the English language, précis of its major reports which it denominates as English summaries. An additional basis for evaluating the S.P.K. reports is provided by the following excerpts from these summaries published in PKF during 1960 and 1961.

a. "Textiles and Ready-Made Clothing . . . The fall in prices that has occurred in American cotton does not seem to have had any appreciable effect on the prices of the fabrics for the autumn market in 1959" (PKF 1960, No. 1, p. 39).

b. "Meat Trade . . . Thus, in spite of its dependence on the shifts in the world market prices this branch of trade has a very rigid price system. It is the organizations in the private-owned trade and the enterprises in the producer and consumer cooperative fields that control the fixing of prices, and the competition between different retail trading firms seems primarily to be concerned with quality and service" (PKF 1960, No. 1, p. 40).

c. "The Weekly Press . . . In the course of 1959 the selling price of the periodicals covered by the investigation went up by an average of 13 per cent. In conjunction with the introduction of the purchase tax [of 4.2 per cent] additional rises in prices were effected in the first quarter of 1960 to the extent of 6.5 per cent.

"Taken as a whole for the sale of single copies and for subscriptions these advances in price may be estimated to correspond to an increase in the annual sales value of nearly 34 million kroner [$6,800,000], of which 8–9 million kronor [$1,600,000–$1,800,000] represent purchase tax" (PKF 1960, No. 5, p. 335).

d. "Hearing Aids . . . For charging a recommended price for hearing-aid spectacles the importers' and the retailers' combined average margin, in terms of an increment on the import price was 133 per cent. For other types of aid the total increment amounted to 134 per cent.

"The auditory centres (a special type of retailer) have not applied the prices recommended by the importers and their prices have been considerably lower than those [suggested]. For instance, the recommended prices for apparatus other than hearing-aid spectacles were about a third lower in 1959" (PKF 1960, No. 8, p. 551).

e. "The Cemented Carbide Cartel . . . The domestic market for *hard-metal tips* is dominated by the firms that have come to the agreement. In regard to *standard tools,* the cartel has not such a free hand in its price policy as in regard to hard-metal tips. The fact is that these tools are manufactured by about twenty smaller firms not belonging to the cartel. As to *special tools* there has been in force under the main agreement the provision (which was suspended while the investigation was going on) that the prices of special tools were to be fixed according to agreed principles and that members of the cartel receiving inquiries for offers were to contact one another in cases in which the estimated sum covering an offer to effect delivery amounted to a certain specified minimum value.

"Thanks to its powerful position on the market the cartel is able to give its price fixing such weightages that in all essentials the profit is gained on the sales of hard-metal tips. The sale of tools brings in a far lower profit and in some cases does not even fully cover the costs of production. This diminishes the possibilities for outside producers of tools to compete.

"Since the above report was issued the agreement on prices within the carbide cartel (Cartel Register No. 503) according to an announcement from the Fagersta Bruks AB has been annulled with immediate effect" (PKF 1960, No. 9, p. 611).

f. "The TV and Radio Trade . . . Under hire purchase, the average price of TV sets is 1,472 kronor [$294.40]—after a 3 per cent reduction in price and including the hire-purchase increment. The corresponding cash price—after a 9 per cent bargain reduction—would be 1,277 kronor [$255.40]. If instead of paying by instalments a hire-purchase buyer had chosen to take up a loan in order to pay cash, he would have needed to borrow 992 kronor [$198.40], i.e., the difference between the cash price and the down payment of 285 kronor [$57.00] he would have to make under hire purchase. The difference between the cash price and the hire-purchase price, 195 kronor [$39.00], may then be said to represent interest on the 992 kronor. Under hire purchase the payments are effected successively in the course of 15 months. Thus, if he took up a cash loan to be paid off month by month for an equally long period, the buyer might have paid up to 29–30 per cent interest without losing on the deal.

"According to the survey, the hire-purchase transactions represent a third of the number of sales and comprise 42 per cent of the turnover in the trade" (PKF 1961, No. 1, p. 69).

g. "Ready-made Clothing in 1960 . . . Recommended prices are fixed on a relatively large scale in the Swedish ready-to-wear industry, especially in regard to men's shirts, of which nearly a third are put on the market at recommended prices. The percentage increments applied by the manufacturers when recommending resale prices to merchants are as a rule higher than those which the retail trade applies when pricing similar articles independently. A similar observation was made by the Board in the course of an investigation in 1959, when the opinion was expressed that in cases—such as here— in which the recommended prices are very largely followed in the trade there was a risk of their having the same effect, from the competitive aspect, as the now prohibited fixed gross prices. Since the year's survey has revealed the same situation as between the recommended margins and the independent margins, that fact has lent further support to this opinion" (PKF 1961, No. 2, pp. 119–120).

h. "Plastics . . . Owing to the imports being on so large a scale the foreign sellers' price policy strongly influences the fixing of the prices of the plastic articles produced at home.

"Three out of the six agreements which the State Price and Cartel Office have entered in the Register of Cartels are still in operation.

"One of these contracts made in 1958, contains a clause to the effect that the foreign contracting parties shall not charge a price below that quoted quarterly by the Swedish contracting party, 'taking into consideration the trend of prices on the world market.' . . .

"The Price and Cartel Office expresses the view that the important economic role played by plastics is bound to deteriorate if their prices cannot be freely fixed owing to a lack of effective competition. It appears from the investigation that price restrictions already exist in the form of agreements that hinder competition not only in Sweden but also in Denmark and Norway" (PKF 1961, No. 3, p. 222).

i. "Knitted Wear . . . the percentage mark-up has been found to be, as a rule, higher on price-recommended goods than on articles for which the prices have been freely fixed but which have been comparable in view of the purchase price. For ladies' nylon stockings it has been possible to make comparisons between price-recommended and non-price-recommended goods which have the same technical description (density of mesh and fineness of thread). These comparisons have shown that the former have almost without exception fetched both higher prices and higher percentage mark-ups" (PKF 1961, No. 5, p. 345).

j. "Restrictive Practices in the Furniture Trade. A number of cases of restrictive practices in the furniture trade have been investigated by the State Price and Cartel Office. It appears from the inquiry that furniture dealers who enter into price competition run the risk of being shut off from the delivery of a number of articles which they would like to market and being forced to substitute for them products that are not quite of an equivalent value. The rest of the furniture dealers consider that they are frequently prevented from marketing the same manufacturers and models as the firms that carry on restrictive practices. The manufacturers are faced with the choice of either selling firms indulging in restrictive practices and losing other customers or partially to exclude those who enter into price competition.

"The Office of the Commissioner for Freedom of Commerce has asked for this inquiry after receiving a complaint from, in the first place, a firm in Stockholm which encountered difficulties in effecting purchases after having made relatively heavy reductions in their prices in the autumn of 1960. This firm stated that the manufacturers had apparently been subjected to pressure by a number of furniture dealers. Similar statements were also received from some other retailers. The inquiry has brought to light the fact that altogether 36 manufacturers all over the country have either wholly or in part cut off competing firms from deliveries. It has been found that the reported circumstances in the furniture trade may be said to render it difficult or impossible for certain dealers to succeed in their efforts to reduce costs and thereby to give the consumer the benefit of not inconsiderable price reductions" (PKF 1961, No. 8, p. 619).

B. The Commissioner for Freedom of Commerce

The Commissioner for Freedom of Commerce is the pivotal agency under the 1953 Act controlling restraints of competition. He is appointed by the King in Council and is required to have judicial experience pursuant to Section 14.

In general the Commissioner functions as a sort of supervisor of the enforcement of the law, as the instigator of investigations, as the focal point for complaints from the public, and as the representative of the public interest in proceedings before the Freedom of Commerce Board.

The Commissioner may on his own initiative start an investigation either using his own staff or, more ordinarily, by instructing the State Price and Cartel Office to undertake an inquiry. An investigation may be based on knowledge which the Commissioner has himself obtained, a scrutiny of the Cartel Register, or a complaint from the public.

Once the Commissioner has determined to his satisfaction that a particular practice falls under the provisions of the 1953 Act, particularly Section 5, he has the power to request that the Board order the parties to negotiate to terminate or modify the practices in question. In many instances the parties to a restraint of trade will terminate or modify as soon as they are aware of the inquiry that is underway. Others wait until called before the Board.

1. PRIVATE COMPLAINTS

From 1954 through 1960 the Commissioner received 838 complaints from private parties concerning restraints of trade. A little more than one-fourth of the complaints, 218, involved matters considered to be not within the purview of the 1953 Act. Various technical and formal reasons led to the dismissal of 33 complaints, and an additional 30 were set aside temporarily for special consideration. Of the balance, 170 were not considered because the restraint of trade was either terminated or modified at some stage of the inquiry or during negotiation with the Commissioner. An additional 32 complaints were withdrawn by the complainants for reasons unknown and not pursued further by the Commissioner. The matters presented to the Freedom of Commerce Board for the period 1954 through 1960 by the Commissioner totalled 37, out of the initial 838 complaints. The balance of 318 complaints, which are unaccounted for, represent a sort of backlog of postponed cases whose fate is not clearly indicated by the Commissioner's annual reports.

Against the total of 838 private complaints one may contrast the 27 inquiries carried out on the Commissioner's initiative during 1954–1960. The Commissioner may determine that a complaint does not warrant his proceeding further with the matter. In such instances an opinion is issued, giving the reasons why the Commissioner does not feel he should take action, and published in PKF. A private complainant may, despite an adverse opinion from the Commissioner, seek the aid of the Freedom of Commerce Board under the provisions of Section 16 of the 1953 Act. The instances in which the Board has taken jurisdiction after an adverse opinion from the Commissioner are relatively rare.

The private complaints do not generally concern restraints which are the subject of registered cartel agreements. They usually originate from refusals to deal, alleged discriminations in trade terms, and practices that are more usually vertical than horizontal.

Section 5 of the 1953 Act is the formal basis for the Commissioner's decision whether or not to proceed with a complaint from a private person. The key words, from the point of view of statutory interpretation, are "harmful effect" and "public interest." More realistically the Commissioner seems to be using standards such as "sound business judgment" and "reasonable business practices" in arriving at a determination that a complaint does not warrant further action on his part, either in the form of negotiation or in the form of a proceeding before the Freedom of Commerce Board.

Often the determinative of the Commissioner's approach is the nature of the product that is the subject of the complaint. Thus, if a luxury cosmetic is sold to only a few selected shops and refused to others, the Commissioner will be likely to perceive the existence of sound business reasons for the discrimination, a lack of "public interest," and an absence of "harmful effects." More clearly, when scientific or technical aspects of a product underlie a selective policy of choosing outlets, he is likely to dismiss a complaint from one not chosen as an outlet. This attitude of the Commissioner is to be distinguished from the general antipathy of Swedish authorities to general limitations on freedom of entry into a trade or profession.

The Commissioner recognizes that one may refuse to deal with a poor credit risk for reasons of sound business practice, and such a discrimination is not treated as a harmful restraint. If competitive products are available, similar to the withheld commodity in price and quality, the complaint may be dropped. Technical reasons for discrimination grounded on efficient distribution, rationalization, and a reduction in cost of goods are all usually accepted by the Commissioner.

When an importer restricts his sales to his regular customers because of seasonal shortages of fruit, his act is considered a sound business judgment. The losses of those who have been refused are weighed against the burdens that might be placed on the importer by a contrary opinion of the Commissioner.

Finally, monopoly or economic power standing alone are not reasons for the Commissioner to take action. Only where an abuse of this power can be shown is he likely to take cognizance of a complaint.

It is apparent from the opinions of the Commissioner that he makes a thorough and careful study of the business practices involved in the cases brought to his attention. In the majority of the dismissed complaints his decision is generally grounded on the soundness of the business practice, the necessity of it, and the lack of a direct harmful effect on the economy or the complainant. However, in some few instances the Commissioner apparently feels that it would be an uneconomic and imprudent use of his time to pursue a matter which is *de minimis* and less important than issues which he finds more pressing.

2. THE COMMISSIONER AND CARTELS

One of the duties of the Commissioner is to examine the Cartel Register and to investigate those cartels whose actions fall within the provisions and definitions of Section 5 of the 1953 Act. After investigating, he may ask the Board to order a negotiation to end the harmful restrictive practices.

From 1954 through 1960, 838 private complaints were the main source of the Commissioner's activity, while during the same period he examined on his own initiative only 221 cartel agreements. Table 7 illustrates the apparent trend toward a reduced use of the Cartel Register as a source for inquiries by the Commissioner.

The percentage figures used in Table 7 are derived from the relationship between the total number of cartel agreements examined by the Commissioner each year and the annual totals for the resulting actions.

TABLE 7: COMPARATIVE ANALYSIS OF CARTEL REGISTRATIONS
STUDIED BY THE COMMISSIONER

	1954	1955	1956	1957	1958	1959	1960
Total cartel registrations	1247	1617	1695	1726	1754	1789	1831
Total agreements in effect at year end	691	893	859	845	859	879	892
Total agreements terminated that year	102	168	112	45	14	15	29
Total registered agreements studied by Commissioner	46	38	56	32	10	14	25
Modified or terminated to Commissioner's satisfaction	25	4	25[1]	10	2	4[2]	7
Percentage	54%	11%	45%	31%	20%	28%	28%
Considered unimportant	6	2	3	7	____	1	6
Percentage	13%	05%	05%	22%	____	07%	24%
Leading to proceedings before Board	2	4	1	3	____	____	2
Percentage	04%	11%	02%	09%	____	____	08%
For further study	13	28	27	12	8	9	10
Percentage	28%	73%	48%	37%	80%	65%	40%
Private complaints studied	69	95	104	119	154	149	148

[1] The agreements listed in the Commissioner's report actually total 43, with 27 terminated and 16 altered, but 25 is given numerically as the total (PKF 1957, No. 2, p. 101).

[2] The named agreements actually total 6 with 3 terminated and 3 altered (PKF 1960, No. 1, p. 47).

These figures would indicate that a trend is developing in which the Commissioner's efforts are being concentrated on situations brought to his attention by the public rather than on those which are found by studying the Cartel Register. One inevitable result of this policy is to place pressures on those industries distributing or producing consumer goods rather than on basic industries involved in restraints. Even where the Commissioner applies himself to a study of the Cartel Register, this emphasis on consumer goods is apparent, as is demonstrated by Tables 8 A and 8 B.

Table 8 A reflects the nature of the products or trades involved in the cartel agreements which have been altered or terminated after scrutiny by the Commissioner during the period 1956–1960. Table 8 B indicates the nature of the practices involved in the terminated or altered agreements. The totals in the tables may exceed the totals in the preceding tables because individual agreements may involve more than one product and more than one restraint of trade.

One result of the trend toward reliance on the public to guide the direction of the Commissioner's inquiries is that restraints in the manufacture or distribution of capital goods and of goods bought only indirectly by the public at large seem to be generally undisturbed. The small staff available to the Commissioner has to give

TABLE 8: RESULTS OF THE COMMISSIONER'S ACTIVITIES

A. *Number of Agreements Terminated or Altered Each Year*

Product or Service	1956 T	1956 A	1957 T	1957 A	1958 T	1958 A	1959 T	1959 A	1960 T	1960 A
General Food	3	--	1	--	--	--	--	--	--	--
Dairy	9	7(1)	--	--	--	--	--	3	--	--
Meat	2	--	--	--	--	--	1	--	--	--
Transport	1	--	--	1	1	--	--	--	--	--
Grain	1	--	--	--	--	--	--	--	--	--
Automobiles	3	5	--	--	--	--	--	--	--	1
Iron and Steel	3	--	1	--	--	--	--	--	--	--
Tools	1	--	--	--	--	--	--	--	--	--
Machinery	2	--	1	--	--	--	--	--	--	--
Building Materials	2	--	--	2	--	--	--	--	1	--
Photographic	--	1	--	--	--	--	--	--	--	--
Shoes	--	1	--	--	--	--	--	--	--	--
Pastry	--	--	--	--	--	--	--	--	2	--
Hairdressing	--	1	--	--	--	--	--	--	--	--
Mineral Oil	--	--	--	--	--	--	--	--	1	--
Printing	--	--	2	--	--	--	2	--	--	--
Optical	--	--	--	--	--	--	--	--	1	--
Fur	--	--	1	--	--	--	--	--	--	--
Cemented Carbide	--	--	--	--	--	--	--	--	1	--
Millinery	--	--	--	1	--	--	--	--	--	--
Electrical	--	--	--	--	--	1	--	--	--	--

(1) One registration involved thirteen agreements and another sixteen.

B. *Incidence of Restrictive Practices in Agreements Terminated or Altered Each Year*

Restriction	1956 T	1956 A	1957 T	1957 A	1958 T	1958 A	1959 T	1959 A	1960 T	1960 A
Price Fixing	12	10	3	3	1	--	2	3	7	2
Market Division	5	6	1	--	--	--	1	1	--	--
Exclusive Dealing	10	7	1	--	--	--	--	1	--	--
Joint Agencies	--	--	1	--	--	--	--	--	--	--
Freedom of Entry	6	6	1	--	--	--	1	1	--	--
Miscellaneous	2	1	3	--	--	--	--	--	--	--

priority to the private complaints, and only by enlarging the staff will it be possible to reach nonconsumer restraints.

3. THE COMMISSIONER AND FREEDOM OF ENTRY

The Commissioner is frequently concerned about general problems of freedom of entry, although this concern is not clearly indicated by the statistics. In 1954 the Commissioner asked the Board of Trade, functioning as the predecessor of the State Price and Cartel Office, to study problems of freedom of entry into the retail trade in food. This investigation resulted in an eighty-page report published in Näringsfrihetsfrågor 1955 (No. 5). The findings of the Board of Trade have greatly influenced the Commissioner, and there is little doubt that a freedom-of-entry complaint at the retail level will invoke the interest and activity of the Commissioner.

The concern of the Commissioner with these problems can be understood if one examines some of the conclusions reached in the Board of Trade's report, conclusions which, with some variations, may be applied to other highly organized branches of retailing. Restriction on freedom of entry is a long established Swedish trade technique, and changes are slow.

The restraints on freedom of entry in the grocery trade date back to an agreement of the early 1930's, which was revised in 1950. The agreement was entered into by the national associations representing the food processors, the food wholesalers, and the existing food retailers. Its purpose was to control the establishment of new grocery stores, branches of those in operation, and the creation of new grocery departments in existing stores selling other products. The agreement did not control changes in ownership.

The agreement operated through twenty-six Cooperation Committees at the local level and a Permanent Central Committee to which appeals from the local committees could be made. The local committees and the Central Committee normally consisted of a chairman from outside the trade and representatives of processors, wholesalers, and retailers. The Central Committee also included a consumer representative and an employee representative, both with the power to vote; similar representatives served on a few local committees without a vote.

The agreement established four considerations that had to be examined in passing on a request for permission to open a grocery store or a grocery department in an existing store: (1) The applicant must have a minimum knowledge of bookkeeping and must have at least three years of actual experience in the grocery trade or in a similar trade; (2) The applicant must prove adequate financial resources to meet the expected demand of his store; (3) The premises contemplated for use as a grocery store must meet minimum local standards established by the local committee; (4) The general economic conditions of the district, particularly the number of potential customers, must justify the opening of a new store, and the size and management of existing stores must be given attention so as not to allow the mere existence of an older store to serve as a reason for refusal of permission.

The operation of this agreement in the grocery trade from 1936 to 1954 resulted in the processing of more than 6,600 applications by local committees. On an annual basis the average was 600 applications a year in the late 1930's, decreasing during World War II, reaching a new high of about 700 per year in 1945 and 1946, and then tapering off to about a 200-per-year average for 1947–1954. The percentage of refusals was at a high in 1936 with 61 per cent of 667 applications turned down and then diminished to a refusal rate of 22 per cent on applications in 1954. The average percentage of refusals for 1936–1954 was 46 per cent.

The Board of Trade concentrated its analysis on the committees' handling of applications during 1952 and 1953. It found that out of the 376 applications received by the local committees, 101 were refused; thus the rate of refusal was 27 per cent. During this period the Central Committee heard 55 appeals, reversed the local committees 20 times, and upheld them in 35 cases.

Local committees were found to base their refusals of permission on more than one of the four considerations set forth in the agreement. The fourth consideration, general economic conditions, was utilized in 74 per cent of the cases, while the first consideration, the applicant's personal qualifications, was used only 60 per cent. The other two considerations were used approximately 50 per cent of the time. The Central Committee was shown to have developed some modifications in the third criterion, the standards for the store's premises. The fourth consideration, when it was cited, served as the dominant reason for refusing to grant permission to enter the trade.

A survey of the actual state of the grocery trade showed that, despite the undertaking by wholesalers not to supply unapproved stores, a not inconsiderable number of unapproved stores seem to have opened. In recent years about one-half of the unsuccessful applicants opened stores, but three-fourths of these have had serious difficulty arising from the boycott by the wholesalers. One device which kept some grocers in business, although inconvenient, was that of buying from wholesalers outside their district. Of course, the grocer had extra transportation costs with which to reckon. Another method was to purchase from one or several of the few independent wholesalers whose stock was quite narrow or to purchase from other retailers or from consumer cooperative stores. All of these devices served to reduce the margins of the independent, unapproved dealers.

The 1950 version of the cartel agreement limiting freedom of entry into the grocery trade was placed on the Cartel Register on 13 May 1953 as No. 922. The agreement was terminated on 1 March 1956, but the Commissioner does not claim credit for this action. By 31 March 1956 related cartel Registrations Nos. 923, 924, and 925 were terminated as a result of investigation and action by the Commissioner. Agreements Nos. 923, 924, and 925 dealt with freedom of entry in various regions of Sweden and covered fish, fruit, and baked goods as well as general groceries.

The termination of the agreements has not brought an end to problems of freedom of entry into the grocery trade in which new forms of retailing are developing in Sweden. These problems will be considered in the section concerned with refusal to deal.

C. Jurisdiction of the Freedom of Commerce Board

The Freedom of Commerce Board (Näringsfrihetsrådet) is the ultimate authority in the hierarchy of agencies administering the Swedish legislation for control of restrictive business practices.

The nine-member Board and its highly efficient secretariat have four major tasks: 1) to pass on requests for exemptions from the ban on resale-price maintenance and the prohibition of bidding cartels, 2) to decide cases of harmful restraints of trade and to supervise negotiations where such a restraint is found to exist, 3) to hear appeals from decisions of the Commissioner not to present cases to the Board, and 4) to advise the government on matters relating to restrictive trade practices and legislative questions.

The Board operates with procedures that might be termed quasi-judicial. When cases of alleged restraints of trade are brought before it, the Commissioner acts as prosecutor; counsel often represents the defendant. Written and oral pleadings, evidence, and proof are presented in public as if before a court. The chairman, appointed by the King in Council, has legal training and is a distinguished lawyer with judicial experience. The vice-chairman, under the provisions of Section 8 of the 1953 Act, also must have had legal training.

Opinions issued by the Board and currently published in PKF are judicial in appearance and character. Though the Board lacks the power to prohibit restraints of competition, its decisions are final and may not be appealed. This finality applies as well to decisions refusing applications for derogations from the prohibitions of resale-price maintenance and tender cartels.

Prior to the publication of PKF, Board opinions were published in Näringsfrihetsfrågor (Freedom of Commerce Questions, NFF).

1. LEGISLATIVE PROHIBITIONS AND EXEMPTIONS

Swedish law prohibits only two restraints on competition—vertical resale-price maintenance and tender cartels. Neither prohibition is absolute and it is within the province of the Freedom of Commerce Board to permit exemptions from the operation of the prohibitions. Horizontal price fixing is within the jurisdiction of the Board and is prohibited only when it has a vertical effect.

a. Prohibition of resale-price maintenance

The practice of resale-price maintenance in Sweden became widespread in the early 1920's, at a time when the trend was toward the increased distribution of trademarked goods. Initially manufacturers of trademarked goods merely announced a price and then sold their products to retailers at a cost which generally allowed a 30 per cent profit on the announced price. Because retailers soon wanted higher profit margins and greater protection against competition, they organized in the mid-Twenties and called on manufacturers to discuss prices and profit margins. Not all manufacturers were happy with the price policies dictated by retailers, and some evidence suggests—for example, the statements made by the Federation of Swedish Industries—that the 1953 legislation banning resale-price maintenance reflects this dissatisfaction. Furthermore, after World War II Sweden saw the evolution of new modes of distribution that cut across traditional commodity and trade lines. Thus, previously established profit margins based on traditional overhead concepts lost their meaning at the retail level. These are some of the forces that led to the ban on resale-price maintenance.

Another force of considerable political and economic impact was the central body of the cooperative movement, Kooperativa Förbundet. The consumers' cooperatives with 3,000 retail stores and their allied producers' cooperatives had long preached against resale-price maintenance, and the rebates on purchases by members were, in fact, contrary to the price-maintenance schemes. However, rebate rates of about 3 per cent were generally ignored by manufacturers. The producers' coops set maximum prices, such as those set for margarine in 1921, but which in the majority of cases were obeyed as minimum prices. Although forced to operate close to the maintained price level, the Kooperativa Förbundet, as a tenet of faith, continually opposed resale-price maintenance. Prior to 1953, resale-price maintenance covered about one-third of all foodstuffs and housewares sold at retail in Sweden.

Maximum prices have always been legal in Sweden, and in the majority of cases they are also treated as minimum prices. Vertical fixing of resale prices is now prohibited under the terms of Section 2 of the 1953 Act, which also gives the Board power to grant exemptions. A derogation may be granted on a showing that a fixed minimum price will benefit the consumer through lower prices or will otherwise contribute to the public interest. Section 4 further permits a derogation on the strength of what it denominates as special reasons.

1. EXEMPTIONS REFUSED. From its creation in 1954 through 1960, the Board has passed on twelve requests for exemptions from the ban on resale-price maintenance and has refused six. The commodities involved in the unsuccessful application are corsets and brassières (Näringsfrihetsfrågor 1955 [NFF], No. 2, Case 1); contraceptives (NFF 1955, No. 2, Case 4); radio receivers (NFF 1955, No. 2, Case 5); margarine (NFF 1955, No. 2, Case 9); paper patterns (NFF 1955, No. 2, Case 10); and water (NFF 1955, No. 6, Case 19).

The applicants requesting exemptions for radio receivers, who individually and through an association represented almost all of the importers and domestic manufacturers of radio sets, advanced the argument that lack of fixed resale prices would lead to price competition injurious to the consumer. The alleged consumer's injury would be in the form of poorer service that would flow from the reductions in profit margins at retail. This argument was not accepted by the Board.

In both the radio and contraceptive cases the argument was also made that some injury might accrue to manufacturers because without price control some retailers might charge more than the recommended price. The Board, not willing to accept this argument, noted that the right to fix maximum prices still rests with the manufacturer and that he may exercise this right.

Other arguments made to the Board and rejected are those against loss leaders and predatory price cutting. The Board has not found substance in such arguments sufficient to warrant an exemption.

2. EXEMPTIONS GRANTED. The six exemptions that have been granted from the ban on resale-price maintenance represent three commodities, each of which has won a renewal on its exemption: sheet music (NFF 1955, No. 2, Case 8; NFF 1955, No. 6, Case 21; PKF 1958, No. 6/7, Case 6); books (NFF 1955, No. 2, Case 8; NFF 1955, No. 6, Case 20; PKF 1958, No. 6/7, Case 5); and newspapers (PKF 1959, No. 5, Case 6; PKF 1960, No. 6, Case 4). Acting in its capacity as advisor to government departments, the Board has also given its approval to price fixing in the trade in Baltic herring (NFF 1955, No. 2, Case 6; NFF 1956, No. 6, Notice 1; PKF 1959, No. 1, Case 15; PKF 1960, No. 1, Case 14; PKF 1960, No. 9, Case 9).

The exemptions have been granted with conditions designed to eliminate other restraints on trade whose effects might be amplified if resale-price maintenance were not permitted. One such condition is the placing of a maximum price ceiling on certain low-priced books sold in ordinary shops. In all cases some social good was thought to be accomplished by the granting of the exemption.

As we have seen, the case for exemption for books has also successfully been made in Norway and Denmark. In general the view is that the maintaining of profit margins on popular books will enable the subsidization of less popular books that are both culturally and socially desirable. Moreover, the rather limited market for books in the Swedish, Danish, and Norwegian languages outside each of the relatively small countries makes it imperative that a sound book publishing and book retail trade be maintained.

The government's objective in granting an exemption to the book trade is to ensure the economic feasibility of the publication and stocking of books of high quality for which demand may be limited. If the number of published titles is a valid index, the rate of annual increase in Sweden indicates that the policy has succeeded. The sheet-music exemption is justified on grounds similar to those applicable to book publishing.

The special exemption for newspapers is for an experimental form of distribution in the southwest region of Sweden around Malmö. The intention is to provide wider distribution of newspapers and to encourage news dealers by improving return privileges. This trial form entails a degree of cooperation as to resale prices which is justified if it improves the availability of newspapers in the district.

The Baltic herring exemption is a reflection of the protection given to fishing activities and of the problems of a seasonal and risky business.

3. THE EFFECT. The evidence that the ban on resale-price maintenance has been effective is to be found in the competitive prices of consumer goods that are necessities. Various new forms of marketing have been introduced. A Swedish housewife may now do her supermarket shopping entirely by telephone. The goods are delivered at discount prices that are often below those charged by the consumer cooperatives, and the evidence of price competition in consumer goods is clear. The picture is less clear in other lines though a study made in 1958 of the technical-chemical products sold to consumers, such as waxes, polishes, cosmetics, and dentifrices, showed smaller retail profit margins and lower consumer prices after the ban on vertical price fixing (PKF 1958, No. 8, p. 501).

Generally the S.P.K. studies of recommended prices since 1955 have shown that in many lines the recommended prices on trademarked goods are the actual selling prices, with some regional variations which normally reflect higher rates of price deviation in Stockholm.

Based on reports appearing in Pris- och Kartellfrågor from 1957 through 1961, Table 9 reflects the general degree of observance of recommended prices. It is understood that all recommendations, pursuant to law, are made with the statement that one is free to sell at a lower price. The recommended price may and does appear in advertising.

The percentages reflect the amount of the total volume of business —in both trademarked and not trademarked goods and in services— done at prices recommended by the manufacturer, trade association, or importer.

TABLE 9: OBSERVANCE OF SUGGESTED PRICES SINCE 1955

0%	1–10%	21–30%	31–40%
Hearing aids Cash sales of radio and TV sets	Leather clothing	Men's shoes Men's trousers Ski pants Men's shirts	Cotton clothing Ladies' hose

61–70%	81–90%	91–100%
Sport coats Branded foods	Shoes generally Socks Underwear Outerwear	Optical goods Woolen ready-made clothing Motor-scooter spare parts Credit sales of radio and TV sets Driving school instruction Bread and rolls

4. HORIZONTAL PRICE FIXING. The Board's most recent opinion concerning the hardware trade made it clear that within limitations, as reflected in the negotiations, a trade association with 950 members and 16 local organizations may issue a catalogue with 40,000 recommended prices—for example, 9,000 for screws and 2,500–3,000 for bolts and nails (PKF 1961, No. 5, Cases 4 and 5).

The view of the Board was that, with the multiplicity of items that a hardware dealer must carry, the catalogue served a useful function in leading to rational practices on the dealer's part. Nevertheless, the Board negotiated an agreement to end the practice of depriving members of the right to use the catalogue if they sold below the recommended prices.

In contrast to this view of the Board are two opinions of the Commissioner concerning catalogues in the brick and the tile industries. These catalogues were issued by the trade associations, whose agreements are registered in the Cartel Register, Register No. 1742 for bricks, and Register No. 1773 for tiles. The tile association, representing about half of the industry, agreed to stop its price catalogue on the strength of the Commissioner's view that the printing and use of the catalogue was probably inconsistent with the 1953 Act. However, the Commissioner dropped the complaint against the brick-industry trade association, noting that only 15–20 per cent of the trade was involved. He was influenced also by testimony that, despite the catalogue, there was no price cooperation (PKF 1961, No. 2, p. 128).

The decision in the hardware case was made after the Commissioner had considered the brick and tile industries. At this time one cannot say whether the tile decision will eventually be reversed. Horizontal price fixing with a definite vertical effect is subject to control; otherwise it is not banned.

b. Prohibition of bidding or tender cartels

The second of the two forms of restraints of trade prohibited by the 1953 Act is the bidding or tender cartel. Again the Board has power to grant an exemption under the provisions of Section 4, and as in all other cases its ruling may not be appealed.

The specific practice banned by Section 3 is the entering into or the carrying out of an agreement requiring consultation or other forms of cooperation among entrepreneurs before any of them bid on a contract to supply a commodity or a service.

The classic Swedish tender cartel, which is the target of the ban, operated through some form of central office or agency, often in a trade association. This office served as a clandestine clearing house for exchange of price-list information between members of the cartel. The office administered a rotation system, designed to give each cartel member a guaranteed share of all business obtained through bids.

When there was a contract to bid on, the central office advised the firm whose turn it was to get the contract of the amount to bid in order to be successful. Other members of the cartel would submit bids at higher prices. The scheme was kept hidden from the one asking for bids.

This practice led to higher than necessary prices and completely destroyed the competitive features of offering business on a bid basis. The results of tender cartels were determined to be incompatible with free enterprise and were therefore prohibited by legislation.

The legislation bars only agreements for regular consultation and it is silent as to individual instances of consultation before submitting a bid where no agreement is in effect. Further, it would seem that the prohibition does not reach bids made as a result of one consultation in the absence of an agreement to consult.

From 1954 through 1960 the Board has passed on five requests for exemptions from the ban on tender cartels and in each case an exemption or its equivalent has been granted.

The first request, coming from a group of retail grocers in a country district, asked permission to make an agreement to collaborate for the purpose of bidding to supply municipal institutions in that district. The argument made on behalf of the petitioners was that without this agreement they would be unable to bid individually, but with such an agreement they could bid against other existing individual larger suppliers and the cooperatives. In this instance the cartel was approved for three years because it was believed that competition would be enhanced and prices lowered (NFF 1955, No. 2, Case 13).

A similar petition by a butchers' association was granted on like grounds (NFF 1955, No. 6, Case 24).

Underwriters of aviation insurance were given an exemption on the theory that the costs to the public would in the long run be less if aviation-insurance resources and activities were pooled. In essence the idea of rationalization in risk sharing seemed to have some merit for the Board (NFF 1956, No. 5, Case 6).

Three meat marketers' associations petitioned the Board for permission to cooperate on a regular and effective basis in bidding to supply the Swedish Army with canned meats. No individual meat-marketing association alone could bid with ease on an entire contract, such as the Army normally opens to bidding. The petitioners argued that, if the exemption were granted, they could divide the filling of the order among themselves in a way that would ensure the best use of time, labor, and machinery. They claimed, further, that their cartel would assist in keeping prices, wages, and employment at optimum levels. The Commissioner and the Army supported the petition, and the Board granted an exemption for three years on the ground that the public interest would be well served by the tender cartel (PKF 1957, No. 2, Case 4).

In 1960 the Board issued a long opinion which passed on alternative requests from the Swedish Wool Manufacturers Marketing Association, a form of joint sales agency. The Association first pleaded that its relationship with the individual wool producers who created the Association did not come within the purview of Section 3 of the 1953 Act. However, if the Board were to find that the relationship was subject to Section 3, the Association wanted an exemption. The Board found that this section did not apply (PKF 1960, No. 9, Case 8).

At the heart of the Board's opinion was its finding that the producers, who accounted for a majority of the production of woolens, had given the Association the exclusive right to enter bids for the supplying of a large number of woolen products, including the exclusive right to bid on Army contracts. The exclusive agent was given authority to sell the products and to allocate orders among the producers. The independence of the entity in law and in fact was crucial in the Board's opinion.

The Board drew a distinction between a legal person given the task of bidding on behalf of the members and a legal person acting independently of the members, having been given the authority so to act. The Board interpreted the intent of Section 3 as being to reach clandestine bidding arrangements which were unknown to those to whom the bids were submitted. Section 3 thus did not apply in the wool case because the entire arrangement was out in the open.

One may infer that the Board is not too troubled by the concentration of economic power in a joint agency, and that it sees little danger of abuse of economic power when it is obvious or apparent that the bidding is the result of collaboration.

The Board, apparently not fully satisfied with its own decision, hedged it with a variety of safeguards. First, the Board said that its decision concerning nonapplicability of Section 3 did not mean immunity from a proceeding under Section 5 to determine whether the arrangement had harmful effects on competition. Presumably, if such a restraint of competition were found, Section 3 applied also. Second, the Board made it clear that it was prepared to distinguish between a bona fide, independent sales agency and a sham arrangement.

Thus, the relationship between a bona fide and independent sales agency and its creators is not within the purview of Section 3.

The guidelines are now fairly clear as to what is intended by the ban on tender cartels. In an industry that might be classed as an oligopoly, consultation on tenders on an *ad hoc* basis is permitted and may in fact continue as long as the parties trust each other. The case of the Swedish Wool Manufacturers Marketing Association has set the precedent for those desiring more formal protection against competition.

c. Enforcement of the bans on resale-price maintenance and tender cartels

Under Section 29 of the 1953 Act anyone attempting to enforce resale-price maintenance or to operate a tender cartel without an exemption may be penalized by fines or imprisonment. The procedure in cases where there has been a violation, under Section 31, is to have the public prosecutor bring an action in the regular courts at the request of the Commissioner for Freedom of Commerce or with his approval.

With the decision of the Board in the Swedish Wool Manufacturers Marketing Association as a precedent, the Commissioner would in similar cases be faced with the problem of whether to follow the Board's reasoning that such cases are not within the purview of Section 3 or to leave it to the courts' determination. It is this possibility of independent action by the Commissioner and the courts that raises some doubt as to the true value of the ruling by the Board in the wool case.

From 1954 through 1960 the Commissioner has referred thirty-five cases of criminal violation of Sections 2 and 3 of the 1953 Act to the public prosecutor. Some of the earlier cases may be viewed as test cases in which the maintenance of retail prices on imported goods pursuant to a contract with a foreign supplier was tested. In such cases the rule was that such contracts violated the *ordre publique* of Sweden and were hence not enforceable. Almost all of the thirty-five cases have involved resale-price–maintenance violations, and the peak year was 1957 with eighteen cases, all involving price fixing. One of the four cases in 1960 involved a tender cartel.

Violations of the prohibition on resale-price maintenance are sometimes brought to light in the course of the investigation and presentation of refusal-to-deal cases before the Freedom of Commerce Board. In one case a German manufacturer of HO-gauge electric trains and accessories bound his general import agent in Sweden to an agreement ensuring that his catalogue retail prices would be obeyed. A retailer who had been refused supplies because he cut prices complained. When the agent learned that the Commissioner had brought the retailer's case to the Board, he promptly offered to supply the retailer. Nevertheless, the agent was convicted of having violated the ban on vertical price fixing (PKF 1958, No. 4, Case 4).

In an economy as active as that of Sweden and with a public educated to ferret out price fixing, the total of prosecutions is remarkably small.

2. NEGOTIATIONS TO ELIMINATE RESTRAINTS ON COMPETITION

The Freedom of Commerce Board is entrusted, by operation of Sections 1 and 5 of the 1953 Act, with the duty to determine in a given

case, brought by either the Commissioner or by a private party under
the provisions of Section 16, whether a restraint of competition with
harmful effects as defined in Section 5 is in existence. If the Board,
following the procedures established by Sections 15 through 25, finds
such a restraint of competition, it may order that negotiations take
place either before the Board or in minor cases in the presence of
the Chairman of the Board. Generally all proceedings of the Board
are public.

The Board does not have the power to order parties to take action
in the event negotiation fails to bring results. However, there is a
degree of reserve power in Section 21. It empowers the King in
Council, after the failure of negotiations and upon the request of the
Board, to impose a maximum price on the goods in question for one
year. This reserve authority has not been exercised. Thus, we may
conclude that the Board is satisfied that negotiations have not failed
in the major cases.

In the period 1954–1960 the Board had forty-one requests asking
it to determine the existence of a restraint of competition. In twenty-
one cases the restraint, which had been the subject of the complaint,
was eliminated prior to a decision by the Board. The Board dismissed
twelve cases as not evidencing a harmful restraint or a matter within
its competence, and it had a backlog of two cases awaiting decision.
The balance of six cases are those in which negotiations were requested and obtained.

Not every restrictive trade practice or restraint of trade reaches the
level of the statutory concept of restraint of competition in Section 5
of the 1953 Act. Thus, reasonable restraints, along with exemptions
to the Act, are permissible. Only those practices which the Board
denominates as restraints of competition are subject to its authority
to order negotiation for the purpose of termination of such restraints.

By definition a restraint of competition must have harmful effects
and must be contrary to the public interest. The statute has been interpreted to mean that both elements are necessary in finding adversely to a practice.

a. Harmful in effect

Section 5 provides the criteria for determining whether the effects
are harmful. Three conditions are listed which are deemed to indicate individually the existence of harmful effects: unduly affecting
the formation of prices, restraining business productivity, or imped-

ing or preventing the trade of others. The proof of any or a combination of these three elements will mean a finding of harmful effects and then it must further be determined that the harmful effect is contrary to the public interest, if the Board is to order negotiation for the purpose of terminating the restraint.

The high degree of selectivity that flows from the definition is evidenced by the relatively few cases, less than six a year on the average, that are filed with the Board.

1. ON PRICE FORMATION. In 1946 a group of experts was formed into a special governmental body, the Commission on Freedom of Entry, for the purpose initially of examining freedom-of-entry problems. Later it was entrusted with the task of drafting legislation for the control of restraints of competition, which in turn led to a comprehensive report filed in 1951 upon which much of the 1953 Act was based. The 1956 amendments to the Act stem from the 1955 report made by another commission established in 1954 to study price-control problems.

The Commission on Freedom of Entry found that harmful restraints of trade caused abnormally high prices. The Commission suggested that it was possible to determine through calculation the presence or absence of an unduly high price, and hence a restraint, by obtaining the ratio between net profit and the enterprise's invested capital funds and invested reserves. This concept of net profit included what is termed "hidden profits," and the valuation of invested funds and reserves was to be made on a replacement basis. The Commission further suggested that in determining the fairness of cartel-established prices one should compare prices for the same goods in those localities or countries where competition existed.

Both methods of calculating whether prices were too high and hence harmful were rejected when it came to the point of enacting the 1953 Act. It has been left to the Freedom of Commerce Board to develop its own view of whether a restraint has unduly affected the formation of prices so as to constitute a harmful effect, but the Board has seldom decided such cases. Mere price rigidity or horizontal price agreements are not in themselves sufficient to constitute the restraint of competition. Thus a horizontal price agreement between a Swedish manufacturer of goods and importers of the same goods whereby the Swedish manufacturer is prevented from offering discounts based on cost savings is not likely to be treated as a restraint of competition with harmful effects contrary to the public interest.

2. ON BUSINESS PRODUCTIVITY. A restraint on business productivity constitutes a harmful effect because it leads to impaired efficiency. The concept was intended to be applied only in a limited number of cases. In short the target was cartels which protected the inefficient producer or seller. In the view of the Commission on Freedom of Entry the legislation should indicate that a shortage of supply of goods was evidence of a hampering of efficiency. The Commission's recommendation was not incorporated in the 1953 Act. It was the view of some legislators that the proposition—a shortage of supply is evidence of inefficiency—was common knowledge and therefore superfluous. Thus it was omitted from the 1953 Act.

One of the few cases dealing with the question of efficiency and of a restraint on business productivity involved also the separate question of whether the formation of prices was affected. The Board was faced with a cartel agreement dividing sales territories for beer and soft drinks in the far northern reaches of Sweden, Lappland, and Norrbotten, which are sparsely settled areas with relatively long distances between settlements. The Board said that in theory and in principle it opposed such market-sharing agreements, but it found that this agreement was not harmful because the division resulted in prices no higher than in those districts where markets were not divided. Thus, in light of the costly transportation in the area, one could find that prices had in fact been lowered through the cartel agreement. The Board found that neither was efficiency of business impaired nor was the formation of prices adversely affected (PKF 1957, No. 2, Case 1).

Among the reasons ascribed for the relative scarcity of cases in this category is the publicity given to such cartel arrangements, and in turn the reaction of the public, which has served to limit drastically the number of cartels that could fall under the provisions of Section 5. Those cartel agreements that promote rationalization and specialization are not likely to be considered within this context.

3. ON FREEDOM TO TRADE. Impediments to trade is the major category into which the vast majority of Board cases fall. It encompasses issues arising from refusals to sell and limitations on freedom of entry. The Commission on Freedom of Entry considered this to be the key provision of the legislation for it reflected the existence of the very problems that afflicted free enterprise. The correctness of this view is attested by the work load of the Board.

a. New forms of distribution. The emergence in Sweden of new

forms of distribution has resulted in pressures from traditional retailers on suppliers to refuse to deal with the newcomers. Among the
new modes of distribution is the telephone-retailer who receives orders for groceries, produce, and usual supermarket items on the phone
and then delivers. Deliveries can be scheduled for evening hours for
those who work. The retailer's prices with such a service, taking into
account the minimum size of an order, may run less than those of the
consumers' cooperatives.

The Freedom of Commerce Board deems the emergence of new
and cheaper forms of distribution essential and recognizes that a full
opportunity for experimentation is essential to the strength of the
Swedish economy. In order to avoid the possibility of retailer reprisals
against a few suppliers utilizing the new modes of distribution, the
Board has sought through negotiations to assure that each wholesaler
bears an equal burden, so that no wholesaler will suffer a boycott
from traditional retailers. One example of such a case involves the
refusal to deal with Sparköp of Sundsvall (PKF 1959, No. 1, Case 14;
negotiations reported: PKF 1959, No. 4, Case 5).

Ordinary discounting of prices is another form of distribution that
the Board deems worthy of the chance to prove itself. Thus, a manufacturer who refused to sell wallpaper to a discounter, ostensibly because he wanted to limit the number of retailers, but actually because
of pressure from competitors of the discounter, was found to be re-
restraining competition with harmful effects. The Board found his
refusal to be contrary to the public interest. Through negotiations the
manufacturer agreed to deliver to another store owned by the discounter, from which he could then deliver to his cut-rate establishment (PKF 1957, No. 9, Case 10; negotiations reported: PKF 1958,
No. 9, Case 7).

On the other hand, not every new form of distribution is entitled,
in the view of the Board, to the benefit of its intervention. In various
communities civil servants, or other groups with something in common, have joined together in purchasing societies which are designed
to lower the costs of distribution to the closed membership of the
society. Refusals to supply such purchasing societies are not considered incompatible with the public interest, as the membership in
the society is limited and not open to the public. If the societies were
open to the public, the Board has indicated that it would take a different view. This matter has been explored in two cases (PKF 1959,
No. 3, Case 2; PKF 1960, No. 4, Case 3).

b. Legitimate refusals to deal. The Board's interest in making it possible for newcomers to enter a trade is not a reason for it to discourage the prudence and good judgment of suppliers. An ex-convict, whose conviction had related to sharp practices in the automobile trade, was not entitled to demand supplies when he entered the telephone-home-delivery grocery trade. After the Commissioner refused to bring the case to the Board, the complainant brought it forward on his own initiative. The Board recognized that the ex-convict's attempt to enter the discount grocery trade was a factor in the suppliers' refusing to deal. However, the validity of the personal objections was considered to be worthy of primary recognition, and the restraint was found to be lacking in harmful effects (PKF 1958, No. 10, Case 11).

In the course of determining that a refusal to deal is not a restraint of competition with harmful effects, the Board makes a full study of the conditions surrounding the alleged restraint. Thus, in determining that a refusal to sell repair parts for business machines was based on the need for technical competence on the part of the repairers, the Board also inquired into the level of prices and the monopoly conditions in the trade. It found that prices were reasonable, that monopoly power was not abused, and the rational and technical organization of the trade provided benefits that exceeded any possible restraint (PKF 1958, No. 2, Case 1).

Other refusals have been permitted when the matter involved was not of great public significance or where the quantity of trade or the nature of the outlet did not justify supplying the complainant. The Board in general seeks to preserve freedom of choice on the part of suppliers when the refusals are rational, rather than arbitrary, when they reflect sound business judgment, and when they do not impede the public interest in fostering competition (PKF 1959, No. 6, Case 9; PKF 1960, No. 6, Case 5).

c. Concentrations of economic power. One of the more difficult problems with which the Board has been faced arose in the complex of arrangements tying the advertising agencies to the newspaper publishers. These long standing arrangements were the subject of Board concern from the time of its opinion in June of 1956 (NFF 1956, No. 6, Case 9) to the conclusion of negotiations announced in March of 1958 (PKF 1958, No. 4, Case 5).

The Swedish Newspapers Publishers Association entered into an agreement with certain advertising agencies which were treated under the agreement as the only agencies authorized to place advertising in the newspapers and to receive commissions. The authorized agencies were those that met certain standards established by the publishers as to professional competence and financial stability. Only authorized agencies could receive a commission from the newspapers on placing advertising, except for locally placed small advertising. No rebates to advertisers were permitted but fee splitting with consultants was allowed.

An emphasized part of the arrangement was the freedom of the individual newspaper to establish its own across-the-board rate schedule, from which no individual deviations were allowed and which had to be published.

The basic complaint was from advertising agencies which were not accepted by the publishers but which wanted to place advertising. They could not be compensated by the newspapers for their work and thus argued that their freedom to enter the business was restricted. Large advertisers with their own publicity departments having prepared all of the materials were unable to realize any of the economies to which they felt they were entitled.

The Board found that the entire scheme was in restraint of trade and contrary to the public policy. All three harmful effects were found to be individually present in the arrangement. However, that part of the agreement that related to the newspapers' freedom to establish a general rate scale and the prohibition of individual discounts was not attacked.

The newspaper publishers argued that the arrangement was essential to maintain business on an orderly basis. They further argued that without such arrangements small newspapers would be at the mercy of big advertisers and the free press would be in danger.

The negotiations resulted in a compromise agreement under which the financial qualifications and standards that had to be met to qualify as an authorized agency would be readjusted through the findings of an impartial board. For those advertisers who wished to place their own advertising directly, without the use of an agency, a central office was created. The commission that the publishers would give this office would be less than that given to the agencies on the theory that the functions of the office would be fewer than those of an agency. The advertisers operating through the central office would receive, after the office paid regular dividends on the capital stock and after taxes, a proportionate share of the central office's net profit.

This arrangement did not entirely please the advertisers who felt that they should be able to exercise control over the central office. The Board, however, felt that the entire arrangement should be tested before any attempt to make further alterations. At this writing the "test" continues.

d. Monopolies. Sweden has only one sugar refiner and this enterprise prior to 1956 sold only through wholesalers. Hemköp, one of the originators of the telephone-and-delivery form of distributing groceries, purchased quantities of sugar greater than those ordered by many wholesalers, but it had to buy through wholesalers under the refiner's terms of doing business. Hemköp, enlisting the aid of the Commissioner, complained before the Board that the monopoly's discrimination in failing to give retailers their deserved discount impeded trade and the development of new forms of retailing. Before the Board came to its decision, the refiner agreed to sell directly to retailers at wholesale prices if their purchases were sufficiently large (NFF 1956, No. 6, Case 10). Thus, the principle may have been established that a mere functional discount may not be maintained when other dealers enter the field and otherwise qualify. Only a Board decision can determine the actual existence of such a principle.

Monopolies exist in purchasing as well as in selling. In another case a municipality controlled the solely licensed distributor of beer for resale in shops. It was found to be discriminating by its refusal to allow the distributor to buy beer from one of three breweries capable of delivering in the district. The municipal authorities argued that restricting the supply to only two sources was necessary to its policy of promoting temperance through the sale of beer at no profit to the distributor. The Board found that the restriction was inconsistent with the temperance objectives and did not further them, and that the restriction was contrary to public policy. The negotiations following the Board's finding resulted in the excluded brewery being given permission to deliver to those shops which wished to sell its products (PKF 1959, No. 3, Case 1; PKF 1960, No. 2, Case 1).

Bottled goods play a large part in the "jurisprudence" of the Freedom of Commerce Board. Another monopoly case concerned the sole manufacturer of a malt liquor—porter, a dark brew with a sweet flavor. The brewer of porter had arranged for distribution through a number of breweries that would serve to resell porter along with their other products. A brewery complained that it had been discriminated against in not being allowed to resell porter. The defense was that a selective selling scheme was necessary, and that one reseller of porter was already in the district where the complainant did business. The Commissioner indicated that the complainant had need of the porter to complete his line, and that the system of distribution would not suffer if the complainant were added. The brewer of porter complied and before the opinion of the Board came down, the agreement to deliver was reached (PKF 1957, No. 2, Case 5).

The outcome of the porter case may be a factor in the development of a novel policy by the Swedish government as demonstrated in the treatment of problems arising in the distribution of Coca-Cola, discussed in the case studies.

e. Regulated trades. Dentistry in Sweden is subject to government licensing, and most dentists are members of a trade association. Before this association was brought to the attention of the Board, it barred from membership those professionals operating clinics which employed several dentists as well as dentists with branch offices. The bar extended also to dental surgeons who worked in clinics with other dentists or who worked in a dentist's branch office. This means of preserving the individual practice of dentistry was designed, according to the association, to protect the public against unqualified dentists. The Freedom of Commerce Board found that in actuality the restrictions made it difficult, if not impossible, for clinics to obtain dentists. Consequently, economies and technical advantages to be derived from a group practice were withheld from the public, and hence the restrictive practice impeded the progress of the profession and was contrary to the public interest. The Board also noted that the public was protected by the governmental licensing authorities, that the people would continue to be so protected, and that it saw no apparent need to supersede such authorities (PKF 1958, No. 2, Case 2).

The resulting negotiations led to a compromise in which membership was open to those practicing with other dentists in a clinic, as long as the term "clinic" was not used. Furthermore, the dentists working in a branch office and those having a branch practice were accepted to membership if the main office and the branch were located within the geographic area of one local dental association or, at the most, within the districts served by two local associations (PKF 1960, No. 1, Case 13).

f. Exceptions. The Board has had no case involving the question of what restraints of competition may be permitted when related to a patent. The Commissioner of Freedom of Commerce has dealt with the issue on a hypothetical basis. On the strength of some of the comments accompanying the legislation which became the 1953 Act, the Commissioner expressed in a short note the view that the use of the patent as a lever for restrictions that do not naturally flow from the monopoly would probably be considered a restraint (PKF 1959, No. 1, Case 19).

Trademarks have been the subject of the Board's scrutiny and of opinions from the Commissioner in cases concerning orange-flavored soft drinks. Twice the Commissioner has refused to take a case involving trademarked soft drinks before the Board. In both situations the availability of the extract to the bottler-complainant, albeit without the right to use the trademark, was given greater weight than the question of whether a trademark license intrinsically deserved protection (NFF 1955, No. 2, Case 7; PKF 1957, No. 2, Case 5).

A third complaint concerning the trademark policy involved in the orange–drink controversy led the Commissioner to bring a case before the Board. The resulting decision, according to some commentators, established the rights of a trademark owner on a firm basis. As in the earlier cases, the bottler who was refused the right to sell under the trademark was allowed to purchase the extract and manufacture the identical drink for sale under a different mark. The Commissioner took the position that a trademark owner had a right to use his mark as he pleased, so long as he did not use his mark to prevent competition between those in the same business. The concept of competition, in the view of the Commissioner, embodies the thesis that all who enter a trade should have an equal opportunity to sell the same products.

The Board took the position that it could not apply the concept of restraint of competition to trademarks or to trademark licenses, even though the licenses were not specifically recognized in the trademark statute. Even in cases where there are many licensees—two hundred were in this one—a licensor who does not use his mark as a lever to cause restraints of competition will be permitted to choose his licensees. The Board's view was that it could not touch normal restraints derived from the operation of the trademark law without special legislation (PKF 1959, No. 6, Case 8).

It would appear from the discussion of Coca-Cola at the end of the case studies that the Board's view is not completely accepted by all of the other authorities concerned with the control of restraints of competition.

Finally, it has been determined that transactions involving real estate, although not now listed as exempt in Section 28 of the Act, are in fact outside the purview of the Act according to the Board (PKF 1959, No. 9/10, Case 10). The Board cited the unamended text of Sections 1, 5, and 25 of the 1953 Act and found that the present ambiguity was derived from the 1956 amendments. Thus, it decided that the legislative intention was to exempt real estate transactions.

b. Contrary to the public interest

The public interest, as it is interpreted in the Board's decisions—particularly in the Swedish Newspapers Publishers Association opinion —is neither a moral nor an ethical issue. In the view of the Commission on Freedom of Entry, the Board is responsible for noting social conditions that justify or excuse the restraint and is in the position of weighing the social consequences of allowing a particular restrictive practice. Unless the Board finds a practice to be contrary to the public interest, it has no basis for ordering that negotiations be undertaken.

As an example, the Commission noted that, although patents may result in higher prices for goods, the social benefits of the patent system outweigh the disadvantages of a higher price. The Commission found that subsidies to agriculture put the State in the position of raising food prices, but emphasized that the social gains to the farmers outweigh the loss to the consumer. Thus, the public interest is purely a policy concept.

The decisions of the Board indicate that it considers boycotts, restrictions on freedom of entry, and abuse of monopoly power to be practices lacking in public interest. The legislation calls upon the Board to apply Kant's categorical imperative to economic and legal questions.

The Board's apparent success in applying a vague test is in part attributable to the variety of experience and expertise that its members bring to its work. The members of the Board in their ordinary duties have opportunities to keep abreast of new problems and current views relating to restrictive practices. The Board or its Chairman give opinions to the government and to international bodies on matters ranging from suggestions for legislation to problems of traffic. Probably not the least of the Board's assets is its staff of exceptional civil servants who, though few in number, are among the most able to be found anywhere.

D. Evaluations of the success of the Swedish legislation

The official Swedish view is that at the present time the legislation is successful in reaching the policy objectives of the government. Thus, a proposal for further legislation, similar to the Robinson-Patman Act in the United States, was not approved by the Freedom of Commerce Board and not passed by the legislature in 1960 (PKF 1960, No. 2, p. 131). The Commissioner and the State Price and Cartel Office also opposed the amendments.

One leading member of the Swedish Bar was of the opinion in 1958 that the legislative system, at least as interpreted by the Freedom of Commerce Board, had brought the full application of the rule of reason to Sweden, although he added that the rule was not as fully utilized in the United States, its country of origin.

One of the Swedish representatives to an international organization gave in 1960 his view of the registration and publication features of the Swedish legislation:

It is obvious that the registration and publication of agreements have considerably contributed to many agreements being abolished or amended. The Cartel Register has also been a valuable source of information for the Commissioner for Freedom of Commerce and, after the intervention of this official, a number of registered agreements have either been abolished or modified to a marked extent. . . . the largest trade organizations have actively promoted the voluntary abolition of such agreements as might be expected to have harmful effects. This voluntary action has been of considerable significance.

As one result of the emphasis on publicity, the representatives of American enterprises are noticeably more willing to speak frankly about their views of the Swedish method of control of restrictive trade practices. One spokesman for a widely held American view stated in 1960:

As for the publicity aspect, which for the time being is the only sanction in Sweden of restrictive practices not specifically prohibited by the existing legislation, I believe it works in a most unfair manner inasmuch as no distinction is made between what we would call in America "ancillary restrictions of trade" which are within the permissive area of American antitrust legislation and other restrictions which are deemed to be harmful. Indeed, one can find instances in which ancillary restrictions are beneficial to competition.

The Swedish legislative provisions apply indiscriminately to practically every kind of arrangement including those which might only remotely result in some restriction on freedom of trade. Thus "fringe" restrictions and ancillaries are subject to registration.

Originally, as may be seen from the Parliamentary debates preceding the adoption of the Swedish legislation, the publicity feature of the registration of restrictive agreements was designed to deter private parties from entering into such arrangements. It is clear that an ordinary member of the public cannot distinguish which kinds of arrangements are desirable or at least harmless, and which kinds of arrangements are harmful to the consumer. The Cartel Register in Sweden thus becomes a sort of black list which unfortunately, as the law stands now, contains not only those arrangements which are generally recognized as harmful restrictions of trade, but equally arrangements which may be considered in effect as restrictive purely as a by-product of the pursuance of an entirely legitimate and desirable business purpose.

With regard to the procedure, the complete absence of judicial review is deplorable because the entire administration of these laws is left to the executive branch of the government which is largely composed of "doctrinaire" elements, and it is practically hopeless to expect to obtain a reversal of a decision of the administrative agencies of the first instance. As to the procedure before the Free Trade Commissioner and the Free Trade Commission, the most striking feature is the complete absence of any power to apply sanctions.

The Free Trade Commissioner's primary function is to mediate between third party complainants and parties to restrictive arrangements. In addition, the Free Trade Commissioner, if he fails to mediate but concludes that there is merit in the third party complaints, then assumes the role and function of public prosecutor before the Free Trade Commission. The Commission has no power of decision and can only make recommendations. The result of this unusual procedural setup is that both the Free Trade Commissioner and the Free Trade Commission always have the tendency of applying whatever moral pressure is at their command towards the working out of a compromise, and this is done regardless of how right or how wrong the parties involved in the proceedings may be.

Another outspoken representative of an American manufacturing enterprise touched a different aspect of the Swedish legislation:

Price maintenance was permitted here earlier, and in 1926 a first attempt at uniform price maintenance was made by a group of Swedish manufacturers in our industry. This attempt broke down entirely, however, at the end of 1927 due to the lack of strong leadership.

In February of 1928, I started a new price maintenance system in Sweden for our company. I met with very stiff resistance during the first four months and, thereafter, on realizing the seriousness of our action and the great advantages that could be realized by all parties, we began to get recognition. We built up a complete price maintenance system tying in both retailers and jobbers.

My system was soon followed by most of the other leading Swedish manufacturers in our line of trade. It worked perfectly until socialistic-minded economists started to oppose it. After considerable discussion with the Swedish State Price Control Bureau all Swedish manufacturers voluntarily agreed to discontinue the system in 1954. Now no price maintenance systems are legally permissible in Sweden. Nothing indicates any trend toward new price maintenance in Sweden.

Finally, another American business representative reflected the degree of effectiveness of the Swedish legislation or at least the competition in his line of business by commenting on the state of his membership in the industry trade association:

The Swedish —— Machines Association has an agreement regarding pricing of standard —— machines in Sweden. We are members of that Association and we are connected to the price arrangement.

There are some companies in Sweden selling —— machines which are not members of the Association, and they are selling at low prices. In order to compete with them we must sell below the prices reported by us to the Association. This has caused some discussion with the Association.

The same business man also commented on the possible disadvantages that might accrue if his company withdrew from the Association: "We cannot see any disadvantages that are presently foreseeable except that it might mean that the prices for standard —— machines might become even lower than they are today."

On the basis of interviews with the managers of American enterprises in Sweden, one may conclude that complaints concerning the indiscriminate nature of the Swedish use of public opinion as a sanction were widespread. The feeling that price levels would drop if horizontal associations were ended was also common. However, most manufacturers have not mourned the demise of price maintenance in Sweden—except those who in one or two lines of trade have been consistent proponents of price maintenance, as is the case in most countries. Many manufacturers have found relief in not having to deal with retailer pressures designed to fix prices sufficiently high in order to ensure high retail profits.

As indicated by the subjects of the cases, the Board has expended its energies for the largest part on problems arising in the distribution of everyday consumer goods at the retail level. Its emphasis seems to be consistent with the interest and concern of the general public.

The old-line cartel agreements in basic goods seem to go on without much interference and with little public interest or comprehension of the effect of such agreements on the economy and competition. When the Commissioner either begins to receive complaints concerning production or obtains staff sufficient to do more than handle current complaints, he will undoubtedly initiate a scrutiny of the old-line production cartels.

III. THE ECONOMIC POWER OF THE KOOPERATIVA FÖRBUNDET: THE COOPERATIVE UNION

No APPRAISAL of the Swedish legislation for control of restraints on competition and of the competitive climate in Sweden is possible without recognizing the special role played by the Cooperative Union since its founding in 1899. No other cooperative movement in any country deserves comparable credit for shaping the competitive profile of the economy.

The Cooperative Union combines production, wholesaling, and consuming cooperatives into one organism. Our analysis of the Union's effect on Swedish competitive patterns emphasizes the producer cooperatives. The consumer cooperatives must be recognized, however, as being prime movers in efforts to keep retail prices at competitive levels.

A. Policy

The participation of the Cooperative Union in production is designed primarily to free consumer products of monopolistic or oligopolistic controls which foster abnormally high prices. The Union professes principles which are to be followed when entering production:

1. Industrial production by Union must be financed by the co-operative movement's own resources; it is better to refrain from entering a new sector of industry than to become indebted to third parties.

2. The fact that Union sells a sufficient quantity of a product to ensure that production would be profitable is not in itself sufficient reason for creating an industrial capacity under Union ownership.

3. Union should not undertake its own production except in those industries in which the cooperative movement has an immediate possibility of mounting an enterprise that at the least is as strong and as technically advanced as the first in the land. Union industrial production must always represent the latest in technology.

4. In its industrial development Union must concentrate all of its abilities and powers on one objective at a time. Only in such a fashion can the necessary internal solidarity and fidelity towards its own production be obtained and maintained in the cooperative movement. It is preferable to be superior to one's competitors in one line than to wear one's self out fighting one's competitors along several fronts and thus obtain only mediocre results.

5. Union should by preference produce those categories of merchandise which are basic necessities and which play a relatively important role in the household budgets of the members.

6. It is preferable that Union produce a relatively small number of articles for the mass of consumer-cooperators than a great number of articles for only a small number of members.

B. Fields of activity

For more than fifty years the Union has entered into the production of a variety of commodities. Generally Union has acted in a new field only after it became apparent that the cooperative movement would suffer from a continuation of the status quo.

The productive facilities of Union are organized as corporations and normally, but not always, the entire share capital is owned by the Union.

1. MARGARINE

Union's first battle set the pattern for the ensuing development of its production facilities. By 1908, nine years after its founding, the 100,-000 members of the cooperatives became a matter of concern to the major food cartels, and manufacturers throughout Sweden were asked to stop serving Union and its wholesaling agency, the Wholesale Society. The consequences of this request were that the traditional agent's commission for marketing of margarine, the right to sell soap on a commission basis, and the earned rebate from chocolate sales were refused Union and the Wholesale Society. The banks were asked to boycott the cooperative movement.

With a small membership and shaky finances Union turned to the public and asked it to boycott the two leading margarine manufacturers. The two producers then suffered a 20 per cent drop in sales, but Union did not consider the battle won. With proceeds from a bond issue floated among its members the Cooperative bought a small margarine factory with an initial capacity of only one-twenty-fifth of the national total. The purchase itself served to drive the cartel price down.

As a result of selectively boycotting the two largest producers, the public turned to the smaller producers who were also members of the cartel. Because the smaller members now had increased sales they, pursuant to the cartel agreement, had to pay the victims of the boycott and reimburse them for their loss of sales. This penalty for producing beyond the quota was not popular with the smaller manufacturers, so the cartel fell apart in 1911 when the agreement was up for renewal. Meanwhile Union, increasing its annual production by 500 per cent, enjoyed the resultant price competition. World War I halted competition.

In the postwar period the old cartel was reconstituted and the margarine price set for Sweden was between 20 and 25 per cent higher than that for neighboring Denmark. Union then erected a new and modern plant that went into operation in 1921. The cartel price of margarine plummeted from 2 kronor 70 öre per kilogram to one kronor 10 öre in a vain effort to drive Union out of business. However, the superior quality of the Cooperative Union's product and the guaranteed outlet provided by the cooperative stores assured that Union would stay in business. The cartel price went back up to 2 kronor 10 öre and Union sold at one kronor 70 öre. No further efforts have been made to dislodge Union, which currently controls about 25 per cent of the margarine production.

With the creation in 1929 of the world's largest international oil and soap organization with headquarters in Britain, Union feared that its margarine production might be terminated by a boycott of essential oils. As a means of ensuring its own production, Union purchased one of Sweden's two vegetable oil factories in 1932. The decision to buy rather than to create was in part dictated by the unwillingness to cause unemployment in the district where the existing factories were located. Moreover, the purchased factory was completely modernized. The vegetable oil factory raised policy problems because not all of its products and by-products could be marketed by consumer cooperatives. Some were marketed as animal feeds through agricultural cooperatives and some were exported. The products sold domestically gave Union a degree of control over private industry ranging from soap to animal feeds. During World War II Union supplied the majority of fats to the Swedish economy, and it served as the single source of supply for the private manufacturers in competition with it.

In 1961 the private margarine manufacturers regrouped in a new cartel agreement, Registration No. 1866, to divide the remaining market among themselves through a quota agreement. The true power to determine price conditions in margarine still rests with Union.

2. GRAIN MILLING

Flour milling was Union's target in 1922, and its entry into the field meant that in 1924 prices of all grades of flour turned downward despite rising costs.

Today Union controls better than 20 per cent of milling capacity. A cartel agreement has recently been concluded dividing the remaining market among the existing producers, Cartel Registration Nos. 1791 and 1792, registered in 1960. Here again Union, which is outside the cartel, is able to keep the consumer price competitive in the face of a market-sharing and quota agreement.

Oatmeal is a primary Swedish commodity. A ten-year cartel agreement was entered into in 1922, and the result was a long period of high prices for the Swedish consumer. Union built its own factory and went into production in 1929. As a result of its action, prices dropped approximately 20 per cent and the cartel terminated.

Today Union produces close to 25 per cent of the oatmeal. The other producers decided, as of July 1959, to establish a market division and quota cartel to last five years, Cartel Registration No. 1793. Of course, the presence of Union makes a horizontal price agreement unworkable.

3. RUBBER GOODS

Rubber shoes and boots were cartelized in Sweden beginning in 1911. At its annual Congress in 1926 Union decided to break this monopoly, and its members authorized another bond issue. The immediate response of the cartel was to drop the price of a pair of men's rubber boots by 27 per cent. The Cooperative Union continued in its resolve to get into the rubber business. Established factories then sought to sell out to Union and by the end of 1926 Union purchased one. Prices on boots continued to drop and finally stabilized at less than one-half of the price which obtained on the eve of Union's decision to enter the rubber business.

The increased competition in the industry meant an increase in employment of over 1,000 workers after Union entered the industry. Today Union's plant not only produces rubber boots, but it is also one of Sweden's big four in the production of automobile tires and accounts for almost 40 per cent of the domestic tire production. Union produces a full line of rubber goods, and the price level of its production ranges between 10 and 15 per cent under its competitors. There is no active current registration for an automobile-tire cartel.

4. LIGHT BULBS

The story of the development of LUMA, Union's answer to the light-bulb cartel, is legendary. Union, in accordance with basic policy, first asked the cartel in 1928 to reduce prices to a realistic level. When the cartel did not agree, Union announced that it would enter production and sell a twenty-five–watt bulb for 85 öre instead of the going price of one kronor 35 öre. Early in 1930, before Union's LUMA plant was in operation, the cartel price dropped 40 per cent. When LUMA entered production in 1931 it sold twenty-five–watt bulbs at 80 öre, a price which the cartel did not try to meet or undercut. LUMA opened factories to supply cooperatives in Norway at Oslo in 1934 and at Glasgow for the British market in 1937. Moreover, it joined forces with the international cartel on terms which gave it patent rights, but under which it retained the freedom to price as it wished in its distribution through cooperatives. However, by joining the cartel, LUMA gave up its right to cut prices in the private sector. Today it produces a third of all types of lighting devices sold in Sweden and serves as a principal supplier of the State and municipalities, while at the same time exporting primarily for consumption by cooperatives. At the present time no Swedish cartel registration involves light bulbs.

5. CASH REGISTERS

A major American maker of cash registers dominated the Swedish market until 1931. When Union began production, prices fell 60 per cent. Union, under the brand name Hugin, produced a machine specifically designed for the Swedish market, and it has been purchased widely outside the cooperative movement and exported. Cash registers are not directly a consumer item, but Union justified its entry into the field in terms of the importance of the machine to its cooperative shops, which were a prime market for exploitation by the high-priced imported registers.

6. CELLULOSE, SYNTHETICS, AND PAPER

Union is established also in cellulose-based industries—synthetic fabrics, textiles, and paper. With an enterprise which it established in 1931, Union began to produce a synthetic wool in 1935. With the coming of World War II, Sweden had only one rayon plant. To meet this monopoly, Union joined with 166 private textile manufacturers to set up their own production, with Union holding 50 per cent of the shares; and their factory turned out its first rayon in 1943. Paper production is based on the complex of forest, sawmills, and paper mills that Union purchased in 1942. In 1951 it began to manufacture cellophane.

7. DETERGENTS AND SOAP

The entry of Union into the soap and detergent fields in 1948 has kept Swedish soap and detergent sales at very competitive prices. Just prior to Union's starting production, the private manufacturers asked the government for permission to raise prices. A few months later with Union in production prices dropped 22 per cent. Today Union controls about 25 per cent of the production of detergents and soaps.

8. MISCELLANEOUS

Union in 1938 asked the monopoly producer of linoleum to reduce his price. Thereupon he did so by 15 per cent and the Union did not enter the field.

Union owns facilities for producing building materials such as sanitary china, heaters, plumbing, wallboard, pipe, and bricks. Other activities include participating in a waxpaper factory, manufacturing preserves and Swedish hard bread, producing superphosphate and nitrogen fertilizers for the Swedish Farmers Purchasing Association, preparing domestic charcoal, and importing coal. Union first began to manufacture major agricultural machinery in 1939. Petroleum, which will be discussed in the case studies, is also a major area of its activity.

C. Conclusion

Union is thus a major influence in the Swedish economy. Indeed, it may be the single greatest influence. Of Sweden's almost 2.4 million families about 1.3 million are cooperative society members. Through the consumer cooperatives Union accounts for fully a quarter of the Swedish retail trade. Union executives sit on the Freedom of Commerce Board, and Union experts serve on the various special governmental committees and commissions which examine problems of restraints on competition. A cardinal feature of Union policy has been to seek the enactment of strong laws designed to curb restraints and terminate monopolies. To this end, the Union continually presses for full and compulsory cartel registration and for laws designed to prevent discriminatory pricing not justified by economies in costs of production or distribution.

The Kooperativa Förbundet, though a major economic power, is not a political power of the same magnitude. The strong control legislation which it has advocated has not been enacted, and the history of Swedish legislation designed to control cartels discloses a considerable time lag between legislative proposals of the Kooperativa Förbundet and enactment.

Nevertheless, one must always reckon with the Union as a potential entrant into any field which it deems to be exploiting the Swedish consumer.

IV. CASE STUDIES OF AMERICAN FIRMS

A. Introduction

The response to questionnaires and requests for interviews in Sweden was by far the best obtained. Out of sixty-five questionnaires sent to American enterprises in Sweden there were forty replies. This same cooperation was reflected in the frankness of the interviews granted by the Swedish managers. No doubt this open approach is a direct result of the high degree of publicity attached to cartel problems in Sweden.

The question of whether publicity was an effective means of freeing competition in Sweden evoked an almost uniform negative response—thirty-seven "no's" and three "yes's." The majority of those replying said that they were not parties to agreements presently on the Cartel Register. There are fewer active registrations involving American enterprises in Sweden than one would expect on the basis of a study of Norwegian and Danish experience. In part the absence of compulsory registration is a factor. Because the Swedish case studies will provide an in-depth view of the problems faced by Coca-Cola, including the entire text of the State Price and Cartel Office public report, certain economies of space have been undertaken.

B. Farm machinery

Classic cartel agreement—Kooperativa Förbundet intervention—Government investigation—competitive conditions

A leader in farm-machinery production is American Firm 201. The industry has gradually moved from cartelization to competition under pressures from the market place and the Kooperativa Förbundet rather than under legislative pressures. The absence of a cartel registration does not have the same significance in Sweden as it does in Denmark and Norway. The present Cartel Register indicates that no agreements are in effect and this situation can be contrasted with Denmark where a variety of restrictions are of concern to the Danish government.

Another indication of the lack of restraints in the industry is the absence of State Price and Cartel Office reports or investigations of the industry. The Monopoly Investigation Bureau of the Board of Trade, the predecessor of the State Price and Cartel Office, published a report in Kartell Registret 1950 (No. 4/5) on the instruction of the government pursuant to a request by the Parliament. Since 1950 no government agency has published a report concerning restraints of competition in the industry.

The production of agricultural implements for both export and domestic purposes is a major Swedish industry dating back to the 1890's. The rate of growth may be seen in the fact that production trebled between 1932 and 1938 and then increased by 50 per cent of the 1938 figure by 1947. The rate of growth has since then been steady and can be measured by the use of tractors on farms of more than five acres; in 1945 30,000 tractors were used on such farms and in 1956 134,000 tractors were in use. Exports of farm machinery are at the rate of about 30 per cent of production.

The subsidiary of American Firm *201* participates in the Association of the Agricultural Machine Trade, which is made up of the eleven largest manufacturers. This group controls more than 75 per cent of the production of farm machinery, thereby overshadowing almost one hundred smaller and somewhat inconsequential firms. The Association dates back to 1907 and has been the subject of two cartel registrations, No. 70 of 16 May 1947, terminated 30 September 1947, and No. 214, registered 22 June 1948 and terminated 1 November 1950. These agreements provided for horizontal price fixing, vertical price fixing, and uniform discount systems. Each agreement was renewable annually, and the termination of the second agreement at about the time the report on the industry was published is not considered a coincidence.

Over the years the industry patterns of distribution have remained fairly static with variations developing from special agreements. Generally the eleven manufacturers have sold directly to dealers, while wholesalers have handled the distribution for the smaller firms. Although the Wholesale Society has generally distributed Kooperativa Förbundet's production, the cooperative-aligned National Federation of Swedish Farmers has purchased a large amount of goods directly.

Prior to the termination of Registration No. 214, the industry had set its gross prices each fall through agreements between manufacturers and wholesalers.

From 1907, the practice of the Association had been to set, during each autumn, the minimum gross prices and the terms of trade to be applied during the coming year. Price and term setting were accomplished through agreements between manufacturers and wholesalers. From 1935 to 1940 the discounts to be given to retailers were similarly set.

During this time there was an agreement between the manufacturers and wholesalers on the one hand and the Federation of Swedish Ironmongers on the other. This agreement gave the Ironmongers an extra discount in return for an undertaking to maintain prices and to sell only machines manufactured by the Association of the Agricultural Machine Trade. This agreement failed because of the conflict of interest created by the wish of some manufacturers to channel their trade directly through retailers rather than through the Ironmongers. One of those who made up the triumvirate dominating the market and seeking sales through direct agencies was the subsidiary of American Firm 201. The products principally involved were sowing and mowing machines, harvesters, and horse rakes.

The entrance of the Kooperativa Förbundet into the production of agricultural machinery in 1939 with its purchase of two factories was another reason for the cartel's failure in 1940. Closely allied with this purchase was the 1943 acquisition of a large factory by the National Federation of Swedish Farmers.

Other cartel agreements in which the members of the Association were also dominant covered harrows, drag rakes, cultivators, Cambridge rollers, and cake breakers. By 1950 once again very little of the trade in all types of agricultural machinery was free of price, discount, and preferential-term agreements except that part controlled by Union or the farmers' own organization.

The Monopoly Investigation Bureau found through an analysis of prices, costs, and rates of return in the 1930's that prices were determined by the various cartel agreements. These agreements fixed prices based on the costs of the most inefficient producers. The agreements, in addition to fixing price, also fixed production quotas and market shares, and the more efficient producers accepted the higher profit margin as compensation for not further expanding their markets. The cartel price policy and the complementary agreements with the wholesalers and Ironmongers also had an adverse effect on the smaller outside firms and on the possibilities of new firms coming into the industry.

The coming of World War II and the introduction of government price control changed the profit and pricing structure of the industry. Price increases were not granted to meet in full the increased costs, so the manufacturers had to exert an effort toward more efficient and rational production with fewer models and more standardized production. In the immediate postwar period, while price control continued, the export market provided the makers of farm machinery with higher profits than did the domestic market, and this tendency then engendered export controls limiting shipments of farm machinery. The rate of return on investment in farm machinery manu-

facture during the 1940's was a third less than it had been from
1935–1939.

The interlocking agreements between the Ironmongers and the
manufacturers came to an end at the beginning of 1950. The National
Federation of Swedish Farmers and the Kooperativa Förbundet as
producers and purchasers of farm machinery changed the modes of
distribution and rendered an arrangement such as that with the Ironmongers meaningless.

The cartel agreements have come to an end, though apparently
the trade association continues to exist with the major machinery
manufacturers as members. The public record would indicate that
the industry operates free of restraints on competition with a high
degree of price competition.

C. Toilet articles

Cartel agreement—Freedom of entry—Resale-price maintenance—Franchise—Refusal to deal—Commissioner's decision—Price
competition—Horizontal price fixing

American Firm 23 was a party to the agreement of April and June
1945, registered as No. 11 and known as "Kelifa." It terminated on 31
January 1950. The cartel encompassed the broad class of chemical-
technical, proprietary toilet articles and included all of the various
trade associations whose members dealt in such goods. Its objective
was to ensure that resale prices were maintained on a broad list of
trademarks. Of the twenty-four marks of foreign origin several were
the property of Firm 23.

The agreement established a governing board made up of representatives from the chemical-technical manufacturers' association,
the wholesalers' association, and the hairdressers' association. The
manufacturers involved totalled twenty-eight.

The governing board had the task of overseeing each trade association's policing of the various trademarks so as to ensure the observance of prices. The board also passed on whether one was
entitled to be treated as an authorized wholesaler, and of 263 applications it fully granted 56 and partly granted 26. This was both a
horizontal and vertical cartel.

The cumbersome organization could not withstand the pressure of
new distribution techniques, and the key feature of resale-price maintenance was rapidly falling into disrepute shortly before the 1953

Act, effective 1 July 1954, ended resale-price maintenance in Sweden. Both Firm 23 and Firm 25 participated in the various agreements designed to maintain the market in razor blades and allied lines. Cartel Registration No. 253 represents an agreement entered into in October 1948 and terminated in 1960, which began its existence as a means of ensuring that dealers in stainless-steel razor blades maintained resale prices. Actually by operation of law this agreement terminated when resale-price maintenance was banned on 1 July 1954, but the official termination date is given as 1960 by the State Price and Cartel Office. Agreement No. 256 commenced during August 1946 and ended in December 1949. It established a uniform discount system for the sale of safety razors and blades and placed a variety of restrictions on the modes of distribution including a ban on giving premiums for advertising purposes, such as gifts to customers. Firm 25 participated in Registration No. 251, a vertical and horizontal price-fixing agreement for razor blades. The agreement was made in December 1942 and terminated by operation of law on 1 July 1954, but here again the Cartel Register gives 1960 as the official termination date, despite a report giving the 1954 date (PKF 1958, No. 6/7, p. 365).

American Firm 21, which specializes in luxury-priced cosmetics for women and a high-priced line of men's toilet articles, was the subject of a complaint brought to the Commissioner. A Stockholm retail perfumer complained that it was denied delivery of the American firm's cosmetic line. Firm 21 admitted the discrimination and asserted that it maintained a selective form of distribution. The selection process required that retailers be able to perform a high degree of service, and to that end the supplier provided special courses for the retailers and their staffs. This training program was essential but costly, and the cost factor made it necessary to limit retailers in given trade areas. Inasmuch as a trained retailer was already in the complainant's trade area, the supplier had refused either to train or to deliver goods. The Commissioner found that the complainant had available alternate sources of supply for equally salable goods, and closed the case as not being suitable for presentation to the Board (PKF 1959, No. 7, Case 8). American Firm 21 is not recorded as ever being a party to a registered agreement.

The growth of competitive selling at the retail level has been a major factor in terminating the various restrictive arrangements in the toiletry, cosmetic, and soap industries. The fifth price list issued in September 1959 by Hemköp, the Stockholm telephone-home-delivery supermarket, reveals that articles bearing the trademarks of all those enterprises formerly involved in various registered agreements are for sale at prices which are less than the recommended prices by 10–19 per cent for shampoos, 20–32 per cent for razors and blades, 15–19 per cent for shaving creams, 5–30 per cent for shaving lotions, 6–11 per cent for bath soap, and 9–14 per cent for toothpaste.

The luxury articles carried by retail perfumers are not equally subject to price competition. Cartel Registration No. 1800 of 2 June 1960 discloses a horizontal agreement among 270 perfumers to maintain recommended prices and to combat unfair competition. Apparently this agreement has been effective.

D. Office machines

Horizontal price and discount cartel—Bonuses—Agency classification—Recommended prices—Price competition

The two largest American producers of office and business machines, Firms 52 and 54 operate in Sweden through subsidiaries. One stays aloof of the cartel arrangements and the other participates in all cartel agreements.

In 1947 Firm 52 registered because of its agreements with the lessees of its machines, under No. 472, which was terminated that year. The agreements called for the exclusive purchase of cards to be used in machines from the lessor of the machines. This firm is cited, in the report made after the 1956 investigation of the trade in office machines, as having always refused to join the cartel agreements (NFF 1956, No. 6).

Firm 54 participates directly and indirectly in three active cartel registrations, Nos. 25, 26, and 646; it also participated in the now terminated No. 27.

Cartel Registration No. 25 for the Office Machine Trade Association dates from October 1938, and its agreement was last reported revised in November 1960. Essentially the Association operates a horizontal price-fixing and uniform discount system for typewriters and other machines. Although it dropped the policy of joint determination of price in 1953, essentially it obtains the same result through the use of three standard agent classifications, standard discount systems for each class, and regulations for sales to governmental agencies. Provision is now made for periodic deposit of price lists with the Association. Since the method of calculation revolves around the "standard" typewriter, the uniformity remains on the basis of recommended prices subject to the possible vagaries of competition at the retail level.

Conditions are also established for the trade in outdated models, demonstrators, and used machines.

The members of cartel agreement No. 25 also participate in a separate agreement registered as No. 26, which concerns the pricing of repairs on office machines. The members agree to a recommended price list and to limitations which authorize the distribution of parts only to those agents who are qualified to do the work. This agreement was also revised as of November 1960.

Finally, Cartel Registration No. 646, the third agreement in which Firm 54 participates, establishes price fixing, sole agencies, and exclusive dealing for office furniture. As the November 1960 revision of the registration discloses, the agreement is designed to rationalize the trade and distribution of office furniture. The agreement operates through agents who are classified by size, and each class receives a different discount ranging from 5–19 per cent. It also utilizes an aggregated rebate or bonus system, giving a 5 per cent bonus for annual purchases of a minimum of $3,000 and up to 15 per cent for $12,000.

The abandoned Cartel Registration, No. 27, was a price-fixing agreement with controls over freedom of entry into the trade of selling office equipment and supplies. The parties to the agreement were the Office Machine Trade Association, the Association of Office Supplies Manufacturers, and two associations of retail dealers in office supplies and machines. The agreement terminated in June 1947.

Despite the attempts to limit competition, the members of the Office Machine Trade Association recognize, at least privately, that the competition at the retail level, emanating in part from the trade in imported machines, causes the agreements to have only limited effect except in the sale of high-priced, low-volume machines. One has the impression that the agreements remain as a means of lessening, rather than stopping, the inevitable price competition at the retail level, which in turn creates pressures for lower prices on the suppliers.

E. Tires

Trade association—Uniform discounts and rebates—Recommended prices—Price competition—Registration not required

Sweden has four domestic manufacturers of tires, of which two are subsidiaries of American Firms 92 and 94. In addition, tires are imported by eighteen firms of which the American enterprises are petroleum Firm 33 and tire producers, Firms 93 and 95. All the importers and three of the manufacturers are members of the Rubber Tire Association.

Until the end of 1952 this Association was party to agreements with a number of retail associations, Cartel Registration No. 381, and with automobile dealers, No. 382, which provided enforcement of resale-price maintenance, a discount system, and exclusive-dealing arrangements in the sale of tires.

Since that time there has been no active registration involving manufacturers or importers of tires.

The fourth Swedish manufacturer of tires is owned by the Kooperativa Förbundet, and its presence is a prime factor in the high degree of competition in the tire trade.

In 1958 the State Price and Cartel Office reported its investigation of the trade in tires. It found that both the members of the Rubber Tire Association and the Union's factory gave the dealers bonuses based on annual purchases which ran up to 15 per cent. In addition, it had evidence that recommended prices were not followed and that price competition was extensive at the retail level. Also, the factory prices were found to reflect fluctuations in world rubber prices with Union's factory prices consistently lower than those of its competitors. The evidence of sufficient price competition warranted the finding that, despite a uniform discount and bonus policy, the Association was not subject to cartel registration (PKF 1958, No. 4, pp. 203–238; addendum: PKF 1959, No. 9/10, pp. 541–544). The view that competition prevailed in the industry was underscored by an opinion from the Commissioner for Freedom of Commerce (PKF 1959, No. 9/10, Case 16).

Thus, there exists for the tire industry, except for the producer controlled by Union, an association of manufacturers and importers which currently agrees on rebates and discounts and which suggests identical prices for identical sizes and qualities of tires. This association is not considered sufficiently effective, in view of retail competition, to warrant the State Price and Cartel Office requiring that it register on the Cartel Register.

Because Swedish law does not contain a compulsory registration provision, this situation is the closest approximation of a determination under Norwegian or Danish legislation that a registration need not take place. Many other arrangements may not be registered because information has not been requested, but in this case the industry was thoroughly investigated and full information was available. It was on the strength of that information that the Commissioner decided not to request the Board to order negotiations to terminate the restraints.

F. Motion pictures

Freedom of entry—Price fixing—Control of noncommercial films—Uniform distribution contracts

The distribution and exhibition of motion pictures in Sweden are the subjects of restrictive and complex agreements, but the industry has been the target of governmental action in only one instance. This was a refusal-to-deal case involving American Firm 66, and it was settled prior to a decision by the Freedom of Commerce Board (NFF 1955, No. 2, Case 11).

In 1941 the industry, except for the American distributors, participated in an agreement designed to control the freedom of entry into the exhibition of motion pictures in all Sweden. The Federation of Swedish Film Producers entered this agreement with the Association of Cinema Proprietors and two groups of theatre circuit operators. Anyone wishing to open a cinema for the showing of films licensed by the Federation of Swedish Film Producers or wanting to increase the capacity of an existing theatre had to present his application to a committee. An impartial chairman and four representatives of the producers and theatre owners respectively comprised this committee. An adverse decision could be appealed to an arbitration commission composed of one member chosen by the appellant, one by the appellee, and a third member whom the parties mutually chose. Other provisions of the agreement dealt with unfair competition, pirating of personnel, and attempting to hire a theatre away from an authorized exhibitor.

This agreement is no longer in force, and no agreement now specifically or literally limits freedom of entry.

From 1934 to 1954 an agreement, Cartel Registration No. 639, was in effect to maintain the price of theatre tickets. The parties to this agreement were all of the American and Swedish firms distributing films in Sweden and the members of the Cinema Proprietors Association. The same parties comprised the Film Control Association.

Today three interrelated agreements are in effect, Cartel Registration Nos. 640, 641, and 643.

No. 640 is a rather wide-ranging and all-embracing agreement between the members of the Film Control Association and various cinema proprietors. Prices for all classes of tickets, a variety of run-and-clearance restrictions, regulations governing the showing of double features and other attractions with a feature film, and terms for the use of advertising films are established. Essentially No. 640 creates a model distribution agreement which all of the parties are bound to use in their individual dealings.

The agreement described in Cartel Registration No. 641 is complementary to No. 640. It covers such items as prohibitions and restrictions on renting to tent theatres and advertising limitations, calculated by the circulation of the newspaper in which the advertising is to be placed. Most matters relative to the advertising and exploitation of films are covered by this agreement.

Cartel Registration No. 643 serves to control noncommercial, documentary, and art film distribution and showing, particularly films printed on sixteen-millimeter stock. In addition, it limits the types of theatres in which such films can be shown, sets ticket prices when admission is charged, and governs the conditions under which no admission may be charged. Those entitled to show noncommercial films are limited in the number of films they may show each year. The limitation is computed on the basis of a five-year average.

Thus, it can be seen that effectively the cinema exhibition and distribution industry is fully self-regulated. The theatres are normally open for two shows each evening in the larger cities and closed the rest of the time.

Some legal commentators have noted a marked inconsistency between permitting ticket prices to be set, apparently on a copyright theory, while requiring dealers in copyrighted books to obtain an exemption from the ban on resale-price maintenance. Those who see some illogic in the result recognize the conceptual difference between the licensing of an opportunity to view a copyrighted film and the outright purchase of a book.

G. Radio and television receivers

Trade association—S.P.K. investigation—Uniform rebates—
Price competition—Terminated registration

In 1957 American Firm *301*'s Swedish subsidiary became a member
of the twenty-year-old Swedish Radio Suppliers Association. This Association had twenty-five members, representing 90 per cent of the
domestic producers of radio and television receivers and allied products, such as phonographs, and of the importers of similar products.
The members of the Association participated in an agreement registered in 1948 as No. 183.

Essentially the agreement called for a uniform system of discounts
and rebates to dealers. The practice of fixing prices, which had been
employed prior to 1 July 1954, had to be replaced by a policy of only
recommending prices. As a replacement, the Association began a
system of fixing the retailer's rebates on the basis of his total annual
purchases, calculated in terms of the recommended price. Thus, a
dealer in radio apparatus who sold between 10,000 and 25,000 kronor
worth received a 19 per cent rebate, calculated on a recommended-
price basis. The same total value of sales of television receivers gave
a 15 per cent rebate. At the other extreme were annual radio-receiver
sales of 600,000 kronor or more which entitled one to a 28 per cent rebate; for television it was 24.5 per cent.

Dealers were expected to channel their purchases primarily to a
member of the Association in order to qualify, and the percentage
that each dealer was obligated to buy from a supplier varied from
year to year, as did the rebate scale. Most dealerships were on a controlled basis designed to limit freedom of entry to a selected group.

The production and distribution of radio and television receivers
are included, along with food and petroleum products, among the
major areas of continuing interest of the State Price and Cartel Office.
In 1957 the industry was thoroughly investigated and the resulting
reports were published in PKF 1957 (No. 6, pp. 225–368) and PKF
1958 (No. 1, pp. 3–58). A short addendum to the original report was
published in PKF 1958 (No. 5, pp. 307–324). Then in 1960 the State
Price and Cartel Office restudied the industry and trade and made
public its findings in PKF 1961 (No. 1, pp. 9–40).

The latest of the reports reflected the high degree of competition at
the retail level of the radio and television receiver trade. From 1953
to the end of 1960 the trade in receivers had annually increased 700

per cent in terms of value of products sold; from 1957 to 1959 the turnover doubled. Television sets accounted for the bulk of the increase, and prices decreased by 20 per cent from 1956 to 1959 despite the increase in the size of sets. Radio receiver prices also dropped.

By 1960 the price structure had become fairly stable, and in terms of the suggested price of a television receiver the import or factory costs represented 57 per cent of the price. The supplier's margin was 17 per cent and the average margin available to the retailer as a percentage of the recommended price was 26 per cent. For radio receivers the factory or import costs were also 57 per cent of the recommended retail price; but the supplier's margin was only 12 per cent and the retailer's margin, if he followed the recommended price, averaged at 31 per cent. These margins are derived after averaging in the results of the operation of the Swedish Radio Suppliers Association rebate scheme.

In practice the State Price and Cartel Office found that the recommended prices were not followed, so that the average reduction of the recommended price for television receivers on cash sales averaged 9 per cent, leaving the dealer a 17 per cent margin. For sales on credit the reduction averaged 3 per cent. In radio cash sales the average reduction was 9 per cent of the recommended price and for installment credit sales only 2 per cent, leaving the dealer 22 per cent and 29 per cent margins respectively. Installment credit sales are a third of the transactions in the trade and represent 42 per cent of the value of the annual turnover.

The continually developing high degree of competition in the trade was evident in all of the reported investigations, and it was equally clear to some of the members of the Association who saw little advantage to binding themselves to a common rebate scheme. Obviously, rebate competition and other forms of supplier competition could assist some suppliers in encouraging retailers to push their sets. Thus, one of the main members broke away in 1960, and shortly thereafter the State Price and Cartel Office was notified that by the end of 1960 the agreement, No. 183, was no longer in effect.

Although some horizontal agreements are designed to ensure the following of recommended prices among some dealers, and although the Swedish Radio Suppliers Association continues, the Commissioner for Freedom of Commerce saw no reason to require negotiations concerning the limited amount of cooperation that presently exists (PKF 1961, No. 5, Case 10).

The members of the Swedish Radio Suppliers Association were among the first to petition the Board for an exemption from the prohibition on resale-price maintenance. The suppliers argued that reduced margins at retail would impair technical service to customers. This argument was rejected and the Swedish consumer is apparently not finding any disability in his service (NFF 1955, No. 2, Case 5).

The history of competition in the radio and television trade raises questions of whether the preoccupation of the State Price and Cartel Office was a factor in engendering public interest in competitive prices in the trade or whether the investigations were the result of such price competition. At the least it can be said that there is an interaction. Certainly the evidence is clear that the trade is now operating on minimum margins and that there are more suppliers and a larger volume of business than ever before. The degree of price competition in the larger Swedish cities approaches that found in the discounting in major metropolitan American areas. It may well be that certain products and certain consumption habits lend themselves to the same distribution patterns.

H. Automobiles

Concentration—Horizontal competition—Vertical rigidity—Special investigations

Sweden is a producer and importer of automobiles. Only two American firms play any considerable role in the Swedish automobile market. Firm *102* is among the three dominant suppliers in Sweden, while Firm *101* plays a lesser role and is not registered. No association of automobile importers or producers is registered.

Firm *102* operates under Cartel Registration No. 1603, which is for the standard agreement between its import agent and its authorized new car dealers. The agreement prohibits competition among franchised dealers and restricts each dealer to his own sales district. Dealers agree not to sell competing brands of new cars and not to use any spare parts other than those manufactured by or authorized by Firm *102*. Firm *101* has no similar agreement registered, but the absence of registration may be due to lack of a request rather than lack of such an agreement.

The automobile trade has been of interest to the State Price and Cartel Office. Each facet of the trade, each price margin, and each detail has been publicized fully in a series of detailed reports (PKF

1958, No. 4, pp. 239–250; PKF 1958, No. 8, pp. 481–500; PKF 1959, No. 2, pp. 87–122; PKF 1959, No. 6, pp. 389–398; PKF 1959, No. 9/10, pp. 526–540; PKF 1960, No. 7, pp. 431–508). Automobile repair shops, also among the subjects covered in the reports, have engaged the attention of the Commissioner (PKF 1960, No. 2, Case 6; and PKF 1961, No. 2, Case 17). Significantly the Commissioner recently concluded, after reviewing the various studies made by the State Price and Cartel Office, that the trading margins in the automobile trade require further study. To that end the School of Business Administration at Göteborg has been asked to make a full economic analysis (PKF 1961, No. 7, Case 11).

In 1959 the three major suppliers to the Swedish market accounted for 65.7 per cent of the sales. American Firm *102* held 20.5 per cent of the market with the three brands which it imported from the United States, Germany, and the United Kingdom. In 1957 American Firm *102*'s three marks accounted for 26 per cent of the total sales, and the single mark utilized by American Firm *101* had 14 per cent of the market. In 1957 American Firm *102* had 99 franchised dealers, and they each averaged 319 sales of new cars a year. American Firm *101* had 95 dealers and they averaged 160 sales a year. All in all there were 1,020 new car dealers in Sweden in 1957, and they individually averaged 133 sales a year.

One aspect of the Swedish trade in automobiles that is indicative of Swedish buying habits is the percentage of cash sales. For American Firm *102* 61 per cent of the sales of its cars at retail were for cash and 82 per cent of all sales were with trade-ins. American Firm *101*'s cars sold for cash in the amount of 55 per cent, and 80 per cent of all sales were with a trade-in. One small German car was sold for cash in 63 per cent of the cases but trade-ins were involved in only 35 per cent of the sales.

If the dealer follows recommended prices, his nominal margins were 25.1 per cent for Firm *102*'s cars without accessories and 25.7 per cent with accessories. For American Firm *101*'s cars without accessories the margins were 23.2 per cent and 23.9 per cent with accessories. For the eighteen brands of cars sold in Sweden the average dealer's margin was 22.1 per cent for cars without accessories, and for those with accessories 22.6 per cent.

The deviations from recommended prices for automobiles are not considered to be very significant in Sweden. The cars of American Firm *102* sold on the average 7.6 per cent under the recommended price without a trade, and only 1.1 per cent under with a trade. For the cars of American Firm *101* the figures were 6.2 and 0.9 per cent respectively and for the automobile trade as a whole the average was 4.3 and 0.9 per cent.

Table 10 provides information in regard to the price range of vehicles available and the degree of price competition among the eighteen brands on the market. These statistics offer a basis for an evaluation of the role of the American firms in Sweden.

TABLE 10: 1957 PRICE RANGES FOR PASSENGER
AUTOMOBILES IN SWEDEN

Firm and Number of Brands	Mean Price Including Accessories	
	With Trade-in	Without Trade-in
American Firm *102* (3)	8,696 kr. ($1,740)	9,822 kr. ($1,965)
American Firm *101* (1)	8,613 kr. ($1,726)	9,226 kr. ($1,845)
A Swedish firm (1)	9,968 kr. ($1,995)	11,047 kr. ($2,210)
A German firm (1)	6,846 kr. ($1,370)	6,974 kr. ($1,395)
A Swedish firm (1); a German firm (2)	11,051 kr. ($2,210)	11,220 kr. ($2,240)
A British firm (3); a French firm (3); a German firm (2); an Italian firm (1)	7,415 kr. ($1,483)	8,693 kr. ($1,738)
Averages	8,144 kr. ($1,629)	9,734 kr. ($1,947)

Sales of cars in Sweden are on the rise with 1957 bringing a 30 per cent increase over the previous year and 1958 registering an 8 per cent gain. The sale of secondhand cars is a relatively new phenomenon in the Swedish market, and that trade doubled from 1956 to 1958. Automobile dealers have average profits, after taxes, of from a minimum of 8.0 to 11.4 per cent if one calculates profit in terms of yield on capital accounts. As calculated on the basis of working capital, before tax and plus interest payable, the minimums and maximums were 8.1 to 10.6 per cent. The dealers handling the cars distributed by the three industry leaders in Sweden, including American Firm *102*, were able to show the most consistent profit records with the least fluctuation from dealer to dealer. The dealers of other brands reflected wider variations. The State Price and Cartel Office believes that profit and consistency are more directly related to the mark of the car sold than to the size of the dealership.

The average gross margins on the sale of new and secondhand cars and trucks were 10.5 per cent in 1956 and 8.5 per cent in 1958. The average retail gross profits on spare parts was 23 per cent and the gross profit on repairs was 32 per cent. Most firms operate on a low self-financing level with about four-fifths of the balance-sheet total represented by borrowed capital, of which 60 per cent is short-term debt.

The present method of automobile distribution in Sweden might benefit from some attempt at rationalization, and it is apparently toward this end that the Commissioner is directing the inquiry which will be made by the economists at Göteborg.

The evidence would indicate that there is a degree of competition among importers and manufacturers of automobiles. The rigidity lies in the exclusive-dealership arrangements designed to discourage competition among dealers in the same brands of cars. This "trademark monopoly," as it is denominated by the Commissioner, is another matter of concern underlying his request for an inquiry. Furthermore, the study will be directed to the rigidities in the vertically recommended prices, deviations from which are not as great as in other lines.

I. Petroleum

Heating-oil rebates—Price competition—Tenant's heating fee—Horizontal recommended-price agreement—Exclusive-dealing contracts

Sweden is entirely dependent on crude petroleum imports. The interest of the Swedish government in the refining and distribution of petroleum is evidenced by the 1945 directive of the Parliament calling for a special committee to investigate the petroleum cartel. The committee's report, Handeln med Olja, published in Statens Offentliga Utredningar 1947 (State Official Investigations, SOU, No. 14, Stockholm), has been well summarized in "The International Petroleum Cartel" (Staff Report to the Federal Trade Commission, Committee Print No. 6, 82d Cong., 2d Sess., Select Committee on Small Business, U.S. Senate, 22 August 1952, pp. 280–311).

The Swedish committee found that international cartelization had been the major factor in the Swedish petroleum trade. There was evidence that it was on the way to becoming so again. The domestic trade was found to be devoid of competition. The committee also found that the Kooperativa Förbundet's petroleum organization was forced to follow the cartel's lead because of dependence on the cartel for supplies. The majority of the committee suggested that the State take over the petroleum trade as a state monopoly.

Today the horizontal competition in the Swedish retail petroleum trade is clearly in evidence, and apparently the government is not concerned with agreements to divide the Swedish market or to establish quotas. No registration for a horizontal cartel, arrangement, or association at the importation or refining level appears in the Cartel Register. The only indication of rigidity is the usual identity of prices for goods of like grade and quality. Some commentators call this price identity evidence of "price leadership" while others believe it is proof of competition.

The use of oils of various grades for heating households and buildings has increased in Sweden during the postwar years. In 1953 heating oils represented only 0.2 per cent of the fuels for domestic heating, and today the consumption exceeds 70 per cent. It is this rapidly growing sector of the petroleum trade which presently preoccupies the Swedish State Price and Cartel Office.

The only studies or scrutinies of the petroleum trade made in recent years have related to analyses of the rebates in heating oils. Early studies concerning heating oils were published in SOU 1951 (No. 32) and SOU 1956 (Nos. 46 and 58). In 1958 the State Price and Cartel Office began to investigate the rebates given to some consumers of heating oils through a study of the situation in Stockholm (PKF 1958, No. 10, pp. 615–633). A study of rebates in twenty-six municipalities appeared in PKF 1959 (No. 3, pp. 207–214). An updating of the use of rebates in Stockholm was reported in PKF 1959 (No. 4, pp. 267–274). Stockholm, Göteborg, and Malmö plus twenty-four other cities were resurveyed in 1960 and 1961 (PKF 1961, No. 3, pp. 201–214).

The reports indicate that all companies selling heating oils—which include American Firms 32, 33, and 34—give varying rebates to landlords with large numbers of flats and to individual householders. The largest number of rebates, 90 per cent, are given in Stockholm and in all cities the rebates are given to more than 50 per cent of the consumers. The number and value of rebates has steadily been increasing, while at the same time the list prices on all grades of heating oils have been dropping. In 1957–1958 the average rebate was 6 per cent, and in 1958–1959 it was 13 per cent.

Although within a given locality most suppliers grant about the same proportion of rebates and at about the same rates, apparently they have no objective standard on which either the entitlement of a given customer to a rebate or the size of the rebate is necessarily based. Of course, the trends in rebates may be correlated to quantities consumed.

One effect of the publicity given to the rebates has been to drive prices down, and the petroleum organization of the Kooperativa Förbundet has taken advantage of the publicity to take the lead in dropping its list prices for all classes of fuel oil.

Another effect of the publicity was the increased demand by consumers for rebates for themselves. The biggest problem created by the publicity was that of the landlords who, according to Swedish tradition, charge their tenants a supplemental heating fee, based on the published fuel prices. The supplemental fees did not give the tenants the advantage of the rebates which were relatively secret until 1958. Protest was made by the National Tenants Association which led to an agreement with the National Association of Property Owners. Provision is now made for calculating the supplemental heating fee on the basis of the average rebates. This calculation is to be submitted to the State Price and Cartel Office, and the Office has decided to make an annual published survey of the rebate averages, so as to assist in the operation of the agreement.

Four major American firms are involved—32, 33, 34, and 35—in the retailing of petroleum products through service stations. They compete with the Kooperativa Förbundet's organization, which controls an estimated 17 per cent of the Stockholm trade and 10 per cent nationally, with a Dutch owned refiner who controls 425 service stations, with a British refiner with 975, and with two Swedish firms which together have 750 stations. Most service stations are members of the Swedish Gasoline Dealers National Association. The Association has registered an agreement, No. 1777, which is designed to ensure that the members abide by their suppliers' recommended prices, and that recommended prices be obeyed for all products and services.

The exclusive-dealing contracts between the suppliers and the service stations are also registered. American Firm 32 has registered its agreements with some 200 service stations under No. 1778. Under the standard agreement only those petroleum products which the refiner chooses to market in a given station may be sold there, and no petroleum product of a competing brand may ever be sold. All tires, batteries, and accessories (T.B.A.) must either bear the refiner's mark or be approved by the refiner. No advertising matter other than that supplied or approved by the refiner may be placed in the stations. The contract is nontransferable. There is no evidence that Firm 32 resisted registration in Sweden as it had elsewhere.

American Firm 35 has Registration No. 1780 for its exclusive-dealing arrangements with 135 stations. The provisions are generally the same as those in No. 1778 except that certain petroleum products, refined by others and sold under marks not controlled by Firm 35, may be furnished by the station if expressly requested by the customer. As to T.B.A. the dealer is bound to sell the refiner's branded items only if the prices and terms he offers are as good as those available elsewhere to the dealer.

American Firm 33 has contracts with 1,500 service stations and they are classics of their type. Absolutely no form of direct or indirect benefit to any competitor is countenanced. The restrictions on T.B.A. are as complete as possible and reflect the great emphasis placed on the firm's own T.B.A. brand all over the world.

Finally American Firm 34 has registered exclusive agreements with 2,000 service stations, No. 1784. It is fully as restrictive as No. 1783, and it contains in addition clauses about price. Under these clauses the dealers are to receive price lists from the company and they are notified, pursuant to law, that they have no obligation to obey the prices. This price provision represents the maximum that can be done without running afoul of the prohibition against resale-price maintenance.

Despite the attempt of the service stations to maintain recommended prices, the influx of cheaper gasoline into Sweden from West German sources and the relative freedom of the Kooperativa Förbundet's petroleum organization have created a tendency toward lower gasoline prices. Nevertheless the evidence is that the major refiners are trying to hold the line.

The general view is that within Sweden there is no present evidence of market-sharing, quota arrangements, or other horizontal understandings among the refiners and importers. It is recognized that the Swedish market must reflect crude prices and other factors beyond its control. However, it is not expected that the refiners will again undertake arrangements such as those reported in 1947. Such a backward step would quickly revive the demand for a state-controlled petroleum monopoly.

J. Miscellaneous

The absence of compulsory registration means that one cannot attribute too much significance to the absence of agreements, yet one cannot help but recognize that a significantly large number of American enterprises in Sweden are absent from the Cartel Register.

Some indication that the absence of registrations is meaningful may be derived from the large number of cancelled and terminated registrations. Some of these have already been noted in prior sections. Others that have been cancelled, Nos. 890 through 919, were a series of agreements between lessees of shoe-making machinery and the lessor, American Firm *801*. Some of the agreements dated back to 1907 and were renewed for either ten or twenty years at a time. In general the agreements were designed to prevent lessees from using machines leased or manufactured by a competitor of the lessor.

Another group of terminated agreements involved dental goods. These agreements involving American manufacturers, Nos. 857, 860, and 866, were part of a series of originally oral agreements—between foreign suppliers and Swedish importers—which fixed prices and conditions of supply for the goods involved. The effect of the series of vertical agreements was in fact horizontal. In a sense No. 866 was unique because the parties included not only the American producer of X-ray machines, but also the manufacturer with the same trademark located in Germany, and the terms for Sweden were apparently decided among them.

Several odd registrations remain on the register, such as No. 847 between two importers of abrasives and a Swedish manufacturer. This agreement provides for the calculations of price lists on the basis of a formula bottomed on a 1923 price list by a leading American exporter, Firm *702*.

Finally, American Firm *401*, a major producer of photographic equipment and film, was the subject of a case brought before the Freedom of Commerce Board (PKF 1959, No. 4, Case 4). The American firm was charged, along with three others controlling 80 to 90 per cent of the market, with having refused to deliver to Hemköp, the telephone-delivery discount supermarket. Prior to a decision by the Freedom of Commerce Board, the suppliers agreed to deliver. The 1959 price list of Hemköp shows that some brands of film are sold at about 15 per cent below the suggested price. Film manufactured by Firm *401* is not listed.

In 1958 the Commissioner asked the State Price and Cartel Office to initiate an investigation into the extent to which vertically suggested prices for film and photographic equipment produced by American Firm *401* were followed in the retail trade. The investigation was completed on 14 February 1958, but, for reasons that are not yet disclosed, the report was never published (PKF 1959, No. 2, Case 2, p. 201).

K. Coca-Cola

1. INTRODUCTION

No effort at identity disguise is here attempted, at the specific request of the Western European Area office of the Coca-Cola Export Corporation.

On a world-wide basis Coca-Cola is organized on a uniform pattern and has a form of doing business that is almost uniquely its own creation. The actual bottling of the beverage trademarked Coca-Cola or Coke is entrusted to independent firms under franchise arrangements. Here in the United States the Coca-Cola Company provides the franchised bottlers with a syrup from which the beverage is prepared and bottled under instructions from the supplying company. Outside of the United States franchised bottlers receive a concentrate from which the beverage is prepared under instructions. Their source of supply and instructions is a separate corporation, the Coca-Cola Export Corporation. The franchised bottlers, both inside the United States and abroad, distribute and sell the bottled beverage in certain territories defined in an agreement known as the "Bottler's Agreement."

The Bottler's Agreement is essentially an agreement licensing the bottler to use the trademark "Coca-Cola" and related marks in connection with bottling and sale of the beverage "Coca-Cola." The consideration for the license is the bottler's undertaking to develop fully the Coca-Cola business and to satisfy every demand for the bottled beverage in the territory or territories allocated to him.

The legal structure of the industry, at least as far as this particular beverage is concerned, is made up of a series of vertical agreements. The head of the vertical line is occupied by the Coca-Cola Company which owns the Coca-Cola trademark and formula. Next comes the Coca-Cola Export Corporation which is the owner of the sales rights to the product outside of the United States. The end of the line is the local bottler.

This legal structure and its operation had been until 1958 the classic example of the way in which a large business could be operated without falling afoul of the letter or spirit of the antitrust laws of any country in the world. In 1958, the structure was attacked almost simultaneously both in Norway and in Sweden. In both countries was a demand that the Bottler's Agreement be spread on the Cartel Register. The Norwegian and Swedish governmental views are so closely akin that no effort will be made to separate them, and the discussion hence will deal primarily with the Swedish treatment of the issues.

The Bottler's Agreements were attacked on two grounds. In the first instance the right of the owner of the trademark to grant exclusive territories was questioned, and secondly ancillary restrictions designed to protect the trademark were put in issue. Putting it another way, the State Price and Cartel Office took the position that both classes of objected-to features in the Bottler's Agreements constituted restraints of competition that justified registration of the agreements under the provisions of the 1956 Act. Obviously Coca-Cola wished to resist this characterization of their agreements, even if it were true that mere registration did not mean a finding that the restraint of competition was per se harmful.

The view of the State Price and Cartel Office was that the overall effect of the series of vertical Bottler's Agreements was, as to territorial exclusivity, the equivalent of a horizontal agreement to divide territory. A further objection was that the territorial limitations imposed on the bottler constituted an unreasonable restriction on his freedom. As to the clauses designed to protect the trademark, the argument was that the restrictions exceeded those permitted under national trademark legislation and under laws designed to prevent unfair competition.

The appeal against registration will probably not succeed in Norway, and it did not succeed in Sweden. In Sweden the appeal was taken to the King in Council under the provisions of Section 13 of the 1956 Act. The King in Council on 25 September 1959 ordered that the summary of the cartel registration be printed. With what may have been a sense of history, the cartel registration number assigned to Coca-Cola was 1776. The summary was published in PKF 1959 (No. 9/10, pp. 546–548), and the registration is predated to the time of the original demand, 30 September 1958.

Two summaries of Cartel Register No. 1776 have been published, the first of which is cited above, and the amended version is published in PKF 1961 (No. 10, pp. 819–820).

2. THE FIRST CARTEL REGISTER SUMMARY

The complete first summary (PKF 1959, No. 9/10, pp. 546–548) reads as follows:

Cartel Reg. No. 1776

Reg. 30 September 1958

According to a decision of His Royal Majesty of 25 September 1959 the following summary is published.

Summary of agreements between the Coca-Cola Export Corporation and the Coca-Cola Company, both of the U.S.A., (here called Corporation and Company) and the Soft Drink Bottlers listed below, and between the Corporation and the 60 so-called Distributors concerning exclusive dealing and territorial divisions in the distribution of Coca-Cola.

Principal Agreements with the Following Soft Drink Bottlers

	Entered	Agreement Effective from
Mineralvattenfabriks AB Tre Kronor, Sundbyberg	25/3 1953	1/6 1953
Björkens Vattenfabrik AB, Göteborg	25/3 1953	1/7 1953
Vattenfabriks AB Kronan i Malmö, Malmö	25/3 1953	1/7 1953
Mineralvattenfabriken Liljan AB, Sundsvall	1/4 1954	1/4 1954
Krönleins Vattenfabriks AB, Jönköping	1/4 1954	1/4 1954
Sveabryggeriers Vattenfabrik i Filipstad AB, Filipstad	15/6 1954	15/6 1954

Each agreement is effective for a period of ten years and the Bottler may renew for a further ten-year period. In certain cases the agreement can be terminated immediately through notice, as for example where there is a conflict with Swedish law.

Company manufactures and sells its Concentrate from which the Syrup is prepared and it also manufactures and sells the Syrup which is employed in the manufacture of the Soft Drink. The Company owns the trademarks Coca-Cola and Coke which distinguish the Concentrate, Syrup and Beverage, as well as a trademark on the form of the bottle in which the Beverage is marketed. Each Bottler prepares and bottles the Beverage for resale and distribution within a territory in which the Corporation along with the Company authorize the Bottler alone to sell the Concentrate, Syrup, and Beverage.

The American Firms and the individual Soft Drink Bottlers have agreed in part as follows.

1. The Corporation and the Bottler will at all times recognize the validity of the trademarks and the ownership thereof by the Company.

2. The American Firms authorize the Bottler exclusively to prepare and bottle the Beverage and to sell and distribute the same only in that territory which is described in the agreement.

· · · · · · · · · · · · ·

4. The Bottler covenants and agrees:

a) To buy of or through the Corporation all of the quantities of Concentrate or Syrup required to supply fully every demand for the Beverage within the territory *and not to* resell the Concentrate or Syrup,

· · · · · · · · · · · ·

c) To prepare the Beverage for distribution and sale only in such distinctive bottles and with such crown seals as the American Firms prescribe, *and to* purchase these articles only from such manufacturers as are authorized by the American Firms,

· · · · · · · · · · · ·

f) To employ only those trucks which the American Firms approve,

· · · · · · · · · · · ·

i) Not knowingly to sell or distribute the Beverage to anyone for the purpose of resale outside the territory without the consent of the Corporation,

j) (1) Not at any time to manufacture, bottle, sell, deal in, or otherwise be concerned with any concentrate, syrup, or beverage which is likely to be substituted for, passed off for or as an imitation of, the Concentrate, the Syrup, or the Beverage, *or* (2) Not at any time to manufacture, bottle, sell, deal in, or otherwise be concerned with any product under any get-up or in any container which is an imitation of the get-up or container used by the Company, or which is likely to be confused or used in unfair competition therewith or passed off therefor, (3) Not at any time to produce or be concerned with any product under any trademark or designation which is an imitation or infringement of Coca-Cola and Coke. It is understood that the use of the word "Coca" during the life of the agreement and thereafter in any unauthorized form would constitute infringement and unfair competition, but the right of the Bottler to use the word Cola after the termination of the agreement shall not be affected either favorably or unfavorably.

· · · · · · · · · · · ·

(7) The Bottler will only do such advertising on his own account of the Beverage as is authorized or approved by the American Firms.

· · · · · · · · · · · ·

Supplemental Agreement with the Six Bottlers

In separate supplemental agreements the Corporation and the Company have declared themselves as being desirous of authorizing persons or companies, to be called Distributors, to distribute and sell Coca-Cola within certain defined territories, outside of the territory assigned to the Bottler in the Principal Agreement as his exclusive territory. The Supplemental Agreement contains in this regard a regulation of significance, namely that the respective Bottlers are authorized to prepare and sell Coca-Cola only to such Distributors as the Corporation has designated as being authorized to purchase from the Bottler.

Agreement with Distributors

The Corporation has through an agreement with all of its 60 Distributors —generally breweries—authorized them to buy Coca-Cola from a specific named Bottler and to distribute and sell the Beverage in a stipulated territory.

The above Cartel Register summary is a literal rendering of some portions of the Bottler's Agreement, and it is a characterization of the legal effect of certain clauses. One gains the impression that the summary slants a bit in the direction of making it appear that the American firms seek to make vassals of the bottlers. For purposes of comparison one may examine the following full paragraph which in the summary above is given as 4. f).

To invest in, set up, maintain, and operate such plant, trucks, and other equipment within the Territory as shall be satisfactory to the Corporation and/or the Company, and sufficient in all respects to meet and satisfy fully every demand for the Beverage within the territory, and at all times to conform to the standards, hygienic and other, set by the Corporation and/or the Company, and to comply with all legal requirements; and to permit the Company and the Corporation, their officers or agents, at all times to enter upon and inspect the plant, equipment, and methods used by the Bottler, to ascertain whether the Bottler is complying with the terms of this agreement, and especially whether it is complying strictly with the standards prescribed by the Company for the Beverage.

3. THE AMENDED CARTEL REGISTER SUMMARY

The second summary (PKF 1961, No. 10, pp. 819–820) reads *in toto* as follows:

Cartel Reg. No. 1776

Reg. 30 September 1958

Agreements between the Coca-Cola Export Corporation and the Coca-Cola Company, both of the U.S.A., (here called Corporation and Company) and all of the following Soft Drink Bottlers, namely . . . [the bottlers listed are those in the last Summary, ed. note], and between the Corporation and each of sixty so-called Distributors concerning exclusive dealing along with territorial division in the distribution of Coca-Cola (see Part 9–10/ 1959). Entry 26/4 1961. Through separate supplemental agreements of 1 September 1960 to the Principal Agreements, between the Company and the Corporation and the Swedish Bottlers, the Bottlers have been allotted additional authorized territory. In this connection the Company and the Corporation have recently authorized certain persons or companies to distribute and sell Coca-Cola within certain stated districts within the extra allotted territory, and the Bottlers have been authorized to supply these Distributors. Bottlers have also individually been given the right to choose Distributors within the newly licensed territories. The Corporation has, however, reserved to itself the right to disapprove such a Distributor, and the Bottler, after receipt of notice of disapproval is obliged to discontinue to sell to such Distributor.

The Bottler is to keep the Corporation informed about such Distributors which it supplies and will provide monthly reports of sales made to such Distributors as it appoints.

Until further notice these provisions do not affect Mineralvattenfabriken Liljan AB.

4. COMPLAINTS TO THE COMMISSIONER

The changes reflected in the Bottler's Agreements as shown in the second summary, are a direct result of complaints made to the Commissioner and of criticisms made by the State Price and Cartel Office.

The complaints lodged with the Commissioner by those who are not authorized to be distributors caused him to request the State Price and Cartel Office on 4 February 1960 to make a full investigation of the distribution of Coca-Cola. This survey led to a full report by the Office, published in June 1961 (PKF 1961, No. 4, pp. 272–307), entitled Selective Selling of Coca-Cola: *Certain Problems of Competition* (S.P.K. Report). The complete translation of this report follows this section, and it is left to the reader to evaluate finally the impact, objectivity, and value of such a report.

The complaints from those not authorized to be distributors are along the line that it is impossible to compete fairly and fully if one is a brewery and one cannot include Coca-Cola in the line of products that one delivers to one's customers. In a sense the complaint is that Coca-Cola has become a public utility and should be available to all middlemen.

5. THE STATE PRICE AND CARTEL OFFICE REPORT: SELECTIVE SELLING OF COCA-COLA

The extent to which trademarks are exempt from the operation of the law concerning restraints of competition is clear only with respect to one type of case. Where the owner of a trademark for a soft-drink concentrate will not supply a bottler, the Board has ruled that such a refusal to deal or mode of selective selling is not a harmful restraint of competition (PKF 1959, No. 6, Case 8). The Board's decision has been characterized as a recognition of the rights of an owner of a trademark, even including his right to license which is not specifically granted by statute.

In our case the refusal to deal takes place at the distributor level, instead of the bottler level, and it is difficult to find a basis for a result different from that in the cited case. There is no allegation or evidence that any retailer has been refused an opportunity to purchase for resale. Indeed, it is the bottler's obligation under the Agreement to see that the beverage is available to all who need or want it at the retail level.

At the least there appears to be some confusion in policy between the cited decision of the Board and the attitude of the State Price and Cartel Office. Only if the Commissioner were to bring a complaint before the Board would it be possible to ascertain the precise degree to which the State Price and Cartel Office is correct in its attitude.

Some of the statements made in the Report itself, primarily in its own Summary, are at least open to question if not argument. A few of these will be examined, so as to provide a context for a study of the Report.

The S.P.K. is of the opinion that a system of selective selling coupled with territorial divisions is unique and the inference is that "uniqueness" is somehow bad. Territorial-franchise agreements, common in most countries, are not bad unless related to restraints of trade or coupled with them. In the Coca-Cola case there are no related price agreements or other restrictive practices. It is not likely that any objection would be raised if every bottler were his own distributor and in turn assigned territories to his own salesmen. Such a territorial division is normal and not usually questioned. The use of a limited number of distributors would seem to be economically sound and designed to provide the widest coverage with the least amount of effort on the part of the bottler. It is highly probable that the demands on a bottler to supply every distributor with a small quantity of the beverage will be more costly than supplying larger quantities of beverage to a few accounts.

Cartel arrangements involving territorial divisions have long been a feature of the brewing trade in Sweden, and at least one case is cited in an earlier section, II. **C**. 2. *a*. 2, in which territorial divisions in sparsely populated areas were approved by the Board. Many of the rigidities derived from the historical, brewery cartel arrangements still continue. Possibly the State Price and Cartel Office believes that it could obtain more popular support for an attempt to demolish such rigidities if the ostensible target were a less entrenched product than beer. In fact, the rigidities in the brewing trade are greater than those that might result from the trademark-bottomed territorial divisions in this case.

The Summary in the Report seems to ignore the fact that all of the bottlers prepare and bottle other soft drinks and beer in addition to Coca-Cola. All of these products are in competition with Coca-Cola, and the bottler is free, as far as Coca-Cola is concerned, to use any form of distribution he wishes for the competing products. Competitors of these bottlers, including the complaining would-be distributors, are not assumed by the State Price and Cartel Office to have a right to the other trademarked goods that the Coca-Cola bottler produces.

The Summary seems to assume that Coca-Cola is a monopoly. This assumption could be made concerning any branded or patented product. It would seem elementary that anyone exploiting a trademark has a sort of monopoly which is recognized by law.

It would also seem that this legal monopoly should bring with it the right to exercise judgment, either sound or unsound, as to the best method of distribution, as long as the public is not injured through operation of restrictive arrangements designed to counter the interest of the consumer.

The discussion of price in the Report's Summary is somewhat hard to follow. It is suggested that prices for Coca-Cola are kept high, yet maximum prices are stipulated by the Corporation, as is legal in Sweden, so as to prevent prices from going too high, and thereby reducing concentrate sales by the Corporation. If prices for Coca-Cola were too high, then sales would reflect this fact, but the inconsistent complaint in the Summary seems to be that Coca-Cola has been too successful in the exploitation of its trademark.

Finally, one gets the impression that the State Price and Cartel Office is asking for less competition rather than more. The burden of the S.P.K.'s views and of those complaining to the Commissioner is that the complainants should not be forced to compete by trying to sell or produce a product competitive with Coca-Cola. They are asking that they be insulated from such a burden, and they are suggesting that free enterprise includes freedom from failure. Experience in other countries has shown that competitive products may be and are being sold in competition with Coca-Cola.

Further comments and questions will undoubtedly occur to the reader as he examines the case made by the State Price and Cartel Office. The comments appearing above are not intended to be exhaustive.

As 1961 ended the Commissioner had not indicated how he would dispose of the complaints brought by those seeking the right to be distributors of Coca-Cola.

The translation of the Report which follows is literal rather than literary, so as to convey as much of the feeling of the original as is possible.

SELECTIVE SELLING OF COCA-COLA
Certain Problems of Competition

How the investigation arose

At the request of the Commissioner for Freedom of Commerce the Price & Cartel Office has previously carried out an investigation into the trade in Coca-Cola. The report thereon was submitted to that Office in 1958. It contains a survey of the trade's organization and price fixing and also an account of action taken in restraint of trade, *inter alia*, in the form of refusal-to-effect delivery as a consequence of selective selling. In conjunction with the investigation a record was entered in the Cartel Register, under No. 1776, of certain contracts concerning exclusivism in addition to a division of territory for the sale of Coca-Cola. A summary of these contracts is printed in Pris- och Kartellfrågor 1959 (September-October issue). Selective selling has found expression mainly by means of the American trademark owners concerned having appointed certain companies to sell Coca-Cola, each within its own territory in the country, primarily to retail merchants.

In a letter dated 4 February 1960 the Commissioner's Office requested the Price and Cartel Office to undertake a supplementary investigation into the distribution of Coca-Cola, with a view to enabling the Commissioner to take up a definitive attitude towards the question as to whether the restrictive trading practices have any harmful effect within the meaning of the law.

The report on the subsequent inquiry having been prepared in all essentials and communicated to the companies concerned for their views, the Coca-Cola Export Corporation announced in a letter to the Office dated 1 February 1961 that the contracts entered in the Cartel Register had been amended to the extent that the "distributor's letter" had ceased to apply. Instead a direct contractual relationship between distributor and bottler had been established, whereby the bottlers commissioned the distributors to buy and sell the beverage. At the same time the territory for which a bottler has obtained the sole right to sell the beverage has been widened. However, the Office has not yet (16 February 1961) received any detailed particulars of the changes effected in the system of contracts, and in consequence the following statement of the case has reference to the circumstances prior to that date.

THE ORGANIZATION OF THE COCA-COLA TRADE

The trade in Coca-Cola is essentially organized by way of cartel agreements, as mentioned above. Coca-Cola was first put on sale in Sweden in 1953. The beverage is manufactured in this country by six producers, called bottlers. It is produced with the aid of a concentrate, which under the contracts is supplied by two American companies, the Coca-Cola Export Corporation and the Coca-Cola Company. The six bottling companies are the following:

> Mineralvattenfabriks AB Tre Kronor, Sundbyberg
> Björkens Vattenfabrik AB, Göteborg
> Sveabryggeriers Vattenfabrik i Filipstad AB, Filipstad
> Krönleins Vattenfabriks AB, Jönköping
> Vattenfabriks AB Kronan i Malmö, Malmö
> Mineralvattenfabriken Liljan AB, Sundsvall.

These bottling companies manufacture and bottle Coca-Cola for sale and distribution with sole rights under their contracts, each within its own territory, comprising the home district and neighborhood, herein called the local district. Within the local districts the bottling companies effect delivery mainly to retailers. In Sundsvall, however, bottlers nowadays have no such local sales. Further, the bottling companies are authorized under their contracts to manufacture and sell Coca-Cola to distributors which have been authorized by the American corporations to sell in allotted districts. The distributors, usually breweries, are about sixty in number. They are authorized to purchase Coca-Cola from a certain bottler and to distribute and sell the beverage each within his own area. The distributors, whose areas differ in size, sell to retailers, though some also sell directly to the consumer. The contracts stipulate that maximum prices be charged by the bottling companies and distributors for their Coca-Cola sales.

In addition to sales in their local districts, the bottling companies in 1957, according to the earlier investigation, sold Coca-Cola to distributors in a number of districts, divided by bottlers' territories.

Bottlers in:	The Distributors' Districts:	
	No.	Main Distribution
Sundbyberg	17	East Sweden from and including Gästrikland to South Småland
Göteborg	9	The West Coast and parts of Västergötland
Filipstad	13	Värmland, Dalsland, Närke, Dalarna
Jönköping	5	Parts of Småland and Västergötland
Malmö	10	South Sweden
Sundsvall	11	Norrland
	65	

The number of distributors and their districts are still largely the same, with certain exceptions, especially in Norrland. The distributors in East, West, and South Sweden are named in the accompanying lists (c. the sketch-map).

To a considerable extent very close relations exist between bottling companies and distributors, not only through their trade in Coca-Cola, but also in other respects as a result of the group conditions prevailing in the trade. As far as the bottlers are concerned, apart from those in Norrland, the group membership is as follows:

Bottlers in:	Belong to:
Sundbyberg	AB Stockholms Bryggerier (the Stockholm Group)
Göteborg	AB Pripp & Lyckholm (the Göteborg Group)
Filipstad	AB Pripp & Lyckholm (the Göteborg Group)
Jönköping	AB Pripp & Lyckholm (the Göteborg Group)
Malmö	AB Malmö Förenade Bryggerier

As to the group conditions otherwise, in thirteen out of the seventeen distribution areas that are handled by bottlers in Sundbyberg the distributors consist of firms within the Stockholm Group. The distributors in seventeen of the total of twenty-seven sales areas under bottling companies in Göteborg, Filipstad, and Jönköping are included in the Göteborg Group. Of the ten distributors under bottlers in Malmö seven are owned by AB Malmö Förenade Bryggerier. Further, Hammars Glasbruk AB, the sole manufacturers of Coca-Cola bottles in Sweden, until a short time ago belonged to the Stockholm Group.

Case Studies 259

AUTHORIZED COCA-COLA DISTRIBUTORS UNDER BOTTLING
COMPANIES IN EAST SWEDEN

Bottlers in Sundbyberg
Distributors (17 districts)

AB Gefle Förenade Bryggeri AB	Södertälje Bryggeri AB
Upsala Bayerska Bryggeri AB	Nyköpings Bryggeri AB
AB Västerås Bryggerier	Askersunds Bryggeri AB
Norrtelje Ångbryggeri AB	AB Norrköpings Förenade Bryggerier
AB Enköpings Ångbryggeri	AB Nya Centralbryggeriet, Linköping
Eskilstuna Bryggeri AB	AB Visby Bryggeri
Arboga Bryggeri AB	Kalmar Bryggeri AB
AB Stockholms Bryggerier (2 districts)	AB Växjö Bayerska Bryggeri

AUTHORIZED COCA-COLA DISTRIBUTORS UNDER
BOTTLING COMPANIES IN WEST SWEDEN

Bottlers in Göteborg
Distributors (9 districts)

AB Axvalls Ångbryggeri	Vänersborgs Bryggeri
Strömstads Bryggeri	Utsikten Bryggeri, Uddevalla
AB Nya Vattenfabriken, Alingsås	A. Karlsons Bryggeri AB, Lysekil
Krönleins Bryggeri, Trollhättan	AB Sandwalls Ångbryggeri, Borås
Bryggeri AB Falken, Falkenberg	

Bottlers in Filipstad
Distributors (13 districts)

Mora Bryggeri AB	Avesta Bryggeri AB
AB Falu Ångbryggeri	Norlings Bryggeri AB, Örebro
AB Wasabryggeriet, Borlänge	Karlskoga Ångbryggeri
Ludvika Bryggeri	Kristinehamns Bryggeri AB
Filipstads Bryggeri AB	Karlstads Bryggeri AB
Bryggeri AB Fryksdalen, Torsby	Arvika Bryggeri AB
Åmåls Bryggeri AB	

Bottlers in Jönköping
Distributors (5 districts)

Tranås Bryggeri AB	Bryggeriet Victoria, Falköping
Hjo Bryggeri	Nässjö Bryggeri AB
AB Värnamo Bryggeri	

AUTHORIZED COCA-COLA DISTRIBUTORS UNDER
BOTTLING COMPANIES IN SOUTH SWEDEN

Bottlers in Malmö
Distributors (10 districts)

AB Förenade Bryggerierna i Karlskrona	AB Klosterbryggeriet, Ystad
Finlands Bryggeri, Kristianstad	Trelleborgs Bryggeri AB
AB Hässleholms Bryggeri & Maltfabrik	Lunds Bryggeri AB
Klippans Bryggeri	Eslövs Bryggeri
AB Läskedrycksfabriken Necken,	AB Skånebryggerier, Hälsingborg
(Appeltofftska Bryggeri AB,	
Halmstad)	

According to information available to the Office, the bottling company at Sundsvall is now owned, after transfers effected in 1959 and 1960, by a number of Norrland breweries.

Practically all the bottling and distributing companies in the Coca-Cola trade belong to the Swedish Brewers Association or the Swedish Mineral Water Manufacturers National Federation, or to both those organizations. In view of the observations that follow, two other organizations will be dealt with in this connection: a) the Association of Breweries Liable to Excise Duty, whose members consist of about twenty beer breweries, and b) the Malt Liquors and Soft Drinks Federation with some two hundred members, which brew a malt liquor known as small beer. The companies belonging to these two organizations work on the whole in competition with the groups mentioned above, *inter alia*. Eight members of the former organization, and in the latter only three (in Upper Norrland) have obtained authorization as distributors of Coca-Cola. Both the Association of Breweries Liable to Excise Duty and the Malt Liquors and Soft Drinks Federation are members of the Swedish Industrial Association.

THE REFUSAL BY AUTHORIZED SELLERS OF COCA-COLA TO EFFECT DE-
LIVERIES THROUGH BREWERIES AT SKRUV AND KOPPARBERG, ETC.

Under the very terms of the above-mentioned contracts the bottling companies, as far as concerns deliveries outside the local districts, are debarred from selling Coca-Cola to any other distributor than the one who is authorized by the Corporation.

In the previous survey certain reports were dealt with which had been sent to the Commissioner for Freedom of Commerce and the Price and Cartel Office on various cases of refusal-to-effect delivery and questions of discrimination in the Coca-Cola trade. Such reports had been received from AB Förbundsbryggeriet Södra Sverige, Skruv, and Kopparbergs Bryggeri AB, Kopparberg, among others. These companies, that is to say, complained that they had been the victims of restrictive trading practices

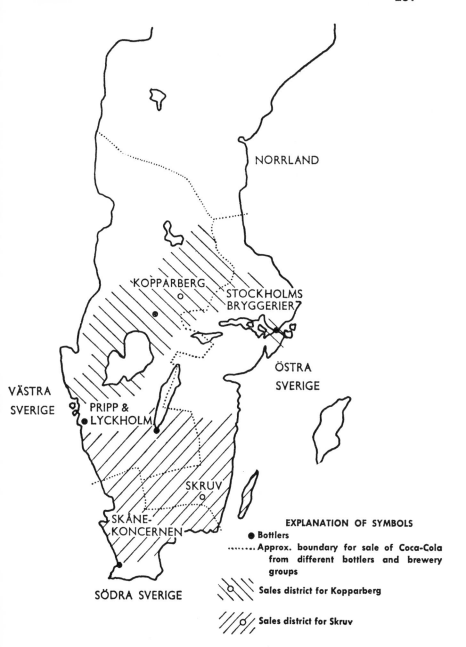

NORRLAND

KOPPARBERG
STOCKHOLMS
BRYGGERIER

ÖSTRA
SVERIGE

VÄSTRA
SVERIGE

PRIPP &
LYCKHOLM

SKRUV

SKÅNE-
KONCERNEN

EXPLANATION OF SYMBOLS
● Bottlers
.... Approx. boundary for sale of Coca-Cola
from different bottlers and brewery
groups

Sales district for Kopparberg

Sales district for Skruv

SÖDRA SVERIGE

Coca-Cola Sales Districts

*(the place of manufacture and the brewery group and the
sales districts of the Skruv and Kopparberg breweries)*

of the kind mentioned. Of the problems that have come to the knowledge of the authorities concerning the refusal-to-effect delivery in the Coca-Cola trade, those that affect the companies at Skruv and Kopparberg are of the widest scope in view of their selling organization. The present investigation is in fact intended to throw light on the problems of current import relating to competition insofar as they apply primarily to those companies, which hereinafter will as a rule be called Skruv and Kopparberg. The activities carried on by these companies, their selling organization, and development were reported on after an investigation made some time ago by the Monopoly Investigation Bureau, functioning under the Swedish Board of Trade, into the question of discrimination in the supply of porter to Skruv. A report on the investigation has been published. (Närings-frihetsfrågor 1956, No. 2. Cf. Pris- och kartellfrågor 1957, No. 2, p. 121 et seq., re the hearing of the matter by the Commissioner for Freedom of Commerce and the Freedom of Commerce Board).

Skruv and Kopparberg, whose production consists for the most part of Pilsener beer (lager), are owned by breweries manufacturing small beer. In the middle of the 1940's a number of small-beer breweries had begun to supply their customers with Pilsener beer as well, though in most cases only as a limited service to their customers since the small-beer breweries, when buying Pilsener, did not usually obtain a retailer's discount. At that period some small-beer brewers in Central Sweden who had hitherto purchased Pilsener from AB Sveabryggeriers i Filipstad (now belonging to AB Pripp & Lyckholm) were informed that they could not count upon receiving further supplies of Pilsener. In view of this situation they bought a Pilsener brewery, Kopparberg, which is now owned by about twenty small-beer brewers, mainly in the provinces of Västmanland, Dalarna, Värmland, and Uppland. For similar reasons Skruv has come into small-beer brewers' ownership. The majority of the shares in the latter firm are owned by about one hundred of the small-beer breweries in the seven counties in South Sweden. Skruv and Kopparberg belong to the Association of Breweries Liable to Excise Duty and to the Malt Liquors and Soft Drinks Federation. In the matter in hand they are also represented by the Swedish Industrial Association, of which those organizations are members, as mentioned above. In regard to Skruv's and Kopparberg's sales districts, reference is made to the sketch-map.

Since Skruv and Kopparberg have not been authorized to act as distributors of Coca-Cola, they have not been entitled to buy the beverage direct from any bottler. Nevertheless, on one occasion Skruv has been allowed to buy from the bottler at Jönköping. They have not been able, however, to buy from the nearest distributors, who as far as Skruv is concerned consist of breweries at Växjö and Kalmar. The distributors at those places, who obtain Coca-Cola from the bottler at Sundbyberg, are among the affiliations of AB Stockholms Bryggerier belonging to the same Group as the bottling firm. However, while Kopparberg has not been allowed to buy Coca-Cola from any distributor, Skruv has for some years been permitted to buy from a distributing firm, Askersunds Bryggeri AB, which during those years had been independent as far as the Stockholm Group was concerned. In its representations to the Office in 1958 Skruv stated that its sales of Coca-Cola then amounted to about 300,000 bottles per annum. Skruv went on to make the following statement:

> We buy our requirements of Coca-Cola from Askersunds Bryggeri, and they in their turn buy the beverage from Stockholm. We have to pay 27 öre per bottle free delivery in Askersund, but we should only have to pay about 20 öre per bottle if we were allowed to purchase the beverage direct from the factory at Jönköping. We are thus forced to pay a very heavy excess price, besides which, we have to bear quite unnecessary transport costs, which add to the price. The article is now conveyed in large trucks direct from the factory in Stockholm to the brewery at Askersund, where we meet the carrier with an equally large truck, whereupon reloading takes place immediately for transport to Skruv. The Coca-Cola manufacturers appear to be not unaware of the manner in which we obtain the beverage, but so far we have not heard anything from Askersunds Bryggeri about the risk they run of being precluded from effecting delivery on account of their selling to us.
>
> We find ourselves in an extremely precarious position in consequence of our large sales of Coca-Cola, seeing that our being precluded from purchasing it would immediately lead to the great majority of our shareholders, the soft-drink brewers, all of whom buy from us their entire requirements of malt liquors, and in many cases soft drinks as well, besides practically all the Coca-Cola, also finding themselves in an untenable position. What it would lead to if our shareholders are unable to market Coca-Cola would be simply this, that they would first be deprived of the Coca-Cola market, which in view of the purchase price they pay does not involve any loss but, on the contrary, means a profit to them; but what is worse, they run the risk of losing their market for malt liquors and soft drinks, since the absence of Coca-Cola is immediately exploited by the authorized Coca-Cola merchants to induce the retailers of the drinks in question to purchase all kinds of drinks from them.

As from March 1959 Skruv has been completely shut off from deliveries of Coca-Cola from Askersunds Bryggeri AB, that firm having passed into the possession of the Stockholm Group on 1 February 1959.

Kopparberg has purchased Coca-Cola from the Grängesberg brewery, which functions as an agent for the Ludvika brewery, which in its turn acts as distributor for the bottler at Filipstad. Like Skruv and Kopparberg, the Grängesberg brewery is a member of the Malt Liquors and Soft Drinks Federation. According to information received from Kopparberg, the Grängesberg brewery was excluded from obtaining supplies of Coca-Cola

as from 30 September 1959 because it sold to Kopparberg and others.
Since then Kopparberg has not marketed Coca-Cola.

In its representations to the Price and Cartel Office in March 1958 the
Federation just referred to reported that its members were making "con-
stant complaints that they are not entitled . . . to purchase the beverage
in question from those firms in Sweden which manufacture Coca-Cola
drinks." According to the Federation, group formations in the brewery
trade were using Coca-Cola as a means of restricting competition as far as
concerned other beverages in the trade. If the Federation's members
wished in conjunction with the sale of their own products to supply their
customers with Coca-Cola as well, they had to procure it in roundabout
ways and pay an "excess price" for it. The Federation requested that the
Price and Cartel Office "cooperate in ensuring that all companies which
have obtained permission in this country to sell and keep in stock beverages marketed by the malt-liquors and soft-drinks trade received the same
treatment as the Coca-Cola company." At the same time the Federation
enclosed letters on the subject from certain of its members, including
Kopparberg, the latter complaining that its twenty-odd agents, consisting
of soft-drinks breweries holding a permit to keep lager beer in stock and
manufacturing their own mineral waters and soft drinks, were debarred
from the possibility of purchasing "Cola drinks," and that they were thus
prevented from "offering much-needed competition." The term "Cola
drinks" in the letter apparently refers to Coca-Cola. Kopparberg added,
among other things, the following observations:

> There are many shopkeepers, sweetshops, fruitstalls, and confec-
> tioners who, faced with the threat of not being able to obtain Coca-
> Cola, have refused to allow us and our agents to sell to them products
> of our own manufacture for the reason that we have not been in a
> position to supply them with Cola drinks. . . . At present the procedure
> is as follows: Our agents are compelled—surreptitiously, so to speak—
> to buy Coca-Cola from the draymen who are employed by the Coca-
> Cola monopoly and to pay the maximum price, and then—likewise
> surreptitiously—actually to supply their own customers free of charge.

In the year 1960 the Office received information concerning the following cases. A brewery, a member of the Malt Liquors and Soft Drinks
Federation, had supplied beverages to a People's Hall Society, among other
customers, during the period from the beginning of the 1950's up to the
spring of 1957. Coca-Cola, however, was delivered by a competitor. The
competitor, an authorized distributor of Coca-Cola, made a request to be
allowed to supply the Society as from the autumn season of 1957. The
minutes of the council of the Society contained an entry on this subject,
among other things, to the effect that the former brewery had effected the
deliveries in a satisfactory manner without the least cause for criticism, so
that the Society intended to continue giving the same brewery its custom.

However, according to the minutes the competing brewery pointed out that "it was bound to supply a portion of the drink that was not marketed by" the former brewery. As from the new season the council decided to purchase all drinks from the firm that has herein been called the competing brewery, and which also sold Coca-Cola.

The same brewery member of the Malt Liquors and Soft Drinks Federation has further stated that for a period of about twenty years it had alone been supplying beverages to a People's Park, and in this connection has made the following observation:

> During the past few years, however, the deliveries have been divided up between ourselves and a competing firm merely for the reason that the Park council considered that it was obliged to supply its public with Coca-Cola as well. During the current year our share in the deliveries has been restricted to only one single occasion during the entire season.

Finally, reference may be made to another case concerning a brewery belonging to the Malt Liquors and Soft Drinks Federation, and which had been granted authorization to distribute Coca-Cola. It has previously been mentioned that three members of that Federation had received similar authorization. The bottler from whom the brewery bought Coca-Cola has formerly obtained from the distributors concerned a certain contribution toward advertising costs. The bottler firm informed the brewery that as from 1 November 1960 the contribution towards advertising costs would be raised. In conjunction herewith these partners in the bottling company who distributed Coca-Cola had decided not to raise the market price of the beverage. The Federation member in question, who is not a partner in the bottling company, considered that the higher contribution to costs, while the selling price remained unchanged, would involve a substantial reduction of his margin of earnings. He felt himself unfairly treated. The Swedish Industrial Association, of which the Federation affected is a member, reported the matter to the Office. On this point the bottling company has stated that the contribution towards the cost of advertising Coca-Cola is the same per bottle for partners as for other customers.

THE PROBLEMS PRESENTED

The statement of the case given in the preceding pages has indicated in the main the starting-point for the investigation reported on herein. The question under consideration turns on the consequences of the selective marketing system practised in the trade in Coca-Cola. Authorization given by the American corporation concerned is in principle, and also in practice, necessary for a firm in the brewery and soft-drinks trade to be able to include Coca-Cola among its assortment of beverages. It may, of course, be inconvenient for a brewery not to be in a position, when selling malt liquors and soft drinks to retailers, as through mobile shops to consumers, to supply Coca-Cola as well. As a result, large numbers of customers may be compelled to purchase from several suppliers, and some customers may find it to their interest to stop buying from a brewery that does not include that drink in its assortment of mineral waters. Thus, Coca-Cola might to some extent be said to assume a key position. It is to be noted, however, that the beverage in question appears to represent a mere fraction of the total quantity of soft drinks sold. The number of various kinds of soft drinks, and even of malt liquors, reckoned in brands, is relatively large, and it happens in this trade, as in others, that different manufacturers have different brands. No supplier is likely to sell all brands in the market. Moreover, there are drinks which, having the word "Cola" in the name, such as Mexi-Cola for instance, may be calculated to compete with Coca-Cola. Probably, too, the possibility exists for the Skruv and Kopparberg breweries themselves to manufacture drinks which in a similar way could be sold in competition with Coca-Cola. Nevertheless, this article, by means *inter alia* of extensive advertising in Sweden as abroad, may have achieved such popularity among a large number of consumers as to have acquired, to some extent, an exclusive position. In this way Coca-Cola, irrespective of the very small proportion which it represents of the turnover in the trade, may be an important competitive article in the malt-liquors and soft-drinks market generally. An important factor in this respect is that through the system of authorization the drink has essentially been reserved for companies within the leading brewery groups in the country. Coca-Cola might thus very well have some part to play in the competition between these groups on the one hand and, on the other, outside suppliers in the trade, among whom may be noted the breweries at Skruv and Kopparberg and their associated companies. The Skruv and Kopparberg breweries assert that the competition which they are able to offer both in malt liquors and in soft drinks depends more or less on whether they are to be able to include Coca-Cola in their assortments. On the other hand, it would appear that the demands made by the Skruv and Kopparberg breweries to be allowed to sell Coca-Cola aim at intervening in the business of the organization that is already established for the sale of that beverage, and which endows each authorized distributor with a monopolistic position in the district allotted to him. Thus, the existing division into marketing areas for Coca-Cola might possibly collapse if the companies at Skruv and Kopparberg, which sell their own products to breweries in a considerable number of counties, were allowed to supply Coca-Cola as well. The already existing sales organization for Coca-Cola is no doubt actually, in all essentials, adequate for meeting the consumers' demand for the drink. If Coca-Cola is regarded as an important competitive instrument, the problem facing the present investigation is to seek to elucidate whether the interest in maintaining competition with such Groups as AB Stockholms Bryggerier and AB Pripp & Lyckholm justifies taking a position in favor of the Skruv and Kopparberg breweries' claims to be allowed to sell Coca-Cola. To that extent, then, the task will be to endeavor to ascertain how significant a part the Skruv and Kopparberg breweries play as a competitive factor on that portion of the malt-liquors and soft-drinks market in which they are already established, primarily perhaps in regard to lager beer. It is worth pointing out, however, that especially in malt liquors the group companies mentioned are up against competition from several quarters. According to information published in the report on the Inquiry of 1954 into the Breweries (SOU 1959, No. 46, p. 59 et seq.), beer is sold, on an average, from about six breweries in each county. The largest number of companies are to be found in Stockholm City and County (8), Jönköping County (11), Kronoberg County (9), and Skaraberg County (9). Of these, Jönköping and Kronoberg Counties represent the main portions of Skruv's sales area. The report gives a list (p. 175 et seq.) of the Group Companies and the independent breweries in the country.

The Commissioner for Freedom of Commerce has requested that the supplementary inquiry into the matter be undertaken in all essentials on the basis of the principles formulated during deliberations that have taken place between the said Commissioner and the State Price and Cartel Office. Thus, attention should be paid to the following problems, among others:

1. Does the selective sale of Coca-Cola make it possible to evade the gross-price prohibition by having recourse as distributors, in the main, to companies which may conceivably desire in their own interests to maintain the maximum prices quoted in the contracts?

2. In regard to malt liquors and soft drinks generally, can price competition be found to exist between, on the one hand, the Coca-Cola sellers who are authorized by contract and, on the other hand, such companies as Skruv and Kopparberg and their partners? Is it possible to ascertain whence the initiative in carrying on any existing price competition has come? In connection with these problems an account should be given of the trend of Coca-Cola prices.

3. Can the price of Coca-Cola be considered to be high in relation to manufacturing and other costs, and is high pricing in that respect rendered possible by the selective-selling method?

4. What extra expenditure have such companies as Skruv and Kopparberg incurred as a result of their having been obliged to procure Coca-Cola in roundabout ways, compared with what the costs would have been had they been allowed to buy direct from the bottler?

Light will be thrown on these questions in the following section. Some introductory considerations may be stated now at once. As to the first question, for instance, this Office has previously pointed out that, notably in East and West Sweden, where the Stockholm and Göteborg Groups have for a long time been predominant in the malt-liquors and soft-drinks market, both the bottling companies and, for the most part, also the authorized distributors exist within the Group structure and are thereby held together by consolidated interests. Under such circumstances it is likely that possibilities exist for a centralized management and for controlling the fixing of prices, due attention being paid to setting the limits in accordance with the contracts. By reason of the problems posed under Point 2 this Office has felt justified in giving some idea of the development of prices, not only of Coca-Cola, but also of other soft drinks and malt beverages. For this purpose certain beverages have been selected as typical examples. The report concerns both nominal and real prices; that is to say, data are given both with and without regard to discounts. In order to throw light on the part played by the Skruv and Kopparberg breweries in the competition, this Office has attempted to make individual price comparisons between each brewery, on the one hand, and a Group brewery or other competitive enterprise in the same or neighboring district on the other. The costs problems touched upon by the Commissioner for Freedom of Commerce are also discussed, though in a more summary fashion.

The Coca-Cola prices reported on in the investigation apply to a bottle size of about nineteen centilitres. During 1960 a larger Coca-Cola bottle containing approximately thirty-six centilitres began to be marketed.

AUTHORIZED COCA-COLA COMPANIES' PRICES FOR MALT LIQUORS AND SOFT DRINKS SOLD TO RETAILERS

Coca-Cola prices recommended by the manufacturers. Under their agreements with the American corporations the bottling companies have undertaken, when selling Coca-Cola to distributors and retailers to maintain certain maximum prices. As already mentioned, the sales to retailers are effected within each bottler's local territory. The agreed maximum prices during the 1950's are quoted in Tables 11 and 12.

In regard to the prices' status as maximum prices the following observations may be made. All the six bottlers have stated that they have applied the maximum prices to retailers without any deviation. Four bottlers have made similar statements regarding the maximum prices charged to distributors. However, two bottlers have deviated from the maximum prices stipulated in the agreements by granting several distributors freight allowances. One of these companies has also deviated by debiting some distributors with an increment to the maximum prices. This company has granted its most remotely situated distributors the highest freight allowances. Sundbyberg bottler has stated that price increments have been applied ever since the autumn of 1956 under a private agreement with the American corporation concerned. Such a private agreement might perhaps be said to imply amended maximum prices. In view of the facts just quoted it would seem as if the bottler companies' market prices have been applied, apart from the freight allowances, as fixed prices, though they have been formally connoted in the contracts as maximum prices.

Prices, freight allowances, and price increments are accounted for by the companies per case of twenty-four bottles. In Tables 11 and 12 the figures have been converted into price per bottle. Concerning price level and the trend of prices the following remarks may be made:

The maximum prices charged to the distributor by most of the bottling companies during various phases of the 1950's were respectively 19, 20, and 23 öre per bottle. However, the Sundsvall bottler demanded one öre higher price throughout the entire period. Two bottling companies have, by granting certain freight allowances and by price increments, deviated from the maximum prices quoted in Table 11.

The bottler at Filipstad has for several years maintained the same price level as the Sundsvall company in respect of all distributors except one. So that with these exceptions the nominal price level has been similar for

TABLE 11: MAXIMUM PRICES CHARGED TO COCA-COLA DISTRIBUTORS

(Charged by bottling companies during the period 1953–January 1960)

Öre per bottle

	Price since beginning of contractual period 1953–54	Amended prices since	
Location of Bottler		*1956–57*	*20/3 1958*
Sundbyberg	20	----	23
Göteborg	19	20	23
Filipstad	19	20 & 21	23 & 24
Jönköping	19	20	23
Malmö	19	20	23
Sundsvall	20	21	24

TABLE 12: AGREED MAXIMUM PRICES CHARGED TO COCA-COLA RETAILERS

(Charged by bottling companies during the period 1953–January 1960)

Öre per bottle

	Price since beginning of contractual period 1953–54	Amended prices since		
Location of Bottler		*1956*	*1957*	*20/3 1958*
Sundbyberg	27	29	----	32
Göteborg	26	28	----	31
Filipstad	26	28	----	31
Jönköping	26	28	----	31
Malmö	26	27	28	31
Sundsvall	27	29	31	34

all bottlers. The prices have been "delivered free ex works." However, the price level is split as a result of the above-mentioned freight allowances and price increments.

The bottling companies' prices to the retailers in the companies' local districts—maximum prices which they have not gone below—have varied during the period between 26 and 34 öre per bottle. Any changes effected have tended upwards. The bottler at Sundsvall has in recent years charged a price of 34 öre to the retailer. Otherwise the bottlers' price to the retailer has been 31 öre. However, in the Sundbyberg bottler's local district, that is to say, Stockholm and neighborhood, the price to the retailer throughout the whole of the 1950's was one öre higher than the other Central Swedish bottling companies' prices to the retailer. The prices in Stockholm have in the course of the years been 27, 29, and 32 öre respectively; in other words, apart from Norrland, the Stockholm prices have been the highest of all.

Soft-drink tax is included in the prices just quoted. During the period up to 20 March 1958 the tax was 21 öre per litre, corresponding to 4.2 öre per Coca-Cola bottle if each bottle is reckoned to contain one-fifth of a litre. To be more precise, a Coca-Cola bottle is said to hold 19.3 centilitres. As from the said date the rate of tax was changed to 33 öre per litre, corresponding to 6.6 öre per bottle. As has been indicated in Tables 11 and 12, the bottling companies' most recent increases in price were effected in conjunction with the said rise in the rate of tax. The Sundbyberg bottler has stated that the change in price effected on 20 March 1958 fully corresponded to the higher tax on soft drinks, the petrol tax, and the introduction of the sugar tax. It may be mentioned that in February 1958 the tax on the consumption of petrol and motor fuel was raised by five öre per litre, and a commodity tax of 20 öre per kilogram was levied on sugar.

After this survey of the bottler companies' prices the Office will now proceed to given an account of the authorized distributors' recommended prices for Coca-Cola sold to the retailer. Like the bottlers, the distributors have undertaken by agreement with the American corporations concerned to maintain certain top prices. When making the earlier investigation the Office wrote to each distributor directly asking for data concerning the highest market prices prescribed for each in the period since the spring of 1957. In their replies a number of distributors have given particulars covering the preceding period as well. The information that has thus come to hand tallies in all essentials with the price data which the Office has previously obtained from the American corporations. When divergences arose, as happened in a few cases, the Office as a rule found an explanation for them.

Tables 13 A–D show the distributors' retail prices in question during the period up to the beginning of 1960. The distributors are grouped in accord with the list, the figures being broken down under the bottling companies from whom they obtain Coca-Cola. Thus, those distributors which belong to the bottling companies in Göteborg, Filipstad, and Jönköping form one group (West Sweden) in view of the fact that these three bottlers belong to one and the same concern, and for the reason that the prices affecting the distributors in question have shown a markedly uniform trend.

In Table 13 A will be found the maximum prices charged to the retailers by the distributors who obtain Coca-Cola from the bottler at Sundbyberg. Originally the prices were 27–32 öre per bottle, and since 20 March 1958, when the tax on soft drinks was raised, they have been 32–35 öre. The lowest price during the first period, 27 öre, had been charged by AB Växjö Bayerska Bryggeri, which is the distributor in central Småland. In the same period AB Visby Bryggeri, the sole distributor on the isle of Gotland, charged the highest price, 32 öre. The Visby Bryggeri is still top of the scale of prices at 35 öre per bottle, having been so since 1958. The next highest price to the retailer has always been charged by the distributor who has the contract for selling in the archipelago outside Stockholm. The distributor in question is AB Stockholms Bryggerier. The most usual price level among the distributors was originally 28–29 öre, and since 1958 it has been 32 öre. A distributor in East Sweden has stated that as from March 1958 his top price was fixed at 32 öre, but at the same time, owing to a deviation combined with a quantity discount, this price was raised to 33 öre. In this case the latter price has been quoted for the said distributor in Table 13 A.

In the Göteborg Group's district (West Sweden) the most common distributor's price to the retailer at the beginning of the period was 27 öre (Table 13 C). This was raised in December 1956 to 29 öre, and then in March 1958, in conjunction with the increased rate of tax on soft drinks,

TABLE 13: HIGHEST PRICES CHARGED TO COCA-COLA RETAILERS

(Charged by authorized distributors during the period 1953–January 1960)

ces in a number of distributor districts

Öre per bottle	1953 or 1954	A. East Sweden			B. Norrland				
		After change of price			After change of price				
		9/11 1956	20/3 1958	1/9 1959	1955	1956	1957	1958	1960
40	--	--	--	--	--	--	--	--	3
39	--	--	--	--	--	--	--	2	--
38	--	--	--	--	--	--	--	3	2
37	--	--	--	--	--	--	--	--	--
36	--	--	--	--	--	--	--	--	--

ontinued on following page)

272   Sweden

(Table 13, continued)

| | A. East Sweden | | | | B. Norrland | | | | |
| | After change of price | | | | After change of price | | | | |
Öre per bottle	1953 or 1954	9/11 1956	20/3 1958	1/9 1959	1955	1956	1957	1958	1960
35	--	--	1	1	--	--	1	4	4
34	--	--	1	1	--	--	1	--	--
33	--	1	5	6	--	1	3	--	--
32	1	1	10	9	2	2	6	--	--
31	--	--	--	--	2	3	--	--	--
30	1	--	--	--	1	5	--	--	--
29	6	15	--	--	5	--	--	--	--
28	8	--	--	--	--	--	--	--	--
27	1	--	--	--	--	--	--	--	--
	17	17	17	17	10	11	11	9	9

| | C. West Sweden | | | D. South Sweden | | | |
| | After change of price | | | After change of price | | | |
Öre per bottle	1953 or 1954	6/12 1956	20/3 1958	1953 or 1954	6/12 1956	Spring 1957	20/3 1958
33	--	--	1	--	--	--	1
32	--	--	26	--	--	--	1
31	--	--	--	--	--	--	8
30	--	1	--	--	--	1	--
29	--	26	--	--	--	1	--
28	3	--	--	1	2	8	--
27	24	--	--	5	8	--	--
26	--	--	--	4	--	--	--
	27	27	27	10	10	10	10

to 32 öre. Only one distributor has quoted a higher sales price in recent years, Axvalls Bryggeri.

In regard to the distributors in South Sweden, primarily in Skåne and Blekinge, their prices to the retailer have risen from an original figure of 26–28 öre to 31–33 öre since March 1958 (Table 13 D). The Karlskrona distributor, selling in Blekinge and south Småland, has throughout almost the entire period recorded the highest price—most recently 33 öre. The next highest price—now 32 öre—has as a rule been quoted by the Halmstad distributor.

In Norrland the price level has been the highest in the country at 29–32 öre in the year 1955 and 35–40 öre at the beginning of 1960 (Table 13 B). The 40 öre price applies to the Kiruna, Gällivare, and Luleå distributor districts. In view of certain changes made in the conditions affecting distributors, particulars regarding a somewhat different number of distributors are given in Table 13 B.

To sum up, it may be stated that a) the distributors' prices for Coca-Cola charged to retailers have been lowest in South Sweden and in that part of the country that is served by the Göteborg Group, b) the price level has been slightly higher in the Stockholm Group's district, and c) it has been highest in Norrland.

As we have explained, the prices quoted are based on information which the Office has obtained upon inquiry as to the highest prices that have been agreed upon between the American corporations concerned and each distributor. At the time of requesting this information the Office also asked whether there had been any deviations from the maximum prices and whether any quantity discounts had been allowed. A number of distributors allow quantity discounts. To judge from the answers, however, opinions differ as to whether such discounts imply deviations from the maximum prices. Some distributors, for instance, have replied that there have been no deviations, but at the same time they have stated that they have allowed quantity discounts. All the answers appear to imply that the contracted maximum prices have been applied as nominal sales prices. Where quantity discounts have been allowed, they have been calculated on those prices. The discount conditions will be dealt with later.

Breweries' list prices of soft drinks other than Coca-Cola and of lager. For the authorized distributors of Coca-Cola that beverage is merely one of the articles in their assortment. As manufacturers or warehousemen in the trade they sell malt liquors and soft drinks generally. Fixing the price of Coca-Cola must be viewed, *inter alia,* in the light of the fact that the distributors are the sole sellers, each in his own district, of the beverage to the retailer. As far as the other beverages are concerned, however, competition is offered on a major or minor scale by other companies. One aim of the present investigation is to throw light on the question as to whether and, if so, to what extent the fixing of the price of Coca-Cola and those of other soft drinks and malt liquors has been influenced by this monopolistic or competitive position held by the sellers. When the Price and Cartel Office asked the distributors for details regarding the price of Coca-Cola, therefore, it also requested information about the distributing companies' prices for other beverages. In regard to soft drinks, the data required for this purpose concerned sugared soda-water, Loranga, and Pommac or corresponding beverages in the respective price Groups 1, 2, and 3 into which they are usually divided. To judge from the particulars sent in, the price of Coca-Cola has approximated to that of soft drinks in price Group 2, including, e.g., Blodapelsin, Champis, and Loranga. Here the comparison has been made between the price per bottle containing respectively one-fifth and one-third of a litre. Further, it has been ascertained that, quite generally, the trend of soft-drink prices in the various groups has in recent years been more or less similar as far as concerns changes in öre reckoned per bottle. For this reason the Office has considered that it could limit the comparison in regard to soft drinks to Coca-Cola and beverages in price Group 2, that is to say, primarily to Loranga and similar drinks. As to malt liquors, lager Class II has been chosen for the purpose of making a comparison. Here, too, it would appear that the distributors, in their capacity of sellers of malt liquors and soft drinks, should be called breweries, even though some of them are solely soft-drink factories or warehouses.

To start with, the Office would like to refer to the picture of the price trend that is presented in Table 14. Seeing that in all essentials the Table concerns the same companies as those which are authorized to sell Coca-Cola, in this connection too they have been grouped according to the abovementioned division of the country into four main districts, although in several cases the competition in regard to beverages other than Coca-Cola even exceeds the limits prescribed for the latter drink. However, the picture presented in Table 14 is drawn more in outline than was Table 13. Thus, the breweries' list prices upon selling to the retailer are accounted for in January 1956 and in January 1960. On the subject of price changes between these points of time the Office would like to make the following remarks. The changes have for the most part been effected upwards, though there have been price reductions in some cases. Nevertheless, the final result for the period is a rise all along the line. As far as the majority of the breweries are concerned, the biggest rise in price and the latest during the period occurred in conjunction with the increase in the malt-liquor and soft-drink tax, which came into effect on 20 March 1958.

For Loranga and similar drinks in price Group 2 all the breweries in South Sweden that were investigated, except one, recommended in January 1956 26 öre per bottle, as the basic list price, when selling to the retailer, whereas most of the breweries in East and West Sweden listed the price at 28 öre. In January 1960 the majority of the breweries in those three parts of Sweden quoted 34 öre as the basic list price to the retailer.

In January 1960 most of the breweries in the parts of the country just mentioned quoted the list price for lager as 34 or 35 öre to the retailer. In January 1960 the corresponding price in West Sweden was 38 öre and in East and South Sweden 40 öre. This difference in price trend and prices between West Sweden on the one hand and East and South Sweden on the other may be partially explained by the fact that, as a rule, the companies in East and South Sweden introduced discounts or increased their discounts during the period, whereas in West Sweden discounts were allowed only in exceptional cases, and then only in districts bordering on East Sweden.

In Norrland the price level has been higher and more widely differentiated. In the other parts of the country a certain coordination has apparently

Table 14: BASIC LIST PRICES CHARGED TO RETAILERS

(Prices for certain malt liquors and soft drinks charged by authorized Coca-Cola distributors in January 1956 and January 1960)

Number of distributors' districts

Öre per bottle	East Sweden 1956	1960	West Sweden 1956	1960	South Sweden 1956	1960	Norrland 1956	1960
Soft Drinks Group 2								
42	--	--	--	--	--	--	--	1
41	--	--	--	--	--	--	--	--
40	--	--	--	--	--	--	--	1
39	--	--	--	--	--	--	--	3
38	--	--	--	--	--	--	--	1
37	--	--	--	--	--	--	--	3
36	--	2	--	--	--	--	--	--
35	--	1	--	--	--	--	--	--
34	--	14	--	26	--	7	--	--
33	--	--	--	1	--	3	--	--
32	--	--	--	--	--	--	2	--
31	--	--	--	--	--	--	4	--
30	--	--	--	--	--	--	--	--
29	3	--	3	--	--	--	3	--
28	10	--	21	--	1	--	--	--
27	2	--	2	--	--	--	--	--
26	2	--	--	--	9	--	--	--
	17	17	26	27	10	10	9	9
Lager Class II								
44	--	--	--	--	--	--	--	2
43	--	--	--	--	--	--	--	3
42	--	1	--	--	--	--	--	--
41	--	1	--	--	--	--	--	2
40	--	12	--	--	--	6	--	2
39	--	2	--	2	--	3	--	--
38	--	1	--	25	--	1	--	--
37	--	--	--	--	--	--	4	--
36	1	--	2	--	1	--	4	--
35	10	--	14	--	9	--	1	--
34	5	--	10	--	--	--	--	1
33	1	--	--	--	--	--	--	--
	17	17	26	27	10	10	9	9

taken place since the middle of the 1950's in the fixing of nominal prices, this being most noticeable in regard to soft drinks.

Discounts allowed to the retailer. In the preceding section an account has been given of the list prices suggested by the breweries, i.e., the authorized Coca-Cola distributors, when selling Coca-Cola, soft drinks belonging to Group 2, and lager Class II to the retailer. However, discounts have been allowed to some extent, so that the actual prices have been lower.

When quantity discounts have been applied, they have been based, according to the date sent in, on öre per bottle calculated on each delivery. In addition, an annual discount has been given in some quarters.

At the beginning of 1956 certain breweries in East Sweden belonging to the Stockholm Group allowed retailers a quantity discount on malt liquors and soft drinks at the rate of one öre as from the 51st bottle, while other breweries in the Group gave a similar discount as from the 71st bottle. One brewery allowed, besides that discount rate, an additional öre per bottle as from the 501st. When allowing this öre discount some breweries made an exception of Coca-Cola. So far as can be gathered from the replies which the Price and Cartel Office has received, a number of breweries both within and outside the Group were not granting at this time, in the beginning of 1956, any quantity discount to retailers either on sales of soft drinks or of malt liquors. Since then, however, an ever-increasing number of breweries have gradually begun to apply a discount system on these lines, so that the situation has as of late been the following: The majority of the breweries investigated in East Sweden allow the retailers a quantity discount of 2 öre as from the 101st bottle. A couple of breweries have framed the rule in such a way that a discount of 50 öre per case is payable after the first 4 cases—which in effect is the same as the rule just mentioned, since a case of malt liquor or ordinary soft drinks contains 25 bottles. One brewery allows a discount of 25 öre per case beyond the first 4 cases. Only a small number of breweries have stated that the quantity discount applies to Coca-Cola as well. One brewery reports that the discount of 2 öre allowed as from the 101st bottle is applicable to Coca-Cola when the brewery distributes that article together with other drinks, but not when it is distributed by the special Coca-Cola vans. However, in the former case, i.e., when a discount is allowed, that brewery charges one öre more per bottle than it does otherwise. Apart from the quantity discounts just discussed, most of the breweries in East Sweden investigated grant an annual-turnover discount varying from 0.5 per cent of the total value of orders between 50,000 and 100,000 kronor up to 2 per cent on the value in excess of one million kronor. The annual discount is calculated, so far as the information received indicates, on the value of orders including purchase tax but excluding quantity discounts. One brewery calculates annual discount on the basis of so many öre per case, viz. from 15 öre per case on orders for at least 200 cases and up to 50 öre per case on orders for at least 4,000 cases.

In West Sweden, where the Göteborg Group is the main producer, as a rule neither quantity nor annual discounts are allowed by the breweries when selling to the retailer. Only four of the breweries investigated there have allowed quantity discounts, e.g., one öre per bottle as from the 51st bottle. One of these companies joined the Group in 1958 and was then incorporated in its price system, so that now it does not apply any discount arrangement. The three other breweries, one of which is a member of the Group, still allow a discount.

So far as the data received indicates, the investigated breweries in South Sweden did not begin to grant discounts on malt liquors and soft drinks when selling to the retailers until 1957. Since October 1959 most of the breweries have paid a quantity discount of one öre per bottle. Only one company, however, pays this discount on Coca-Cola. For the retailer to receive a quantity discount on malt liquors and soft drinks generally, it is usually stipulated that he purchase at least 50 bottles at a time, the discount being calculated at some breweries already on the first of the 50 bottles, and at one of the breweries as from the 51st bottle. Usually the breweries allow an additional annual discount on each bottle, ranging from 1.02 öre if the annual purchase is below 10,000 bottles, to 1.50 öre if it exceeds 150,000 bottles.

In Norrland the majority of the breweries give quantity discounts on malt liquors and soft drinks upon selling to retailers at one or two öre per bottle. One example is a discount of one öre per bottle on a purchase of 100 bottles and 2 öre per bottle when over 200 bottles are bought at a time. Some companies include Coca-Cola among the beverages qualifying for a discount. Others exclude Coca-Cola. Only one brewery in Norrland has reported that it applies an annual discount arrangement. The rate of discount, up to 2.6 per bottle, depends on the size of the total purchases made by the members of the local merchant organization. The brewery in question does not allow any quantity discount on each purchase.

Prices and changes in price owing to discounts. The above is a survey of breweries' list prices and the rules governing discounts upon the sale of malt liquors and soft drinks to the retailer as practiced mainly by such companies as are at the same time authorized to sell Coca-Cola. The Price and Cartel Office will not proceed to discuss the real prices and the changes in prices, that is to say, the prices after deduction for discount. Seeing that the discounts, when they exist, are generally allowable on the basis of quantity at each occasion of effecting delivery, the Office has selected certain quantities for estimating the discount, viz. 200, 300, and 500 bottles. These quantities have also been regarded as weekly deliveries, so that after converting them into annual quantities, consideration could also be given to any existing annual discount when such a discount has been calculated according to the number of bottles. In one group, however, an annual discount is allowed that is based on a certain percentage of the value of the retailer's annual purchases of malt liquors and soft drinks, starting at 0.5 per cent on purchases amounting to at least 50,000 kronor. In the event of weekly deliveries of the size mentioned, no such annual amounts are reached, so that the discount according to value is not reflected in the following calculations. If the discount according to value were taken into account, certain assumptions might have had to be made as to what drinks at different price levels the deliveries comprised. The following may be given as an example of how the annual discount in question works. If the average price per bottle is assumed to be 40 öre, this would require deliveries of about 2,500 bottles per week in order to arrive at the lowest limit for a discount. The discount, 0.5 per cent, then corresponds to 0.2 öre per bottle. In order to reach the highest annual discount, 2 per cent, it would require deliveries, at a price of 40 öre per bottle, of approximately 50,000 bottles per week, the discount then corresponding to 0.8 öre per bottle.

As a background to the observations that follow, the Price and Cartel Office finds it appropriate in this connection to refer to the malt-liquor and soft-drink tax. This tax is levied on the quantities supplied from brewery or factory for the market. As far as concerns the period under examination here, the tax was, to start with, 42 öre per litre on lager Class II and 21 öre per litre on soft drinks. On 20 March 1958 these rates were raised to 48 and 33 öre respectively, which meant an increase per bottle containing one-third of a litre of 2 öre for lager and 4 öre for soft drinks. The raising of the soft-drinks tax from 21 to 33 öre per litre corresponded in the case of Coca-Cola to 2.4 öre per bottle if each bottle is estimated to contain one-fifth of a litre.

During the period from the beginning of 1956 to the beginning of 1960 the changes in price that were effected very largely corresponded to the increase in the tax rate. As a rule, however, the prices have gone up more than would correspond to the higher tax. Table 15 illustrates the price increases excluding tax and taking into account the effect of discounts upon the sale to the retailer of the above-mentioned quantities. The rises are indicated in average (unweighted) for the companies investigated, that is to say, mainly those authorized to distribute Coca-Cola. The increases in the nominal prices, i.e., those that are applied when no discount is allowed, are accounted for both per litre and per bottle. The object of tabulating the rise on a per-litre basis is primarily to eliminate the difference in the size of the bottle when comparing Coca-Cola to other soft drinks.

It appears from the figures that in Norrland and West Sweden the rise in the nominal prices excluding tax per litre has been nearly twice as high for Coca-Cola as for other soft drinks. In East and South Sweden the trend of prices has been approximately the same for Coca-Cola as for other soft drinks. A comparison worked out per bottle shows that the price of Coca-Cola has gone up only slightly more than that of the other soft drinks in Norrland and West Sweden and that the price of Coca-Cola has been raised less than the prices of other soft drinks in East and South Sweden.

If account is taken of existing discounts, which in most cases were initiated during the period for which the comparison is drawn, the rise in prices is less, especially those for beverages other than Coca-Cola, for which latter it is less usual to allow a discount. Thus, in South Sweden the granting of a discount alters the picture, so that the price of Coca-Cola has gone up more than that of other soft drinks. In regard to the rise in prices including tax during the period from 1956 it may be adduced that the increase throughout the country as a whole has been smaller in the case of Coca-Cola than in that of other soft drinks. The reason, of course, is that the most recent tax increase just mentioned represented only 2.4 öre per bottle of Coca-Cola as against 4 öre for other drinks.

As to lager, it may be deduced from Table 15 that nominally the prices have shown the smallest rise in West Sweden, the next smallest in South Sweden, and the biggest rise in East Sweden and Norrland. If the allowing of a discount is taken into account, the sequence starting from the smallest rise will be South, West, East Sweden, and Norrland.

After this survey of the changes in prices from 1956 to 1960, excluding tax and taking into account the allowing of discount, the Office proposes to discuss the prices obtaining in January 1960 including tax and, as just

TABLE 15: PRICE RISE, JANUARY 1956–JANUARY 1960

(Prices of certain malt liquors and soft drinks, excluding tax, effected on an average by the companies investigated when selling to retailer)

			Öre per bottle			
				After any discount allowed on following no. of bottles		
Soft Drinks	No. of companies	Öre per litre	Nominal	200	300	500
East Sweden						
Coca-Cola	18	8.2	1.7	1.4	1.2	1.1
Group 2	16	8.1	2.7	2.1	1.8	1.7
West Sweden						
Coca-Cola	30	12.0	2.4	2.4	2.4	2.4
Group 2	29	6.4	2.1	2.1	2.1	2.1
South Sweden						
Coca-Cola	11	11.2	2.2	2.2	2.2	2.2
Group 2	11	10.6	3.5	2.1	2.0	2.0
Norrland						
Coca-Cola	10	24.0	4.8	4.3	4.1	3.9
Group 2	9	12.3	4.1	3.3	3.1	3.0
Lager Class II						
East Sweden	16	9.6	3.2	2.6	2.4	2.2
West Sweden	29	4.2	1.4	1.4	1.4	1.4
South Sweden	11	7.5	2.5	1.0	0.9	0.9
Norrland	9	11.0	3.7	2.9	2.7	2.5

now, after deduction in respect to discount in cases where applied. As previously, the prices refer to sales to the retailer. In this section the investigation comprises a) the authorized Coca-Cola distributors, b) the bottling companies, and c) the various Groups' main companies operating in malt liquors and in soft drinks generally, that is to say, altogether sixty-nine companies for Coca-Cola, sixty-six for soft drinks in Group 2 and for lager Class II. The result is shown in Table 16 and reflects, *inter alia*, the following position. According to the statements received, fifty-three out of the sixty-nine companies have not allowed any discount on the nominal prices charged for Coca-Cola. In West Sweden only one company has allowed a discount on that beverage. In the said district there have been extremely few cases of a discount being granted even on other drinks. In the other parts of the country nearly all the companies under investigation have allowed a discount on sales to the retailer of drinks other than Coca-Cola, and consequently the prices charged have been below the nominal prices. A summary view of the significance of giving a discount is obtained by taking note of which list prices have been the most commonly applied and comparing them with the most prevalent price level after discount. Among the companies under investigation the list prices per bottle then work out as follows:

Coca-Cola	32 öre in 37 companies and 31 öre in 12 companies
Soft Drink Group 2	34 öre in 50 companies and 33 öre in 33 companies
Lager Class II	38 öre in 29 companies and 40 öre in 20 companies

Thus, no less than fifty companies charge a similar list price, 34 öre per bottle—that for soft drinks in Group 2—and the list prices for the other beverages were similarly in close agreement. This circumstance should be viewed against the background of the powerful Group formation in the trade. Upon the sale of 300 bottles (which is taken here as an example) the price was reduced as a result of discounts in cases where they were allowed, so that the actual prices varied as follows:

Coca-Cola	30.5–32.0 öre in 55 companies
Soft Drink Group 2	30.9–34.0 öre in 55 companies
Lager Class II	37.0–39.0 öre in 56 companies

For each one of the four districts (the Group districts) in the country in respect to which details are given in Table 16 there are also indicated unweighted averages of the prices charged the retailer by the individual companies. To judge from these averages, the prices due to existing discounts were lowest in South Sweden in regard to all the three beverages referred to here. Concerning lager, however, the price level due to the discount was the same in South and West Sweden. At the same time the list price (without discount) for lager was lowest in West Sweden.

Table 16: LIST PRICES AND PRICES AFTER DISCOUNT CHARGED TO RETAILERS

(Prices of malt liquors and soft drinks charged by certain companies in January 1960[3])

re per bottle

	Coca-Cola					Soft Drinks Gr. 2					Lager Cl. II			
		Price when following no. bottles sold					*Price when following no. bottles sold*					*Price when following no. bottles sold*		
No. of Com-panies[1]	*List Price*	*200*	*300*	*500*	*No. of Com-panies*	*List Price*	*200*	*300*	*500*	*No. of Com-panies*	*List Price*	*200*	*300*	*500*
ast Sweden														
1	32	30,8	30,5	30,3										
9	32	32,0	32,0	32,0	1	34	32,8	32,5	32,3	1	38	38,0	38,0	38,0
6	33	32,0	31,7	31,4	12	34	33,0	32,7	32,4	1	39	38,0	37,7	37,4
1	34	32,8	32,5	32,3										
1	35	34,5	34,3	34,2	1	34	34,0	34,0	34,0	1	39	39,0	39,0	39,0
					1	35	35,0	35,0	35,0	1	40	38,8	38,5	38,3
					1	36	34,8	34,6	34,4	11	40	39,0	38,7	38,4
										1	41	39,8	39,6	39,4
[2]18	32,6	32,1	32,0	31,8	16	34,2	33,3	33,0	32,8	16	39,8	38,9	38,7	38,4
Vest Sweden														
3	31	31,0	31,0	31,0	1	33	33,0	33,0	33,0	2	38	37,0	37,0	37,0
1	32	31,0	31,0	31,0						1	38	37,4	37,4	37,4
25	32	32,0	32,0	32,0	2	34	33,0	33,0	33,0	24	38	38,0	38,0	38,0
1	33	33,0	33,0	33,0	26	34	34,0	34,0	34,0	2	39	39,0	39,0	39,0
[2]30	31,9	31,9	31,9	31,9	29	34	33,9	33,9	33,9	29	38,1	38,0	38,0	38,0
outh Sweden														
9	31	31,0	31,0	31,0	2	33	31,0	30,9	30,9	1	38	37,0	37,0	37,0
1	32	32,0	32,0	32,0	1	33	32,0	32,0	32,0	3	39	38,0	37,9	37,9
1	33	32,3	32,2	32,1	3	34	32,0	31,9	31,9	1	39	38,0	38,0	38,0
					3	34	33,0	32,9	32,9	5	40	38,0	37,9	37,9
					1	34	33,0	33,0	33,0	1	40	39,3	39,2	39,1
					1	34	33,3	33,2	33,1					
[2]11	31,3	31,2	31,2	31,2	11	33,7	32,5	32,2	32,2	11	39,5	38,0	38,0	37,9
Norrland														
1	34	34,0	34,0	34,0	1	35	34,0	34,0	34,0	1	39	38,0	38,0	38,0
4	35	35,0	35,0	35,0	2	37	36,0	36,0	36,0	1	40	39,0	39,0	39,0
1	38	36,7	35,8	35,8	1	38	38,0	38,0	38,0	1	40	40,0	40,0	40,0
1	38	37,0	36,8	36,4	1	39	37,7	36,8	36,8	1	41	40,0	40,0	40,0
1	40	39,4	39,3	38,8	1	39	38,0	37,8	36,4	1	43	41,7	40,8	40,8
1	40	39,5	39,3	39,2	1	39	38,5	38,3	38,2	1	43	42,0	41,8	41,4
1	40	39,5	38,0	37,6	1	40	39,4	39,3	38,8	1	43	42,5	42,3	42,2
					1	42	41,5	41,0	40,6	1	44	43,4	43,3	42,8
										1	44	43,5	43,0	42,6
[2]10	37,0	36,6	36,3	36,2	9	38,4	37,7	37,5	37,2	9	41,9	41,1	40,9	40,8

[1] In East Sweden seventeen companies in eighteen districts are concerned.
[2] Total number of companies and average values.
[3] The use of the comma instead of the decimal point is common in Western Europe.

THE PART PLAYED BY THE SKRUV AND KOPPARBERG BREWERIES IN THE COM-
PETITION IN THE MALT-LIQUORS AND SOFT-DRINKS TRADE

The beer trade has been seriously affected by the restrictions on competition in consequence both of legislation and of cartel agreements. During
the 1950's the legislation was liberalized, and a wide complexity of cartel
agreements on a division into districts was annulled. A further important
change making for liberalization in the 1950's was a decree entitling small-
beer breweries to sell ale of another company's brew. The report on the
inquiry into the breweries in 1954 has drawn attention to the fact that the
competitive position on the beer market underwent a change in consequence, and that the purchase by the light-beer companies of a couple
of ale breweries was made with a view to strengthening the associated
companies' position in competition with the already established ale breweries (SOU 1959, No. 46, p. 54). As the report on the breweries mentioned,
the existing conditions in the beer trade may, on the whole, be said to imply
that the breweries' former sales districts have very largely been extended,
and that competitive selling by various companies is going on in most parts
of the country.

The Skruv and Kopparberg breweries, whose customers consist of retailers and consumers in considerable areas in South and Central Sweden
and south Norrland, represent an abundant assortment of the malt liquors
and soft drinks usually sold on the market. As to their present efforts to be
allowed to include Coca-Cola as well in their assortment of beverages, the
problem of the current inquiry is to throw light on these efforts against
the background of the part which the breweries in question are playing
from the competitive aspect on the malt-liquors and soft-drinks market
generally. The first task, therefore, is to consider the Skruv and Kopparberg
breweries' position in this competitive field. For this purpose a comparison
will be drawn between these breweries on the one hand and, on the other,
the rest of the companies under investigation here. The latter are for the
most part those which are at the same time authorized distributors of Coca-
Cola. The comparison has reference to sales to the retailer. A comparison
that is made in regard to the companies' direct sales to the consumer, i.e.,
mobile selling, should be gauged in the light of the insignificant proportion
of the turnover which this form of distribution represents in the total business of a good many breweries, especially the largest Group companies,
so far as can be gathered from the report on the inquiry into the breweries
(SOU 1959, No. 46, p. 59).

Prices charged to the retailer. The Price and Cartel Office has obtained details from ten Skruv partners in central and south Götaland regarding their
prices for malt liquors and soft drinks when selling to the retailer. A summary of the prices of soft drinks in price Group 2 (Loranga) and lager
Class II since 1956 is given in Table 17. Of the ten Skruv companies, four,

viz. those at Jönköping, Växjö, Borgholm, and Åskloster (Halland), have stated that they allow a quantity discount on malt liquors and soft drinks, though the last-mentioned company only in one or two isolated cases. To judge from the figures supplied, the discounts have apparently not been applied from the beginning of the period, but only after the lapse of some time. The discounts are in the case of the Jönköping company 15 öre per case and in those of the Växjö and Borgholm companies one and two öre respectively per bottle, provided 100 bottles are bought at a time.

The question now is how the Skruv companies' prices upon selling to the retailer have compared with the corresponding prices charged by other investigated companies in the trade. In this respect it seems justified to make a comparison with reference to each individual Skruv company. Accordingly, each company has been compared in regard to its prices with a competing company in the same locality or in a neighboring locality.

As regards the breweries' list prices in January 1960, the following observations may be made. Of the ten Skruv breweries two, those at Osby and Jönköping, charged one öre higher per bottle than the competing com-

TABLE 17: LIST PRICES CHARGED BY TEN BREWERIES

(Prices of malt liquors and soft drinks sold to the retailers by ten partners in Ab Förbundsbryggeriet Södra Sverige, Skruv, during the period January 1956–January 1960)

	Number of breweries		
Öre per bottle	1/1 1956–30/6 1957	1/7 1957–19/3 1958	20/3 1958–1/1 1960
Soft Drinks Group 2			
35	--	--	1
34	--	--	4
33	--	1	5
32	--	--	--
31	--	1	--
30	1	1	--
29	1	3	--
28	2	3	--
27	6	1	--
	10	10	10
Lager Class II			
40	--	--	2
39	--	--	6
38	--	1	2
37	--	2	--
36	3	3	--
35	3	4	--
34	4	--	--
	10	10	10

pany in question for soft drinks, and Jönköping for lager as well. Three Skruv breweries, those at Borgholm, Oskarström, and Åskloster, charged the same prices for malt liquors and soft drinks as their competitors. Further, the Skruv brewery at Osby and its competitor charged the same prices for lager. Otherwise the Skruv breweries' list price was one öre lower per bottle. However, the list price of the Skruv brewery at Eslöv for soft drinks was 3 öre lower than that of its competitor. In practically every case the list prices which the Skruv breweries mentioned here, and their competitors applied in January 1960 have been current since 20 March 1958, when the tax was increased by 4 öre for soft drinks and 2 öre for lager per one-third–litre bottle.

The above-mentioned list prices have been applied as sales prices when the retailers' purchases at any one time have not amounted to quantities entitling them to a discount. As will have been gathered from what has been said above, the Skruv breweries in question allow discounts on a smaller scale than their competitors. In Tables 18 A and B comparisons are made between the ten Skruv breweries and their competitors in regard to prices in January 1960 when selling to retailers for a) quantities not entitling to a discount and b) such quantities as, in the case of a considerable number of breweries, entitled the retailer to receive a discount. Prices have been calculated—quantity discounts being taken into account—on purchases of 200, 300, and 500 bottles at any one time. For the purpose of working out such annual discounts as have been allowed, these quantities have been reckoned as weekly deliveries. With the deliveries of the weekly quantities just quoted, the minimum value per annum that would warrant the previously mentioned value discount which one Group allows is not reached. The tables also show changes, usually rises, in prices since the beginning of 1956; the increase in the malt liquors and soft-drinks tax that took place during the period, however, have been deducted, so that the rises in prices quoted here are those which the breweries effected over and above the tax increase. Table 18 A refers to comparisons in cases where the Skruv breweries have charged higher prices than other companies calculated on major deliveries, whereas Table 18 B refers to comparisons in cases where Skruv's prices both for small and for large deliveries have as a rule been lower.

In regard to the comparison made in Table 18 A between the Skruv brewery at Osby and the competing company at Hässleholm, which quoted respectively 34 and 33 öre as their list prices for soft drinks when selling to retailers in January 1960, it may be mentioned that the Osby brewery's price, 34 öre, had been charged ever since 20 March 1958, and that the Hässleholm brewery had also quoted 34 öre as its list price from the same date up to 1 November 1959, when it reduced its price to 33 öre. Thus the Hässleholm brewery's lower price has been current for a relatively short time.

The Kopparberg brewery's products are marketed partly in districts where the Göteborg Group is predominant—viz. in Dalarna, Närke, west Västmanland, Värmland, Dalsland, and also parts of Västergötland and Bohuslän—and partly in certain sections of the Stockholm Group's sales district such as east Västmanland, Uppland, and Stockholm. The brewery owns one of two warehouses and, besides, sells through about twenty agents, which are usually light-beer breweries. All of them buy lager from Kopparberg. About ten agents also buy soft drinks from that brewery. The latter has stated that both it and practically all its agents, here called the Kopparberg breweries, have quoted similar prices when selling to retailers and that, as a rule, discounts have not been allowed; the following comparison is based on this statement. The Kopparberg breweries' competitors in the Göteborg Group have likewise had similar list prices for sales to retailers, and they have not given discounts either (cf. Table 14 concerning West Sweden). Companies in the Stockholm Group which compete with the Kopparberg breweries are breweries at Västerås, Uppsala, and in Stockholm. A comparison between the various categories of suppliers' list prices may be drawn in the following way.

The comparison relates first of all to the Kopparberg breweries and companies belonging to the Göteborg Group. In regard to lager, the former in January 1956 charged a list price to the retailer of 35 öre per bottle and the latter 34 and 35 öre per bottle. The price of 34 öre was raised during 1956 and 1957 to 38 öre, and this price was current also in January 1960. As to soft drinks, Group 2, the price charged by both groups in January 1956 was 28 öre per bottle. The Göteborg Group raised theirs by one öre, first on 1 June 1956 and again on 1 June 1957. The Kopparberg breweries' price was raised by 2 öre on 1 June 1957 and was thus brought into parity with the Göteborg Group at 30 öre per bottle. After that, both groups increased the price to 35 öre on 20 March 1958 and reduced it to 34 öre per bottle on 1 January 1960. Thus ever since 1956 the Kopparberg breweries and their competitors in the Göteborg Group have had, on the whole, the same price level and the same price trend.

Certain breweries buying malt liquors from Kopparberg and which compete with the Stockholm Group have stated that they apply the same list prices as the Group when selling to retailers, thus in January 1960, 34 öre per bottle for soft drinks in Group 2 and 40 öre per bottle for lager. One brewery has advised that it has had lower prices than the Group. However, the Group companies' list prices charged to the retailer for malt liquors and soft drinks were reduced by the allowance of 2 öre discounts, e.g., upon the delivery of the 101st bottle, corresponding to one öre per bottle, and the previously mentioned discount for 200 bottles at a time, plus any discount on annual turnover that may have been agreed upon. Discounting is also used to a certain degree among the Group's competitors.

TABLE 18: COMPARISON BETWEEN PRICES CHARGED BY SKRUV BREWERIES
AND OTHER BREWERIES

(Regarding changes in price, apart from tax, January 1956–January 1960, and prices in January 1960 upon selling to the retailer)

A. Skruv's prices higher than other companies' on the sale of major quantities.
Öre per bottle

Breweries in the following localities	Soft Drinks Group 2			Lager Class II		
		After any discount on following number of bottles			After any discount on following number of bottles	
	Nominal	200	300 & 500	Nominal	200	300 & 500
Osby (Skruv)						
Rise 1956–1960	2	2.0	2.0	2	2.0	2.0
Price in 1960	34	34.0	34.0	40	40.0	40.0
Hässleholm						
Rise 1956–1960	3	1.0	0.9	3	1.0	0.9
Price in 1960	33	31.0	30.9	40	38.0	37.9
Bjuv (Skruv)						
Rise 1956–1960	2	2.0	2.0	3	3.0	3.0
Price in 1960	33	33.0	33.0	39	39.0	39.0
Hälsingborg						
Rise 1956–1960	4	2.0	1.9	3	1.0	0.9
Price in 1960	34	32.0	31.9	40	38.0	37.9
Markaryd (Skruv)						
Rise 1956–1960	2	2.0	2.0	3	3.0	3.0
Price in 1960	33	33.0	33.0	39	39.0	39.00
Klippan						
Rise 1956–1960	4	2.0	1.9	3	1.0	0.9
Price in 1960	34	32.0	31.9	40	38.0	37.9
Oskarström (Skruv)						
Rise 1956–1960	2	2.0	2.0	1	1.0	1.0
Price in 1960	33	33.0	33.0	38	38.0	38.0
Halmstad						
Change 1956–1960	1	-----	-----	----	—1.0	—1.0
Price in 1960	33	32.0	32.0	38	37.0	37.0
Jönköping *Skruv brewery*						
Rise 1956–1960	2	2.0	2.0	1	1.0	1.0
Price in 1960	35	34.4	34.4	39	38.4	38.4
Another brewery						
Rise 1956–1960	2	2.6	2.6	1	1.0	1.0
Price in 1960	34	34.0	34.0	38	37.4	37.4

Skruv's prices in several cases lower than or the same as other companies'.
e per bottle

	Soft Drinks Group 2				Lager Class II			
reweries in e following localities		After any discount on following number of bottles				After any discount on following number of bottles		
	Nominal	200	300	500	Nominal	200	300	500
löv								
ruv brewery								
se 1956–1960	----	------	------	------	2	2.0	2.0	2.0
ice in 1960	31	31.0	31.0	31.0	39	39.0	39.0	39.0
other brewery								
se 1956–1960	4	2.0	1.9	1.9	3	1.0	0.9	0.9
ice in 1960	34	32.0	31.9	31.9	40	38.0	37.9	37.9
xjö								
ruv brewery								
se 1956–1960	2	1.0	1.0	1.0	3	2.0	2.0	2.0
ice in 1960	33	32.0	32.0	32.0	39	38.0	38.0	38.0
xjö Bayerska								
se 1956–1960	2	1.0	0.7	0.4	3	2.0	1.7	1.4
ice in 1960	34	33.0	32.7	32.4	40	39.0	38.7	38.4
rgholm (Skruv)								
ange 1956–1960	----	—2.0	—2.0	—2.0	2	------	------	------
ice in 1960	34	32.0	32.0	32.0	40	38.0	38.0	38.0
lmar								
se 1956–1960	2	1.7	1.4	1.3	3	2.7	2.4	2.3
ice in 1960	34	33.0	32.7	32.4	40	39.0	38.7	38.4
nneby (Skruv)								
se 1956–1960	2	2.0	2.0	2.0	3	3.0	3.0	3.0
ice in 1960	33	33.0	33.0	33.0	39	39.0	39.0	39.0
rlskrona								
se 1956–1960	4	3.3	3.2	3.1	3	2.3	2.2	2.1
ice in 1960	34	33.3	33.2	33.1	40	39.3	39.2	39.1
kloster (Skruv)								
se 1956–1960	2	2.0	2.0	2.0	1	1.0	1.0	1.0
ice in 1960	34	34.0	34.0	34.0	38	38.0	38.0	38.0
lkenberg								
se 1956–1960	3	3.0	3.0	3.0	1	1.0	1.0	1.0
ice in 1960	34	34.0	34.0	34.0	38	38.0	38.0	38.0

Consumer prices. After the comparisons made in the preceding section of the prices charged on sales to the retailer, the Price and Cartel Office now proposes to make a survey drawing certain comparisons in regard to the prices per bottle sold to the consumer in January 1960. In Table 19, for instance, the recommended prices are given based on information obtained from price lists issued by the merchants' county and local organizations. The prices recommended by the manufacturers have been compared with those list prices which, according to information received, have been applied when selling to the consumer by the brewery companies examined here, namely a) such firms as are authorized distributors of Coca-Cola and certain Group companies in addition—all here called authorized—and b) the breweries at Skruv and Kopparberg as well as their partners and agents. The merchant organizations' suggested prices are throughout the country above the breweries' consumer prices for malt liquors and soft drinks. It should be noted that the suggested prices are probably calculated taking into account any existing discount allowances in the form of deferred rebate. Where the organizations have quoted higher suggested prices in cases of deferred rebate, the higher price has been given in Table 19. Further, it may be mentioned that it has not been ascertained in this connection how far the retailers follow the suggested prices nor to what extent the various brewery companies sell direct to the consumer. Table 19 shows, in addition to the suggested prices, by how many öre the brewery companies' list prices fall short of the merchants' suggested prices when selling to the consumer. As to Coca-Cola, only a relatively few authorized distributors have stated that they sell to the consumer. In regard to soft drinks Group 2 and lager, the Table also affords some possibility of making a comparison between the consumer prices of the authorized companies and the Skruv and Kopparberg breweries. It appears, for instance, that Skruv's and Kopparberg's prices in various quarters of the country were in January 1960 equal to, lower than, or higher than those of the authorized companies. The deviations generally amounted to one öre per bottle. It is not possible to infer from Table 19 any marked tendency toward lower consumer prices being charged by either group of breweries.

One or two points are worth recording in regard to the suggested prices in different parts of the country. The merchant organizations' lowest suggested prices for various beverages were as follows:

Coca-Cola
41 öre in Jönköping County
42 öre in Skåne, Halland, Göteborg, Värmland, Dalsland, Karlskoga

Soft Drinks Group 2
44 öre in Stockholm, Linköping, Halmstad
45 öre in Skåne, central Halland, Göteborg, Örebro, Karlskoga, Gästrikland

Lager Class II
47 öre in Jönköping County
48 öre in Halland, Dalarna
49 öre in Skåne, Örebro, Karlskoga

TABLE 19: SUGGESTED PRICES TO THE CONSUMER IN JANUARY 1960

(According to the merchant organizations' price lists, compared with consumer prices quoted by certain brewery companies in the same locality or district and by the respective organization)

re per bottle
A = authorized distributor of Coca-Cola and certain Group companies
S and K = brewery companies that sell beverages from Skruv and Kopparberg respectively
For A, S, and K is given the number of öre by which their list prices when selling to the consumer fall short of the merchant organization's suggested prices.

Locality District	Coca-Cola Sugg. Price	A	Soft Drinks Gr. 2 Sugg. Price	A	S	K	Lager Class II Sugg. Price	A	S	K
ockholm	43	....	44	2	....	....	54	6	....	....
ppsala	45	....	46	4	....	....	52	4	....	....
est of Uppland	45	....	46	4	....	4	55	7	....	7
idermanland	43	1	46	4	....	....	50	2	....	....
orrköping	45	....	48	6	....	....	50	2	....	....
inköping	44	....	44	2	....	....	50	2	....	....
inköping County	41	....	46	5–6	4	....	47	2–3	1	....
ronoberg County	45	....	46	4	3–4	....	51	3	3	....
almar County	44	....	46	4	4	....	51	3	3	....
lekinge	43	....	46	4	1	....	50	1	2	....
kåne	42	....	45	2	2–3	....	49	1	1–2	....
almstad	42	....	44	3	3	....	48	1	1	....
entral Halland	42	....	45	3	3	....	48	2	2	....
öteborg	42	....	45	....	....	....	50	6	....	....
orås	43	....	46	3	....	....	50	6	....	....
änersborg	45	6	50	10	....	7	52	8	....	6
ärmland-Dalsland	42	2–3	46	4–5	....	5	50	4–5	....	5
rebro	43	3	45	4	....	....	49	4	....	....
arlskoga	42	2	45	4	....	3	49	4	....	3
ästerås	46	....	48	7	....	....	51	4	....	....
alarna	44	5	49	7–8	....	6–8	48	0–3	....	2–3
ästrikland	44	....	45	2	....	....	50	3	....	1
älsingland	45	1	47	2	....	....	50	2	....	....
imtland	47	3	51	4	....	....	54	5	....	....
ästerbotten	53–56	....	48	1	....	....	53–55	3–5	....	....
orrbotten	55	....	55	5–8	....	....	57	6–7	....	....

While Stockholm and a couple of other cities thus had the lowest suggested prices for soft drinks in Group 2, Stockholm at the same time had a suggested price for lager—54 öre—which, apart from Uppland, was exceeded only in Norrland. With the exception of Norrland the suggested price for Coca-Cola was highest in Västerås, 46 öre, and that for soft-drinks in Group 2 was highest in Dalarna and Vänersborg, 49 and 50 öre. For the rest, there are apparently quite a few districts with low suggested prices where

Skruv's and Kopparberg's products are sold. This may perhaps be explained by the fact that Skruv's and Kopparberg's partners and agents are probably more concerned with selling direct to the consumer than are the companies belonging to the big groups. If there were a wider difference between suggested price and the breweries' price to the consumer, an increasing number of consumers might make a change and buy their beverages direct from a brewery, which may not be desirable from the retail trade's standpoint.

On the question of the retail trade's margins it may be mentioned in this connection that the difference between the retail trade's purchase prices in the form of the breweries' list prices on the one hand and the merchant organizations' suggested prices on the other was in January in different localities and districts, apart from Norrland, as follows: for Coca-Cola 9–14 öre, soft drinks Group 2 10–16 öre, and lager Class II 9–15 öre per bottle.

RISE IN PRICES IN THE AUTUMN OF 1960

During the latter part of 1960 a relatively all-round rise was effected in the prices of malt liquor and soft drinks sold both to the retailer and to the consumer. For instance, prices were increased, *inter alia*, by the Stockholm and Göteborg Groups, several representatives of the Skruv and Kopparberg breweries and the cooperative enterprise Wärby Hälsobrunn AB. The rise in prices took place partly at the beginning of October 1960 and partly— among the majority of the companies investigated in this connection—on one and the same date in December 1960, viz. on 1 December. As a rule, the price went up by one or two öre per bottle. Some of the companies investigated, however, did not raise their prices on the date in question. The general increase in prices did not affect Coca-Cola.

THE COSTS OF MANUFACTURING AND DISTRIBUTING COCA-COLA AND OTHER SOFT DRINKS AT THE MANUFACTURER'S LEVEL

As has been mentioned before, the Commissioner for Freedom of Commerce has requested the Price and Cartel Office to endeavor to throw light on the question of whether the price of Coca-Cola can be considered high in proportion to the manufacturing and other costs. In this connection the Price and Cartel Office has felt that its inquiry could be confined to asking the companies themselves to give an account of their costs by filling in a questionnaire. The six Coca-Cola bottling companies have sent in data on the subject. For the purpose of comparison similar information has been collected along the same lines concerning other soft drinks partly from Group companies in Stockholm, Göteborg, and Malmö, and partly from the companies at Skruv and Kopparberg. A summary of the reports, relating to the costs in 1959 or in the financial year 1958–1959, is given in Table 20. However, the cost account of one bottling company has not been included because of difference in accounting periods. The other bottling companies have stated that the costs as far as Coca-Cola is concerned amount to an average of 134 kronor per hectolitre, while the costs for soft drinks in Group 2 (Loranga, Blodapelsin, and others) bottled by the five other companies have been 87 kronor on an average per hectolitre. These figures include the soft-drinks tax, which is the same for both categories of beverages—33 kronor per hectolitre. The average costs excluding tax amount to 101 and 54 kronor respectively, which implies that Coca-Cola involves twice as high costs as beverages in Group 2. A comparison between the various cost items in respect of the two kinds of beverages gives, *inter alia*, the following result: On an average, the expenditure on preparing and bottling is practically the same for both categories. The cost of the bottles is more than twice as high for Coca-Cola as for other beverages. On the whole, the same applies to the costs of distribution, marketing, and administration. Advertising costs are five times higher for Coca-Cola than for beverages in Group 2. It should be pointed out, however, that the companies may have had different methods of dividing the costs, so that the subitems in the calculation for the respective beverages are not fully comparable. Apart from distribution and marketing the biggest items relate to raw materials. The raw material costs, which are more or less the same in the different companies for producing the same drink, are well over twice as high for Coca-Cola as for soft drinks in Group 2.

As to the high cost of raw materials for producing Coca-Cola, it may be mentioned that, according to information received, the only earnings which the American corporations concerned receive from the business in Sweden consist of what they derive from exporting the concentrates to the bottling companies.

On the basis of the costs per hectolitre quoted above, the Price and Cartel Office has calculated the costs per bottle and compared them with the companies' selling price per bottle. The average total expenditure quoted in Table 20, 134 kronor per hectolitre, for the manufacture and distribution of Coca-Cola corresponds to 26 öre per bottle containing 19.3 centilitres. In arriving at this figure the sales price per bottle has been calculated, in principle, on the basis of the companies' statements as to the number of bottles sold during the accounting period 1958–1959 and the sales total. The five bottling companies' sales price was thus, on an average, about 23 öre to an authorized distributor and 32 öre to a retailer in the bottlers' local districts, or altogether for these two kinds of marketing 27 öre per bottle. Thus, the last-mentioned average price exceeded the average cost by one öre. One company sent in figures implying that a deficit of about 4 öre per bottle must have arisen, while four companies gave particulars showing a positive difference between selling price and cost, at the most about 2 öre per bottle. The reason for the deficits is apparently largely attributable to heavy distribution and marketing costs.

292 Sweden

Table 20: MANUFACTURING AND DISTRIBUTING COSTS, 1958–1959

(Coca-Cola and soft drinks in Group 2; average values on a kronor-per-hectolitre basis as reported by the companies investigated)

Cost Factors	Coca-Cola (5 companies) Average	Soft Drinks Gr. 2 (5 companies) Average
Raw materials	36.79	17.74
Bottles	7.16	3.24
Processing and bottling	15.10	14.15
Advertising	5.63	1.01
Distribution and marketing	28.25	13.51
Administration	7.55	3.28
Interest on capital	1.21	1.85
Tax on soft drrinks	33.00	33.00
TOTAL	134.69	87.78

EXTRA COSTS INCURRED BY THE BREWERIES AT SKRUV AND KOPPARBERG IN PURCHASING COCA-COLA BY ROUNDABOUT WAYS

As has been mentioned above, one of the functions of the inquiry was to throw light on the question of what extra costs the breweries at Skruv (Förbundsbryggeriet—the Brewery Federation) and Kopparberg have incurred through having been compelled to procure Coca-Cola more or less by roundabout ways compared with what the costs would have been had they been allowed to buy direct from a bottler. The companies are called here, as in earlier connections, by their local names. First as regards Skruv, the following observations may be made. It was already mentioned in an introductory chapter that at one period this company had been allowed to buy Coca-Cola from the authorized distributor at Askersund, which in its turn buys from the bottler at Sundbyberg. The purchases were made during the period from October 1956 to the end of February 1959, when Skruv was excluded from using that source of supply. On one single occasion in 1958 Skruv received a delivery direct from a bottling company, namely, the bottler at Jönköping. Skruv purchased from Askersund and Jönköping a total of more than half a million bottles. For these Skruv paid a price exceeding by an average of 6.5 öre per bottle the price which the bottler at Jönköping charged when selling to his distributors. Calculated thus, Skruv's additional cost amounted to nearly 37,000 kronor. Skruv has estimated that its freight costs from Askersund were about 1.8 öre more per bottle than the freight from Jönköping. The extra cost would thus be increased by 10,000 kronor to nearly 47,000 kronor.

Kopparberg has given the information that during the period from 1956 to the end of 1959, when it was shut off from supplies of Coca-Cola, it bought approximately 230,000 bottles of that article. Kopparberg's purchase price was then 3 öre above that charged by the bottler at Filipstad when selling to his distributors and corresponded to an extra cost of nearly 7,000 kronor for its above-mentioned total purchases.

Next, as regards such small-beer brewers as are partners in Skruv, the Price and Cartel Office has learned in the course of its inquiry that they usually try to obtain Coca-Cola by various roundabout ways in order to supply their customers. Thus, it sometimes occurs that the small-beer brewers buy Coca-Cola in small quantities from different retailers in order to sell to other retailers or, when using mobile shops, to households. It also occurs that, thanks to having personal acquaintances in the trade, draymen in the employ of small-beer brewers succeed in buying Coca-Cola from draymen working for authorized Coca-Cola distributors or from draymen in bottling companies, and that in such cases they can carry on the sale of Coca-Cola as a service article and as a supplement to the rest of the assortment. However, the Office has not ascertained the approximate extent to which this "clandestine" trade in Coca-Cola has been carried on.

The considerable difficulties experienced by breweries which are not authorized to sell Coca-Cola in order to procure that beverage show, therefore, what importance they attach to having Coca-Cola included in their assortments. It should be pointed out, however, that the special costs which the nonauthorized companies have to incur in procuring Coca-Cola are at the same time likely to reduce their competitive ability vis-à-vis the authorized breweries.

Summary (This text is also part of the official report.)

Compared with the conditions in the malt-liquor and soft-drink trade generally, the organization for the trade in Coca-Cola appears to be unique on account of the system of selective selling, combined with a division into districts that has been set up in regard to that beverage. Control is exercised through the instrumentality of the owner of the American trademark. Six companies in this country—bottlers—have a permit to manufacture Coca-Cola, so that in this respect the control applies to the manufacture. For marketing purposes the American corporation has had the country divided into about seventy districts. The bottling works are the sole sellers in their local districts. In each one of the other districts a brewery company is appointed to act as distributor, its position being actually that of sole agent, having the right to buy Coca-Cola from a certain bottler for the purpose of selling to retailers and other customers in the district. It is a fact of importance that the bottler companies are not themselves at liberty to choose their own retail dealers throughout the country. These have been authorized by the American corporation.

The control of the Coca-Cola market has been exercised through contracts, which have been entered in the Cartel Register. Formerly the entire malt-liquor and soft-drink market was distinguished by being divided into districts; this division was carried out in detail by means of a series of contracts, most of which, however, after having been entered in the Cartel Register, were cancelled during the first half of the 1950's. As a result of the Coca-Cola contracts the market for this particular drink has been redivided, in part along lines conforming to the earlier division into districts.

Further, it is characteristic that the right to sell Coca-Cola in most parts of the country has been reserved for the principal brewery groups. For instance, AB Stockholms Bryggerier owns one and AB Pripp & Lyckholm owns three of the six bottling works, and the majority of the distributors in Central Sweden are members of these groups of breweries as affiliates. This means that Coca-Cola is sold almost exclusively under the management of the Stockholm Group in East Sweden and under that of the Göteborg Group in West Sweden.

The monopoly position which the big brewery groups hold in the Coca-Cola trade has been regarded as a problem worrying many outside breweries which sell malt liquors and soft drinks in competition with the Groups. One Group of such competing companies is comprised of Förbundsbryggeriet Södra Sverige, Skruv, and Kopparbergs Bryggeri AB, both brewers of beer, and their partners and agents among malt-liquor and soft-drink companies, especially small-beer breweries in large parts of Central and South Sweden. For some years the companies at Skruv and Kopparberg procured Coca-Cola, although at prices higher than the authorized distributors' purchase prices. However, they were able at that period to some extent to supply their agents with Coca-Cola. In 1959 these companies were entirely shut off from their sources of supply. This exclusion from the market, at the same time, hit all those small-beer brewers who are customers of the companies at Skruv and Kopparberg. The investigation is mainly concerned with the companies just referred to. They belong to the Malt Liquor and Soft Drinks Federation and to the Association of Breweries Liable to Excise Duty, which have other members in a similar situation.

The problem confronting the companies at Skruv and Kopparberg and their agents as well as certain other enterprises in the organizations just mentioned is stated not to be confined to Coca-Cola but concerns their marketing of malt liquors and soft drinks in general,

Coca-Cola playing the part of a competitor in the assortment of beverages. The breweries affected declare that the demand on the part of retailers and consumers is such that the breweries are faced with serious difficulties and even lose customers when Coca-Cola is not included in their assortment. The problem, then, is what possibilities the companies at Skruv and Kopparberg and others have of offering the Group breweries, in the long run, competition on the malt-liquors and soft-drinks market. They have stated that, in order to maintain their market, they are obliged to buy Coca-Cola by roundabout ways, e.g., from certain retail dealers.

This indicates the terms of reference for the investigation. The task has been to endeavor to elucidate whether the cartel agreements on selective selling and division into districts in the trade in Coca-Cola have a harmful effect in view of the degree of importance attaching to the competition which such enterprises as the companies at Skruv and Kopparberg and their agents offer on the malt-liquors and soft-drinks market. A number of queries arise in this connection. The first is what effect the agreements have on price fixing, and whether selective selling concentrated within certain group companies can actually entail a circumvention of the decree prohibiting gross prices. Maximum prices are prescribed in the agreements. In their arrangements for selling to retailers in the local districts all the six bottlers have in fact charged the maximum prices without deviations. Four bottlers have also applied the maximum prices to the distributor without deviations, while two have given freight contributions. Apparently the conclusion can be drawn that the marketing system as regards Coca-Cola has resulted in a fixed and uniform price level on Coca-Cola at the manufacturer's stage as far as concerns the main bulk of the sales.

So far as the Price and Cartel Office has been given to understand, the distributors when selling to the retailer have used the prescribed maximum prices as their list prices, and when discounts have been allowed they have been calculated on the maximum prices. To that extent the agreements have achieved a fixed price level at the distributor stage also.

While bottlers and distributors, each in his own district, hold a monopoly in the sale of Coca-Cola, they have to meet competition from other companies when selling malt liquors and soft drinks generally. The question is whether the monopoly situation in regard to Coca-Cola has been exploited not only in such a way that a largely uniform price level has been established, but also in respect of the height at which the prices are fixed. In view hereof the prices of beverages other than Coca-Cola charged by those breweries that are authorized to sell Coca-Cola have been compared with the prices charged by certain other companies. For this purpose soft drinks in price Group 2 (of the Loranga type) and lager beer Class II have been selected. It appears from the inquiry, in the first place, that the prices of these beverages—the list prices charged to the retailer— are just as uniform as those for Coca-Cola, apart from Norrland. For making further comparisons the Price and Cartel Office has also taken into consideration the system of allowing discounts that exists in the trade, especially in the form of a quantity discount. Such discounts, however, are given to a lesser extent on Coca-Cola than on other drinks. During the period from the beginning of 1956 to the beginning of 1960 such changes as occurred in the prices when selling to the retailer very largely corresponded to the increase in the malt-liquor and soft-drink tax effected during that period. As a rule, however, the prices were raised beyond what corresponded to this higher amount of tax. A study of the price rise, reckoned per bottle, taking into account quantity discounts and excluding tax, gives among other things the following result: The rise in Coca-Cola prices from the beginning of 1956 to the beginning of 1960 was lowest in that part of the country in which the Stockholm Group is predominant, and in the same district was also lower than the increase in the prices of soft drinks in Group 2. In the rest of the country the prices went up slightly more for Coca-Cola than for drinks in Group 2. Lager prices showed the smallest rise in South and West Sweden. On the basis of price computation with due allowance for discount and tax, in January 1960 the prices of Coca-Cola and soft drinks, Group 2, were lowest in South Sweden, while lager prices were lowest in South and West Sweden.

The part played by the Skruv and Kopparberg breweries in the competition is to be viewed in the light of the price conditions just described. The storage depots and breweries belonging to partners in those companies or owned by their agents are also a competitive factor. Comparisons have been drawn between individual Skruv breweries on the one hand, and competing companies (likewise authorized distributors of Coca-Cola) in the same or a neighboring locality on the other hand, in regard to the prices of soft drinks in Group 2 and lager Class II when selling to the retailer. Prices have been similar in some instances, but differences in both prices and price trend have also been observable between the two categories of companies. The Skruv companies have allowed discounts less often than their competitors. In spite of the latter's discounts allowed on large quantities, certain Skruv companies have charged lower prices than their competitors without allowing discounts. The comparisons of prices thus present a picture which, with their slight variations in regard to similar and deviating prices, seems to indicate that price competition does exist on the malt-liquor and soft-drink market. The Kopparberg breweries have, for the most part, maintained the same price level and price trend as their competitors in the Göteborg Group's area, whereas differences in price have occurred if compared with the competitors in the Stockholm Group's area.

The retail trade organizations have to a large extent notified their members of recommended prices when selling malt liquors and soft drinks to the consumer. These prices have been higher than the breweries' own prices when selling to households from mobile shops. As to those breweries which act as agents for the companies at Skruv and Kopparberg, apparently they are, on the whole, more concerned with selling to the consumer than the companies belonging to the main Groups, so that in this respect too they represent an important factor in the competition. In some cases the said breweries acting as agents have charged lower prices to the consumer than to competing breweries, though there have also been cases of higher and similar prices.

With regard to the question of the reasonableness of the Coca-Cola prices, the Price and Cartel Office has made an investigation at the manufacturer's level. The bottler companies' selling prices appear to be high in comparison with costs. On the other hand, the costs are high. Thus, apart from the purchase tax, which is the same for Coca-Cola as that for other soft drinks, the manufacturers' costs for producing and selling by volume are twice as high for Coca-Cola as for beverages in Group 2.

The Coca-Cola trademark has been exploited by the proprietor and his contracting partners for creating a substantial sales organization. As a result, however, Coca-Cola has come to play a part of some consequence not only in the competition for that brand, but also in the competition that has been going on for a long time between various categories of enterprises and group formations on the malt-liquor and soft-drink market.

APPENDICES

Appendix I: Legislation Controlling Restrictive Business Practices

A. DENMARK

THE MONOPOLIES AND RESTRICTIVE PRACTICES CONTROL ACT[1]

No. 102 of 31 March 1955
as amended 25 May 1956, 6 July 1957, and 10 June 1960

PART I

PURPOSE AND SCOPE

1

The purpose of this Act is, by means of public control of monopolies and of restrictive business practices, to prevent unreasonable prices and business conditions and to secure the best possible conditions for the freedom of trade.

2

1) This Act applies to private enterprises, co-operative associations, etc., within trades in which competition, throughout the country or in local market areas, is restricted in such a manner that the enterprises exert or may be able to exert an effective influence on price, production, distribution, or transport conditions.

2) This Act does not apply to wage and labour conditions, nor to price conditions or business activities which, under special legal provision, are regulated or approved by the competent authorities.

PART II

THE MONOPOLIES CONTROL AUTHORITY

3

1) Monopolies and restrictive business practices shall be subject to control by the Monopolies Control Authority, which shall consist of a Board and a Directorate.

---

[1] The statutes and the accompanying notes are based upon official translations obtained from *Guide to Legislation on Restrictive Business Practices,* published in Paris by the European Productivity Agency of the Organization for European Cooperation and Development.

2) In the case of enterprises the economic conditions of which, under special legislation, are subject to control or regulation by other public control organs, the Minister of Commerce may decide that the control prescribed in this Act shall be carried out by the control organ concerned. Such control shall be based on rules laid down by the Minister, regard being had to the special character of the enterprises in question.

4

1) The Board shall consist of a Chairman and up to 14 members. The Chairman shall be appointed by the King. The other members shall be appointed by the Minister of Commerce for a period not exceeding 3 years. The Board shall possess a comprehensive knowledge of business and consumption conditions, including legal, economic, and technical knowledge. The majority of the members of the Board shall be independent of business enterprises and business organisations the conditions of which are directly affected by this Act.

2) No member of the Board shall take part in the decision of a case which directly affects business enterprises or organisations in which he has interests or with which he is connnected. On any given occasion the Board shall decide whether or not a member shall retire during the consideration of a case.

3) If, under the second subsection of this section, or for other reasons, a member is prevented from taking part in the work of the Board, the Minister may appoint a deputy.

4) The Minister shall lay down the Board's rules of procedure.

5

1) The current business of the Board shall be attended to by the Directorate, which shall be headed by a Director appointed by the King. The Director shall not be a member of the Board but shall attend the Board's meetings.

2) The Directorate may call in experts to the extent deemed necessary.

3) Civil servants and other employees of the Directorate shall not have interests in, nor be connected with any business enterprise or trade organisation. Experts called in for advice shall not have interests in, nor be connected with enterprises or organisations directly affected by the case in question.

4) The Minister of Commerce shall issue regulations governing the work of the Directorate.

PART III
NOTIFICATION AND REGISTRATION

6

1) Agreements between enterprises and decisions made by organisations shall be notified to the Monopolies Control Authority provided that these agreements and decisions exert, or may be able to exert, an effective

influence on price, production, distribution, or transport conditions throughout the country, or in local market areas.

2) Individual enterprises or combinations which exert or may exert an effective influence on price, production, distribution, or transport conditions, throughout the country or in local market areas, shall be subject to notification if the Monopolies Control Authority so demands. Restrictive practices of such enterprises or combinations shall likewise be subject to notification when demanded by the Monopolies Control Authority.

7

1) Notification as prescribed in the first subsection of Section 6 shall be effected within 8 days after the agreement or decision in question has been made.

2) Alterations in matters already notified, including alterations in prices, margins, rebates, and quotas, etc., shall likewise be notified within 8 days.

3) In special circumstances, the Monopolies Control Authority may prolong the time limits laid down in the first and second subsections of this section.

8

Agreements and decisions coming under the provisions of the first subsection 6 shall not be valid or enforceable in the Law Courts unless the Monopolies Control Authority has been notified within the prescribed time limit.

9

1) The Monopolies Control Authority shall enter the notifications in a public register. Registration shall not imply any approval of the matter registered.

2) The Minister of Commerce may permit that a registration shall be kept wholly or partly secret if this is warranted by exceptional circumstances.

PART IV
AGREEMENTS, DECISIONS, AND BUSINESS PRACTICES
FIXING MINIMUM PRICES

10

Agreements, decisions, and business practices fixing minimum prices or margins to be observed by subsequent resellers must not be enforced unless the Monopolies Control Authority has approved the agreement, etc., concerned. Such approval may be given if warranted by circumstances of special importance.

PART V
POWERS OF THE MONOPOLIES CONTROL AUTHORITY TO
NEGOTIATE AND TO ISSUE ORDERS, ETC.

11

1) If upon investigation the Monopolies Control Authority finds that

restriction of competition within the meaning of the first subsection of Section 2 results in, or must be deemed to result in unreasonable prices or business conditions, unreasonable restraint of the freedom of trade or unreasonable discrimination in respect of the conditions of trading, the Monopolies Control Authority shall attempt to terminate the said unreasonable restrictions through negotiations with the individual enterprises or combinations concerned.

2) In judging whether prices are unreasonable, regard shall be had to conditions in enterprises which are operated with comparable technical and commercial efficiency.

12

1) If the harmful effects stated in Section 11 cannot be remedied through negotiations, the Monopolies Control Authority shall issue an order to that end.

2) Such an order may cancel, wholly or partly, the agreements, decisions, or practices concerned, and/or prescribe that prices, composition, weight, or measure of articles be indicated by marking or posting and/or order alterations in prices, margins and terms of business, including the fixing of prices and margins which must not be exceeded.

3) In cases where a restriction of competition results in unreasonable restraint of the freedom of trade, which cannot be remedied by the other provisions of this Act, the Monopolies Control Authority may order an enterprise to supply goods to specified buyers on its usual terms for similar sales, provided always that the enterprise is entitled to demand cash payment or adequate security.

4) In the fixing of maximum prices or margins under the second subsection of this section, prices or margins shall not be fixed at a lower level than are required by such enterprises as are mentioned in the second subsection of Section 11 in order to cover their necessary costs including depreciation allowances and remuneration for services in connection with the purchase or replacement, production, storing, marketing, and transport of the commodity, as well as a reasonable net profit, regard being had to the risk involved in the production or sale of the commodity.

5) An order shall state the date as from which it must be complied with.

13

When it is deemed necessary for control purposes, the Monopolies Control Authority may order compulsory invoicing of goods sold to or by resellers. Further, the Monopolies Control Authority may order price-marking or price-posting for important consumer goods in trades where such marking or posting of prices is not practised to a reasonable extent. Before such orders are issued, consumers' and trade organisations concerned shall be consulted.

14

If harmful effects cannot be eliminated through the provisions of Sections 11 and 12, or if other measures are deemed more efficient, the Monopolies Control Authority shall refer the matter to the Minister of Commerce.

Part VI

General Provisions

15

1) The Monopolies Control Authority shall be empowered to call for all such information as may be deemed necessary for its activities, including information necessary for determining whether a given case falls within the scope of this Act. The Monopolies Control Authority may thus call for properly certified extracts from records and accounts and may call in persons to give oral evidence. The Monopolies Control Authority shall further be empowered to demand access to accounts and account books and to carry out, on the spot, investigations necessary for clearing up the case.

2) Any person called in to give evidence about technical secrets may submit to the Chairman of the Board a request that the information shall not be disclosed to all the members of the Board. Paying regard to the circumstances of the case, the Chairman shall then rule to what extent and in what form the information shall be given.

16

If it is found that an enterprise has obtained a profit through transactions contravening a decision of the Monopolies Control Authority, and such profit cannot be confiscated under the third subsection of Section 22, and if it is not found expedient to deduct the said profit from future yields, the Monopolies Control Authority may order that it shall be paid to the State Treasury.

17

1) The decisions of the Monopolies Control Authority shall be given in writing and shall include information about the facts and reasoning which have led to the decisions.

2) A decision having been made, the organisations or individual enterprises concerned shall be given access to the evidence on which the decision of the Monopolies Control Authority has been based, provided that the material in question does not include confidential information regarding the affairs of individual enterprises, or information which cannot be supplied without detriment to the public interest.

18

1) Any complaints against decisions made by the Monopolies Control Authority under this Act shall be submitted to the Monopolies Control Authority but the complaint may demand that the complaint shall be passed on, within 8 days, to an Appeal Tribunal appointed for this purpose by the Minister of Commerce, which Tribunal shall consist of a Chairman

and two members. The Chairman shall possess the qualifications required of a Supreme Court Judge; one of the members shall have knowledge of economics, and one member shall be appointed after consultation with the Joint Representative Council of Danish Traders and the Federation of Danish Industries.

2) No member of the Tribunal shall take part in the decision of a case which directly affects enterprises or trade organisations in which he has interests or with which he is connected. On any given occasion the Tribunal shall rule whether or not a member shall retire during the consideration of a case.

3) The complainant shall upon request be entitled to acquaint himself with the evidence laid before the Tribunal, provided that it does not include confidential information of the affairs of individual enterprises, or information which cannot be supplied without detriment to the public interest. Further, the complainant shall upon request be entitled to appear in person before the Tribunal. Neither complainants nor representatives of the Monopolies Control Authority shall be permitted to be present during the deliberations of the Tribunal.

4) The Minister shall fix rules for the work of the Tribunal.

5) The Tribunal shall, after consultation with the Minister, be given access to all information available from the Monopolies Control Authority and necessary for judging the complaints.

6) After the Monopolies Control Authority has stated its opinion on a complaint, the Tribunal shall decide the case.

7) Except in the case of decisions made under Section 6 and the third subsection of Section 12, the lodging of a complaint against a decision of the Monopolies Control Authority shall not suspend the operation of the said decision.

8) The Tribunal, after consultation with the Minister, shall be empowered to employ assistance to the extent deemed necessary.

9) The complainant may, within 4 weeks after the decision of the Tribunal has come to his knowledge, appeal against it to the Law Courts—in accordance with Section 63 of the Constitution, the High Court (*landsret*) being the court of first appeal. If the Tribunal has altered a decision of the Monopolies Control Authority, the latter shall have a corresponding right to take the decision of the Tribunal to the Law Courts—in the form of an action brought against the complainant.

10) Cases coming under the ninth subsection of the Section shall not be admissible in the courts until the Tribunal has given its decision. If a case is not brought before the High Court within the period stipulated in the ninth subsection of this section, the decision of the Tribunal shall be final.

19

1) The Minister of Commerce shall be authorised to make the necessary arrangements for the implementation of this Act and of the orders

issued under the Act, and shall be authorised to lay down rules for the publishing of a Registration Gazette.

2) The Minister shall give directions as to the submission and publication of reports and other communications to the public regarding inquiries and decisions made under this Act. Before the public is informed about any inquiry made, the Monopolies Control Authority shall give the organisations or individual enterprises concerned an opportunity to express their views on the matter. The Monopolies Control Authority shall submit to the Minister of Commerce an annual report on its activities, which report the Minister shall lay before Parliament not later than the end of October of the following calendar year.

3) The expenses incurred in connection with the work of the Monopolies Control Authority and the Appeal Tribunal shall be provided by the annual Finance Acts.

20

If anyone fails to notify in due time under Section 6, cf. Section 7, or to give the Monopolies Control Authority any information requested under Section 15, the Minister of Commerce may, at the request of the Monopolies Control Authority, order the person concerned to fulfill this obligation under the penalty of a daily or weekly fine which shall be recoverable by distraint.

21

Members of the Board, civil servants and other employees of the Directorate, as well as experts called in for advice, shall be bound under Sections 152 and 263 of the Civil Penal Code, cf. the third subsection of Section 3 of the Civil Servants Act, to observe professional secrecy toward unauthorised persons, on matters which have come to their knowledge through their work.

22

1) Failure to notify as prescribed in this Act and contravention of regulations issued under this Act, as well as noncompliance with an order issued by the Monopolies Control Authority under this Act, shall be punishable by fines or, under aggravating circumstances, by mitigated imprisonment (*haefte*), provided that the offence is not subject to severer penalty under the Civil Penal Code.

2) The same penalty shall apply if anyone, in matters falling within the scope of this Act, gives to the Minister of Commerce, the Monopolies Control Authority, or the Tribunal referred to in Section 18, incorrect or misleading information, or conceals information about circumstances which may be of importance in a given case.

3) Profit obtained by transactions which are liable to penalty under this Act, or an amount corresponding to such profit, shall, by court sentence, be forfeited to the State Treasury.

4) The provisions of Part 69 of the Administration of Justice Act shall

apply to cases under this section to the same extent as in cases brought by the Public Prosecutor.

PART VII
COMMENCEMENT AND TRANSITIONAL PROVISIONS
23

1) Maximum prices and maximum profits which, before this Act takes effect, have been fixed under the Prices of Goods Act, cf. Promulgation Order No. 463 of 14 November 1949, Act No. 233 of 25 May 1951 and Act No. 191 of 30 May 1952, or under the Price Agreements Act No. 378 of 14 November 1952, cf. Act No. 70 of 31 March 1954, and other regulations and rulings of the Price Control Board in accordance with these Acts, shall remain in force until they are repealed in accordance with the provisions of the said Acts.

2) If it is found that an enterprise has obtained a profit as a result of transactions which contravene the provisions of the Acts referred to in the first subsection of this section, the provisions of Section 16 of this Act shall apply.

3) The notifications made to the Price Control Board under the Acts stated in the first subsection of this section, and the register of the Price Control Board, shall be transferred to the Monopolies Control Authority as from the date when this Act takes effect.

24

1) Any increase of prices subject to notification under Part III must not be put into effect without the approval of the Monopolies Control Authority.

2) The rulings of the Monopolies Control Authority, which shall be in accordance with the provisions of Sections 11 and 12, shall be communicated as far as possible within 8 days after the application for a price increase has been made under the first subsection of this section.

3) When warranted by the market conditions, the nature of the commodity, or its relative importance as to the total trade volume, the Monopolies Control Authority can deviate from the provision laid down in subsection 1. This rule shall apply also in respect of agreements and decisions of material importance for the advancement of efficiency, as, inter alia, in the case of structural rationalisation.

1) This Act, which repeals the Price Agreements Act No. 158 of 18 May 1937, shall take effect as from 1 July 1955. Up to that date the Price Agreements Act. No. 378 of 14 November 1952 shall remain in force.

2) The provisions of Part IV of this Act shall, however, only take effect as from 1 July 1956.

26

1) This Act does not extend to the Faroe Islands.

2) For Greenland, such amendments as are deemed necessary in view of local conditions shall be fixed by Royal Order.

THE PRICE SUPERVISION ACT
No. 135 of 25 May 1956

1

1) Upon the request of consumers', manufacturers' or trade organisations, the Monopolies Control Authority may institute inquiries of price and profit conditions within specific fields if the Authority finds good cause to surmise that the price formation results in unreasonable prices.

2) The Monopolies Control Authority shall keep the public informed of the results of the inquiries instituted under the first subsection of this section. Before publication of the results of the inquiries, the Authority shall offer the organisations or individual enterprises concerned an opportunity to express their view on the matter.

2

1) In co-operation with the Supply Office, the Monopolies Control Authority shall endeavour to elucidate how prices for goods manufactured in this country and protected against foreign competition by import regulations compare to corresponding prices abroad.

2) The Minister of Commerce shall pass the results of inquiries made under the first subsection of this section on to the Parliamentary Commission for Supplies.

3

When goods are sold to the consumers in manufacturer's, importer's or wholesaler's ready-made packings, the Monopolies Control Authority may, after negotiation with the consumers' or trade organisations concerned, issue an order to the effect that the packings must be provided with information as to the net weight of the contents.

The provisions of Sections 15, 18 and 22 of the Monopolies and Restrictive Practices Control Act, No. 102 of 31 March 1955, shall apply correspondingly to the issues governed by the present Act.

THE ACT ON STANDARDIZATION MARKS
No. 212 of 11 June 1959

Section 1

Trade organisations can—in accordance with Sections 1–3 of the Act on Trade Marks*—by registration or by use acquire a sole right for their mem-

---

* These sections set out the definition of trade marks to which a sole right can be acquired on registration made by the State Patent Agency, or by use.

bers to apply special distinctive marks to commodities or services offered by the members in their business or profession.

.   .   .   .   .   .

Distinctive marks under the provisions of this Act are called Standardization Marks.

.   .   .   .

Section 5

Registration of a standardization mark can be abolished by the Law Courts if conditions similar to those mentioned in Sections 25 and 36† of the Act on Trade Marks are in evidence, if the standardization mark conflicts with the public interest, or if amendments of the rules governing the application of the standardization mark are not duly notified to the register.

Legal proceedings may be instituted by any interested party. However, legal proceedings for the purpose of abolishing a standardization mark registration for being adverse to the public interest can be instituted by the Minister of Commerce only.

.   .   .   .

B. NORWAY

ACT ON CONTROL OF PRICES, DIVIDENDS, AND RESTRICTIVE BUSINESS ARRANGEMENTS[1]

Dated 26 June 1953
As Amended in Sections 4, 6, 7, 34, 37, 49, and 50
by the Acts of 25 June 1954 and of 28 March 1958
And as Amended in Sections 9, 14, 24, 28, 29, 30, 31,
32, and 42 by the Act of 17 June 1960

CHAPTER I
PURPOSE AND SCOPE OF THE ACT
Section 1: Purpose of the Act

It shall be the purpose of this Act to serve as a means in the endeavour to attain full employment, and the effective utilisation of production potentialities and to assist in counteracting marketing crises and in promoting an equitable distribution of the national income, by:

† These sections set out the conditions under which a registration of a trade mark may be abolished, cf. Act No. 211 of 11 June 1959.

[1] The statutes and the accompanying notes are based upon official translations obtained from *Guide to Legislation on Restrictive Business Practices*, published in Paris by the European Productivity Agency of the Organization for European Cooperation and Development.

a) Promoting such a development of prices as is desirable from the point of view of the public interest and counteracting prices, profits and terms of business* which are unreasonable;

b) Preventing the distribution of higher dividends than are deemed justified;

c) Safeguarding against improper marketing or competitive conditions, and against restrictive business arrangements which are unreasonable or detrimental to the public interest.

Section 2: Scope of the Act

The Act shall apply to business activities of every kind, as defined in Section 60, Point 4, irrespective of the type of goods, services or rights concerned, and irrespective of whether it be private or operated by governmental or local authority. The Act shall not apply to wages and terms for work in the employment of others.

If an activity covered by this Act falls within the scope of other statutory provisions for regulation or control, the King may issue regulations defining the mutual limitation of jurisdiction of the authorities involved.

Regulations issued pursuant to this Act may not be inconsistent with any resolution of the Storting.

CHAPTER II

ADMINISTRATION

Section 3: Administration of Control and Regulations

Within the limits of the resolutions of the Storting according to Section 14, and in so far as the power to make decisions is not otherwise vested in the Storting, the King shall lay down the general instructions governing control and regulations.

The Ministry concerned shall be responsible for implementing the provisions of this Act in accordance with the resolutions and general instructions cited in the preceding paragraph, and shall issue further regulations governing the activities of the authorities exercising control and regulation.

Section 4: The Price Council

The Price Council shall consist of five members, with personal deputies, appointed by the King. Their term of office shall be four years; except that the first appointment of two of the members and their deputies shall be for two years only. Members and deputies are eligible for reelection. The King shall appoint the Chairman and Deputy Chairman of the Council from among its members. After hearing the opinion of the Council, the Ministry may appoint from among the members and deputy members of the Council select committees for consideration of specific matters.

The Chairman or Deputy Chairman and at least three other members

---

* The Norwegian expression *"forretningsvilkår"* covers all terms and conditions, other than the price, which are stipulated in commercial transactions (e.g. terms of payment and delivery, rebates, etc.).

or deputies shall constitute a quorum. A resolution is valid only when not less than three votes have been cast in favour of the decision.

The head of the Price Directorate or his delegate shall attend the meetings of the Price Council and of the select committees, but shall have no vote.

The Price Council is empowered to make decisions as provided for in Sections 23, 33, 34, 37, 40 and 41 of the Act. The King may also authorise the Council to decide other matters. Further, the Price Council shall act as an advisory body in accordance with further regulations issued by the King.

The Price Council shall submit reports to the Ministry on decisions taken. The King shall issue further regulations concerning the organisation and functions of the Price Council and the select committees.

Section 5: The Price Directorate

The Price Directorate shall:

a) Assist in the preparation and implementation of matters decided by the Storting, the King, or the Ministry concerned;

b) Prepare cases for decision by the Price Council and carry out its decisions;

c) Prepare and implement measures of control and regulation within the jurisdiction of the Directorate;

d) Instruct and supervise the control and regulative bodies subordinate to the Directorate, cf. Sections 6–8.

e) Otherwise assist in implementing the Act.

The King shall issue further regulations concerning the organisation and functions of the Price Directorate.

Section 6: The Price Inspectorate

The Regional Offices of the Price Inspectorate shall be responsible for local control and regulation and otherwise perform the duties entrusted to them under this Act. The Ministry may rule that the Price Committee in Oslo shall be directly subject to the jurisdiction of the Price Directorate and take the place of the Regional Offices of the Price Inspectorate in dealing with matters under this Act.

The King shall issue regulations concerning the functions of the Regional Offices under this Act and also concerning the relationship between the Price Inspectorate and Price Directorate.

Section 7: Price Committees in County Districts

Unless otherwise decided by the King, a Price Committee shall be established in each county district. The King may decide that several county districts shall have a joint Price Committee, or that a Price Committee shall have separate divisions to deal with special matters.

The Price Committee shall be elected by the local council for a term corresponding to that of the local elections, and the Committee shall consist of a Chairman, Deputy Chairman, and not less than three other members, all with personal deputies. In a joint Price Committee each district shall have at least two members, elected by the local council concerned, and the committee itself shall elect its Chairman and Deputy Chairman. The composition of the special divisions shall be determined by the King. The provisions of Section 10 of the County District Elections Act of 10 July 1925, shall apply equally to the election of a Price Committee. Before the election of members by a local council, local associations of enterprises, cooperative societies, trade union councils, and such other local organisations as the King may determine, shall have the right to submit proposals within a period to be determined by the aldermen. The king shall decide who shall have the right to propose persons for election as members of the special divisions.

The Price Committee shall take part in the local control and regulation work and perform such other functions as may be required. The general division of the committee shall constitute a quorum when at least one half of the members are present. Decisions shall be made by simple majority vote. The King shall issue regulations concerning the quorum requirements of the special divisions and voting procedure. The provisions dealing with disqualification in Section 16 of the Act of 10 June 1938 concerning Rural Districts, and in Section 15 of the Act of the same date concerning Urban Districts, shall also apply to the members of the Price Committee.

The county district shall defray the expenses incurred by the activities of the Price Committee, and may pay the members of the Committee a reasonable remuneration for their work. Where several county districts have a joint Price Committee, expenses shall be divided among them as proposed by the Committee. In the event of disagreement among the county districts, the county governor shall determine how to divide the expenses after hearing the views of the Regional Office of the Price Inspectorate. The State may contribute towards the expenses to the extent determined by the Storting.

The King may issue regulations concerning the organisation and activities of the Price Committees. Within the limits of regulations issued by the King, the Price Directorate may make orders for the activities of the Price Committees.

Section 8: Other Control and Regulative Bodies

The King may rule that public bodies, including local authorities, other than those mentioned in Sections 4–7, shall assist in the control and regulation activities under the provisions of this Act. The King may issue regulations concerning the functions of such bodies and their relationship to the control and regulative bodies established under this Act.

The King may also determine that association or select committees established or approved shall assist in the control and regulation activities under the provisions of this Act. Any person appointed a member of such select committees or associations, shall have no option but to perform this duty.

The King may rule that enterprises in the sector concerned shall cover approved expenses incurred by such select committees or associations in the performance of their control and regulation duties. The King shall make regulations concerning payments to be made for this purpose and the disposal of the funds. Members may not, without the consent of the Price Directorate, be offered or accept remuneration for the performance of their duties.

The King may issue regulations regarding the functions of the associations and select committees under this Act.

Section 9: Delegation of Authority

The King may authorise the Ministry to act on his behalf under Sections 8, 9 (sixth paragraph), 10, 11, 15 (third paragraph), 24, 25 (first sentence of third paragraph, cf. sixth paragraph), 26 (first paragraph), 30, 42 (first, third and fourth paragraphs), 45 (fifth paragraph), 49 (third paragraph), and 51 (fifth paragraph). In other matters which this Act specifies as cases for decisions by the King, authority may be delegated by the King to the Ministry, the Price Directorate or the regulative bodies cited in Sections 6–8 to issue regulations and orders for supplementing or implementing decisions of the King.

The King may authorise the Price Directorate to act according to Sections 8 (second paragraph), 9 (sixth paragraph), 15 (third paragraph), 24, 25 (first sentence of the third paragraph, cf. sixth paragraph), 26 (first paragraph) and 42 (first, third and fourth paragraphs). This may also be done in cases where the Ministry itself has been authorised to make such decisions. The Ministry may also authorise the Price Directorate to issue regulations supplementary to, or for implementation of the decisions of the Ministry.

The Ministry and the Price Directorate may, within the limits of their authority to make decisions, delegate such powers to the regulative bodies mentioned in Sections 6–8 under Sections 24 and 26 (first paragraph). Furthermore, these bodies may be empowered to issue regulations for supplementing or implementing decisions made by the Ministry or the Price Directorate.

Delegation of authority by the King, the Ministry or the Price Directorate to the bodies mentioned in Sections 6–8 may only be made in respect of matters particularly appropriate for decision by these bodies.

Even if a case falls within the limits of the authority of the Price Directorate, the Directorate shall, if time allows, obtain the approval of the Ministry in decisions involving questions of general principle, unless the Ministry has given prior instructions governing such decisions. Rules for the submission of such cases are issued by the Ministry.

The provisions of the preceding paragraph shall also apply to the relationship between the bodies mentioned in Sections 6–8 and their superior bodies, in accordance with regulations of the King.

In no case may the King authorise others than the Ministry to make decisions in matters concerning the regulation of prices fixed by local authorities for water supply, refuse disposal, gas, electric power, or hospital services, schools and other institutions or enterprises of a monopolistic nature. In case of doubt the King shall rule whether or not a particular matter is of such a nature, and there shall be no appeal from such ruling.

Section 10: Procedure

Before a decision is made in a question of regulation, representatives of the firms or trades to which the regulation shall apply shall be given an opportunity to state their case. If the regulation is to apply to a plurality or to all trades, the central organisations concerned may, instead of the individual branch organisations, be given an opportunity to state their opinion. To the extent deemed necessary for the thorough elucidation of a question, statements shall also be obtained from others.

A regulation case may be determined without prior notification according to the first paragraph when it is in practice unfeasible to give such notice or if to do so would entail the possibility of the contemplated regulation being evaded or of lessening its effectiveness in other respects. Such matters shall, however, also be examined as fully as possible.

The provisions of the preceding paragraph shall also apply to the issue of supplementary regulations under Sections 33, 34, 35 (first paragraph), and 43 (second paragraph).

In the event of disputes under Sections 23, 40 and 41, a party shall be allowed to acquaint himself with the documents submitted by the other party, unless the information given therein concerns technical devices and methods of a secret nature. However, if so requested by one party, the authority concerned may agree not to make available to the second party information given about other matters if special circumstances are involved and such information is not considered to be necessary to enable the other party to protect his interests. To what extent persons interested in other cases shall be allowed to acquaint themselves with documents which have been produced shall be determined in regulations as provided for in the last paragraph of this section.

The Ministry, the Price Council or the Price Directorate may decide that proceedings shall take place in public, when such a procedure is deemed to be in the public interest and the case is such as can be dealt with in public session.

The rules for disqualification in the Judiciary Act of 13 August 1915, Section 106 (Subsections 1–5) and Section 108, shall apply equally to the authorities mentioned in Sections 4, 5, 6 and 8 in their dealings and decisions on cases concerning specific enterprises.

The King may issue further regulations concerning procedure.

Section 11: The Stating of Grounds for Decisions

In regulation cases which concern specific named persons, companies, foundations or associations, the grounds for a decision shall be given if requested by the parties concerned, provided that such action is not in conflict with the provisions on secrecy in this Act, cf. Section 17 (third sentence of the second paragraph), and no other special circumstances hinder divulgence of such information. The grounds shall be given together with the decision or, if this is impracticable, as soon as possible after the decision has been made. No grounds are required to be given in cases where an application is granted by the authorities.

In regulation cases of a general nature an explanation shall, whenever possible, be given of the circumstances which have led to regulation and of the contents and purposes of the regulations.

The King may issue further regulations concerning the grounds for decisions.

The provisions of this section shall not apply to decisions of the Storting.

Section 12: The Price Bulletin

The Price Directorate shall issue an official bulletin entitled the Price Bulletin (*Pristidende*), which shall contain the following:

1. This Act and later amendments and additions thereto.

2. Regulations and orders made by the Storting or by the King pursuant to this Act.

3. Major control and regulative measures of a general nature and other orders of basic importance issued by the Ministry or the Price Directorate pursuant to this Act.

4. Surveys of registered restrictive business practices and of major concerns, cf. Section 35.

The Bulletin may also contain a review of the control and regulation activities, legal decisions involving general principles, and other reports which are considered to be of such importance that they should be made known in such manner. The Ministry may issue regulations concerning the publication of the Price Bulletin and its contents.

The Ministry may prescribe that certain groups of persons engaged in business and business associations shall be required to subscribe to the Price Bulletin and have it exhibited at their place of business or office.

The Norwegian Law Bulletin Act of I April 1876, Section 1, item d, shall not apply to regulations made pursuant to this Act. The King shall determine whether and, if so, to what extent such regulations shall be published in the Law Bulletin.

Section 13: Publication of Other Decisions Made under this Act

The authorities shall ensure that control and regulation orders of a general nature, which are not published in the Price Bulletin, are made properly known by other means.

Any notification of decisions concerning specific named persons, companies, foundations or associations shall be given in writing to the party or parties to whom they apply.

The Ministry may issue further regulations with regard to the publication or other announcement of decisions made pursuant to this Act.

Section 14: Reports to the Storting

At the beginning of each calendar year the King shall submit a report to the Storting on the general instructions on which it is intended to base control and regulation activities in the current year. The report shall, as far as possible, contain a review of control and regulation activities as practised during the past year.

The general instructions so reported, together with any amendments passed by the Storting, may not be changed in any essential respect before a special report has been made thereon, unless such delay is deemed unjustifiable. In that event, a report on the change made shall be submitted as soon as possible after it has been put into effect.

The Storting shall also receive a report every year on control and regulation activities during the past year.

The King shall submit special reports to the Storting on general regulations issued under Section 3, major amendments to such regulations, regulations concerning levies or the reservation of funds under Section 25 (third or sixth paragraph) and particularly important regulations of a general nature under Section 24.

The King shall submit to the Storting every year a statement of accounts for levies under Section 25, with a detailed statement of revenues and expenditures. Unless otherwise provided by the Storting, the statement shall be in respect of the fiscal year.

CHAPTER III

OBLIGATION TO FURNISH INFORMATION

AND MAINTAIN SECRECY

Section 15: Obligation To Furnish Information

All persons shall be obliged to furnish the King, the Ministry and the authorities mentioned in Sections 4–7, or specific representatives appointed by them, with such information as they call for to enable them to carry out their duties under this Act. It may be stipulated that such information shall be given verbally or in writing within such time limit as the authorities or their representatives may determine.

The authorities mentioned above may also require that they themselves or their appointed representatives shall be allowed to examine business documents, correspondence, minutes of proceedings and other books and papers. If necessary, the assistance of the police may be requested to have such documents, etc., surrendered. The authorities may also require that they or their appointed representatives shall be allowed to inspect plants and other real estate or movable property.

The King may authorise representatives of the bodies mentioned in Section 8 to demand information, and to make examinations and inspections according to the first and second paragraphs; provided, however, that such right shall not be given to any person occupying a competitive position in relation to the party concerned.

The party from whom information is required may request that information on technical devices or processes which are secret shall only be given to the head of the Price Directorate, or to a person specially appointed by him to receive such information. This rule shall apply equally to examinations and inspections.

Section 16: Information Required from Authorities Subject to the Obligation To Maintain Secrecy

Any information which is requested under Section 15 (first paragraph) may be furnished to the following authorities notwithstanding the obligation to maintain secrecy which they may otherwise be required to observe:

a) Tax assessment authorities and other tax authorities;

b) Authorities entrusted with the enforcement of the provisions of this Act;

c) Authorities entrusted with the administration of regulations or controls of imports and exports, emergency supply measures, or other public regulation of business activities.

Nor shall the obligation to maintain secrecy be a valid objection to the examination according to Section 15 (second paragraph) of books and documents in the possession of such authorities.

Section 17: Obligation To Maintain Secrecy

Any person who, by virtue of his position or office under this Act obtains information of technical or business secrets, or other matters which are not generally known, shall keep secret the information thus obtained; nor may he make use of such information in his business.

The provisions of the first paragraph apply with the limitations set by the functions of the person concerned under the Act. They shall not thus prevent the giving of the information to others in so far as is requisite for the proper consideration of the case. Information such as mentioned in the first paragraph may be given in the statement of grounds under Section 11 (first paragraph) when this appears to be necessary and justifiable in weighing conflicting considerations. Such information may also be given to authorities entrusted with the enforcement of this Act or with the prosecution of violations thereof.

No person receiving information under the second or third sentence of the second paragraph may make use thereof in his business; nor may he impart this information to others unless such action is a pre-requisite for the exercise of his right of complaint under the Act.

The Ministry, the Price Council, or the Price Directorate may rule that such information as mentioned in the first paragraph may be required to be given or cited in public session, cf. Section 10, or otherwise be made public when such action is considered in the public interest; provided, however, that information on secret technical devices and processes may not under any circumstances be made public.

CHAPTER IV
GENERAL PROVISIONS CONCERNING BUSINESS ACTIVITIES

Section 18: Prices and Other Terms of Business

It is prohibited to accept, demand or make an agreement on prices which are unreasonable; nor may terms of business be demanded, agreed upon, or maintained if they affect the other party unreasonably, or if they are clearly contrary to the public interest.

An enterprise shall be considered to have demanded a price or to have stipulated terms of business when such price or terms have been stated in price lists, advertisements, or other communications to customers, or if they have been announced by price marking, price notices, or by the display of price lists at the place of business, cf. Section 20.

Section 19: Estimates of Costs

Enterprises which submit estimates of costs as a basis for a decision on regulation under this Act shall calculate such estimates in accordance with the regulations which may have been issued by the authority concerned, or explain in detail departures therefrom. If an enterprise has submitted incorrect estimates of costs, or other incorrect information of importance for a decision, this shall be reported as soon as the enterprise becomes aware of the mistake. If costs fall substantially after the submission of an estimate, a report thereon must be submitted, if the regulative provision is still in force or if regulation has not been effected on the basis of the first estimate.

Section 20: Price Marking, Bills, Invoices and Receipts

Retailers selling to consumers shall, as far as practicable, mark the goods with the retail prices or display price lists so that prices are easily seen by the customers.

In wholesale transactions—and in other business when so required by the buyer—the seller shall give the buyer a bill, invoice or receipt.

Section 21: Unnecessary Middleman Activities

Such middleman activities as are unnecessary and raise prices are prohibited; nor may sales be made to buyers who are engaged in such activities.

Section 22: Payment for Licenses, etc.

No payment may, without the consent of the Price Directorate, be demanded or accepted for the transfer of a license or other authorisation, granted or expected to be granted in connection with public control of business activities. This provision shall also apply if the license or the authorisation is transferred together with a business.

Section 23: Refusal of Business Connections

The Price Council may forbid enterprises to refuse to have business connections with another enterprise or with a consumer, if the Council finds that such refusal would be detrimental to the public interest, or that it would have an unreasonable effect on the other party. It is deemed to constitute a refusal when one party is willing to have business connections only on terms which the Council considers to be unreasonable or unusual.

The Council may, if so requested by a party intending to refuse business connections or to urge others to do so, give an advance ruling as to whether such refusal will be forbidden or allowed. Otherwise, the Council cannot make a decision under the first paragraph before refusal is a fact, or threat or incitement thereto has been made.

In order to ensure that the purpose of a prohibition under the first paragraph is attained, the Price Council may issue supplementary regulations, which inter alia can require enterprises to make or maintain business connections on such terms as the Council prescribes, and may prohibit incitement and other complicity in the refusal.

If a refusal of the kind mentioned in the first paragraph or a threat or an incitement thereto has caused financial damage to the other party, the latter may demand compensation. This applies irrespective of whether or not the Council has forbidden such refusal, but not if the Council has decided that such refusal shall be permitted. The provisions of Section 4 of the Boycott Act of 5 December 1947 shall also apply.

The provisions of the first, second and third paragraphs shall not apply to conditions governed by the provisions of the first paragraph of Section 45.

CHAPTER V

GENERAL POWERS TO CONTROL AND REGULATE PRICES, PROFITS AND OTHER CONDITIONS OF BUSINESS

Section 24: General Regulative Powers

1. In furtherance of the purposes cited in Section 1, subsections a) and c), the King may issue regulations:

a) Concerning maximum prices, minimum prices, price freezing, price calculations, discounts, additions, maximum profit margins, terms of delivery and payment, and other provisions with regard to prices, profits and terms of business;

b) Concerning the counteraction of unnecessary middleman activities and unfair competition;

c) Concerning estimates of cost, procedure regarding offers, contracts and settlements, and other regulations which may be needed to facilitate control.

2. In association with regulations under Subsections 1 a) or b) of this section, the King may issue:

a) Regulations requiring that enterprises shall fulfill certain conditions before they take specific prices, profits or definite discounts; or regulations requiring that such action shall be conditional on approval;

b) Regulations prohibiting the sale or offer for sale of goods or services when no price regulations have been issued covering such sale, or when amendment of a regulation is under consideration, provided that such prohibition is considered to be necessary for effective regulations;

c) Regulations providing that goods shall be sold in definite measures or weights and regulations concerning methods of measurement and grading;

d) Regulations concerning the nature and quality of price-controlled goods and services in so far as effective regulation so requires;

e) Such regulations concerning the distribution of production or marketing as are considered necessary in order to prevent unfair treatment of certain consumers or districts.

3. To aid purchasers to appraise prices and qualities, the King may make regulations:

a) Requiring enterprises to mark their goods, display notices and otherwise make known their prices, trading conditions, quality and other properties of their goods or services;

b) Concerning the shape of certain goods, packaging and other external features, and on the grading and measurement of goods offered for sale.

4. Regulations under sub-paragraph 1, 2 or 3 may be issued as general regulations or as regulations of more limited scope.

Section 25: Levies and Reservation of Funds for Price Regulation Purposes

In furtherance of the purposes mentioned in Section 1, Subsection a), enterprises may be required to pay levies for use in the regulation of prices and costs. Such levies may be imposed for use in measures concerning the levy-payers' own business or for measures covering the whole trade or industry or major groups of trades, or for general price regulation purposes.

Such requirements as mentioned in the first paragraph shall be imposed by the Storting when the nature of the levy system is such as to be of major importance to the national economy. In imposing a levy the Storting may stipulate that the King shall determine the amount of the levy and make other regulations thereon.

Any levy system which is not of the kind cited in the second paragraph shall be imposed by the King. Levies may also be imposed by the King in other cases if the King finds it advisable not to await the decision of the Storting. In such circumstances the King may also suspend or amend levy systems which have been imposed by the Storting. The Storting may in any circumstances decide that a levy imposed by the King shall be repealed.

The levies shall be allotted to special funds with the status of independent legal entities, whose moneys are kept separate from the government accounts. The King shall issue by-laws for the funds, and regulations as to their purpose, administration, management of their assets, in and out payments, enforcement of claims, accounting and auditing. If any moneys remain after the original purposes of the funds have been carried out, or if such action is otherwise justifiable, the King may rule that the moneys may be used for other price regulation purposes. It may, however, be stipulated in the by-laws that the purpose cannot be changed, or changed only with the consent of definite organisations or others representing the payers, or organisations or others representing those parties who—according to the original purpose—are intended to benefit from the funds.

If levies which have been imposed under the provisions of the preceding paragraphs are not paid in due time, interest shall be paid thereon at the rate of one half per cent per month from the date when the payment falls due until payment is made.

The Storting or the King, as the case may be, may also require enterprises to set aside funds to be used for such purposes of regulation as mentioned in the first paragraph. The provisions of the first, second and third paragraphs shall apply accordingly to such requirements. The King shall make regulations governing the reservation of such funds.

Section 26: Regulations Concerning Keeping of Accounts and Annual Statements

As part of the system of control of prices and profits and other activities of enterprises, the King may issue regulations concerning the keeping of accounts, annual statements of accounts and annual reports.

The King may issue directives requiring certain groups of enterprises to publish their annual statements.

Section 27: The Relationship between Regulations under Chapter V and under Chapter IV

Regulations issued pursuant to Chapter V shall overrule those of Chapter IV.

CHAPTER VI
REGULATION OF DIVIDENDS IN LIMITED LIABILITY COMPANIES

Section 28: Maximum Dividends and Remuneration to the Officers of Limited Liability Companies

Joint-stock companies may not distribute dividends or make other distributions or payments which may be placed on a par with dividends, exceeding what is justified in view of the provisions contained in the Act of 6 July 1957 on Joint-Stock Companies, Section 106, cf. Section 103 of the Act.

Repayment of share capital written down previously without repayment may not take place without the approval of the Price Directorate.

The remuneration to the officers of a joint-stock company may not exceed an amount which would be reasonable having regard to the work performed and the responsibility of the task.

The expression "joint-stock companies" means companies covered by the Act of 6 July 1957 on Joint-Stock Companies, cf. Section 60, p. 6 of this act.

Section 29: Authority To Resolve on Limitation of Dividends

The Storting may for each individual year make a special resolution on limitation of distribution of dividends and of remuneration to the officers in such companies as mentioned in Section 28.

Section 30: Provisions on Control

The King may lay down such provisions as are found necessary for the control of dividend distribution, including provisions imposing on companies the duty to submit reports on this distribution.

Section 31: Effect of Company By-laws

No shareholder may make a claim against a company because dividends have been limited in violation of the by-laws, when such limitation is a consequence of the provisions of Sections 28 and 29 or of regulations issued pursuant to these Sections.

Additional dividends may not be distributed without the approval of the Price Directorate, for previous years when limitations have been in force.

CHAPTER VII
RESTRICTIVE BUSINESS ARRANGEMENTS

Section 32: Supervision of Restrictive Business Arrangements and Dominant Enterprises

In furtherance of the purposes mentioned in Section 1, Subsections a) and c), the Price Directorate shall supervise restrictive business arrangements and dominant enterprises. The Directorate shall, inter alia:

a) Control that the provisions of this chapter regarding compulsory registration are observed, and carry out the prescribed registration.

b) Collect other information which may elucidate competitive conditions and the effects of restrictive business arrangements;

c) Examine such information about dominant enterprises and restrictive business arrangements as are obtained from reports or in other ways;

d) Implement or propose such general or special measures of regulation or control under the Act as are found necessary for terminating improper conditions in business, for improving the organisation, or otherwise promoting the development for the general good.

e) Assist enterprises endeavouring to implement arrangements in so far as these are deemed likely to further the purposes mentioned in Subsection d) and such assistance is permissible under the terms of the Act.

Section 33: Obligation To Report Restrictive Business Arrangements

Under specific regulations issued by the King, there shall be reported to the Price Directorate:

1. Associations of enterprises which regulate, or have for their purposes to regulate, prices, profits, calculations of costs, terms of business, production or distribution within the realm;

2. Restrictive agreements or other arrangements made by enterprises without the organisation of an association with a separate board, if the agreement or arrangement has such purpose or such effect as mentioned in Subsection 1);

3. Restrictive provisions made by enterprises subject to the obligation to report according to Section 34, when the provisions have such purpose or such effect as mentioned in Subsection 1).

The obligation to report shall apply irrespective of whether the arrangement is implemented by means of binding or guiding provisions or by other means. Unless otherwise prescribed by the King, the obligation to report shall also apply to an association, agreement, arrangement or provision which has come into being in pursuance of legislation.

The obligation to report according to Subsection 1) rests with the board of the association. If the registered office is outside the realm, the obligation to report rests on the representative of the association and its members within the realm. The obligation to report restrictive agreements and other arrangements mentioned in Subsection 2) is incumbent on every participant who is engaged in business activities within the realm as well as any representatives within the realm of participants domiciled abroad. The obligation to report restrictive provisions mentioned in Subsection 3) rests with the enterprise which has made such provisions.

The report shall contain a detailed description of the restrictive business arrangements and information on matters of importance for the supervision of such arrangements. In addition to the initial or principal report, supplementary reports shall be submitted on changes or new circumstances. The regulations governing reports shall contain further provisions on the data to be furnished.

The reporting regulations may contain provisions for exemptions from the obligation to report restrictive business arrangements which are of so little significance that there is no call for supervision.

In cases of doubt, the Price Directorate shall determine whether an association, agreement or other arrangement or a provision is of such kind as to be subject to the obligation to report. The decision of the Directorate may be appealed within 14 days to the Price Council, which has the power to reverse the decision.

Section 34: Obligation of Dominant Enterprises To Report

Under regulations issued by the King, the following enterprises shall submit a report to the Price Directorate:

1. Enterprises which must be assumed to produce or distribute at least one quarter of the total production or distribution in the realm of one or more commodities produced or distributed by the enterprise, or of services provided by it. If an enterprise has controlling influence over enterprises within the realm other than those which are operated in its own name, all the enterprises concerned shall be considered as one in determining the question of obligation to report;

2. Persons who own or are responsible for the running of enterprises which are subsidiaries or subject to the controlling influence of:

a) A foreign firm which may be assumed to have substantial influence on the prices in one or more countries of one or more commodities or services, or which is associated with an association of firms which, together, may be assumed to have such influence;

b) Association of foreign firms or of Norwegian and foreign firms which may be assumed to have such influence as mentioned under a).

The provisions of the last sentence of Subsection 1) shall apply equally.

3. Enterprises which, although not coming under Subsections 1) or 2), have received specific instructions from the Price Directorate to submit a report, because they are engaged in activities which are of such importance for one or more trades within the realm that special supervision is considered by the Directorate to be necessary. The obligation to report does not apply to Government monopolies.

The report shall contain a detailed account of the nature and extent of the activities which are carried on, of the connections existing between the firms or the firms operated by a person in his own name and other firms or associations of firms as well as other matters of importance for the supervision thereof. In addition to the principal report, supplementary reports shall be submitted on any changes or new circumstances. Further details of particulars to be reported shall be given in the regulations governing reports.

The reporting regulations may contain provisions for exemptions from the obligation to report if such business activities as mentioned under Subsection 1) are of so little significance that there is no call for supervision.

In case of doubt, the Price Directorate shall decide whether an enterprise has an obligation to report under the provisions of Subsections 1) and 2) of the first paragraph. If there is justifiable doubt as to there being an obligation to report, no such obligation shall exist until the Price Directorate has made a decision.

A decision of the Price Directorate under this section may be applied within 14 days to the Price Council, which has the power to reverse the decision.

Section 35: Registration

Reports submitted under Sections 33 and 34 shall be entered in a register kept by the Price Directorate. The register shall also include reports which have been, or will be submitted in accordance with registration regulations under the Act concerning Control of Restrictive Business Arrangements and of Unreasonable Prices, dated 12 March 1926, or the Temporary Act of 30 June 1947 concerning Price Control and Control of other Business Activities, cf. the third paragraph of Section 61 of this Act. The Price Directorate may also include in the register any surveys or accounts of conditions which have been reported or other documents which may elucidate them. It may be requested by the person or institution furnishing the particulars that information about secret technical devices and processes shall not be registered. The King shall issue regulations on registration.

If the Price Directorate obtains knowledge of circumstances which are subject to compulsory reporting, but have not been reported, a temporary registration may be made until a report has been received.

On application to the Price Directorate any person may acquaint himself with the contents of the register. Extracts may be obtained against the payment of a charge according to rates to be prescribed by the Ministry.

According to regulations issued by the King, the Price Directorate shall publish in the Price Bulletin surveys of cases which are subject to compulsory reporting and have been registered by the Directorate.

*Section 36: Prohibition of the Implementation of Restrictive
Business Arrangements Before a Report Has Been Submitted*

It is forbidden to implement or to participate in the implementation of restrictive business arrangements which are subject to the obligation to report, under Section 33, before they have been reported to the Price Directorate in the prescribed manner. Until a report has been submitted, the agreements are not valid.

Section 37: Duration of Restrictive Business Arrangements

An agreement to participate in a restrictive business arrangement as mentioned in Section 33, Subsections 1 and 2, may only be concluded for a maximum period of one year, or with a term of notice not exceeding three months, unless otherwise approved by the Price Council.

Section 38: Annual Accounts and Annual Reports

Enterprises participating in an association, agreement or other arrangement which is subject to the obligation to report under Section 33, shall submit each year to the Price Directorate their annual statement of accounts together with a report on activities during the year, provided that:

a) The share capital of the enterprise or its net capital stock and funds according to the books at the end of the last accounting year amounted to not less than 1 million kroner, or

b) The enterprise concerned has been required by the Price Directorate to submit annual accounts and annual reports.

Enterprises obliged to submit reports under Section 34 shall in any case submit accounts and reports as mentioned in the first paragraph.

Accounts and reports as mentioned in the first paragraph, cf. the second paragraph, shall be submitted within four months after the expiry of the accounting year. Joint-stock companies shall submit their accounts and reports within 14 days after these have been approved by the Annual General Meeting, but no later than 14 days after the expiry of the time allowed under the Joint-Stock Companies Act for the adoption of the annual accounts by the General Meeting. In the case of joint-stock companies and other companies with limited liability, the accounts and report shall be signed by the Council, and in the case of other companies, by not more than three of the responsible members, and in the case of a one-man business by the owner. If the business has an auditor, the accounts shall bear documentation from the auditor stating that they have been audited.

The annual accounts shall be compiled in accordance with regulations issued by the Price Directorate within the limits of any instructions issued under Section 26. The Price Directorate may prescribe that the accounts shall be submitted on certain forms.

Persons who are running several firms shall submit separate accounts for each firm as far as practicable.

The annual report shall contain a further explanation of the accounts and a survey of activities during the year.

If an enterprise holds shares or other participating documents in other firms, this shall be stated in the annual report or in a special appendix thereto, together with a list of the firms concerned, the capital thereof, and how many shares or other participating documents are held, as well as the nominal value of such shares or participating documents.

Section 39: Restrictions in Respect of Tenders

Enterprises which are members of an association which regulates or controls prices or terms of tenders, shall—when submitting a tender— inform the prospective purchaser inviting tenders of the implications of the regulation or control.

The provisions of the first paragraph shall apply equally when restrictive business agreements or other arrangements have been made, or when provisions have been made thereunder, regarding the regulation or control of tendered prices or terms.

Section 40: Coercive Measures Applied to Members

If a restrictive association has imposed a fine or other penalty on a member, or demanded indemnity for the violation of a restrictive provision, the Price Council may—on receipt of a complaint or on its own initiative—reduce or cancel the penalty or indemnity, if it is considered by the Council that it would be contrary to the public interest to enforce the provision by coercive means, or that the consequences of the penalty or indemnity for the member concerned would be unreasonable.

The provisions of the first paragraph shall apply equally to penalties or indemnities for the violation of restrictive agreements or other arrangements and of restrictive provisions made under such agreements or arrangements, or by dominant enterprises which are subject to the obligation to report according to Section 34.

Section 41: Exclusion of Members and Refusal To Admit Members

If a restrictive association has excluded or refused to admit an enterprise as a member, the Price Council may—on receipt of a complaint or on its own initiative—reverse the exclusion or direct the association to admit the enterprise concerned as a member, provided that the Council is of the opinion that the exclusion or refusal is unfair to the enterprise concerned, or that it is contrary to the public interest.

The provisions of the first paragraph shall apply equally with regard to participation in restrictive agreements and other arrangements.

Section 42: Amendments in, and Abolition of Restrictive Business Arrangements and Prohibition of such Arrangements

The King may amend or abolish any provision which has been made by a restrictive association if it is deemed likely to have a harmful effect on production, distribution or other business activities within the realm, or the provision must otherwise be considered unreasonable or detrimental to the public interest. Such prohibitions or requirements as are deemed necessary to ensure that the purpose of the abolition or amendment is achieved may be issued in connection with the decision.

If the measures taken according to the preceding paragraph do not achieve their purpose, or are not considered to be sufficient, the King may dissolve the association. Prior to such a dissolution an opinion shall be obtained from the Price Council. In connection with the dissolution of an association, the King may also order the dissolution of a company considered to be part of the association or through which the latter operates. The King shall issue regulations governing the implementation of the dissolution of the association and/or the company. The King may also issue such prohibition and requirements as are deemed necessary to ensure that the purpose of the dissolution is achieved.

The provisions of the first paragraph shall apply equally to restrictive business agreements and other arrangements, and to restrictive provisions made under such agreements or arrangements or by dominant enterprises which are subject to the obligation to report under Section 34.

The King may forbid particular associations or groups of enterprises, particular dominant enterprises subject to the duty to report or enterprises in particular trades to carry out restrictive business provisions, agreements or arrangements when such regulations may be assumed to have such effects as mentioned in the first paragraph or when prohibition is found necessary to further such competition as is desirable from the public point of view. On similar conditions the King may lay down general prohibition of particular types of restrictive business arrangements. On such conditions as mentioned in the first and second sentence the King may also lay down other provisions for the counteraction of restrictive business arrangements or particular types of restrictive business arrangements.

Section 43: Restrictive Business Arrangements Applicable to Foreign Countries

The provisions of Sections 32, 33, 35, 36, 37, 40 and 41 shall not apply to:

a) Restrictive business associations which have their registered office within the realm, but which have only made, and whose only purpose is to make restrictive business provisions applicable to other countries, or to trade and commerce between other countries;

b) Restrictive business agreements, arrangements or provisions made by enterprises within the realm, when such agreements, arrangements and provisions are of the nature mentioned under a);

c) The participation by Norwegian enterprises in foreign restrictive business associations, agreements or other arrangements of the nature mentioned under a).

The Price Directorate shall supervise such restrictive business arrangements as mentioned in a) and b), with a view to counteracting conditions which may have a detrimental effect on Norwegian interests, or which may be assumed to be contrary to obligations undertaken by Norway in an international agreement. Similar supervision shall be exercised in respect of the participation by Norwegian enterprises in such restrictive business arrangements as mentioned in c). The King may issue regulations concerning the obligation to report as a basis for supervision.

Section 44: Foreign Restrictive Arrangements

If the Price Directorate obtains knowledge that measures detrimental to Norwegian interests are being put into effect through foreign restrictive business arrangements, the matter shall be reported to the Ministry.

CHAPTER VIII
COUNTERACTION OF REGULATIONS. FORCED SALES
FEES FOR ASSESSMENTS. DISTRAINT

Section 45: Counteraction of Regulations

Unless 14 days have passed since notification to the Ministry, no organization of enterprises may put into effect a stoppage, reduction or realignment of economic activities likely to be contrary to statutory regulations and which are of essential importance to the supply situation in the realm or major part thereof. In cases of doubt, the King shall determine, with binding effect, whether a stoppage, reduction or realignment comes within the provisions of this paragraph.

When advance notice has been given according to the first paragraph, the Storting—or the King, if the Storting is not in session—may determine that the time allowed according to the first paragraph shall be extended by up to one month. Such decision shall be made before the expiry of the time limit stated in the first paragraph.

In the event of a dispute between the authority concerned and an organisation of enterprises with regard to the lawfulness or interpretation of a regulative order, action may not be taken to settle the dispute by means of stoppage, reduction, or realignment of economic activities; nor may any such action be taken in a dispute concerning the validity or interpretation of an agreement on which regulative orders are based.

It is unlawful to incite to the implementation or continuation of such action as mentioned in the third paragraph. It is also unlawful to incite to the implementation or continuation of such action as mentioned in the third paragraph before the expiry of the time limit stated in the first and second paragraphs.

The King may prohibit the stoppage, reduction, or realignment of economic activities likely to counteract controls under this Act. Such prohibition shall not apply to circumstances covered by the provisions of the first paragraph.

Section 46: Determination of Prices in Cases of Forced Sales
Expropriation, and Repurchase according to Allodial Right

Unless regulations to the contrary have been made under this Act, prices higher than those permissible in voluntary sales may not be accepted in a forced sale. An auction bid may be confirmed notwithstanding the provisions regarding time limits in the Act of 13 August 1915, Section 148, concerning forced sales, when the Court has found it necessary to postpone decision on confirmation having regard to the determination of the price.

In cases of expropriation and repurchase according to allodial right, the price shall be determined on the basis of current price regulations.

Section 47: Payment of Fees for Assessments and Surveys

The Ministry may rule that fees shall be paid at specified rates for assessments or surveys made pursuant to this Act at the request of any interested party.

Section 48: Distraint

Unpaid amounts for the expenses of an association or a committee under Section 8, subscription fees for the Price Bulletin under Section 12, a price regulation levy under Section 25, and fees for assessments and surveys under Section 47, plus interest and costs, may be obtained by process of distraint.

CHAPTER IX

REVIEW OF DECISIONS

Section 49: The Right of a Superior Authority To Review
Decisions on own Initiative

The King or the Ministry may, on its own initiative, amend or cancel a decision made by the bodies mentioned in Sections 4–8, or instruct the bodies concerned to do so.

The Price Directorate has a similar right regarding decisions made by the bodies mentioned in Sections 6 and 7, or those mentioned in Section 8, when the latter are under the jurisdiction of the Directorate. This provision also applies to the Regional Offices of the Price Inspectorate in respect of decisions made by the Price Committees or by bodies mentioned in Section 8 when the latter are under the jurisdiction of the Regional Office.

The King may issue regulations on the examination of decisions by superior bodies.

Section 50: Review of Decisions on Appeal

Decisions of a Price Committee or a Regional Office of the Price Inspectorate containing a directive to, or refusal of an application from a particular enterprise, or which otherwise specially affect a particular enterprise, may be appealed against to the Regional Office of the Price Inspectorate or the Price Directorate as appropriate. If such a decision has been made by a body mentioned in Section 8, an appeal against it may be made to the controlling authority to which the body concerned is subordinate, under regulations issued by the King.

In the case of decisions made by the Price Directorate or the Ministry, of the nature mentioned in the first paragraph, an appeal may be lodged by the enterprise concerned with the Ministry or the King, as appropriate. A decision made by the Price Directorate or the Ministry on an appeal is final.

There is no appeal against decisions of the Price Council taken under Sections 10, 17, 23, 33, 34, 37, 40 and 41: nor against decisions in other matters in which the authority to make decisions has been vested in the Council under the second sentence of the fourth paragraph of Section 4, unless otherwise provided in regulations issued by the King.

Section 51: Procedure in Appeal Cases

An appeal under Section 50 must be lodged within 14 days from the day on which the decision is made known to the enterprise concerned.

The appeal shall be presented to the controlling authority which has made the decision. If the authority concerned finds no grounds for a repeal or amendment, the case shall immediately be transmitted to the competent authority for considering the appeal.

The case shall be decided without unjustifiable delay. The provisions of Section 10 shall have equal application. Grounds for the decision taken shall always be given. An appeal shall not have the effect of suspending the execution of the decision appealed against unless so determined by the controlling authority which has made the decision or by superior authority. The King may issue regulations concerning appeal procedure.

CHAPTER X

PENALTIES AND FORFEITURE

Section 52: Penalties Imposed on Individuals

Any person who wilfully violates provisions of, or regulations made pursuant to this Act, or which are maintained thereunder, and which are not concerned with the organisation and functions of the regulating or controlling authorities, shall be liable to a fine or to imprisonment up to one year, or both. The same penalty shall apply to any person who wilfully aids or abets in such violation. Any person who has purchased goods, a right, or a service for an unlawful price, shall only be liable to penalty as accessory if he has encouraged or incited to the violation.

In particularly serious circumstances, the offenders may be sentenced to imprisonment for up to three years, to which penalty may be added a fine. In determining whether such circumstances exist, particular consideration shall be given to whether the violation is extensive in nature and of considerable duration, whether it has been committed or continued despite a warning by a public authority, whether incorrect accounts or other records have been kept, whether an attempt has been made to conceal the offence by, inter alia, neglecting to keep accounts, giving false information, whether a wrongfully procured or manufactured trade mark, legitimation or similar document has been used, and whether the offender has previously been punished for violation of legislation concerning prices, trust control, supplies, or rationing.

Any person who through negligence violates any provisions or regulations mentioned in the first paragraph, or who aids or abets in such violation, shall be liable to a fine.

It may be stipulated in the regulations issued under this Act that a violation thereof shall not entail penalty.

Section 53: Penalties Imposed on Corporate Bodies

If a punishable offence mentioned in Section 52 has been committed by any person who has acted on behalf of a corporate body, a foundation or an association, the corporate body, foundation or association may be sentenced to a fine and deprivation of the right to carry on business, provided, however, that this shall only be done when the violation has been committed in furtherance of the interests of the corporate body, foundation or association, or they may be assumed to have had substantial advantage from the violation. The provisions of Section 28 of the Penal Code shall not apply to fines imposed under this section.

Section 54: Penalties for Breach of Secrecy Obligations

Any person who wilfully divulges or makes use of information in violation of the provisions of this Act, or aids or abets therein, shall be liable to a fine or imprisonment up to one year, or both. If the violation has been committed through negligence, the offender shall be liable to a fine.

Section 55: Application of the Provisions of the Penal Code in Respect of Public Service

Participation in duties of control or regulation under this Act shall be regarded as public service in relation to the provisions of the General Civil Penal Code of 22 May 1902, Chapters 11, 12, 33 and 34.

Section 56: Forfeiture of Unlawfully Paid Excess Price, etc.

If any person has charged a higher price than is lawful under provisions contained in or regulations issued under, or maintained by this Act, an amount which the court considers to be equivalent to the excess price shall be forfeited. This provision shall apply irrespective of whether or not the circumstances entail criminal liability.

The excess price shall be forfeited either by the person who has taken the unlawful price, or by the person or institution on whose behalf or for whose benefit he acted, or from both these parties. If the amount is confiscated from both parties, the Court may either divide the responsibility between them, or it can hold them both jointly and separately responsible for the whole amount or part thereof. The provisions of this paragraph shall apply equally when more than one person is implicated in the circumstances giving rise to the forfeiture.

In the amount so forfeited no deduction may be made for the unlawful excess price paid by the responsible party for goods for sale, raw materials or means of production, or for services received, unless:

1. The part of the excess price concerned has been confiscated from the supplier, or

2. The offender can prove that he was not aware that the prices paid by him, or accepted by him, were excessive, and further that he has exercised such care as might be expected in the circumstances.

A deduction shall be made in respect of amounts which the responsible party is ordered, by decision of the Court or by order of the magistrate, to repay the aggrieved party. This shall also be done if the responsible party has made such repayment in advance and he either proves that he was obliged to do so under the provisions of Section 59, or proves that repayment took place before the matter was raised by the police or the controlling authority concerned.

If the entire amount has been declared to the tax authorities, a deduction shall be made corresponding to the increase in public taxes and duties which the excess price has imposed on the responsible party. The Public Prosecutor shall notify the tax authorities concerned of any deduction which has been made in accordance with the provisions of this paragraph.

Proceedings for forfeiture under this section may not be instituted when five years have lapsed since the excess price was obtained, unless a criminal offence has been committed.

The provisions of this section shall apply equally when, in violation of provisions contained in, or regulations issued under this Act, or maintained by this Act,

1) a lower price than the minimum price has been paid, or

2) compensation has been taken for the transfer of licences or other authorisations, which have been given or are expected, or

3) company dividends received have been excessive.

Section 57: Forfeiture of Excess Profits due to Incorrect Computation of Costs

Any excess profit obtained because the authorities have determined the regulated price at a higher level than they would otherwise have done, or if they have refrained from putting regulations into effect, may be forfeited by the party which has contributed to this condition by:

1. Submitting computations of costs or other information which—in the light of conditions prevailing when the information was given—contain substantial errors, or

2. Failing to submit obligatory reports stating that the costs have become substantially lower than in computations previously submitted.

Such excess profits may also be forfeited by the party on whose behalf the offence has been committed. Such forfeiture may take place irrespective of whether or not any criminal liability has been incurred by anyone. The provisions of the second, fifth and sixth paragraphs of Section 56 shall apply equally.

Section 58: Application of the Provisions Concerning Penalty and Forfeiture in Violation of Previous Regulations

The provisions for the imposition of penalties in this Act shall also apply in respect of violations of orders issued in, or pursuant to the Regulations on price control of 12 September 1940, the Provisional Order of 8 May 1945 concerning the control of prices and other business activities, or the Provisional Acts of 14 December 1946 and 30 June 1947 concerning the control of prices and other business activities, provided, however, that no person may be sentenced to a more severe penalty than might have been imposed according to the penal provisions in force at the time when the offence was committed.

The provisions of Section 56 shall also apply to offences committed before the entry into force of this Act, provided, however, that the amount forfeited may not exceed the maximum amount which might have been forfeited under the provisions in force at the time of the offence.

Proceedings which have been instituted before the entry into force of this Act for the payment of money to a price adjustment fund in accordance with Section 15 of the Provisional Act of 30 June 1947 concerning the Control of Prices and other Business Activities, shall be adjudicated under the provisions of the said Act. In proceedings which are instituted after the entry into force of this Act in respect of previous cases, forfeiture according to Section 57 may be made in so far as payment could have been required under Section 15 of the Act of 30 June 1947.

Section 59: Repayment of Unlawful Excess Price

Anyone who has paid a higher price than is lawful may demand repayment of the excess price unless, having regard to the circumstances of the case, he is considered to be responsible to a considerable extent for the violation.

A demand for reduction of the agreed price to the lawful price or for repayment of the excess price shall not entitle the other party to annul the agreement,

1) if the transaction is a part of the regular commercial sale of goods or services to consumers,

2) if the annulment would have unreasonable effects having regard to the degree of guilt of both parties and to the other circumstances of the case.

CHAPTER XI

INTERPRETATION. ENTRY INTO FORCE. TERRITORIAL APPLICATION

Section 60: Interpretation

In this Act the following expressions have the meanings hereby respectively assigned to them, namely:

1. "Price" shall mean compensation of any kind irrespective of whether any other terms are used, such as remuneration fee, honorarium, freight, rate, rent, etc.;

2. "Goods" shall mean movable or immovable property, including ships, aircraft and electric power;

3. "Services" shall mean all kinds of services for which compensation is received, except work in the employment of others;

4. "Business activities" shall mean all kinds of permanent or occasional economic activities for gain;

5. An "enterprise" shall mean any party—whether an individual, a corporate body, a foundation or an association which carries on business activities;

6. "Joint-stock company" shall be deemed to include limited partnerships and joint-stock shipping companies.

Section 61: Entry into Force

This Act shall enter into force on 1 January 1954. Regulations may nevertheless be issued pursuant to this Act at any earlier date, provided such regulations do not enter into force before the Act itself, except in so far as they are concerned with the organisation of the bodies for exercising control and regulation.

As from the entry into force of this Act, the Act to provide for the control of Restrictive Arrangements and of Unreasonable Prices dated 12 March 1926 is repealed. The Provisional Act of June 1947 concerning the Control of Prices and other Business Activities shall continue to apply until this Act enters into force.

Regulations issued or maintained pursuant to the above mentioned Acts of 12 March 1926 and 30 June 1947 shall—in so far as they are in force on 1 January 1954—continue in effect until amended or repealed pursuant to this Act or by special regulations issued by the King. Until such time as the Storting has made a decision under Section 28 of this Act, the provisions concerning the limitation of dividends under the Provisional Act of 30 June 1947 shall continue to have effect.

The King shall determine whether and to what extent the provisions of this Act and regulations made hereunder shall apply to Svalbard (Spitzbergen).

ROYAL DECREE OF 18 OCTOBER 1957

In pursuance of Section 24 of the Act of 26 June 1953 on control of prices, dividends and restrictive business arrangements, the following provisions concerning resale price regulation are hereby laid down:

Section 1: Definition of Resale Price Regulation

The terms "resale price regulation" in these provisions means the action of a supplier or of an association or group of suppliers, or several such associations or groups in concert, to issue guiding or binding resale prices or guiding or binding directives to the dealers on the determination of their prices or profits. Resale price regulation as defined herein is considered to exist, whether or not a supplier has made specific mention of the prices or profits to be taken, or which ought to be taken on resale, if the supplier has made out invoices on the basis of gross prices which are so determined that dealers would normally use them as resale prices.

The term "supplier" in these provisions means a person or persons engaged in the business of making sales to dealers. Association of such suppliers is referred to as a suppliers' association. A group which is formed by agreement between such suppliers without the organisation of a separate board is known as a suppliers' group. The term "dealers" in these provisions means persons engaged in the business of reselling, wholesale or retail.

Resale price regulation by one single supplier is designated as individual resale price regulation. Resale price regulation by a suppliers' association or group, or by several suppliers' associations or groups in concert, at the same or at different stages of production or distribution is designated as collective resale price regulation.

Section 2: Provisions Governing Individual Resale Price Regulation

Unless exception has been granted under Section 9 a supplier may not effect such resale price regulation as mentioned in Section 1.

The provisions of the preceding paragraph shall not, however, prevent a supplier from giving advice to dealers on their prices and profits, provided that the supplier makes it clear to the dealers that they are free to take lower prices or profits. This must be stated specifically in the written notices to the dealers on the prices or profits on which advice is given.

The Price Directorate is empowered to prohibit such advisory activity as mentioned in the second paragraph, if the Directorate considers that the condition laid down is not observed or that pressure has been exerted contrary to the provisions of Sections 5 and 6, or that the activity is assumed to result in too high prices or profits, or in other ways will counteract an effective price competition.

Section 3: Provisions Governing Collective Resale Price Regulation

Unless exception has been granted under Section 9 suppliers' associations or groups may not effect such resale price regulation as mentioned in Section 1. This applies irrespective of the nature of the regulation involved, whether it is guiding or binding.

Section 4: Provisions Governing Foreign Resale Price Regulation

Unless an exception has been granted under Section 9 resale price regulation by a foreign supplier may not be practised within the realm.

The provision of the preceding paragraph shall not, however, prevent a foreign supplier or his representative in the realm from giving advice to dealers on their prices or profits, provided that the foreign supplier or his representative in the realm makes it clear to the dealers that they are free to take lower prices or profits. This must be stated specifically in the written notices to the dealers on the prices or profits on which advice is given.

The Price Directorate is empowered to prohibit such advisory activity as mentioned in the second paragraph, if the Directorate considers that the condition laid down has not been observed or that pressure has been exerted contrary to the provisions of Sections 5 and 6, or that the activity is assumed to result in too high prices or profits, or in other ways will counteract an effective price competition.

Resale price regulation by foreign suppliers' associations or groups may not be practised in the realm unless an exception has been granted under Section 9.

If foreign suppliers, suppliers' associations, or groups have effected resale price regulations which according to the provisions in the preceding paragraphs, cf. Section 9, may not be practised in the realm, the representative of the supplier, or of the suppliers' association or group, must inform the Norwegian dealers in writing that they are not committed by the regulation activity and that they are free to take lower prices or profits than those fixed by the foreign supplier, suppliers' association or group. The representative shall send such notice to all his clients. Similar notices shall be given by the importers to the dealers to whom they sell the goods.

Section 5: Prohibition of Inducing Dealers To Take Definite Prices or Profits

Suppliers, suppliers' associations or groups or their representatives, may not, by refusal of business connections or by the use of other methods of compulsion or by threats to use such measures or through appeals or in any other way, endeavour to induce dealers to observe definite prices or profits, if an exception has not been granted under Section 9. These provisions apply irrespective of whether the prices or profits are fixed by suppliers, suppliers' associations or groups or by others, as, for example, associations or groups of dealers.

Section 6: Prohibition of Inducing Suppliers To Effect Resale Price Regulation

Dealers or associations or groups of dealers may not, by refusal to purchase from specific suppliers or by threat of such action or through appeals or use of other measures, endeavour to induce suppliers, suppliers' associations or groups, or suppliers' representatives to effect or assist in effecting resale price regulation which is prohibited under these provisions.

Section 7: Terms of Business Which Form Part of Regulation of Dealer's Prices and Profits

The terms[1] of these provisions which prohibit regulation by suppliers of dealers' prices or profits are also applicable to guiding or binding regulation by suppliers, suppliers' associations and groups of the trading conditions of dealers in so far as such conditions must be regarded as forming part of the regulation by suppliers of dealers' prices or profits. This also applies to the provisions of Sections 5 and 6.

Section 8: Special Provisions for Resale Price Regulation Effected in Pursuance of Act or Resolution of the Storting

For resale price regulation effected in pursuance of an act or a resolution of the Storting, the provisions of Sections 1–7 apply, with the limitations arising from the act or the resolution or from rules issued in pursuance of the act or the resolution.

Section 9: Exceptions

The Price Directorate is empowered to grant exceptions from the pro-

---

[1] The Norwegian expression "forretningsvilkår" covers all terms and conditions other than the price which are stipulated in commercial transactions (e.g. terms of payment and delivery, rebates, exchange values of trade-ins, etc.).

visions of Sections 1–7, when such exception is deemed advisable on account of special circumstances and is consistent with the public interest.

The Price Directorate can determine such conditions and issue such rules as are considered necessary to prevent an exception from having as its consequence too high prices or profits or improper distribution or competitive conditions, or otherwise having effects which are considered to be contrary to the public interest.

The Price Directorate is further empowered to repeal at any time an exception which has been granted, if the conditions laid down or the rules issued are not observed, or it is considered that the exception results in such improper effects as mentioned.

Section 10: Provisions Concerning Implementation

The Price Directorate is empowered to issue such rules as are regarded as necessary or expedient for the implementation of the provisions of Sections 1–9, including provisions on advertisement of supplier regulated prices or profits, and rules designed to put an effective stop to existing resale price regulation which is contrary to these provisions.

Section 11: Entry into Force

These provisions enter into force as from 1 May 1958. Notwithstanding, the Price Directorate is empowered immediately to make decisions under the provisions to the extent that such decisions are considered to be necessary or expedient for the preparation of the implementation of the provisions.

ROYAL DECREE OF 1 JULY 1960

By Royal Decree of 1 July 1960 the following provisions governing restrictions of prices and rates of profit and restrictions in respect of tenders were laid down under the Act of 26 June 1953 on Control of Prices, Dividends and Restrictive Business Arrangements, as amended:

Section 1: Prohibition of Regulation of Prices and Profits, Additions and Rebates

Associations or groups of enterprises may not establish or maintain such regulations for the sale of commodities or for the rendering of services as entail:

a) The fixing of prices or profits or the issuing of directions as to how the enterprises themselves may determine their prices and profits;

b) The stipulation of additions or rebates apart from ordinary cash discount;

c) That enterprises shall report to a joint body their prices, profits, additions or such rebates as are covered by b);

d) Other regulations with regard to prices, profits, additions or such rebates as are covered by b).

The provisions contained in the first paragraph apply regardless of the manner in which the restrictive arrangements come into being, whether through written or oral provisions, agreements, decisions or arrangements, or whether they are implemented in any other way. The provisions also apply to guiding regulations.

Associations or groups of enterprises may not in their constitutions or by-laws or in other decisions establish or maintain provisions which reflect the aim to implement such regulations as are prohibited under the provisions of the first paragraph, cf. second paragraph, or establish or maintain other provisions involving such regulations.

The provisions contained in the first, second and third paragraphs apply regardless of whether the enterprises themselves are members of the association or group, if the association or group is established or the restrictive arrangement put into effect by persons acting on behalf of the enterprises.

Section 2: Prohibition of Regulations in Respect of Tenders

Associations and groups of enterprises may not establish or maintain regulations with regard to prices or terms for tenders concerning the sale of commodities or the rendering of services. Nor may such associations or groups establish or maintain provisions stating that particular enterprises may not submit tenders or provisions allocating tenders between particular enterprises or establish or maintain other regulations with regard to tenders.

The provisions contained in Section 1, second, third and fourth paragraphs, also apply to restrictions in respect of tenders.

Section 3: Prohibition of the Exercising of Influence on Enterprises with Regard to Prices or Profits, Additions or Rebates

Associations or groups of enterprises may not by refusal of membership, imposing of fines or the application of other coercive measures or by threats to make use of such measures or by recommendations or in any other way try to influence their members or other enterprises to charge higher prices or profits or grant other additions or rebates than they themselves find reason to do.

Nor may associations or groups of enterprises in such a way as mentioned in the first paragraph try to influence their members or other enterprises with the aim of restricting the competition with regard to tenders, cf. Section 2.

Nor may such influence as mentioned in the first and second paragraphs be exercised by the members of an association or a group or by any person who is employed by the association or group or who otherwise is acting on behalf of the association or group.

Section 4: Provisions Governing Foreign Restrictive Business Arrangements

Enterprises in this country may not take part in restrictive business arrangements of such kind as described in Sections 1 and 2, which are made by a foreign association or group for the sale or delivery of commodities or the rendering of services within this country.

Representatives in this country for such associations or groups as mentioned in the preceding paragraph or for enterprises which are members of such an association or group, may not try to influence Norwegian enterprises, which have a corresponding business to the members of the foreign association or group, to charge higher prices or profits or grant other additions or rebates than they themselves find reason to do for the sale or delivery of commodities or the rendering of services in this country. Nor may such representatives try to influence Norwegian enterprises with the view to restricting the competition in respect of tenders.

The term "influence" in these provisions means such actions as described in Section 3, first paragraph.

Section 5: General Exemptions from the Provisions Contained in Sections 1 to 4.

The provisions contained in Sections 1 to 4 shall not apply to:

a) Exports;
b) Sale or delivery of Norwegian products of agriculture, forestry or fisheries from producers or producers' organisations in agriculture, forestry or fisheries;
c) Banking services and insurance services;
d) Sale or delivery from a joint sales organisation established by an association or group of enterprises or for the settling of accounts between such an organisation and the members.

The Ministry of Wages and Prices may lay down detailed rules to determine which sales or deliveries shall be considered to be covered by the exemption under b) above.

The exemption stated under d) shall only apply to an organisation approved by the Ministry of Wages and Prices, as a real sales organisation for the association or group of enterprises concerned. The Ministry may withdraw an approval if it turns out that the preconditions for such an approval have not existed or are not in existence any more.

Section 6: Authority To Grant Exemptions from the Provisions Contained in Sections 1 to 4

The Ministry of Wages and Prices may grant exemptions from the provisions contained in Sections 1 to 4:

a) If the restrictive business arrangement is considered necessary for an extensive technical or commercial co-operation between enterprises and this co-operation is considered to entail the lowering of costs or the improvement of products or otherwise the promotion of rationalisation desirable from the public point of view;
b) If the restrictive business arrangement is considered necessary to protect the economic activity in a sector against such methods of competition as are unfair or detrimental to the public interest;

c) If the restrictive business arrangement otherwise is called for on account of specific circumstances and is considered to be in accordance with the public interest.

Generally exemptions shall be granted only for a limited period of time.

The Ministry may stipulate such conditions or issue such rules as are considered necessary to counteract that an exemption leads to too high prices or profits or entails other conditions which are considered unreasonable or against the public interest.

The Ministry may withdraw a grant of exemption if the exemption is no longer considered necessary or if the conditions stipulated or rules issued are disobeyed or the actions taken under the exemption turn out to have entailed such condition as mentioned in the preceding paragraph.

Section 7: Definitions

The term "group of enterprises" in these provisions means a group established by two or more enterprises through agreements or arrangements without the organisation of an association with a separate board.

The term "ordinary cash discount" means such a discount as is normally granted in the trade concerned by cash payment or payment within 30 days. A rate exceeding 3 per cent shall under no circumstances be considered as ordinary cash discount.

Section 8: The Relation to the Provisions on Resale Price Regulation

The rules contained in these provisions shall not apply to such cases as is covered by the provisions on resale price regulation laid down by Royal Decree of 18 October 1957.

Section 9: Provisions Concerning Implementation

The Ministry of Wages and Prices is empowered to issue such rules as are regarded as necessary or expedient for the implementation of the provisions of Sections 1 to 6, cf. Sections 7 and 8, including provisions designed to put an effective stop to existing regulations which are contrary to these provisions.

The Ministry may wholly or partly delegate its authority under Sections 5 and 6, cf. Section 11, to the Price Directorate.

Section 10: The Competence of the Ministry and the Price Directorate

The rules contained in these provisions entail no limitation in the authority vested with the Ministry and the Price Directorate to make decisions under Sections 24 and 42 of the Price Act, cf. Section 9, paragraph 5, of the Price Act.

Section 11: Entry into Force

These provisions shall enter into force on 1 January 1961, the provisions in Section 2, cf. Sections 3 to 10, however, on 1 September 1960. The Ministry is empowered to make decisions immediately under the provisions to the extent that such decisions are considered to be necessary or expedient for the preparations of the implementation of the provisions.

C. SWEDEN

ACT TO COUNTERACT RESTRAINT OF COMPETITION IN BUSINESS IN CERTAIN INSTANCES[1]

Act of 25 September 1953
Sections 1, 5, 6, 21, 25, 26, 29 as amended 1 June 1956;
Amendments taking effect 1 January 1957

INTRODUCTORY PROVISIONS

Section 1

For the purpose of promoting competition in business such as is desirable in the public interest, it is provided hereunder that certain types of restraint of competition shall be prohibited, and in addition that it shall be the duty of the Freedom of Commerce Board to endeavour through negotiation to eliminate the harmful effects of restraints of competition submitted for its consideration.

THE PROHIBITION OF CERTAIN TYPES OF RESTRAINT OF COMPETITION

Section 2

Unless otherwise provided by law, an entrepreneur may not, without the permission of the Freedom of Commerce Board, require a reseller to maintain a specified minimum price in the resale of a commodity in Sweden, or otherwise specify a price as a guidance to the establishment of resale prices in Sweden, unless it is clearly stated that a price lower than that price may be charged.

Section 3

An entrepreneur may not, without the permission of the Freedom of Commerce Board, enter into or carry out an agreement stipulating that consultation or other forms of cooperation shall take place between a number of entrepreneurs before any one of them submits a tender for a contract to supply a commodity or to render a service in Sweden.

Section 4

The permission specified in Sections 2 and 3 may be granted only if the restraint of competition can be expected to result in lower costs, substantially benefiting consumers, or otherwise to contribute to the public interest, or if there are other special reasons for granting such permission.

The Freedom of Commerce Board may withdraw a permission granted,

---

[1] The statutes and the accompanying notes are based upon official translations obtained from *Guide to Legislation on Restrictive Business Practices,* published in Paris by the European Productivity Agency of the Organization for European Cooperation and Development.

in the event of abuse or if the circumstances under which it was granted have materially changed.

NEGOTIATIONS TO ELIMINATE THE HARMFUL EFFECTS OF RESTRAINT OF COMPETITION

Section 5

The negotiations specified in Section 1 hereof may take place in cases when restraint of competition other than that specified in Section 2 and 3 is found to have harmful effects.

A restraint of competition shall be deemed to have a harmful effect if, contrary to the public interest, it unduly affects the formation of prices, restrains productivity in business, or impedes, or prevents the trade of others.

Section 6

Without the permission of His Majesty,* negotiations may not deal with effects arising outside Sweden from restraint of competition. Such permission may be granted only so far as it is required as a result of agreements with Foreign Powers.

Section 7

The Freedom of Commerce Board shall consist of a Chairman and eight members.

Section 8

The Chairman and two members shall be appointed by His Majesty for a specified period from among persons who cannot be regarded as representing either the interests of entrepreneurs or the interests of consumers and employees. The Chairman and the member appointed Vice-Chairman of the Board shall have legal training and judicial experience. The third member shall have special knowledge of business problems and conditions.

For each of these members of the Board, His Majesty shall appoint two deputies with the same qualifications as the member concerned.

Section 9

The remaining members shall be appointed by His Majesty to serve for a period of three years. Three of them shall be selected from among persons who represent the interests of entrepreneurs, and three of them from among persons who represent the general interests of consumers and employees.

Each member shall have a sufficient number of deputies appointed and selected in the manner indicated above.

Section 10

When a member of the Board, or his deputy, as referred to in Section 9, resigns from the Board, a person shall be apointed by His Majesty for the

* "His Majesty" here . . . refers to the King in Council of State, i.e., essentially His Majesty's Government in parliamentary parlance.

remainder of the term for which the retiring member or deputy was appointed.

Section 11

Persons under a legal disability and persons against whom bankruptcy proceedings have been instituted may not serve as Chairman or as members of the Board.

Section 12

A quorum of the Freedom of Commerce Board shall be constituted when the Chairman, the two members referred to in Section 8, and one representative of the interests of entrepreneurs, and one representative of the interests of consumers and employees are present. An equal number of representatives of the interests of the entrepreneurs and of representatives of the interests of consumers and employees must be present when a decision is taken by the Board.

Notwithstanding the provisions of the first paragraph hereof, the Chairman, on behalf of the Board, may deal with or take decisions regarding matters of minor importance, and conduct preliminary proceedings in other matters.

Section 13

The rules applicable to the challenge of judges shall, so far as appropriate, apply to the challenge of the Chairman and members of the Board.

Section 14

A Commissioner for Freedom of Commerce shall be appointed by His Majesty for a specified term. The Commissioner shall have legal training and judicial experience.

Rules of Procedure of the Freedom of Commerce Board, etc.

Section 15

Application for the permission specified in Sections 2 and 3 shall be made in writing. The application shall state the grounds on which the request is submitted and other circumstances considered relevant by the applicant. The Commissioner for Freedom of Commerce shall be heard on the application.

A person who has been granted permission must be given an opportunity to state his views before such permission is withdrawn.

Section 16

The Commissioner for Freedom of Commerce shall initiate the negotiations specified in Section 1.

If in a certain case the Commissioner decides not to initiate negotiations, an entrepreneur who is directly affected by the restraint of competition in question, or an association of consumers or employees, may apply for the institution of negotiations.

Section 17

Applications for the institution of negotiation proceedings shall be made in writing, stating the reasons for such application.

Section 18

When application for negotiation proceedings has been lodged, the Freedom of Commerce Board shall give the applicant and the opposing party an opportunity to state before a meeting of the Board, their views as to whether the statutory grounds for negotiation proceedings exist. The Commissioner for Freedom of Commerce shall be invited to attend such meeting even if he is not the applicant. Nevertheless, if it is obvious that the application does not merit consideration, it may be rejected without having been discussed at a meeting of the Board.

A meeting may be preceded by such oral or written preliminary proceedings as the Board considers necessary.

Section 19

If it is found at the meeting provided for in Section 18 that the conditions specified for negotiation proceedings do exist, the Board shall decide that negotiation proceedings be held.

Section 20

The negotiation proceedings shall take place at a meeting of the parties before the Freedom of Commerce Board, or, if it is considered appropriate and the case is not of great importance, before the Chairman of the Board. The Board or the Chairman may also hold meetings with the parties separately. The negotiations shall in all cases conclude with a meeting of the parties before the Board.

Section 21

If the negotiations are completed without it being possible to eliminate the harmful effects of the restraint of competition, the Board shall, if the matter is deemed to be of major importance, so inform His Majesty.

If the harmful effect is manifested by a particular price being obviously too high, having regard to costs and other circumstances, and if the matter is found to be of public importance, His Majesty, upon the request of the Freedom of Commerce Board, may specify a certain maximum price which may not be exceeded by an entrepreneur without permission of the Board. Such a decision by His Majesty shall relate to a specific period of time, which shall not exceed one year.

Section 22

The Freedom of Commerce Board may order a party to proceedings to appear before the Board, on pain of a fine, and to produce to the Board any books, correspondence or other documents which may be of importance in the case.

This requirement shall not imply any obligation to divulge trade secrets of a technical nature.

Section 23

Meetings of the Freedom of Commerce Board dealing with cases under the present Act shall be public. Where it is likely that a trade secret may be divulged or that the negotiations may be impeded if a meeting is held in public, the Board may rule that the meeting shall be held in camera.

The Board may rule that the proceedings of a meeting held in camera shall not be disclosed.

Deliberations prior to decision shall be conducted in private unless the Board decides that they may be conducted in public.

Section 24

No appeal shall lie from decisions of the Freedom of Commerce Board in cases under this Act.

Section 25

The Commissioner for Freedom of Commerce as well as the Freedom of Commerce Board may call upon the authority referred to in the Act concerning the obligation to submit information as to conditions of price and competition, for assistance in the investigation of matters which may be of importance to negotiations under this law.

Section 26

Within the meaning of this Act, any person is an entrepreneur who professionally:

—Makes, buys or sells any commodity;

—Carries on the business of rendering any service to others;

—Writes insurance, or carries on the business of borrowing or lending money, or

—Deals in foreign or domestic currency or in stocks, bonds, or other securities;

—Transfers or licenses incorporeal property rights;

—Licenses the right to use any commodity or utility, or

—Carries on a hotel or boarding-house business for which an official licence is required.*

The provisions relating to entrepreneurs shall also be applicable to associations of entrepreneurs.

Section 27

The provisions relating to agreements are also applicable to by-laws adopted by associations of entrepreneurs and to other rules and regulations instituted by such associations.

* Such licence is required for all hotels and boarding-houses which are not managed entirely by the members of one family of not more than three persons.

Section 28

This Act does not apply to agreements between employers and employees concerning wages and other conditions of work.

PENALTIES, ETC.

Section 29

Any person who intentionally violates the provisions of Sections 2 and 3 shall be liable to daily fines,* or if the violation is grave, to imprisonment for not more than one year, or daily fines.

Any person who, after a decision has been made by His Majesty under Section 21, paragraph 2, concerning the price of a commodity, service or utility, intentionally or by gross negligence, demands or receives a higher price than that specified in the decision, or in a special permission granted by the Freedom of Commerce Board, shall be subject to daily fines. If the violation of the law is grave, the punishment shall be imprisonment for not more than one year, or daily fines.

Any person guilty of an offence punishable under the second paragraph shall, in the absence of special circumstances, be obliged to surrender to the Crown the value of the consideration received or agreed upon, or, if special reasons so warrant, a specified proportion of that value.

A master is liable for violations specified in the second paragraph committed by persons in his household or employ, as if the violation had been committed by himself, where the violation takes place with his knowledge and on his desire.

Section 30

Any person who, without good reason, discloses information which under a ruling by the Board may not be divulged shall be liable to daily fines.

Section 31

In the case of the offences referred to in Section 29, proceedings may be instituted by the public prosecutor only on the request, or with the approval of the Commissioner for Freedom of Commerce.

Section 32

Proceedings against the Chairman or a member of the Board, or the Commissioner for Freedom of Commerce, for abuse of office shall be brought before the Svea Court of Appeal.

Section 33

His Majesty may issue such detailed provisions as are required for the administration and enforcement of this Act.

* Under Swedish law, fines are frequently related to the daily income of the violator of the law.

ACT CONCERNING THE OBLIGATION TO SUBMIT INFORMATION AS TO CONDITIONS OF PRICE AND COMPETITION
(ACT OF 1 JUNE 1956)

Section 1

In accordance with the provisions of this Act, entrepreneurs are obliged to submit such information as is required to promote the public knowledge of conditions of price and competition in the national economy.

Other persons are also obliged to submit information in the manner and to the extent prescribed for entrepreneurs where, owing to special circumstances, this is necessary for the verification or completion of information to be submitted by entrepreneurs.

Section 2

Within the meaning of this Act, any person is an entrepreneur who professionally:

—Makes, buys or sells a certain commodity;

—Carries on the business of rendering any service to others;

—Writes insurance, or carries on the business of borrowing or lending money, or deals in foreign or domestic currency or in stocks, bonds or other securities;

—Transfers or licenses incorporeal property rights;

—Licenses the right to use any commodity or utility, or

—Carries on a hotel or boarding-house business for which official licence is required.

The provisions relating to entrepreneurs shall also be applicable to associations of entrepreneurs.

Section 3

An entrepreneur shall be bound to submit, upon request, to such public authority as is designated by His Majesty information about such restraint of competition as is specified in the request, and which concerns his activity and relates to the conditions of price, production, commerce or transport in Sweden, and information on prices, revenues, costs, profits and other conditions affecting the general price structure.*

Section 4

The obligation to submit information under this Act does not imply any duty to disclose trade secrets of a technical nature.

Section 5

Detailed provisions concerning the extent of the obligation to submit information as well as the manner and time for its accomplishment shall be made by the authority. Under such provisions the authority may order an entrepreneur to produce agreements in restraint of competition, books, cor-

---

* More accurately, "the formation of prices."

respondence and other documents. Any person who is obliged to submit information may also be summoned to appear before the authority.

The authority shall take care to avoid imposing unnecessary burdens on entrepreneurs in fulfillment of the obligation to submit information.

Section 6

If a request to submit information is not complied with, the authority may subject the defaulting person to an appropriate fine.

Fine in case of default may also be prescribed in connection with orders to produce or summonses under Section 5.

Section 7

Any person who, on being summoned under Section 5, appears before the authority, is entitled to witness allowance according to rules laid down by His Majesty.

Section 8

All agreements in restraint of competition in respect of which information has been submitted, or which have otherwise become known to the authority, shall be entered upon a register (the Cartel Register).

When a decision to register an agreement has been made, the authority shall forthwith notify all parties to the agreement.

The provisions relating to agreements are also applicable to by-laws adopted by associations of entrepreneurs and to other rules and regulations instituted by such associations.

Section 9

Any information acquired in the course of employment or other service with the authority concerning commercial and operative conditions and business arrangements may not be revealed to any greater extent than that required for the purposes of such employment or service.

Section 10

Any person who intentionally, or by gross negligence, fails to submit information in accordance with this Act within the time prescribed, or in the fulfilment of that duty gives wrong information, shall be punished by daily fines.

If the violation of the law is grave, the punishment shall be imprisonment for not more than one year, or daily fines.

Section 11

Any person who intentionally, or negligently, violates the provisions of Section 9, or makes undue use of information which he is obliged to keep secret under that Section, shall be punished by daily fines or imprisonment, if he is not subject to liability under the general penal code.

Such offences may not be prosecuted by a public prosecutor except upon request of the injured party. If the offence is one which falls under the general penal code, the provisions of that code concerning the right to sue are applicable.

Section 12

When court actions are brought to recover fines under Section 6, or when violations under Sections 10 or 11 are alleged, and proceedings in public might be damaging to any person as a result of the disclosure of commercial or operative conditions and business arrangements, the court may rule that the proceedings shall be conducted in private.

Section 13

An appeal shall lie to His Majesty against any decision by administrative authority under this Act.

Section 14

This Act does not apply to agreements between employers and employees concerning wages or other conditions of work.

Section 15

His Majesty may issue such further regulations as may be necessary for the application of this Act.

This Act shall come into force on 1 January 1957. This Act repeals the Act of 29 June 1946 concerning the supervision of restrictive practices in the national economy.

ROYAL PROCLAMATION LAYING DOWN CERTAIN REGULATIONS UNDER THE ACT CONCERNING THE OBLIGATION TO SUBMIT INFORMATION AS TO CONDITIONS OF PRICE AND COMPETITION
(Proclamation of 19 October 1956)

As authorised by the Act of 1 June 1956 concerning the obligation to submit information as to conditions of price and competition, it is ordered by His Majesty as follows:

Section 1

The authority to procure information under the Act of 1 June 1956 concerning the obligation to submit information as to conditions of price and competition is vested in the Banking and Stock Exchange Inspection Office as regards banking and stock exchanges, the Insurance Inspection Office as regards insurance, and the State Price and Cartel Office as regards other sectors of economic life.

Witness allowances for appearance before any of the said authorities in accordance with Section 7 of the aforementioned Act shall be drawn from public funds and shall be determined by the authority according to the general rules governing the payment of witness allowances from public funds.

Section 2

The Cartel Register provided for in Section 8 of the Act of 1 June 1956 concerning the obligation to submit information as to conditions of price and competition, shall be the responsibility of the Banking and Stock Exchange Inspection Office as regards banking and stock exchanges, of the Insurance Inspection Office as regards insurance, and of the State Price and Cartel Office as regards other sectors of economic life.

This proclamation shall come into effect on 1 January 1957. The following proclamations are hereby repealed, viz., of 29 June 1946 (No. 451) directing the Board of Trade to exercise supervision under the Act of 29 June 1946 (No. 448) concerning the supervision of restrictive practices in the national economy, and of 20 December 1946 (No. 774) directing the Banking and Securities Exchange Inspection Office and the Insurance Inspection Office to exercise supervision under the same Act.

Appendix II: Forms Used To Obtain Data

SCHOOL OF LAW[1]

THE UNIVERSITY OF TEXAS

AUSTIN 12, TEXAS

E. ERNEST GOLDSTEIN

Dear Sir:

This letter and questionnaire are being sent to American affiliated firms in your country and in other Western European countries which have legislation controlling restrictive business practices. This request for information arises out of a Ford Foundation grant which will enable me to spend a year, beginning in September 1959, in Europe preparing a book, on the actual effect of such legislation on American firms.

I am a Professor of Law at the University of Texas, and my special fields include antitrust law and international trade. Prior to coming to the University, I spent the period from 1952 to 1954, in Europe as a member of the group representing the United States in the development of the various productivity programs and in the creation of the European Productivity Agency. During the summers of 1956 and 1958, I did research in Europe, primarily at the governmental level, as a preliminary to the present effort.

In order to schedule and plan my research it seemed advisable to obtain certain basic information prior to my leaving the United States, thus, the attached questionnaire.

Your cooperation is requested with the understanding that there will be no direct or indirect identification of your firm in any resulting publications. Moreover, your confidence will at all times be respected in my dealings with other firms or representatives of any government.

Please fill out and return the questionnaire, by airmail if possible, at your earliest convenience. Even if it is not possible to answer all questions, return of the questionnaire would be helpful. It is particularly important that I receive a reply to the last question which deals with the possibility of a future interview with you and your key personnel.

[1] This letter accompanied all questionnaires sent in the spring of 1959 to Denmark, Norway, Sweden, France, Germany, Ireland, Austria, the Netherlands, and the United Kingdom.

May I thank you in advance for your help, and may I assure you that your assistance will eventually serve to provide much needed information for other American firms concerned with foreign operations.

Sincerely,

E. Ernest Goldstein

E. Ernest Goldstein
Professor of Law

DENMARK QUESTIONNAIRE[2]

It would be greatly appreciated if you would provide the answers to as many questions as possible and return the questionnaire to Professor E. Ernest Goldstein, Law School, University of Texas, Austin, Texas, U.S.A.

If there is insufficient space for some of your answers, please use either the reverse of one of these pages or an additional sheet of paper.

1. Please indicate the approximate extent of American interest in your firm. None ...., Less than 50%........, More than 50%.........

2. Does your firm belong to any association or participate in any arrangement or agreement which has been registered with the Monopltilsynet under the provisions of Lov nr. 102 af 31. marts 1955 om Tilsyn med Monopoler og Konkurrencebegraensnunger? Yes........, No.........

(If the answer to No. 2 is No, please omit questions 3 through 11.)

3. Does your firm's name appear in any registration statement? Yes........, No.........

4. Please describe the arrangement or association, as for example, restrictions on price competition (other than resale price maintenance), rebate system, limitation of entry, quotas, joint sales agencies, division of markets, allocation of customers, profit pooling, etc.

5. At the time when your firm commenced operations was a similar arrangement or association in existence? Yes........, No.........

6. Please list the advantages enjoyed by your firm through its participation in the arrangement or association.

7. Please list the disadvantages suffered by your firm by reason of its participation in the arrangement or association.

[2] Similar questionnaires, adapted to local conditions, were sent to American firms in Norway, Sweden, France, Germany, Ireland, Austria, the Netherlands, and the United Kingdom.

8. Please list the disadvantages your firm would suffer if it withdrew from the arrangement or association.

9. If your firm were free today to decide whether or not to participate in the arrangement or association, would your firm participate? Yes........, No.........

10. Has the public nature of the registration procedure caused any hardship or difficulties? Yes........, No.........

11. During the past 5 years has any practice or policy under the arrangement been modified, banned, or questioned by the Danish Government? Yes........, No.........

a. If the answer is Yes, please indicate the nature of the practice or policy and the kind of action taken by the Government.

b. Did any resulting publicity affect your business adversely? Yes........, No.........

c. If any appeal was taken from the Government's action, please indicate the nature of the appeal and the outcome.

12. Has the publicity given to the Government's actions against practices in another industry, for example a decision adverse to exclusive dealing or boycott arrangement, caused your firm to change its practices or policies? Yes........, No.........

a. If the answer is Yes, please indicate what practices were changed and the reasons for change.

13. Has your firm, or the industry in which your firm participates by arrangement or association, requested the right to maintain resale prices at the consumer level? Yes........, No.........

a. If the answer is Yes, did the government approve the resale price maintenance? Yes........, No.........

14. If your firm produces consumer goods, has it been required by operation of other laws to post or mark its prices? Yes........, No.........

15. Has your firm been required to register because of its "dominant" position in its industry? Yes........, No.........

a. If the answer is Yes, please indicate the extent to which such a registration has affected your practices or policies.

16. Does your firm qualify as one which must have prior approval from the Government before it may increase prices? Yes........, No.........

a. If the answer is Yes, have you ever requested such approval? Yes........, No.........

b. Was your request Refused........, Approved........, Approved with modifications ....?

17. Does your firm participate in any international arrangements which affect or regulate competition, including limitations on exports? Yes........, No.........

a. If the answer is Yes, please indicate the general nature or character of the arrangement and the countries involved.

b. If this international arrangement is registered in any country or countries, please indicate the name or names of the country.

c. If any country listed above in "a" is a member of the European Economic Community (Common Market), do you expect that the coming into force of the anti-trust provisions of the Treaty of Rome, Articles 85–90, will make it necessary to modify or abandon the agreement? Yes........., No..........

18. To the extent that you have knowledge of the laws governing competition which are in effect in other countries, please indicate which, if any, of the following countries has a control law which you prefer to that of Denmark. Netherlands........., Austria........., Germany (Federal Republic)........., Norway........., Sweden........., United Kingdom........., Eire........., France........., United States..........

a. If you have placed a check opposite one or more countries, please indicate the features of the laws which you find desirable.

19. Please indicate those aspects, if any, of the Danish laws governing competition and of the administration of those laws which you would wish to have improved or changed.

20. How would you characterize the climate of competition in your industry in Denmark? No competition........., Too much competition........., Insufficient competition ...., Sufficient competition.......... (More than one item may be checked.)

21. Under certain circumtances the Patent Laws of Denmark provide for the compulsory licensing of patents. Have such laws affected your business practices or policies? Yes........., No..........

a. If the answer is Yes, please indicate in what way the law has affected your business practices or policies.

22. If you are willing to permit me to discuss these matters with representatives of your firm during the autumn of 1959, please give the name, address, and telephone number of the person with whom I should arrange the appointment.

Index

secures Coca-Cola from, 262, 263, 292; sale of malt liquors in, 267; Skruv brewery in, 283; soft-drink and malt-liquor prices in, 286, 288, 289
judge: as head of Price Council, 92
judicial notice: use of, in Price Council hearings, 99
judicial review: of Price Council decisions, 96–97; of Freedom of Commerce Board decisions, 219

Kalmar, Sweden: Coca-Cola distributor in, 262; soft-drink and malt-liquor prices in, 287, 289
Kalmar Bryggeri AB (distributor): 259
Kant, Immanuel: categorical imperative of, 217
Karlskoga, Sweden: 288, 289
Karlskoga Ångbryggeri (distributor): 259
Karlskrona, Sweden: 272, 287
Karlsons Bryggeri AB, A (distributor): 259
Karlstads Bryggeri AB (distributor): 259
Kelifa: as toilet-article cartel, 231
King, the. SEE King in Council (Norway); King in Council (Sweden)
King in Council (Norway): and control of restrictive practices, 75, 77, 169; nature of, 76, 91; and regulations about registration, 77, 82; and Price Act, 88, 91; delegation of powers of, 88–89; and Price Directorate, 90; procedures of, 91; and Price Council, 92, 96; and price fixing, 95, 105, 106; and Royal Decree of 1 July 1960, 116
King in Council (Sweden): and secret registrations, 175; and appeals from order to register, 176; and Commissioner, 191; and Freedom of Commerce Board, 199; and control of restrictive practices, 208; Coca-Cola's appeal to, 249
Kiruna, Sweden: 272
Klippan, Sweden: 286
Klippans Bryggeri (distributor): 260
Klosterbryggeriet, AB (distributor): 260
knitted-wear industry: S.P.K. report on, 186, 190
Koksexport Norden: and coke industry, 50–51
Kooperativa Förbundet (Sweden): influence of, on trade practices, 200, 201; composition of, 221; policy of, 221–222; and prices, 221–222; influence of, 221–227; and monopolies and oligopolies, 221–222; and financing of cooperatives, 222; and technology, 222; fields of activity of, 222–227, 235; Wholesale Society as agency of, 223; use of boycott by, 223; and food cartels, 223; and Swedish Farmers Purchasing Association, 227; in farm-machinery industry, 228, 229, 230, 231; in petroleum trade, 243–244, 245, 246; in heating-oil trade, 245
Kopparberg, Sweden: 260, 289
Kopparberg Bryggeri AB, Kopparberg: complaint of, against Coca-Cola, 260–264, 282, 292–293, 294; ownership of, 262; sales districts of, 262, 285; as competitor of Coca-Cola, 266; sale of Coca-Cola by, 267; role of, in soft-drink trade, 282–290, 296–297; role of, in malt-liquors trade, 282–290, 296–297; operation methods of, 285; discounts allowed by, 285; prices charged by, 288, 289, 290; manufacturing costs of, 290
Kristianstad, Sweden: 260
Kristinehamns Bryggeri AB (distributor): 259
Krönleins Bryggeri, Trollhättan (distributor): 259
Krönleins Vattenfabriks AB, Jönköping: as Coca-Cola bottler, 257. SEE ALSO Jönköping, Sweden
Kronoberg, Sweden: 267